MW00389300

Critical Thinking and American Government

Critical Thinking and American Government

EXERCISES AND APPLICATIONS

Kent M. Brudney
Cuesta College

Mark E. Weber
Cuesta College

PEARSON

Boston Columbus Indianapolis New York San Francisco Upper Saddle River
Amsterdam Cape Town Dubai London Madrid Milan Munich Paris Montreal Toronto
Delhi Mexico City Sao Paulo Sydney Hong Kong Seoul Singapore Taipei Tokyo

Executive Editor: Reid Hester
Executive Marketing Manager: Wendy Gordon
Production Project Manager: Debbie Ryan
Full-Service Project Management: Dhanya Ramesh, Jouve
Art Director: Jayne Conte
Cover Designer: Suzanne Behnke
Cover Image: Fotolia
Cover Printer: Lehigh-Phoenix Color/Hagerstown
Printer/Bindery: Edwards Brothers

For permission to use copyrighted material, grateful acknowledgment is made on the appropriate page within the text.

Library of Congress Cataloging-in-Publication Data

Brudney, Kent M.
  Critical thinking and American government : exercises and applications / Kent M. Brudney, Mark E. Weber.–1st ed.
    p. cm.
  ISBN-13: 978-0-205-21280-4
  ISBN-10: 0-205-21280-8
    1. United States–Politics and government–Textbooks.   2. United States–Politics and government–Problems, exercises, etc.
  3. United States–Politics and government–Study and teaching (Secondary) I. Weber, Mark E. II. Title.
  JK276.B79 2011
  320.473–dc23
                                        2011037273

0205212808
Copyright © 2012 by Pearson Education, Inc.
All rights reserved. Manufactured in the United States of America. This publication is protected by Copyright, and permission should be obtained from the publisher prior to any prohibited reproduction, storage in a retrieval system, or transmission in any form or by any means, electronic, mechanical, photocopying, recording, or likewise. To obtain permission(s) to use material from this work, please submit a written request to Pearson Education, Inc., Permissions Department, One Lake Street, Upper Saddle River, New Jersey 07458, or you may fax your request to 201-236-3290.

10 9 8 7 6 5 4 3 2 1—CRS—14 13 12 1

ISBN 13: 978-0-205-21280-4
ISBN 10: 0-205-21280-8

CONTENTS

PREFACE

Critical Thinking and American Government was written for students who come to the study of American government unaccustomed to thinking critically and analytically about politics. It was also written for Advanced Placement and college instructors who want their students to grasp American politics in greater depth and with more practical applications than standard survey textbooks provide.

We are happy to have a found a new home at Pearson for *Critical Thinking and American Government.* For our first edition with Pearson, we've updated the exercises with new data and material focusing on important political developments that have occurred in the past four years. There is an updated exercise, for example, that leads students through an analysis of presidential statements during the 2008 presidential campaign. The role of the economy in presidential elections continues to be critical, and the most recent presidential campaign is now incorporated in the exercise on this topic. Perhaps the most significant development since the last presidential election has been the Tea Party movement, and the exercise on earmarks and pork-barrel spending now incorporates coverage of this movement.

We suggest that students and teachers consider a few elements that underpin the critical thinking approach to the study of American politics incorporated in this text. The first element is *discipline-based* critical thinking. Many colleges and universities require students to take a class in critical thinking as one of their degree requirements. Unfortunately, those classes are often taught in isolation from any academic discipline, which is a bit like teaching writing without a language to work with. This text grounds the development of critical and analytical thinking skills in the discipline of political science.

Second is the *integration* of critical thinking into the introductory American politics course. The critical thinking exercises in this text are grouped in chapters that match those in most standard survey texts. The exercises allow students and teachers to delve critically and analytically into topics typically covered in the introductory course. Examples include tracing African American representation in Congress using data sets, analyzing the Electoral College through popular and electoral vote results, assessing the president's war power by categorizing and quantifying the use of armed force abroad, and investigating incumbency using data on reelection rates. Students and teachers will find that the exercises complement their studies in class and in the standard text.

The third element in our approach is the *regular assignment* of critical thinking exercises. This text allows students to *practice* analytical inquiry within political science on a regular basis, thereby deepening their knowledge and understanding of the discipline and course material. We recognize that the term *homework* conjures up in many students' minds images of bleak, unending drudgery. But that won't be the case here. These critical thinking exercises offer a wide variety of approaches that our students find interesting and challenging.

The fourth element is *actively engaging* the subject. The introductory American government course is often constrained by its reliance on the instructor's description and analysis of the subject matter. But no matter how effective a survey text—or how dynamic an instructor—description without active engagement brings students up short. Our students want to confront, apply, manipulate, and actively problem-solve within the discipline. This text provides that opportunity.

For teachers in the natural sciences and mathematics, it is evident that students must embrace the subject—actively and regularly—to learn it. Imagine teaching math by describing numeric problems with a PowerPoint® presentation and not requiring students to practice solving problems that embody the concepts and relationships explained in class. Science students have their labs; math students have their proofs and problems. Why should a midterm and final exam alone suffice for students of American politics?

The fifth element is that these critical thinking exercises are designed to facilitate the measurement of student outcomes and assessment. The authors have misgivings about the simplistic market-based model of outcomes and assessment, which too often comes from those without classroom experience. This text is anchored, however, in the classroom and builds on what teachers know from their everyday experience: Successful student learning requires clear objectives and regular assessment. Instructors need to know whether students are mastering the required skills and subject matter of the discipline. We believe that our text is consistent with the most useful research on outcomes and assessment as well as the new scholarship of teaching and learning.

A NOTE ON THE STRUCTURE OF THE TEXT

Each critical thinking exercise begins with a one- to three-page introduction, broadly explaining the topic and preparing students to tackle the critical thinking assignment. The introduction is followed by critical thinking questions based on a wide variety of primary sources: Supreme Court opinions, legislation, the *Federalist Papers,* public opinion polls, apportionment and population tables, presidential and congressional election results, data on campaign spending, among others. The critical thinking questions are calibrated carefully to lead students to engage these sources successfully. The exercises focus on data interpretation and analysis, the discovery of basic relationships among variables, and the ability to read critically, to summarize information concisely, to formulate generalizations and hypotheses, to draw logical inferences, to assess the strength of opposing arguments and positions, and to practice obtaining and analyzing *reliable* sources on the Internet.

AN IMPORTANT NOTE TO INSTRUCTORS

Appendix 1 in this text is a guide to using this critical thinking approach. It includes suggestions on selecting and assigning exercises, integrating the exercises into the introductory class, getting students started, employing the exercises as group work, and evaluating the exercises.

ACKNOWLEDGMENTS

We are indebted to reviewers, colleagues, and students for the new approaches, exercises, and topics they have suggested. We thank them, too, for pointing out problems in previous editions, allowing us to clarify and amend where necessary. Phyllis Brudney's expertise helped us get the mathematics right. Of course, remaining sins of omission or commission are ours alone. Our thanks go to the professionals at Pearson, most especially our editor, Reid Hester, who could not have been more encouraging. Most of all, we thank John Culver for co-authorship of the first two editions with Wadsworth. He has been sorely missed, but his good work is still evident in several exercises.

Governing Principles and Ideologies

EXERCISE 1.1   Reading the Constitution

INTRODUCTION

The U.S. Constitution establishes the fundamental principles, processes, and structures of the U.S. political system, including representative government, republicanism, popular sovereignty, and individual rights; the process of checks and balances; and the structures of separation of power and federalism. The Constitution grants power to government institutions, to officeholders, and to citizens, and it constrains all of them in their exercise of power. Under the Constitution, sovereignty is divided among the people, the state governments, and the national government, thus preventing a concentration of power that could endanger the liberties of citizens.

That the Constitution has endured for more than two centuries is a function of four extraordinary innovations in the theory and practice of republican government. First, American constitutions were written. This innovation was employed in creating state constitutions and later the Articles of Confederation and the Constitution of 1787. Written constitutions were a significant departure from the British model, a vague body of law and precedent, some written and some not. During the colonial and revolutionary periods, Americans had found that an informal constitution was a weak and unreliable guarantor of citizens' liberties. So they insisted that their constitutions be written.

Second, the American constitutions were separate from and superior to the government they sought to restrain. This, too, was a departure from the British model. In England, citizens customarily looked to Parliament to protect their liberties from the abuse of power by the king. But Americans learned from their experience with state governments between 1776 and 1787 that duly elected legislatures and even citizens themselves might abuse power and had to be restrained by a higher authority. Their written state and federal constitutions would be that separate and paramount authority.

The third innovation was a process for creating and then amending the written documents. A constitution separate from and superior to the government could not be created or altered by the government it was meant to control. So Americans located the power to create and alter the Constitution of 1787 in special conventions of citizens that were separate from the national and state governments in existence at the time.

Article V of the Constitution of 1787 divides the amendment power between the national and state governments, on one hand, and popular conventions of citizens, on the other. Popular conventions have been employed only once since the adoption of the Constitution, when the Twenty-First Amendment, which repealed Prohibition, was ratified by popularly elected conventions in the states in 1933. But their inclusion in the Constitution illustrates the conviction of Americans that fundamental law must be separate from the institutions of government.

The fourth innovation was *judicial review*, the power of judges to say what a constitution means and to strike down government actions that conflict with the authority of the Constitution. Judicial review was rooted in the belief that the nation's fundamental law is both separate from and superior to the government. Clearly, government officials cannot evaluate their own performance against the standards set forth in the Constitution. The framers, or authors, of the Constitution could have made the people the instrument for assessing the government's compliance with the Constitution. But they, like many Americans at the time, held a dim view of democracy and feared the consequences of locating power in the citizenry.

Actually, judicial review is nowhere mentioned in the Constitution of 1787. But the concept of a fundamental law that binds the government pointed to the need for interpretation by some impartial body. Judges at the state government level were the first to exercise judicial review. In 1803, the U.S. Supreme Court asserted the power for the first time, striking down a law passed by Congress. In *Marbury v. Madison,* Chief Justice John Marshall claimed for the Supreme Court the power to interpret the Constitution: "A law repugnant to the Constitution is void." The exercise of judicial review confirmed that Americans had elevated the fundamental law above their government and had found a practical way to maintain that separation.

The framers intended the Constitution to be the foundation for "A New Order of the Ages," yet it is a surprisingly brief and often ambiguous document. Both its brevity and ambiguity suggest the wisdom of its authors: They did not want the document to be so detailed that it would constrain policymakers in future generations, tying them to the interests and issues of the founding period. The framers knew that a free people facing ongoing political change would cast off any document that could not be adapted to new circumstances. The spareness of the Constitution has helped it endure as the fundamental law in the United States for over 200 years.[1]

Some of the matters on which the Constitution is ambiguous are important. The interests of those at the Constitutional Convention were often too diverse to reconcile through bargaining and compromise. Ambiguous language allowed the parties to agree on issues that, if dealt with specifically, would have deadlocked the convention. Since 1787, ambiguities in the Constitution have been sorted out in the practice of U.S. political life and through interpretation by the federal courts. Still, the meanings of certain phrases—"necessary and proper" (Article I, Section 8) and "equal protection" (Fourteenth Amendment), for example—are likely always to be contested.

On a number of important matters, the Constitution is silent. The framers did not explicitly confer the right to vote on anyone. The right to vote is implicit, of course, in the Constitution's guarantee that every state will have a republican form of government and in the Constitution's references to the election of representatives, senators, and the president. But until the Fifteenth Amendment was ratified in 1870, state governments alone determined who could vote in their respective states. Subsequent amendments granted the right to vote to women and citizens of age 18 or older. The framers did not set out the role that political parties should play in the political system or a process for canceling treaties. Over the years, state legislatures and Congress have defined, in law, the functions and responsibilities of parties in the electoral arena. And it wasn't until the late 1970s that the treaty issue was resolved. In 1978, President Jimmy Carter abrogated (canceled) a mutual defense treaty with Taiwan without securing the approval of the Senate. A group of senators challenged the president's action in court. In *Goldwater v. Carter* (1979), the Supreme Court ruled that the case involved a political question and refused to decide the matter. With both the Constitution and the Supreme Court silent on the authority to abrogate treaties, it seems that authority is now the president's by virtue of a president's having claimed it and successfully exercised it.

The Constitution offers neither law nor much guidance on current social issues. It was the Supreme Court that legalized abortion in *Roe v. Wade* (1973). And the courts are now in the process of examining issues such as gay marriage and the right to die. Judges will have to look deeply into the Constitution and their own notions of truth and justice to determine how to rule on these matters.

ASSIGNMENT, PART A: THE CONSTITUTION'S BASIC PROVISIONS

The following questions will familiarize you with the organization of the Constitution and several of its provisions. Consult the Constitution in the appendix of this text. In your answers, always cite the number of the relevant article or amendment. Preview the questions below before you read the Constitution so that you know what to be looking for as you read the document.

1. Read each article of the Constitution. In just one sentence, state the general purpose or subject of each article.

Article I: _____

_____

Article II: _____

_____

---

[1]By contrast, many state constitutions suffer from excessive detail. They often run on for hundreds of pages, with arcane specifications confused by scores of amendments. They are commonly documents that only legislators, lawyers, and judges can make sense of.

Article III: _____

_____

Article IV: _____

_____

Article V: _____

_____

Article VI: _____

_____

Article VII: _____

_____

2. In the Constitution of 1787—the unamended document—how many times do the words *slave* and *slavery* appear?

_____

3. The powers the Constitution specifically grants to the branches of government or to office-holders are called *enumerated powers.*

　a. Identify one enumerated power of the president.

　_____

　b. Identify one enumerated power of the vice president.

　_____

　c. Identify one enumerated power of Congress.

　_____

4. a. How were U.S. senators chosen before the Seventeenth Amendment was ratified in 1913?

　_____

　_____

　b. How have U.S. senators been chosen since 1913?

　_____

　_____

5. a. Identify one power that the Constitution prohibits Congress from exercising.

　_____

　b. Identify one power that the Constitution prohibits the states from exercising.

　_____

6. According to the principle of checks and balances, each branch of government must have some degree of scrutiny and control over the other branches. With the exception of the judiciary, the Constitution accomplishes that by giving each branch roles in the affairs of the others.[2] Look at the first two articles of the Constitution, and identify one of each of the following types of checks and balances:

　a. A power that the executive branch holds over the legislative branch

　_____

    b. A power that the executive branch holds over the judicial branch

_____

    c. A power that the legislative branch holds over the executive branch

_____

    d. A power that the legislative branch holds over the judicial branch

_____

7. a. What are the two ways that amendments to the Constitution can be proposed?

_____

_____

_____

    b. What are the two ways that amendments to the Constitution can be ratified?

_____

_____

_____

8. Article V of the Constitution of 1787 singles out two matters that are beyond the reach of the amendment process. What are they?

_____

_____

_____

9. Read the twenty-seven amendments to the Constitution. Identify, by number, one amendment that:

    a. extended individual rights.

_____

    b. extended civil rights (including voting rights).

_____

    c. prohibited certain practices by the states.

_____

10. The Twenty-Fifth Amendment describes the sequence of events that would install the vice president as acting president against the will of the president. Outline that sequence of events.

_____

_____

_____

---

[2]The Constitution specifies no role for the judiciary in the functions of the legislative or executive branches. The power of judicial review was claimed by Chief Justice John Marshall in his decision in *Marbury v. Madison* (1803). See Exercise 9.1.

_____

_____

_____

_____

_____

11. Identify one term in the Constitution that you do not understand. Look up the meaning of the term, and define it here.

_____

_____

ASSIGNMENT, PART B: MAJORITY AND SUPERMAJORITY

Essential to the functioning of government and to balancing the relative powers of its three branches are the numeric requirements the Constitution sets forth for overriding a presidential veto, ratifying treaties, and carrying out other tasks and procedures. The three numeric requirements specified in the Constitution are the simple majority and two supermajority levels, two-thirds and three-fourths. The simple majority and two-thirds margins apply to the number of House and Senate members actually casting votes, not to the total number of votes residing in each body. For example, the requirement for passing legislation in the House is a simple majority, or 50 percent plus one, of the number of votes cast. There are 435 members in the House, so a simple majority is 218. But 218 votes are needed to pass a bill only if all 435 members vote. If only 400 members vote on a bill, then 201 votes would satisfy the simple-majority requirement.

1. a. What bodies have the power to override a presidential veto?

_____

b. What margin is required to override a presidential veto?

_____

2. a. What body has the power to ratify treaties?

_____

b. What margin is required to ratify treaties?

_____

3. To *impeach* means "to bring charges against" or "to indict."

a. What body has the power to impeach the president?

_____

b. What margin is required to impeach a president?

_____

4. a. What body has the power to convict the president of charges brought against him in the impeachment process and thereby remove him from the presidency?

_____

    b. What margin is required to convict and remove a president?

_____

5. a. What body has the power to accept or to reject a president's nominations to the Supreme Court?

_____

    b. What margin is required to elevate a president's nominee to a seat on the Supreme Court?

_____

6. a. If no candidate for the presidency wins a simple majority of the total number of electoral votes, what body has the power to choose the president?

_____

    b. What margin is required to choose the president?

_____

7. The Constitution requires that the House and the Senate have a simple majority of their members present to conduct legislative business. This is called a quorum requirement. If the House can muster only the minimum requirement for a quorum, what number of votes would be needed to pass a bill?

_____

8. The Constitution specifies a three-fourths majority for just one process. What is it?

_____

EXERCISE 1.2   The Framers of the Constitution and Republicanism

INTRODUCTION

The U.S. Constitution established a republic. The framers chose the republican form of government over all other forms, including monarchy, aristocracy, and democracy.

Americans have often differed over the practice of republican government. But they have agreed in large part on the fundamental principles and elements of republican government:

- *Republican government is limited.* The powers of government are constitutionally restricted to reduce the possibility of tyranny. In the Constitution, the framers set limits on the powers exercised by each branch of government (legislative, executive, and judicial), on the powers exercised by the national government over the states, and on the powers exercised over individuals.
- *Republican government is representational.* The government's exercise of power over citizens is legitimate only when elected officials represent their interests in legislative bodies. The framers' historical model for representative government was rooted in the representative institutions of the Roman Republic. They even named the U.S. Senate for the Roman Senate. But republicanism offered no standard position on four difficult issues:
  1. How many constituents should each legislator represent?
  2. Should legislators be responsible to their constituents, to their own conscience, or to the public interest?
  3. Should representatives of the people be elected by the people themselves or by intermediate institutions (e.g., the Electoral College)?
  4. Who should be eligible to vote for legislators?

  On the issue of the direct popular election of representatives (number 3 in the preceding list), the framers were divided. The Constitution has always provided for the direct popular election of members of the House of Representatives, but U.S. senators were chosen by members of their state legislature until the Seventeenth Amendment was ratified in 1913. Remember that the framers didn't think too highly of the public's ability to handle political power wisely. So they chose not to expand the right to vote beyond the voting qualifications the states had previously established for the largest branch of each state's legislature. The Constitution of 1787 did not guarantee voting rights. That issue was left to the states. Later, a series of constitutional amendments, Supreme Court decisions, and popular movements democratized representation and expanded the eligible electorate. Today, because of the gradual expansion of a constitutionally guaranteed right to vote, we refer to the United States as a representative democracy or as a democratic republic. But the framers did not refer to the constitutional order they founded as a democracy: They used the term *republic*, though it did include some representative democracy in the House of Representatives.
- *In republican government, the people are sovereign.* Sovereignty means ultimate authority. Republicans believe that the people at large create, authorize, and empower government, and they also believe that government must be accountable to the people. A government rooted in the people cannot act without the consent of the people. The word *republic* comes from the Latin *res publica* ("the public thing"), which means that government is a common enterprise, originating from and belonging to the people. Thomas Jefferson made the principle of popular sovereignty clear in the Declaration of Independence: "Governments are instituted among Men, deriving their just powers from the consent of the governed. . . . Whenever any Form of Government becomes destructive of these ends, it is the Right of the People to alter or to abolish it, and to institute new Government."

ASSIGNMENT

The following questions require a close reading of the Constitution. Consult the U.S. Constitution in the appendix of this text.

  1. Identify three significant elements of the unamended Constitution of 1787 that embody the republican principle of limited government. (This excludes from your response the Bill of Rights,

the first ten amendments to the Constitution, which was ratified in 1791, as part of a compromise to secure the ratification of the Constitution.) Explain and support your answers.

_____

_____

_____

_____

_____

_____

2. Three institutions in the new government embodied the framers' commitment to the principle of representation: the House of Representatives, the Senate, and the presidency. Identify below the system of representation the framers established for each institution by answering this question: Was it representation by direct popular election, or was representation filtered through the choice of some intermediate body? If the latter, identify that intermediate body and describe its role.

House of Representatives: _____

_____

_____

Senate: _____

_____

_____

President: _____

_____

_____

3. Identify three amendments to the Constitution that expanded democratic representation, and explain what each amendment accomplished.

_____

_____

_____

_____

_____

_____

4. Identify one passage in the Constitution that expresses the republican principle of popular sovereignty.

_____

_____

EXERCISE 1.3   Contemporary American Political Ideologies

INTRODUCTION

The labels we use to describe political thought are often loaded with connotations—either positive or negative—depending on who's wielding the label as a political weapon and on who's listening. Republicans, for example, have turned *liberalism* into a term of disparagement by associating that label with big government, moral irresponsibility, and a lack of will to defend the nation. Democrats have tried to discredit *conservatism* by linking that label to practices such as racism, the oppression of women, religious fanaticism, and favoritism for the rich.

A *political ideology* is a set of coherent, deeply felt political beliefs and values through which individuals interpret political events and decide what is politically right and wrong. Despite the utility of the labels in making sense of political issues and actors, most Americans are not ideologues: They may hold ideological positions on particular issues, but they do not think of their politics in ideological terms. Most Americans are pragmatists—positioned in the middle of the political spectrum—and are unlikely to judge issues or candidates by a set of consistent political beliefs. They care more about solving problems pragmatically than they care about ideological dogma about how to solve problems. Indeed, Americans historically have rejected political movements and candidates that appeared too ideological. Some public opinion polls suggest, however, that Americans have become increasingly ideological in the first decade of the twenty-first century.

Ideological labels do help voters sort out a bewildering array of political arguments, and to some extent they do reflect political positions, especially among political elites, whose positions tend to be more ideological than other Americans. There is abundant evidence that elected representatives in Congress and in state legislatures have become increasingly more ideological than the electorate. This helps us to understand why legislative bodies are becoming more and more polarized and why they find compromises difficult.

The task of identifying ideological positions has become more difficult in recent decades as the relatively simple divisions of the New Deal era—based largely on the economy and the role of government in the economy—have fragmented into more diverse and complex thinking about the economy; moral, religious, and social issues; and foreign policy, especially in the wake of 9/11 and the war on terrorism.

Here are brief definitions of seven ideologies prominent on the American political landscape today. Recognize that the descriptions are simplified.

> *Liberalism.*   Liberals generally support strong government action in a broad array of contemporary problems, from economic policy to civil rights. But liberals are likely to oppose strong government action when they believe it threatens civil liberties—freedom of speech, for example, or the individual's right to privacy. Liberals believe that government must play an active role in creating equal opportunity, through antidiscrimination laws, through affirmative action programs, and through initiatives to assist the disadvantaged. Liberals pin their hopes for a just and progressive society on action by the national government because of its superior power, reach, and resources. Liberals favor progressive income taxes as a means of assisting the most disadvantaged, and they believe that all levels of government should prevent and punish market practices that hurt consumers and threaten the environment. Liberals want foreign and defense policies that depend less on military and unilateral action and more on diplomacy and multilateralism, especially through the United Nations. Liberals were heartened by the presidential election of 2008 and the congressional elections of 2006 and 2008, when the Democratic Party gained large majorities in Congress and won the presidency. Many believed that these victories signaled the beginning of a new area of active government, perhaps a new New Deal. But their hopes were dashed by ongoing economic recession, by a president who often pursued a centrist approach, and by the Republican tidal wave in the 2010 midterm elections.
>
> *The Left Wing.*   From the 1930s to the 1960s, the American Left supported socialist, or Marxist, economics (public ownership of the means of production and the redistribution of wealth to foster economic equality); opposed U.S. imperialistic, interventionist foreign policy; and sought to eradicate racism in the United States. In the decades since, with the increasingly conservative trend in U.S. politics and the end of the cold war, the left has splintered into a number of movements, each with its own passionate critique or indictment of U.S. society.

Among those left-wing movements are radical feminism (denouncing patriarchy in all its manifestations), radical environmentalism (damning the ethos of acquisitiveness and the rape of nature), and radical multiculturalism (censuring social, economic, and belief systems that marginalize people of color). Recently, left-wing organizations have attacked economic globalization, which they believe cheats developing nations, hurts U.S. workers, and damages the environment. The left wing has opposed the Bush and Obama administrations' unilateral ("imperialistic") actions in world affairs.

Conservatism.   Conservatives want to reduce the role of government in the nation's economic affairs. For conservatives, government's chief roles are to defend the nation from foreign attack, maintain law and order, and protect citizens from immediate threats to their health and safety. Conservatives decidedly favor government spending on national security over social programs. Although many conservatives have made peace with the main components of the welfare state—Social Security and Medicare—many want those programs to be contained or even scaled back and partially or wholly privatized. Conservatives today are split on budgetary policy. Supply-siders, like George W. Bush, advocate across-the-board tax cuts—even a flat tax—which, they believe, will stimulate economic growth. Fiscal conservatives, on the other hand, worry about budget deficits. Rather than cut government revenues, they want to see existing programs downsized. Conservatives argue that affirmative action improperly creates special rights for minority groups. Most conservatives believe that individual liberties must be balanced against the government's responsibilities to protect national security and to defend core American values (e.g., the Patriot Act, which significantly broadened governmental powers of search and seizure and reduced fair trial rights), or Judeo-Christian values (e.g., government support to religious organizations that render social services). Conservatives support a foreign policy that muscularly advances U.S. interests abroad and protects U.S. prestige—unilaterally and preemptively if necessary. Conservatives worry that multilateral organizations, like the United Nations, may undermine U.S. sovereignty and constrain America's freedom to act on the world stage. During the Obama Administration, conservatives have broadened their attack on the growing responsibilities of the federal government, especially in the wake of the healthcare reform of 2010. The ambitious Obama Administration's package of federal programs led to the rise of the Tea Party movement—populist allegations that the Obama/Democratic program constituted a socialistic and anti–states' rights subversion of the framers' constitutional ideals. Some have proposed a constitutional amendment that would allow a vote of two-thirds of state legislatures to nullify a federal program.

Neoconservatism.   Neoconservatism took a prominent place in U.S. foreign policy after 9/11. Neoconservatives want to secure and advance the cultural and moral traditions of the United States—particularly freedom and democracy. The justification for U.S. intervention in Iraq was largely the result of strong neoconservative voices in the Bush Administration. Neoconservatives call for a renewed commitment to individual responsibility—a value that they believe has been eroded by liberal policies. Their influence in Washington has declined with weakening public support for the wars in Iraq and Afghanistan, and with the election of President Obama.

Christian Conservatism/Evangelical, Born-Again Christianity.   Conservative Christians have been a major political force in the United States beginning in the 1980s. Their votes contributed significantly to George W. Bush's election in 2000 and his reelection in 2004. Adherents of this ideology/theology promote so-called traditional moral values against a perceived assault on them by a hedonistic, media-driven culture. Christian conservatives believe that the United States was founded on and owes its greatness to Judeo-Christian principles. They oppose abortion rights, they favor government aid to students who attend religious schools, and they have mobilized in opposition to gay marriage. With the rise of the Tea Party movement, the Christian Conservatives' center-stage role in U.S. politics has been moved to stage right within the Republican Party.

Libertarianism.   Libertarians are more consistent in their view of government activism than are either liberals or conservatives. Both liberals and conservatives favor government activism but in different kinds of policy. Liberals favor active government in enforcing civil rights, programs to help the disadvantaged, and government regulation of the economy, whereas they favor less government in civil liberties (e.g., free speech), in national security policy, and the vigorous pursuit of U.S. interests abroad. Conservatives, favor active government in protecting national security, maintaining law and order, and the muscular defense of U.S. global interests, whereas they favor less government in regulation of the economy, new programs to help the disadvantaged (e.g., healthcare reform), and the enforcement of civil rights. Libertarians favor minimal government involvement in all areas of policy. Although they recognize the need to defend the nation, their primary value is individual liberty, which they believe is threatened as much by the government's zealous protection of national security and economic regulations as it is by the government's attempts to restrict civil liberties or the right of same-sex couples to marry. Ron Paul, a libertarian and a long-time member of the House of Representatives from Texas, who ran for the Republican presidential nomination in 2008, criticized Republicans for their support of the wars in Iraq and Afghanistan as much as he criticized Democrats for their reliance on government to solve the nation's economic problems.

The Right Wing.   The Right in the United States includes groups with different agendas, but it is united in its opposition to social diversity and to governmental encroachments on private property rights. Right-wing ideologues contend that the national government has established a tyranny over the individual; white Christian males are believed to be those most oppressed. Many right-wing groups embrace doctrines of racial supremacy; others are anti-Semitic. In recent years, several right-wing groups have come to believe that armed resistance—including terrorism—is necessary to liberate the United States from perceived sources of oppression. Timothy McVeigh, a self-described right-winger, was involved in the 1993 bombing of the Alfred P. Murrah Federal Building in Oklahoma City.

ASSIGNMENT

1. Listed below are five hypothetical statements. Identify the ideology each statement reflects. Explain and support your answer.

a. "Marriage must be legally defined as only between a man and a woman."

_____

_____

_____

b. "If elected, I will get government off your backs and release the great economic energy of the American people."

_____

_____

_____

c. "So long as I am president, no American shall go to bed hungry, no American shall suffer the burden of discrimination, and no American shall fall ill without the benefit of medical help."

_____

_____

_____

d. "To make America safe from terrorism, we must first make the Islamic world safe for democracy."

_____

_____

_____

    e. "The war on terrorism should not provide a pretext for a governmental assault on the liberties of the American people."

_____

_____

_____

    f. "The government that governs best governs least."

_____

_____

_____

    2. *Web-Based Question.* Go the Directory of U.S. political parties at http://www.politics1.com/parties.htm.

    Web addresses sometimes change. If you can't locate a website, try an external search (e.g., Google) to find the website. Configurations within a website often change. If you can't find a particular link or article, for example, try an internal search of the website as well as an external search. Be resourceful! If you still can't find what you're searching for, move on to the next question.

    The site briefly describes the ideologies of the two major political parties in the United States, Democratic and Republican, and more than thirty minor parties. The site also provides a link to each party's website. Search the directory for a political party that exemplifies each of the political ideologies identified above. Explain and support your answer.

Liberalism: _____

_____

_____

The left wing: _____

_____

_____

Conservatism, or neoconservatism, or Christian conservatism: _____

_____

_____

The right wing: _____

_____

_____

Libertarianism: _____

_____

_____

3. *Web-Based Question:* Go to the websites of the following organizations. Identify the ideology each organization exemplifies. Explain and support your answer. You might need to navigate around the website to determine the ideology.

Religious Freedom Foundation: http://www.rfcnet.org/news/default.asp

_____

_____

_____

Change: http://www.change.org

_____

_____

_____

Project for the New American Century: http://www.newamericancentury.org/

_____

_____

_____

United for a Fair Economy: http://www.faireconomy.org/

_____

_____

_____

Minutemen Project: www.minutemanproject.com/

_____

_____

_____

Tea Party Movement: http://teapartypatriots.ning.com/

_____

_____

_____

Cato Institute: http://www.cato.org/

_____

_____

_____

4. *Web-Based Question.* To find your ideology, take the "World's Smallest Political Quiz" at http://www.theadvocates.org/quiz. What was the result? Do you think the quiz was accurate about you? Why or why not?

_____

_____

_____

_____

_____

EXERCISE 1.4   Direct Democracy via the Web

INTRODUCTION

In a direct democracy, every citizen is a ruler: Citizens—not elected representatives—make law. Direct democracy was practiced in the ancient Greek city-state of Athens, but large segments of the population were excluded: women, slaves, the foreign-born, and the young. The Athenian statesman Pericles (ca. 495–429 B.C.) said, "We do not say that a man who takes no interest in politics minds his own business; we say that he has no business here at all."[1] The major theoretical defense of direct democracy was made by philosopher Jean-Jacques Rousseau (1712–1778), who argued, in *The Social Contract*, that the moment citizens surrender their will to a representative, they become slaves to that representative. Only the individual can represent his or her own will.

The framers of the Constitution were vehemently opposed to direct democracy and excluded it from the Constitution. In *Federalist No. 10*, Madison wrote: "[S]uch democracies have ever been spectacles of turbulence and contention; have ever been found incompatible with personal security and the rights of property; and have in general been as short in their lives as they have been violent in their deaths." The U.S. Constitution continues to reflect Madison's view: The Constitution has not been amended to allow direct democracy.

In contrast, since about the beginning of the twentieth century, Americans have been enthusiastic practitioners of direct democracy in many of their state and local governments. Many state constitutions provide for the *initiative*, which allows voters to originate and enact laws no matter what their elected representatives think, and the *referendum*, which allows voters to approve or repeal laws passed by their representatives. These take the form of *propositions* on the ballot in the states that provide for the initiative and referendum. Neither practice conforms precisely to the Athenian understanding of direct democracy because citizens do not assemble to debate proposed legislation. Measures that do pass are subject to modification or even nullification by the courts. Still, vestiges of Athenian-like direct democracy survive in parts of the United States—especially New England—where town business, such as spending and local ordinances, are decided by citizens directly in public meetings.

ASSIGNMENT

Direct democracy like that in Athens or in a New England town meeting has been practiced only in small political communities.[2] There are two reasons for this: First, the logistics—too many citizens would make it difficult for assemblies to function, and too vast a territory would make it unlikely that many citizens could travel to the assemblies. Second, smaller communities facilitate the establishment of trust and friendship among citizens, bonds that are important in the exercise of direct political power. The size and complexity of the modern nation-state would seem to prohibit the practice of Athenian-like direct democracy today. Not so, say the supporters of direct democracy, who point to the possibility of using the Internet and other social media to create a virtual assembly of a community of citizens. Reading 1.4.1 presents one version of Web-based direct democracy. Study the model and answer the questions that follow.

READING 1.4.1
A Model of Web-Based Direct Democracy

A blue-ribbon commission of citizen-experts with broad experience in voting technology would develop the software required to enable eligible voters to cast their ballots over the Internet. Voters without Internet access would vote via the Internet at local polling places. In assessing this model of direct democracy and answering the questions below, assume that this system of Internet voting is perfectly accurate and absolutely secure against any kind of

---

[1]Quoted in Thucydides, *The Peloponnesian* War (Baltimore: Penguin Books, 1954), p. 119.
[2]Athens, at its most populous, had about 100,000 residents, some 20,000 of whom were citizens.

tampering or fraud: The point of this exercise is not to debate the merits or weaknesses of the technology, but rather to explore the benefits and the drawbacks of expanding the political power of citizens.

In addition to voting for president and their representatives in Congress, voters would be empowered for the first time in the history of the nation to vote for or against national ballot propositions—in other words, to directly enact national laws. These national legislative propositions could be placed on the Internet ballot by an act of Congress, by executive order of the president, or by citizen petition. The petition route would require a number of digital signatures equal to 5 percent of all eligible voters. The legislative propositions would be written in clear and concise language. For example, the voters might be asked, "Should all Americans be guaranteed insurance that covers 80 percent of their health-care costs annually?" or "Should the United States send troops to Iran to force compliance with nuclear nonproliferation agreements?" By a simple majority (50 percent plus one vote), the results of the Internet vote would be binding on the nation.

To be effective in increasing the political power of citizens, this system of direct democracy would require modifying the existing structure of government. First, the power of Congress to initiate and enact legislation would be substantially curtailed. Congress would perform three main functions in the new direct democracy: placing propositions on the Web-based ballot for citizens to approve or reject, enacting narrowly tailored legislation to implement the propositions passed by the voters, and appropriating money to fund those propositions. The powers of the executive branch would also be circumscribed. Presidents could issue executive orders only for the purpose of implementing the will of the people as expressed through the national legislative propositions. The president would remain commander-in-chief and retain emergency power to deploy troops. However, military action by the president would be subject to a later Internet referendum. The federal courts would retain the power of judicial review—the power to strike down laws passed by Congress or acts of the president that conflict with the Constitution. National legislative propositions enacted under the new system of direct democracy would also be subject to judicial review to protect minority and other rights contained in the Bill of Rights, as well as the integrity of the Constitution itself.

There is no doubt that members of Congress and the president would resent and possibly resist the vast expansion of citizens' power that this system of direct democracy would deliver. To ensure that they would not obstruct the will of the people, members of Congress and the president would be subject to recall from office via an Internet vote. (The ability of voters to recall elected officials from office prior to the completion of their term is provided for in many state constitutions, but not in the U.S. Constitution.) A recall vote would be triggered by a number of digital signatures equal to 5 percent of all eligible voters. A simple majority vote would be required to recall the president or a member of Congress.

Unrestricted media campaigns for and against the new national ballot measures would be allowed. In addition, a bipartisan commission, appointed by the president with the consent of Congress, would be responsible for arranging debates about each proposition in the week preceding the vote. These debates would be broadcast on television and available on the Internet. Participants in each debate would include spokespersons for the pro and con positions and a panel of independent analysts, who would provide expert opinion on the consequences and costs of the proposed measure. Citizens would be free, of course, to debate these national legislative initiatives in Internet chat rooms and through social media.

Of course, establishing this model of electronic direct democracy would require the kinds of changes to the Constitution that could be accomplished only by a new constitutional convention, according to the procedures outlined in Article V of the Constitution (see the appendix of this text).

1. What particular features of the model of Web-based direct democracy would you favor adopting? Why? Explain and support your answer.

_____

_____

_____

_____

_____

_____

_____

_____

2. What particular features of the model of Web-based direct democracy would you oppose adopting? Why? Explain and support your answer.

_____

_____

_____

_____

_____

_____

_____

_____

3. Regardless of the features of any particular model of how direct democracy might look, do you think it's a good idea for the political power of citizens to be expanded so they could make law directly? Your opinion on this question is linked, of course, to your view of human nature generally, and more specifically to your view of citizens' political interest, commitment, capability, and knowledge. Address these matters as you explain and support your position.

_____

_____

_____

_____

_____

_____

_____

_____

_____

_____

4. The model of Web-based direct democracy increases the political power of citizens far beyond anything the framers of the Constitution were willing to consider. But the model checks the power of majorities—and the problem of majority tyranny—by retaining the power of judicial review for the federal courts.

    a. Search the Web for a definition and a current or historical example of majority tyranny and write it here.

_____

_____

_____

_____

_____

_____

    b. In a direct democracy without judicial review, what position might minorities find themselves in? Recognize that there are a wide range of minorities based on race, ethnicity, religion, political ideology, wealth, sexual orientation, among others.

_____

_____

_____

_____

_____

_____

_____

Federalism

EXERCISE 2.1   Creating Federalism

INTRODUCTION

In 1781, American forces defeated the British at Yorktown. A year later Great Britain agreed to recognize the independence of the United States, and in 1783, it signed the Treaty of Paris. The war was over, and Americans were able to give their full attention to this question: What form of government would be most suitable for the newly independent republic?

In 1777, the colonies joined together to fashion America's first national government under the provisions of the Articles of Confederation. Americans were in no mood in 1777 to create a strong central government that might abuse power and suppress the liberties of citizens, as the British government had done. A central feature of the new government was that states would retain their sovereignty, unless the power was expressly delegated to the Congress of the Confederation. The colonies were stingy in their grants of power to the new government, denying to it powers that Americans today take for granted. That first national government, for example, had no executive or judicial branch: All power was vested in Congress, but it was a weak Congress, without the power to tax or to regulate foreign or domestic commerce.

By 1787, many Americans recognized the folly of their experiment with a central government too weak to maintain order, conduct foreign relations, or provide for the general welfare of its citizens. That year, proponents of a stronger central government gathered in Philadelphia to consider revising the Articles of Confederation. Instead, the delegates to the Constitutional Convention went considerably further: They produced a new constitution that vested in the national government many of the powers denied to it under the Articles. The Constitution, then, often rightly cast as a document about liberty, is also a document that *expands* the powers of government. As James Madison wrote, in *Federalist No. 51*, "You must first enable the government to control the governed; and in the next place oblige it to control itself."

Proponents of the new government faced the formidable task of persuading citizens in the thirteen states to ratify the new Constitution. Those proponents, who would have been described most accurately as nationalists, instead called themselves *federalists*. They wanted to emphasize that state governments would retain considerable powers under the new Constitution. Federalists also emphasized that the new national government would be limited and restrained by the separation of powers and by checks and balances. Opponents of the new Constitution, called *antifederalists*, objected, insisting that the document proposed to empower the new national government largely at the expense of state governments. For example, under the Articles of Confederation, the states reserved exclusively to themselves the power to tax. Under the new Constitution—for the first time—the national government would have the power to tax directly. Antifederalists favored decentralized government and the preservation of the powers and prerogatives of the states.

A debate raged in the new nation over the transfer of power to the national government as well as over many other features of the new Constitution. Because the ratification of the proposed Constitution was by no means a foregone conclusion, Alexander Hamilton, John Jay, and James Madison—all federalists—wrote public arguments, under the pseudonym Publius, to defend and promote the Constitution. Eighty-five of their articles were reprinted as *The Federalist*, in 1788, a collection usually referred to as *The Federalist Papers*. The degree to which the arguments advanced in *The Federalist* persuaded the public of the time is debatable, but today the collection remains an essential explanation of the structure and functions of the government established by the Constitution.

Federalism has remained a contentious issue from the founding period, to the Civil War, to the New Deal, to the civil rights movement, and to our current debates about federal versus state power in health care policy, gun regulation, and education, to name a few.

ASSIGNMENT

The Articles of Confederation were written in 1777 and became law in full force with Maryland's ratification in 1781. Study Reading 2.1.1, which contains excerpts from the Articles, then answer the questions that follow the reading.

READING 2.1.1
Excerpts from the Articles of Confederation

    I. Stile [legal designation] of this Confederacy shall be "The United States of America."

    II. Each state retains its sovereignty, freedom, and independence, and every power, jurisdiction, and right, which is not by this Confederation expressly delegated to the United States, in Congress assembled.

    III. The said States hereby severally enter into a firm league of friendship with each other, for their common defense, the security of their liberties, and their mutual and general welfare, binding themselves to assist each other, against all force offered to, or attacks made upon them, or any of them, on account of religion, sovereignty, trade, or any other pretense whatever. . . .

    V. . . . . In determining questions in the United States in Congress assembled, each State shall have one vote.

---

1. a. Confederations have been likened to alliances. Alliances are organizations in which the member nation-states act in concert only when they agree to act together. What language in the Articles suggests an alliance of the states rather than a union of the states?

_____

b. In a unitary form of government, power flows from the central government. In a federal form of government, some powers belong to the central government and some to regional or state governments. In a confederal form of government, power flows from regional or state governments. What language in the Articles suggests that power flows from the states?

_____

_____

c. What language tells us that, under the Articles of Confederation, states were represented, not people?

_____

_____

d. What institution under the U.S. Constitution to this day embodies the representational principle of the Articles?

_____

_____

Federalist No. 45, written by James Madison, appeared in the *New York Packet* on January 29, 1788. In the article, Madison sought to dispel the fear that the new constitution would undermine the powers and prerogatives of the state governments. Study Reading 2.1.2, which contains excerpts from *Federalist No. 45*, then answer the questions that follow it.

READING 2.1.2
Excerpts from *Federalist No. 45*, by James Madison

Having shown that no one of the powers transferred to the federal government is unnecessary or improper, the next question to be considered is, whether the whole mass of them will be dangerous to the portion of authority left in the several States.

. . . [I]f the Union, as has been shown, be essential to the security of the people of America against foreign danger; if it be essential to their security against contentions and wars among the different States; if it be essential to guard them against those violent and oppressive factions which embitter the blessings of liberty, and against those military establishments which must gradually poison its very fountain; if, in a word, the Union be essential to the happiness of the people of America, is it not preposterous, to urge as an objection to a government, without which the objects of the Union cannot be attained, that such a government may derogate from the importance of the governments of the individual States? Was, then, the American Revolution effected, was the American Confederacy formed, was the precious blood of thousands spilt, and the hard-earned substance of millions lavished, not that the people of American should enjoy peace, liberty, and safety, but that the government of the individual States, that particular municipal establishments, might enjoy a certain extent of power, and be arrayed with certain dignities and attributes of sovereignty? . . .

We have seen, in all the examples of ancient and modern confederacies, the strongest tendency continually betraying itself in the members, to despoil the general government of its authorities, with a very ineffectual capacity in the latter to defend itself against the encroachments. Although, in most of these examples, the system has been so dissimilar from that under consideration as greatly to weaken any inference concerning the latter from the fate of the former, yet, as the States will retain, under the proposed Constitution, a very extensive portion of active sovereignty, the inference ought not to be wholly disregarded. . . .

The State governments may be regarded as constituent and essential parts of the federal government; whilst the latter is nowise essential to the operation or organization of the former. Without the intervention of the State legislatures, the President of the United States cannot be elected at all. They must in all cases have a great share in his appointment, and will, perhaps in most cases, of themselves determine it. The Senate will be elected absolutely and exclusively by the State legislatures.[1] Even the House of Representatives, though drawn immediately from the people, will be chosen very much under the influence of that class of men, whose influence over the people obtains for themselves an election into the State legislatures. Thus, each of the principal branches of the federal government will owe its existence more or less to the favor of the State governments, and must consequently feel a dependence, which is much more likely to begat a disposition too obsequious than too overbearing towards them. . . .

The powers delegated by the proposed Constitution to the federal government are few and defined. Those which are to remain in the State governments are numerous and indefinite. The former will be exercised principally on external objects, as war, peace, negotiation, and foreign commerce; with which last the power of taxation will, for the most part, be connected. The powers reserved to the several States will extend to all the objects which, in the ordinary course of affairs, concern the lives, liberties, and properties of the people, and the internal order, improvement, and prosperity of the State.

The operations of the federal government will be most extensive and important in times of war and danger; those of the State governments in times of peace and security. As

---

[1]The Twelfth Amendment (1804) provided for the election of the president by electors chosen by the public, and the Seventeenth Amendment (1913) provided for the popular election of U.S. senators.

the former periods will probably bear a small proportion to the latter, the State governments will here enjoy another advantage over the federal government. The more adequate, indeed, the federal powers may be rendered to the national defence, the less frequent will be those scenes of danger which might favor their ascendancy over the governments of the particular States.

2. a. Identify two arguments Madison made to support his contention that a strong central government with independent powers is necessary.

_____

_____

_____

_____

b. Identify three arguments Madison made to support his contention that the Constitution is not a threat to the powers and prerogatives of the state governments.

_____

_____

_____

_____

_____

_____

The distribution of power between the national and state governments in the United States today is governed by several key passages in the Constitution, the Supreme Court's interpretation of those passages, and legislation enacted by Congress and the state legislatures. Two clauses in the Constitution are particularly important. Go to the copy of the U.S. Constitution in the appendix of this text. Study Article I, Section 8. Pay close attention to the last clause, which gives Congress the power "to make all Laws which shall be necessary and proper for carrying into Execution the foregoing Powers, and all other Powers vested by this Constitution in the Government of the United States, or in any Department or Officer thereof." Look next at the Tenth Amendment: "The powers not delegated to the United States by the Constitution, nor prohibited by it to the States, are reserved to the States respectively, or to the people." Compare these provisions with Article II in the Articles of Confederation: "Each State retains its sovereignty, freedom and independence, and every power, jurisdiction, and right, which is not by this confederation expressly delegated to the United States in Congress assembled."

3. a. Article II of the Articles of Confederation uses the phrase _expressly delegated_ to limit the power of the central government. Even though the Tenth Amendment was meant to protect the power of the states, its authors omitted the word _expressly_, so that it refers to only the powers "delegated to the United States," not "expressly delegated." What is the significance of the omission of the word _expressly_?

_____

_____

_____

_____

b. In Article I, Section 8 of the Constitution, how might the last paragraph—the *necessary and proper* clause—pave the way for the expansion of federal powers not expressly delegated to the federal government?

_____

_____

_____

_____

During the Obama Administration, and particularly with the passage of health-care reform, some state legislatures and governors (usually Republican) argued for the so-called Repeal Amendment to the Constitution. The Repeal Amendment reverberates with theories going back to the Articles of Confederation and Nullification prior to the Civil War. The theory of nullification, argued by southern states, maintained that each state had the prerogative to nullify federal laws that the state did not want to be enforced within its boundaries. The Repeal Amendment states, "Any provision of law or regulation of the United States may be repealed by the several states, and such repeal shall be effective when the legislatures of two-thirds of the several states approve resolutions for this purpose that particularly describe the same provision or provisions of law or regulation to be repealed."

4. a. Many of the proponents of the Repeal Amendment believe that they are carrying out the intentions of the framers of the Constitution by reasserting states' rights against a federal government that has exceeded its constitutional powers. Considering the background to the creation of federalism described in the introduction to this exercise and Madison's argument in *Federalist No. 45,* do you think that the framers of the Constitution would support the amendment? Explain and support your answer.

_____

_____

_____

_____

_____

b. Do you think that Congress should propose, and the states should ratify, this amendment? Explain and support your answer.

_____

_____

_____

_____

_____

EXERCISE 2.2   Reforming K–12 Education: The Disputed Role of the Federal Government

INTRODUCTION

Who determines whether students have learned their lessons? And how should that learning be determined? These questions are at the heart of the current controversy about the effectiveness of K–12 education in the United States. Public opinion polls show that Americans are deeply dissatisfied with pubic education. Cross-national test scores in science, math, and language skills show that American students compare unfavorably with students in other countries. The widely publicized results of Third International Mathematics and Science Study (2010)[1] showed U.S. twelfth-graders scored sixteenth in math and nineteenth in science. An emerging consensus is that the United States does not have world-class schools, which bodes poorly for our economic competitiveness in a global marketplace that demands high-level educational skills.

The issue of who determines whether students have learned their lessons has proved to be politically contentious. The United States is one of the few economically advanced countries with a tradition of state and local control over primary and secondary education. Early in the republic's history, parents and private schools controlled the practice of education. As public school systems expanded during the nineteenth and early twentieth centuries, local and state governments set standards, curriculum, and teacher education requirements. The federal government did not claim a significant role in determining educational policy until after World War II.

The creation of the Department of Health, Education and Welfare (HEW) in 1953 signaled that educational policy had become a matter of national concern. That concern escalated into a crisis of confidence after the Soviet Union launched *Sputnik*—the world's first orbiting satellite—on October 4, 1957. Many Americans feared that the Soviets might surge ahead of the United States to conquer outer space. As part of a broad response to ensure that the United States would not be left behind, President Dwight Eisenhower proposed, and Congress approved, federal funding for the expansion of science, mathematics, and foreign language education. As indicated by its title, the National Defense Education Act of 1958 was sold to Congress and the public as a national security measure. The act endorsed a greater federal role in determining national educational policy by increasing federal funding for schools and universities. Not only were many students now receiving federal aid, but many colleges and universities, in order to be eligible for federal dollars, responded to the federal government's interest in expanding their curricula in science and mathematics.

The expansion of the national government's role in education continued as a result of President Lyndon Johnson's War on Poverty. In the Educational and Secondary School Act of 1965, Johnson sought to expand and equalize educational opportunity by providing federal aid in the form of *categorical grants* to states and to school districts. Categorical grants fund specific projects, and they come with strings attached, thereby giving the national government greater control over educational policy. By 1979, during Jimmy Carter's presidency, the federal role in education had become so large that Congress established a separate Department of Education.

During Ronald Reagan's presidency (1981–1989) and later during the Republican ascendancy in Congress (beginning in 1995), conservatives led a backlash against the growing role of the national government in traditionally state and local government affairs, including education policy. As part of the rebellion against "big government," Republicans sought to provide a larger percentage of federal aid to education in the form of *block grants*, which give state and local officials more control over how federal money is spent than they had with categorical grants. (See Box 2.2.1.)

With more studies showing the United States falling behind other countries—especially the 1983 U.S. Department of Education's stinging critique of the performance of the nation's public schools, *A Nation at Risk*—federal aid to education became a prominent issue in the 2000 presidential campaign. Mounting evidence showed declining test scores and complaints came from employers about the lack of math, science, and writing skills in the workforce, so candidate George W. Bush charged that President Bill Clinton and Vice President Al Gore were responsible for an "education recession."

---

[1] http://nces.ed.gov/timss/

BOX 2.2.1   Three Ways the Federal Government Has Delivered Aid to State and Local Governments

- **Revenue sharing.** The federal government returned federal tax dollars to the states with few strings attached. The states could use the money as they wished to supplement state revenues. Though started as a Republican approach in the Nixon Administration to end heavy-handed federal regulations on the use of federal funds, revenue sharing was abolished during the Reagan Administration. With his tax-cut plan and his proposal to increase federal spending on defense, Reagan argued that the federal government could no longer afford to distribute revenue-sharing funds.
- **Block grants.** These grants have been the hallmark of the Republican approach to federal funding to the states since the Reagan Administration. Funds are awarded in general policy areas (e.g., highway construction funds), but the states may decide on which programs and projects to use the funds. Block grants come with relatively few restrictions. Republicans and conservatives generally favor this approach. (See Exercise 1.3.)
- **Categorical grants.** Beginning in the Johnson Administration, funds were delivered directly to projects at the local level, including school districts. Funds were awarded for the project's consistency with federal policy objectives. Categorical grants come with abundant rules, regulations, and accountability procedures. Usually categorical grants require matching funds from the governmental entity seeking the funding. Most federal aid—over 80 percent— is still delivered in the form of categorical grants. Democrats and liberals generally favor this approach. (See Exercise 1.3.)

Bush advocated a hybrid approach to federal aid to education, containing both categorical and block grant elements. Having criticized Democratic candidate Al Gore's proposals as imposing too many federal mandates on the states, Bush appeared to tilt toward the block grant approach, allowing states to set their own goals for improvement, with the Department of Education monitoring whether the states were making progress toward meeting their own goals. But Bush's position that schools that failed to meet standards should lose their federal aid and that their students should then be free to transfer to successful schools was closer to the intrusive, strings-attached approach usually associated with Democrats. Bush especially insisted that public schools be held accountable for improving test scores for racial and ethnic minorities. Lack of funding has led some states to claim that the program is an unfunded federal mandate, which Congress had prohibited in 1995.[2] Bush also favored a school voucher program that would allow students in poorly performing schools to use federal funds to enroll in private schools. Except for the school voucher proposal, Bush's plan was signed into law as the No Child Left Behind (NCLB) Act of 2001.

Because NCLB has never been fully funded, transfers of funds to successful schools have been difficult, especially in large urban districts, where successful schools are already overenrolled. Lack of funding combined with higher standards has raised concerns in many states. Utah has since enacted a law that exempts the state from provisions that conflict with Utah's own educational goals or that require additional funding by the state. More troubling has been the trend of many states purposefully lowering their standards in order to increase their chances for meeting federal requirements for continued funding. One recent study suggests that, although student scores have improved after the implementation of the NCLB Act, the rate of improvement has begun to decline.[3]

Barack Obama, in his 2008 campaign, promised substantial revisions of NCLB, which was a response to criticisms from a variety of groups that NCLB was too inflexible, too punitive, and too deferential to states that were lowering standards and showing little progress toward improving public schools. The thrust of the Obama reforms, led by his secretary of education, Arne Duncan, has been increased flexibility with regard to the measurement of improved teaching and learning, while moving to greater federal control in defining what steps states must take to improve public education. This is particularly evident in the Race to the Top block grant program, in which states competed for billions of dollars in federal aid based on their willingness to meet sweeping federal guidelines for overhauling public education, including teacher evaluation. One clear sign of the

---

[2]In 2005, the largest teachers' union and several school districts across the country sued the Department of Education for requiring states to meet standards without providing the necessary funding. See Sam Dillon, "Teachers' Union and Districts Sue Over Bush Law," *New York Times,* April 21, 2005, p. A.1. Several states, including Connecticut, have filed such suits. In July 2010, the Second Circuit Court of Appeals rejected the Connecticut suit.

[3]Greg Winter, "Study Finds Shortcoming in New Law on Education," *New York Times,* April 13, 2005, p. A. 15.

trend toward an increased federal role is that, as of July 2010, twenty-seven states had adopted national standards for student learning. This dramatic departure from the tradition of state and local control over educational standards was, in part, a response to the Obama Administration's Race to the Top competition, in which extra points were added to the state's application for the federal grant if the state had adopted the standards. (Governors and state school superintendents had recommended the standards less than two months earlier.) Nevertheless, many states refused to cooperate with the Race to the Top program, and many groups were highly critical of what they saw as federal preemption of a reserved power of the states.

On March 14, 2011, President Obama announced that he would ask Congress to overhaul NCLB to provide more flexibility for state and local governments and to provide more federal funding. In return for more flexibility, the Obama Administration would ask for improvement in the quality of testing and additional accountability for school principals.

ASSIGNMENT

This assignment asks you to think of improvement of public education in terms of the ongoing dispute over federal versus state and local control of public education. Study Reading 2.2.1, "Excerpts from President Obama's Speech to the National Urban League" (July 29, 2010), and Reading 2.2.2, "Governor Perry [of Texas]: Texas Knows Best How to Educate Our Students" (January 13, 2010), in which the governor announced that Texas would not apply for Race to the Top funds. Then answer questions 1 to 3.

READING 2.2.1
Excerpts from President Obama's Speech to the National Urban League (July 29, 2010)[4]

Too many of our children see college as nothing but a distant dream—because their education went off the rails long before they turned 18. These are young people who've been relegated to failing schools in struggling communities, where there are too many obstacles, too few role models. . . .

That's why I want to challenge our states to offer better early learning options to make sure our children aren't wasting their most formative years, so that they can enter into kindergarten already ready to learn . . . .

. . . I think the single most important thing we've done is to launch an initiative called Race to the Top. We said to states, if you are committed to outstanding teaching, to successful schools, to higher standards, to better assessments—if you're committed to excellence for all children—you will be eligible for a grant to help you attain that goal.

And so far, the results have been promising and they have been powerful. In an effort to compete for this extra money, thirty-two states reformed their education laws before we even spent a dime. The competition leveraged change at the state level. And because the standards we set were high, only a couple of states actually won the grant in the first round, which meant that the states that didn't get the money, they've now strengthened their applications, made additional reforms. Now thirty-six have applied in the second round, and eighteen states plus the District of Columbia are in the running to get a second grant.

[The Race to the Top has] forced teachers and principals and officials and parents to forge agreements on tough, and often uncomfortable issues—to raise their sights and embrace education. For the most part, states, educators, reformers, they've responded with great enthusiasm around this promise of excellence. But I know there's also been some controversy about Race to the Top. Part of it, I believe, reflects a general resistance to change. We get comfortable with the status quo even when the status quo isn't good. We make excuses for why things have to be the way they are. And when you try to shake things up, some people aren't happy.

---

[4]Retrieved from http://www.whitehouse.gov/the-press-office/remarks-president-education-reform-national-urban-league-centennial-conference

Now, there's also the question of how hard our teachers should push students in the classroom. Nations in Asia and Europe have answered this question in part by creating standards to make sure their teachers and students are performing at the same high levels throughout their nation. That's one of the reasons that their children are doing better than ours. But here at home, there's often a controversy about national standards, common standards—that violates the principle of local control. Now, there's a history to local control that we need to think about, but that—that's the argument.

So here's what Race to the Top says: Instead of Washington imposing standards from the top down, let's challenge states to adopt common standards voluntarily, from the bottom up. That doesn't mean more standards; it means higher standards, better standards, standards that clarify what our teachers are expected to teach and what our children are expected to learn—so high school graduates are actually prepared for college and a career. I do not want to see young people get a diploma but they can't read that diploma. . . .

So, yes, our federal government has responsibilities that it has to meet, and I will keep on making sure the federal government meets those responsibilities. . . .

You've got to want it. You've got to reach out and claim that future for yourself. And you can't make excuses.

READING 2.2.2
Governor Perry [of Texas]: Texas Knows Best How to Educate Our Students (January 13, 2010)[5]

Gov. Rick Perry today announced that Texas will not submit an application for federal Race to the Top education funds. Despite tremendous education successes, Texas' application would be penalized by the U.S. Department of Education for refusing to commit to adopt national curriculum standards and tests and to incur ongoing costs.

"Texas is on the right path toward improved education, and we would be foolish and irresponsible to place our children's future in the hands of unelected bureaucrats and special interest groups thousands of miles away in Washington, virtually eliminating parents' participation in their children's education," Gov. Perry said. "If Washington were truly concerned about funding education with solutions that match local challenges, they would make the money available to states with no strings attached."

Texas' curriculum standards, which determine what students are taught in Texas classrooms, are set by the elected State Board of Education (SBOE). The SBOE recently adopted one of the nation's first college- and career-ready curriculum standards in core subjects after receiving widespread input from Texas education and business leaders.

"I wholeheartedly support the governor's decision," Texas Education Commissioner Robert Scott said. "This one-time grant program would result in mandates for districts that would last for decades."

Through Race to the Top funding, the U.S. Department of Education seems to be coercing states like Texas to suddenly abandon their own locally established curriculum standards in favor of adopting national standards spearheaded by organizations in Washington, D.C. While Texas could be eligible for up to $750 million in Race to the Top funding, it would cost Texas taxpayers upwards of $3 billion to realign our education system to conform to the U.S. Department of Education's uniform vision for public education.

"Texas has been working to implement research-based education reforms for years, culminating with great solutions for Texas children, and we should qualify for Race to the Top funding

---

[5]Retrieved from http://governor.state.tx.us/news/press-release/14146/

based on what we have already accomplished," Rep. Rob Eissler, Public Education Committee chairman, said. "Instead, Texas will be penalized in its Race to the Top application for not complying with the federal government's concepts about what is best for the children of Texas. In short, the two things I worry about in education are fads and feds, and this combines both."

Developing Texas' workforce is imperative to maintaining our position as a national leader in job creation and our future prosperity. . . . The governor recently announced a $160 million initiative to expand the number and scope of Texas Science, Technology, Engineering and Math (T-STEM) academies, an initiative he established in 2005, as well as fund STEM scholarships. Building on successful initiatives like T-STEM academies helps ensure future generations of Texans have the educational foundation necessary to compete and excel in the increasingly competitive global economy.

Source: Used by permission of the Office of the Governor Rick Perry.

Now answer questions 1 to 6, based on Reading 2.2.1 and 2.2.2.

1. What is President Obama's defense of the Race to the Top program? In particular, how does he defend common, higher educational standards?

_____

_____

_____

_____

_____

2. On what grounds does President Obama argue that the federal government is not *imposing* national standards?

_____

_____

_____

_____

_____

3. What are Governor Perry's criticisms of the Race to the Top program?

_____

_____

4. What kind of federal aid to education would Perry support?

_____

_____

5. On what grounds does he contend that improvement in education policy is best left to the state of Texas?

_____

_____

_____

6. Are you more persuaded by Obama's or Perry's argument? Why?

_____

_____

_____

_____

Question 7 is based on Figure 2.2.1. Study the pie chart and then answer question 7.

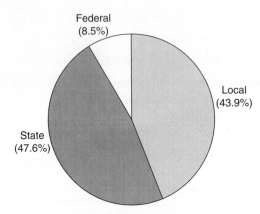

FIGURE 2.2.1   Percentage Distribution of Revenues for Public Elementary and Secondary Education in the United States, by Source: Fiscal Year 2007. *Source:* U.S. Department of Education

7. In 2007, a relatively small portion of the total funding for education came from the federal government. Knowing that categorical grants make up most of federal funding for education, what feature of those grants makes the federal government's role more prominent than its 8.5 percent share would otherwise suggest?

_____

_____

_____

Question 8 is based on Figure 2.2.2. Study the line graph on the next page and then answer question 8.

8. Refer to the introduction to Exercise 2.2. What policy innovations explain the relatively rapid rise in federal spending (inflation-adjusted) on primary and secondary education beginning in 2001 and continuing through 2007?

_____

_____

_____

Questions 9 to 12 are based on Table 2.2.1. Refer to the table when answering questions 9 to 12.

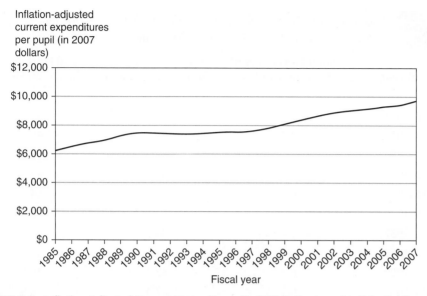

Inflation-adjusted
current expenditures
per pupil (in 2007
dollars)

Fiscal year

FIGURE 2.2.2 Inflation-Adjusted Current Expenditures (in 2007 Dollars) per Pupil for Public
Elementary and Secondary Education in the United States: Fiscal Years 1985–2007. *Source*: U.S.
Department of Education

TABLE 2.2.1	Revenues for Public Elementary and Secondary Schools (School Years 1939–1940 to 2006–2007)		
School Year	**Federal Percentage of Education Funding**	**State Percentage of Education Funding**	**Local Percentage of Education Funding**
1939–1940	1.8	30.3	68.0
1941–1942	1.4	31.4	67.1
1943–1944	1.4	33.0	65.6
1945–1946	1.4	34.7	63.9
1947–1948	2.8	38.9	58.3
1949–1950	2.9	39.8	57.3
1951–1952	3.5	38.6	57.9
1953–1954	4.5	37.4	58.1
1955–1956	4.6	39.5	55.9
1957–1958	4.0	39.4	56.6
1959–1960	4.4	39.1	56.5
1961–1962	4.3	38.7	56.9
1963–1964	4.4	39.3	56.3
1965–1966	7.9	39.1	53.0
1967–1968	8.8	38.5	52.7
1969–1970	8.0	39.9	52.1
1970–1971	8.4	39.1	52.5
1971–1972	8.9	38.3	52.8
1972–1973	8.7	39.7	51.6
1973–1974	8.5	41.4	50.1
1974–1975	9.0	42.0	49.0
1975–1976	8.9	44.4	46.7
1976–1977	8.8	43.2	48.0
1977–1978	9.4	43.0	47.6
1978–1979	9.8	45.6	44.6

(Continued)

TABLE 2.2.1	Revenues for Public Elementary and Secondary Schools (School Years 1939–1940 to 2006–2007) (*Continued*)		
School Year	Federal Percentage of Education Funding	State Percentage of Education Funding	Local Percentage of Education Funding
1979–1980	9.8	46.8	43.4
1980–1981	9.2	47.4	43.4
1981–1982	7.4	47.6	45.0
1982–1983	7.1	47.9	45.0
1983–1984	6.8	47.8	45.4
1984–1985	6.6	48.9	44.4
1985–1986	6.7	49.4	43.9
1986–1987	6.4	49.7	43.9
1987–1988	6.3	49.5	44.1
1988–1989	6.2	47.8	46.0
1989–1990	6.1	47.1	46.8
1990–1991	6.2	47.2	46.7
1991–1992	6.6	46.4	47.0
1992–1993	7.0	45.8	47.2
1993–1994	7.1	45.2	47.8
1994–1995	6.8	46.8	46.4
1995–1996	6.6	47.5	45.9
1996–1997	6.6	48.0	45.4
1997–1998	6.8	48.4	44.8
1998–1999	7.1	48.7	44.2
1999–2000	7.3	49.5	43.2
2000–2001	7.3	49.7	43.0
2001–2002	7.9	49.2	42.9
2002–2003	8.5	48.7	42.8
2003–2004	9.1	47.1	43.9
2004–2005	9.2	46.9	44.0
2005–2006	9.1	46.5	44.4
2006–2007	8.5	47.6	43.9

Source: U.S. Department of Education.

9. a. What percentage of total K–12 funding in 1939–1940 came from the federal government?

_____

b. What percentage of total K–12 funding came from the federal government in 2006–2007?

_____

c. What is the percentage increase in the federal share of K–12 funding from school year 1939–1940 to 2006–2007? (To find the percentage increase, subtract the 1939–1940 number from the 2006–2007 number. Then divide the result by the 1939–1949 number.)

_____

10. a. What percentage of total K–12 funding in 1939–1940 came from state governments?

_____

b. What percentage of total K–12 funding came from state governments in 2006–2007?

_____

c. What is the percentage increase in the state share of K–12 funding from fiscal year 1939–1940 to 2006–2007? (To find the percentage increase, subtract the 1939–1940 number from the 2006–2007 number. Then divide the result by the 1939–1949 number.)

_____

11. a. What's the long-term trend? Are elementary and secondary schools coming to rely more on federal or state dollars?

_____

_____

12. Does the growth in the federal share of K–12 funding versus the growth in the state share of K–12 funding confirm the notion of an expanding federal role in education? Explain and support your answer.

_____

_____

_____

Web-Based Information.   To answer questions 13 to15, you'll need a list of presidents with their years in office. A list of presidencies is available at http://www.enchantedlearning.com/history/us/pres/list.shtml. (Note: If this website is no longer available, try a Web search for a similar list. There are many such sites.)

13. Between which successive school years did the largest increase in the federal share of K–12 funding occur? Who was the president at that time?

_____

14. Between which successive school years did the largest decrease in the federal share of K–12 funding occur? Who was the president at that time?

_____

15. Are your answers to questions 11 and 12 consistent with the assessment that Republicans favor a smaller federal role in education and Democrats favor a larger federal role in education? Be specific.

_____

EXERCISE 2.3 The Amendment Process

INTRODUCTION

Many forces have propelled constitutional change: social and political movements, public opinion, political leadership, and court decisions, among others. The framers recognized that an amendment process was necessary to make the Constitution's fundamental law both flexible and enduring. The functions of government and the allocation of political power would have to be adjusted as the nation evolved and faced new challenges. The threat of tyranny—the abuse of power—surely would arise from quarters and situations the framers had not anticipated, and the Constitution would have to be able to meet those threats.

The problem, of course, was where to locate the immense power to alter the nation's fundamental law. To vest the power of amendment exclusively in elected officials would be foolish: A primary objective of the Constitution is to restrain those very officials. To vest the power of amendment directly in the citizens would raise the threat of majority tyranny and would likely result in transitory popular interests corrupting the nation's fundamental law. In the end, to guard against abuse of the amendment power, the framers divided it more extensively than any other power and subjected it to a supermajority requirement found nowhere else in the Constitution. James Madison claimed in *Federalist No. 53* that the amendment mechanism guarded "equally against that extreme facility, which would render the Constitution too mutable, and that extreme difficulty, which might perpetuate its discovered faults."

The amendment process established by Article V consists of two distinct phases: proposal and ratification. Changes to the Constitution do not take effect until the requirements of both phases have been satisfied. There are two ways to satisfy the requirements of each phase. Amendments to the Constitution can be *proposed* by a two-thirds vote in the House and Senate or by a constitutional convention called by Congress at the request of two-thirds of the states— this latter route to bypass an unresponsive Congress. The *ratification* phase of the amendment process requires approval by three-fourths of the state legislatures or by special ratifying conventions in three-fourths of the states. Congress decides which path a proposed amendment will follow in the ratification phase. (See Figure 2.3.1 for a diagram of the amendment process.)

The three-fourths requirement for ratification is extraordinary: It is the most stringent numeric margin in the Constitution. It makes changing the nation's fundamental law a very difficult task, one that can be accomplished only with widespread support in Congress and the states. It also increases the probability that changes to the Constitution will prove enduring, that transitory popular passions are unlikely to be written into fundamental law. And for the most part, that has been the case. Only the Eighteenth Amendment has been repealed. Of course, the supermajority requirement also can block what's right and just: It took women well over a century to obtain the right to vote through the Nineteenth Amendment (1920).

One authority estimates that over 11,000 amendments have been introduced in Congress.[1] Recent amendments that were not approved by Congress include one to allow devotional Bible reading in public schools and one to prohibit burning the American flag as a form of protest. Only thirty-three amendments have completed the proposal phase of the amendment process. Of those, only twenty-seven have been ratified. The first ten amendments—the Bill of Rights—were proposed by the First Congress as a gesture of conciliation to the remaining opponents of the new government. They were ratified by the state legislatures in 1791. The seventeen subsequent amendments were adopted between 1795 and 1992.

The states have never achieved the two-thirds requirement (thirty-four states) necessary for Congress to call a second constitutional convention. They came close when opposition developed to the Supreme Court's decision in *Reynolds v. Sims* (1964), which required the reapportionment of state legislatures on the basis of population (see Exercise 6.4). By 1967, thirty-three state legislatures had petitioned Congress to call a constitutional convention. Their objective: to use the amendment process to reverse the ruling in *Reynolds*. But a thirty-fourth state legislature never gave its assent. Thus, all of the Constitution's twenty-seven amendments have been proposed by Congress.

---

[1] J. W. Peltason, *Understand the Constitution* (New York: Harcourt, 1997), p. 188.

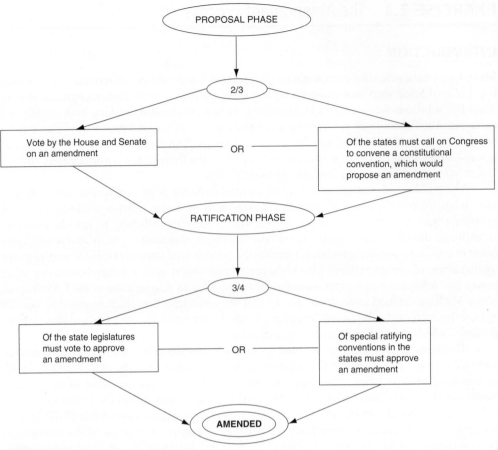

FIGURE 2.3.1 The Amendment Process

All but one of the twenty-seven amendments have been ratified by the state legislatures. The Twenty-First Amendment (1933), which repealed the Eighteenth, was routed by Congress through and then approved by special ratifying conventions in the states instead of by the state legislatures. Members of Congress believed that supporters of Prohibition (the "drys") controlled too many state legislatures, and that repeal would be more likely if the matter was decided in special ratifying conventions. Delegates to the ratifying conventions ran on "wet" or "dry" slates, so the conventions reflected the voters' will in each state.

Great power can be achieved by amending the Constitution, but proponents of constitutional change often have found their victories less than complete. In the case of Prohibition, the amendment was later repealed. Advocates of women's suffrage were disappointed following the ratification of the Nineteenth Amendment in 1920 that the voting rate for women remained below that for men until the 1950s. The Supreme Court narrowed the scope of the Fourteenth Amendment (1868) so severely in the late nineteenth century that racial discrimination remained a legal reality in the South until the 1960s. The Fifteenth Amendment (1870), which guarantees the voting rights of blacks, was not implemented across the nation for nearly 100 years after its ratification. Even today, efforts to suppress the African American vote are widespread.[2] These examples show that constitutional change is effective only in the presence of political and social change.

Congress has charged the National Archives and Records Administration (NARA) with managing the ratification process. NARA's website (www.archives.gov) offers information that should help you understand the amendment process.

---

[2]See, for example, "The Long Shadow of Jim Crow: Voter Intimidation and Suppression in American Today" at www.naacp.org.

ASSIGNMENT

The Constitution stipulates two-thirds and three-fourths majorities for the proposal and ratification phases, respectively, of the amendment process. We might assume, then, that changing the Constitution requires the support of a very large number of the nation's citizens. Questions 1 to 8 test that assumption. These questions also highlight the politics of the different systems of representation in the House and Senate. To answer these questions, you need to consult Table 2.3.1, which lists the population of each state and its representation in the House based on the 2010 census.

TABLE 2.3.1	Population and Representation in the House by State, 2010 Census Data	
State	**Population**	**Number of Representatives in the House**
Alabama	4,802,982	7
Alaska	721,523	1
Arizona	6,412,700	9
Arkansas	2,926,229	4
California	37,341,989	53
Colorado	5,044,930	7
Connecticut	3,581,628	5
Delaware	900,877	1
Florida	18,900,773	27
Georgia	9,727,566	14
Hawaii	1,366,862	2
Idaho	1,573,499	2
Illinois	12,864,380	18
Indiana	6,501,582	9
Iowa	3,053,787	4
Kansas	2,863,813	4
Kentucky	4,350,606	6
Louisiana	4,553,962	6
Maine	1,333,074	2
Maryland	5,789,929	8
Massachusetts	6,559,644	9
Michigan	9,911,626	14
Minnesota	5,314,879	8
Mississippi	2,978,240	4
Missouri	6,011,478	8
Montana	994,416	1
Nebraska	1,831,825	3
Nevada	2,709,432	4
New Hampshire	1,321,445	2
New Jersey	8,807,501	12
New Mexico	2,067,273	3
New York	19,421,055	27
North Carolina	9,565,781	13
North Dakota	675,905	1
Ohio	11,568,495	16
Oklahoma	3,764,882	5

(*Continued*)

TABLE 2.3.1	Population and Representation in the House by State, 2010 Census Data (*Continued*)

State	Population	Number of Representatives in the House
Oregon	3,848,606	5
Pennsylvania	12,734,905	18
Rhode Island	1,055,247	2
South Carolina	4,645,975	7
South Dakota	819,761	1
Tennessee	6,375,431	9
Texas	25,268,418	36
Utah	2,770,765	4
Vermont	630,337	1
Virginia	8,037,736	11
Washington	6,753,369	10
West Virginia	1,859,815	3
Wisconsin	5,698,230	8
Wyoming	568,300	1
Total*	309,183,463	435

*This is the total 2010 apportionment population. The populations of the District of Columbia, Puerto Rico, and the U.S. island areas are excluded from the apportionment population because they do not have voting members in the House.

Consider an amendment to the Constitution that would change the basis of representation in the House. Under this amendment, the bargain struck at the Constitutional Convention between the large and small states—the Great Compromise—would be nullified. The amendment under consideration here would revise Article I, Section 2 to abolish population-based representation in the House and instead make representation there equal for every state by increasing the size of the House to 500 members and awarding ten seats to each state.

1. How many seats in the House would California lose under the terms of this amendment?

_____

2. How many seats would Alaska gain?

_____

3. Consider first the fate of this amendment in the *proposal* phase of the amendment process. The proponents of the amendment introduce it in the House and Senate, hoping to marshal the required two-thirds support.

  a. Use the data in Table 2.3.1 to determine the number of votes cast in the House and Senate for and against *proposing* the amendment. Assume that members of Congress vote solely on the basis of the amendment's effect on their state's voting power in the House and that they do not consider other issues raised by the amendment. California, for example, would vote against the amendment because it would lose 43 of its 53 seats in the House. Wyoming, on the other hand, would vote in favor of the amendment because it would gain nine seats in the House. Assume that Washington, the only state with ten representatives in the House— and so nothing to gain or lose—votes in favor of the amendment.

  Vote in the House: _____

  Vote in the Senate: _____

b. Does the vote in the House meet the two-thirds requirement?

_____

c. Does the vote in the Senate meet the two-thirds requirement?

_____

d. Will the amendment be forwarded to the states for possible ratification and incorporation into the Constitution?

_____

e. Why is the outcome of the vote in the Senate strikingly different from the vote in the House? Explain and support your answer.

_____

_____

_____

_____

_____

_____

_____

4. On Figure 2.3.2, plot the relationship between population and political power in the House. Begin with the group of twelve states with the largest populations. On the vertical axis of the graph, mark the total number of votes in the House that these states command. On the horizontal axis, mark the percentage of the nation's population in these twelve states. That number is about 60 percent. From the location you established on the vertical axis, draw a line to the right, stopping

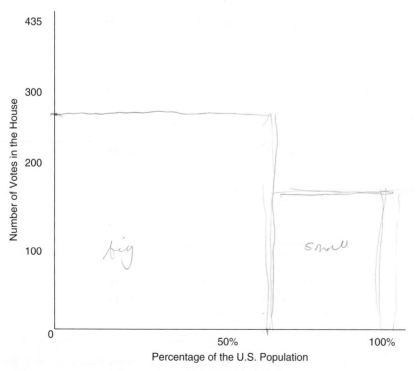

FIGURE 2.3.2 Population and Political Power in the House

when it intersects the line you'll draw up from the location you established on the horizontal axis. Repeat the same process for the group of thirty-eight states with the smallest populations. The thirty-eight smallest states have about 40 percent of the nation's population. Label each rectangle of your graph: small states and large states.

On Figure 2.3.3, plot the relationship between population and political power in the Senate for the group of twelve states with the largest populations and for the group of thirty-eight states with the smallest populations. Follow the same process you used for the graph on the House. Label each rectangle.

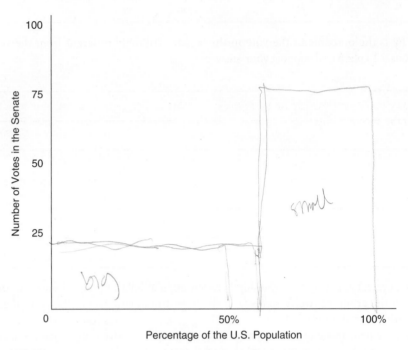

FIGURE 2.3.3   Population and Political Power in the Senate

a. Explain why the shapes of the two rectangles on the House graph are similar.

_____

_____

_____

_____

_____

b. Explain why the shapes of the two rectangles on the Senate graph are so strikingly different.

_____

_____

_____

_____

_____

5. Let's imagine that the proposed amendment to change the system of representation in the House did, in fact, successfully complete the proposal phase of the amendment process. Now consider the amendment's fate in the *ratification* phase of the amendment process. Assume that each state legislature votes solely on the basis of the amendment's effect on the state's voting power in the House: voting for the amendment if that state would gain seats in the House and against the amendment if that state would lose seats in the House. Assume again that the state of Washington votes for the amendment.

a. How many state legislatures would vote to ratify the amendment, and how many would be opposed?

_____

b. Is the number of state legislatures in favor of the amendment sufficient to change the Constitution?

_____

6. What percentage of the nation's population would support the amendment? Assume that popular support is determined by whether a state gains or loses seats in the House under the terms of the amendment.

_____

7. What accounts for the gap between the vote in the state legislatures and popular support for ratifying the amendment?

_____

_____

_____

_____

_____

8. a. Design an alternative to the Constitution's amendment process that gives a less prominent role to the states and that is more consistent with the principles of representative democracy.

_____

_____

_____

_____

_____

b. Make an argument in support of your alternative amendment process.

_____

_____

_____

_____

_____

c. Argue against your alternative amendment process.

_____

_____

_____

_____

EXERCISE 2.4   Is the Federal Government or Are the States in Charge of the Minimum Drinking Age?

INTRODUCTION

The Constitution delegates certain powers to the national government and reserves others to the states. Some areas of responsibility are clearly specified in the Constitution: Article I, Section 8, for example, enumerates the powers that belong to Congress and hence to the national government. Other responsibilities are not as clear. The Tenth Amendment (1791) states: "The powers not delegated to the United States by the Constitution, nor prohibited by it to the States, are reserved to the States respectively, or to the people." American political history is replete with disputes centering on the distribution of those powers. The Health Care Reform Act of 2010 has made this debate more heated than at any time since the Civil Rights era of the 1950s and 1960s, with some states reasserting the Tenth Amendment against what they see as federal overreaching and some conservatives making the argument—not heard since the Civil War—that states should have the authority to nullify federal laws that they do not wish to apply within their borders.

The Supreme Court is the final arbiter in those disputes. But because the political landscape is constantly changing in response to international and domestic events, the Court has not been consistent in its interpretation of the respective powers of the national and state governments. Still, from the mid-1930s to the mid-1990s, the Court consistently found for the national government. At times, it would cite implied powers to support federal claims to power over the states. According to the Court, *implied powers* are those that Congress rightfully infers as its own from the necessary and proper clause of the Constitution. For example, the Court has held it proper for Congress to pass legislation prohibiting racial discrimination in hotels, motels, and restaurants.[1] According to the Court, that authority is implied by the Constitution, which grants Congress the authority to regulate interstate commerce. The Court reasoned that, because travelers use public accommodations as they go from one state to another, the businesses are engaged in interstate commerce and therefore are subject to federal regulation.

In the 1980s, the national government used its allocation of highway funds to the states to try to get the states to restrict the sale of alcoholic beverages. At issue was the minimum drinking age. Although most states set the minimum age at 21, several allowed the consumption of some types of alcoholic beverages at ages ranging from 18 to 20. The national government eventually adopted the argument of Mothers Against Drunk Driving (MADD) that an under-21 drinking age in one state creates an incentive for young people to drive from bordering states to purchase and consume alcoholic beverages and then to return to their home states. Actuarial tables showed that arrests for driving under the influence and drunk-driving accidents among 18- to 21-year-old drivers increased in states that bordered a state with a lower minimum drinking age. Congress subsequently enacted the National Minimum Drinking Age Amendment of 1984. (The Reagan Administration, despite its dislike of federal meddling in state affairs, eventually supported the law.) That statute directed the secretary of transportation to withhold 5 percent of federal highway block grants (see Exercise 2.2) from states where those under 21 could legally purchase or consume alcoholic beverages.

South Dakota, which allowed those 19 years or older to purchase and consume 3.2 percent beer, filed suit in federal court seeking a declaratory judgment that the statute violated the Twenty-First Amendment to the U.S. Constitution, which gives the states the power to impose restrictions on the sale of liquor. South Dakota also contended that the statute violated the spending clause in Article I, Section 8 of the U.S. Constitution because it permitted the federal government to withhold block grant money available to other states. The federal district court rejected South Dakota's claim and was upheld by the U.S. court of appeals. South Dakota then appealed to the U.S. Supreme Court. South Dakota was the plaintiff; the respondent was Elizabeth Dole, then the secretary of transportation. In a 7–2 vote, the justices rejected South Dakota's claim.

Since that decision, all states eventually raised their minimum drinking age to 21, partly because of the lobbying efforts of MADD and partly because the states could not afford to

---

[1]See *Atlanta Motel v. United States* (1964) and *Katzenbach v. McClung* (1964).

disregard federal highway grants. In 2009 and 2010, a debate resurfaced in Vermont about lowering its drinking age, even though it stands to lose millions in federal aid if the current age minimum of 21 is repealed.

The decision in *South Dakota v. Dole* was typical of the Court's deference to federal over state power that prevailed between the mid-1930s and the mid-1990s. But from 1995 to the present, the Rehnquist and then the Roberts Courts, led by a pro-states' rights, conservative majority—often found for the states in federal–state disputes. The shift began with *United States v. Lopez* (1995), in which the Court held that a federal law (the Gun-Free Schools Act of 1990) prohibiting the possession of a gun within 1,000 feet of a school was unconstitutional because it was not within the meaning of commerce that can be regulated by Congress. Nevertheless, in the most controversial case in recent years, *Bush v. Gore* (2000), the Court held that the state of Florida could not recount ballots cast in the 2000 presidential election because a recount would violate the equal protection clause of the Fourteenth Amendment. This departure from the Rehnquist Court's usual deference to states led some critics to claim that the Court's majority was less committed to the principle of states' rights than to a conservative, pro-Republican political agenda. In recent years, the supposedly pro-states' rights Roberts Court has struck down state laws regulating firearms.[2]

ASSIGNMENT

Excerpts from the opinion of the Court (Chief Justice Rehnquist) and the dissenting opinion (Justice O'Connor) in *South Dakota v. Dole* (1987) are reprinted in Reading 2.4.1. Study the decision and answer the questions that follow it.

READING 2.4.1
South Dakota V. Dole, 483 U.S. 203 (1987)

Mr. Chief Justice Rehnquist delivered the opinion of the Court.

In this Court, the parties direct most of their efforts to defining the proper scope of the Twenty-first Amendment. . . . South Dakota asserts that the setting of minimum drinking ages is clearly within the "core powers" reserved to the States under §[Section]2 of the Amendment. . . . The Secretary in response asserts that the Twenty-first Amendment is simply not implicated by §158 [the National Minimum Drinking Age Amendment]; the plain language of §2 [of the Twenty-first Amendment] confirms the States' broad power to impose restrictions on the sale and distribution of alcoholic beverages but does not confer on them any power to *permit* sales that Congress seeks to *prohibit*. That Amendment, under this reasoning would not prevent Congress from affirmatively enacting a national minimum drinking age more restrictive than that provided by the various state laws; and it would follow a fortiori that the indirect inducement involved here is compatible with the Twenty-first Amendment.

These arguments present questions of the meaning of the Twenty-first Amendment, the bounds of which have escaped precise definition. . . . Despite the extended treatment of the question by the parties, however, we need not decide in this case whether that Amendment would prohibit an attempt by Congress to legislate directly a national minimum drinking age. Here, Congress has acted indirectly under its spending power to encourage uniformity in the States' drinking ages. As we explain below, we find this legislative effort within constitutional bounds even if Congress may not regulate drinking ages directly.

The Constitution empowers Congress to "lay and collect Taxes, Duties, Imposts, and Excises, to pay the Debts and provide for the common Defence and general Welfare of the United States." Art. I, §8, Cl. 1. Incident to this power, Congress may attach conditions on the receipt of federal funds, and has repeatedly employed the power "to further broad policy objectives by conditioning

---

[2]See *Haraz v. Ghanbari* (2010).

receipt of federal moneys upon compliance by the recipient with federal statutory and administrative directives." . . . The breadth of this power was made clear in *United States v. Butler* . . . where the Court, resolving a long-standing debate over the scope of the Spending Clause, determined that "the power of Congress to authorize expenditure of public moneys for public purposes is not limited by the direct grants of legislative power found in the Constitution." Thus, objectives not thought to be within Article I's "enumerated legislative fields," . . . may nevertheless be attained through the use of the spending power and the conditional grant of federal funds.

The spending power is of course not unlimited . . . but is instead subject to several general restrictions articulated in our cases. The first of these limitations is derived from the language of the Constitution itself: the exercise of the spending power must be in pursuit of "the general welfare." . . . In considering whether a particular expenditure is intended to serve general public purposes, courts should defer substantially to the judgment of Congress. . . . Second, we have required that if Congress desires to condition the States' receipt of federal funds, it "must do so unambiguously . . . , enabl[ing] the States to exercise their choice knowingly, cognizant of the consequences of their participation." . . . Third, our cases have suggested (without significant elaboration) that conditions on federal grants might be illegitimate if they are unrelated "to the federal interest in particular national projects or programs." . . .

South Dakota does not seriously claim that §158 is inconsistent with any of the first three restrictions mentioned above. We can readily conclude that the provision is designed to serve the general welfare, especially in light of the fact that "the concept of welfare or the opposite is shaped by Congress. . . ." Congress found that the differing drinking ages in the States created particular incentives for young persons to combine their desire to drink with their ability to drive, and that this interstate problem required a national solution. The means it chose to address this dangerous situation were reasonably calculated to advance the general welfare. The conditions upon which States receive the funds, moreover, could not be more clearly stated by Congress. . . . And the State itself, rather than challenging the germaneness of the condition to federal purposes, admits that it "has never contended that the congressional action was . . . unrelated to a national concern in the absence of the Twenty-first Amendment." . . . Indeed, the condition imposed by Congress is directly related to one of the main purposes for which highway funds are expended—safe interstate travel.

This goal of the interstate highway system had been frustrated by varying drinking ages among the States. A Presidential commission appointed to study alcohol-related accidents and fatalities on the Nation's highways concluded that the lack of uniformity in the States' drinking ages created "an incentive to drink and drive" because "young persons commut[e] to border States where the drinking age is lower." . . . By enacting §158, Congress conditioned the receipt of federal funds in a way reasonably calculated to address this particular impediment to a purpose for which the funds are expended.

The remaining question about the validity of §158—and the basic point of disagreement between the parties—is whether the Twenty-first Amendment constitutes an "independent constitutional bar" to the conditional grant of federal funds. . . . Petitioner, relying on its view that the Twenty-first Amendment prohibits direct regulation of drinking ages by Congress, asserts that "Congress may not use the spending power to regulate that which it is prohibited from regulating directly under the Twenty-first Amendment." . . . But our cases show that this "independent constitutional bar" limitation on the spending power is not of the kind petitioner suggests. *United States v. Butler* . . . , for example, established that the constitutional limitations on Congress when exercising its spending power are less exacting than those on its authority to regulate directly.

We have also held that a perceived Tenth Amendment limitation on congressional regulation of state affairs did not concomitantly limit the range of conditions legitimately placed on federal grants.

These cases . . . establish that the "independent constitutional bar" limitation on the spending power is not, as petitioner suggests, a prohibition on the indirect achievement of objectives which Congress is not empowered to achieve directly. Instead, we think that the language in our earlier opinions stands for the unexceptionable proposition that the power may not be used to induce the States to engage in activities that would themselves be unconstitutional. Thus, for example, a grant of federal funds conditioned on invidiously discriminatory state action or the infliction of cruel and unusual punishment would be an illegitimate exercise of the Congress's broad spending power. But no such claim can be or is made here. Were South Dakota to succumb to the blandishments offered by Congress and raise its drinking age to 21, the State's action in so doing would not violate the constitutional rights of anyone.

Even if Congress might lack the power to impose a national minimum drinking age directly, we conclude that encouragement to state action found in §158 is a valid use of the spending power. Accordingly, the judgment of the Court of Appeals is affirmed.

Justice O'Connor dissenting.

The Court today upholds the National Minimum Drinking Age Amendments . . . as a valid exercise of the spending power conferred by Article 1, §8. But, §158 is not a condition on spending reasonably related to the expenditure of federal funds and cannot be justified on that ground. Rather, it is an attempt to regulate the sale of liquor, an attempt that lies outside Congress' power to regulate commerce because it falls within the ambit of §2 of the Twenty-first Amendment.

My disagreement with the Court is relatively narrow on the spending power issue: it is a disagreement about the application of a principle rather than a disagreement on the principle itself.

The Court reasons that Congress wishes that the roads it builds may be used safely, that drunken drivers threaten highway safety, and that young people are more likely to drive while under the influence of alcohol under existing law than would be the case if there were a uniform national drinking age of 21. It hardly needs saying, however, that if the purpose of §158 is to deter drunk driving, it is far too over- and under-inclusive. It is over-inclusive because it stops teenagers from drinking even when they are not about to drive on interstate highways. It is under-inclusive because teenagers pose only a small part of the drunken driving problem in this Nation.

When Congress appropriates money to build a highway, it is entitled to insist that the highway be a safe one. But it is not entitled to insist as a condition of the use of highway funds that the State impose or change regulations in other areas of the State's social and economic life because of an attenuated or tangential relationship to highway use or safety. Indeed, if the rule were otherwise, the Congress could effectively regulate almost any area of a State's social, political, or economic life on the theory that use of the interstate transportation system is somehow enhanced. . . .

As discussed above, a condition that a State will raise its drinking age to 21 cannot fairly be said to be reasonably related to the expenditure of funds for highway construction. The only possible connection, highway safety, has nothing to do with how the funds Congress has appropriated are expended. Rather than a condition determining how federal highway money shall be expended, it is a regulation determining who shall be able to drink liquor. As such it is not justified by the spending power.

The immense size and power of the Government of the United States ought not obscure its fundamental character. It remains a Government of enumerated powers. . . . Because 23 USC 158 . . . cannot be justified as an exercise of any power delegated to the Congress, it is not authorized by the Constitution. The Court errs in holding it to be the law of the land, and I respectfully dissent.

1. What are the three restrictions on Congress's spending power identified in Chief Justice Rehnquist's opinion?

_____

_____

_____

_____

_____

2. On what grounds did the Court find that Congress was not in violation of those three restrictions when it withheld a percentage of block grant highway funds from South Dakota?

_____

_____

_____

_____

_____

3. The Twenty-First Amendment makes the states responsible for regulating the sale of alcohol. But the Court took the position that the Twenty-First Amendment does not present an "independent constitutional bar" to the federal government's effort to encourage the states to raise their minimum drinking age by withholding block grant funding. What was the basis for the Court's conclusion that the Twenty-First Amendment did not stand in the way of the National Minimum Drinking Age Amendment of 1984? Explain and support your answer by citing language from the Court's decision.

_____

_____

_____

_____

4. Congress did not attempt to legislate directly a uniform minimum national drinking age. Does Chief Justice Rehnquist indicate in the Court's decision whether this direct approach would violate the Twenty-First Amendment? Explain and support your answer by citing language from the Court's decision.

_____

_____

_____

_____

_____

5. In her dissent, Justice Sandra Day O'Connor holds that the National Minimum Drinking Age Amendment of 1984 is not "reasonably related to the purpose for which the funds are expended." How does she justify her position? Explain and support your answer by citing language from the Court's decision.

_____

_____

_____

_____

_____

6. *Web-Based Question.* In the late 1990s and again in 2010, the Vermont state legislature considered lowering the minimum drinking age to 18. (Neither time did the effort succeed.) Would you support a bill in your state legislature to lower the minimum drinking age to 18? Why or why not? If you would support lowering the minimum drinking age, would you impose any restrictions on 18- to 20-year-old drinkers that would not apply to drinkers age 21 and older? Before you answer the question, go the website *Debatepedia* to review pro and con arguments about lowering the drinking age: http://debatepedia.idebate.org/en/index.php/Debate:Drinking_age_lowering_of. (If this website is no longer available, try a Web search for a similar site. There are many such sites.)

_____

_____

_____

_____

_____

_____

_____

_____

_____

3

Public Opinion and the Mass Media

EXERCISE 3.1   Public Confidence in U.S. Institutions

INTRODUCTION

Politicians use opinion polls to gauge the public's view of their performance in office, assess public support for particular policies, and determine the strengths and weaknesses of candidates as elections draw near. Some pundits claim that the national obsession with opinion polls has made our political life a popularity contest and turned our electoral campaigns into horse races.

The key to a credible public opinion poll is questioning a statistically significant number of people; most nationwide polls survey anywhere from 600 to 2,000 respondents. The procedure called *random sampling* is based on the mathematical probability that random surveying (e.g., using randomly generated telephone numbers) of a large number of citizens will approximate the views of the whole population. Most polls have a margin of error of ±3 percent. For example, several polls taken early in the 2008 presidential campaign showed Barack Obama's support at 50 percent and John McCain's at 48 percent. That was a statistical dead heat because Obama's support—given the margin of error—might have been as low as 47 percent and McCain's as high as 51 percent. (The polls moved in Obama's favor after the economic meltdown of September 2008. Almost all of them accurately had Obama winning but within the margin of error. He won by 6 percent of the vote.)

Some polls are more problematic than others. A question can be phrased so that it is likely to elicit a favorable or a negative response. Pollsters have found that even the positioning of a question can make a difference. Because many respondents have little interest in or commitment to any of the alternatives posed in a survey, they may "merely choose the option that was mentioned last."[1] Another problem is that some respondents don't answer honestly, and some answer even though they are uninformed.

The least credible polls are so-called *straw polls*. Local media and college newspapers often use straw polls to gauge the popularity of politicians and policies. A straw poll may involve asking as few as fifty people going into a local market who they think is the best candidate in the town's upcoming mayoral election. Even though straw polls interest many people, they are not scientific and they are not reliable. Be cautious, then, of the results of straw polls that are common on the cable news networks and local television news. They're really just telling us what a small section of highly motivated and opinionated viewers think.

ASSIGNMENT

Polls regularly ask Americans about their level of confidence in different institutions. The responses can be charted over time, allowing us to see how public confidence changes in response to major events. Questions 1 to 4 are based on Figure 3.1.1, which shows trends in public trust in government for the last fifty years. Respondents were asked, "How much of the time do you trust in the government in Washington?" Percentages on the graph are those who responded that they trust the government always or most of the time.

---

[1]David W. Moore, "Questionnaire Experiments," *The Gallup Monthly*, December 1995, p. 36.

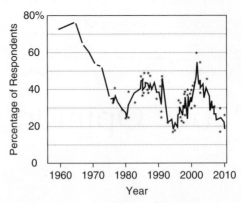

FIGURE 3.1.1   Public Trust in Government: 1958–2010.   *Source:* "Distrust, Discontent, Anger and Partisan Rancor: The People and Their Government", April 18, 2010, the Pew Research Center for the People & the Press, a project of the Pew Research Center. Used by permission of Pew Research Center.

1. What's the general trend of public trust in government from 1958 to 2010?

_____

2. Students of public opinion agree that the Watergate scandal and the defeat of the United States in the Vietnam War undermined public confidence in U.S. institutions in the quarter-century after these major national crises, from 1967 to 2000. Does the graph support that view? Explain and support your answer.

_____

_____

_____

3. Students of public opinion believe that the terrorist attacks of 9/11 and the subsequent war on terrorism rebuilt public confidence—at least temporarily—in U.S. institutions, possibly because of the tendency during wartime to "rally 'round the flag." Does the graph support that view? Explain and support your answer.

_____

_____

4. Historically, public confidence tends to decline as the "rally 'round the flag" effect plays itself out. Notice the sharp decline in public trust after its resurgence in the early 2000s. By 2010, record lows in public trust in government had shown up in poll after poll. The decline in public trust was most evident in the years 2005 to 2010. What two major national crises likely explain that sharp decline best?

_____

Despite the negative perceptions of government expressed in Table 3.1.1, surveys show that the vast majority of Americans continue to expect and sometimes demand that the government solve major social and economic problems—from fixing the economy to expanding educational opportunity. In other words, we hate and love government at the same time. Questions 5 and 6 are based on Table 3.1.1.

TABLE 3.1.1	Reasons for Distrust of Government	
Reason	**Percentage of Respondents Citing Reason**	
Government spending is almost always wasteful and inefficient.	61	
Government accountability for spending is a serious/very serious problem.	75	
Government is run by special interests and is not responsive to ordinary citizens.	70	
Government is more of a hindrance than a help to getting ahead in life.	67	

Source: Ruy Teixeira, "The Public Opinion Paradox," Center for American Progress (www.americanprogress.org), 2010.

5. Which of the above perceptions of government do you agree with? Why? Which do you disagree with? Why? Whether you agree or disagree, include an example from the news or your personal experience that supports your response to each of the reasons.

_____

_____

_____

_____

_____

_____

_____

_____

6. *Web-Based Question.* See how your views about government compare to other Americans' views. Take the "Satisfaction" quiz at http://pewresearch.org/satisfaction/. How do your views compare to the views of Americans in general?

   Web addresses sometimes change. If you can't locate a website, try an external search (e.g., Google) to find the website. Configurations within a website often change. If you can't find a particular link or article, for example, try an internal search of the website as well as an external search. Be resourceful! If you still can't find what you're searching for, move on to the next question.

_____

_____

_____

EXERCISE 3.2   Bias and Accuracy in the News Media: The Case of CBS News and George W. Bush's Military Record

INTRODUCTION

Negative perceptions of the news media are widespread. In 2010, a Gallup poll showed public confidence in the media at an all time low, with only 25 percent expressing "a great deal" of confidence in newspapers and 22 percent in television news.[1]

Part of the news media's credibility problem is the perception that reporters and news organizations have a political or ideological bias. Many Americans believe that coverage is slanted to further a political agenda. One study found that 83 percent of the public perceived the news media as biased.[2] More Americans believe that the media are biased on the liberal side than on the conservative side, but the perception of bias in the news media can stem from the viewer's bias as much as from the media source itself. One study by the nonpartisan Pew Research Center for the Study of the People and the Press found that party loyalty correlates strongly with confidence in particular news providers. For example, among viewers of cable news networks, Republicans tend to find Fox News what it claims to be: "fair and balanced," whereas Democrats have more confidence in CNN.[3]

Conservative Republicans claimed liberal bias in a CBS News *Sixty Minutes* segment, broadcast on September 8, 2004, during that heated and highly partisan presidential race between George W. Bush and John Kerry. Dan Rather—then-CBS anchor and target of conservative critics for his alleged liberal bias—reported that CBS News had obtained a document proving the oft-repeated charges that George W. Bush received favorable treatment in the Texas Air National Guard because of his family connections and that his performance and participation in training were not up to par. For days, Rather defended the authenticity of the incriminating document despite allegations that it was a forgery. Subsequently, CBS News admitted that it was unable to prove the authenticity of the document. The resulting firestorm of criticism engulfed Rather, Mary Mapes (the segment's producer), and CBS News in charges that they were out to get Bush. CBS subsequently appointed an independent panel to review its handling of the story. The panel's report—sections of which are included in this exercise—found numerous sins of commission and omission. Dan Rather retired as anchor of the *CBS Evening News* on March 9, 2005. (At the time of this writing, litigation over Rather's dismissal is unresolved.)

Although conservatives charge that CBS is afflicted with political bias, many experts on journalism argue that the real problem in the story stemmed from a *commercial bias*. According to those critics, the mistakes in the Bush National Guard story stemmed less from political bias than from the high level of competition among news organizations to break a story, any story. Competitive pressures led CBS News to air the story before other news organizations could run it, which compromised the news organization's ability to check the story properly. Many have also noted that the substance of the story—Bush's poor record in the Texas Air National Guard—was never found to be false and that the document was never proved to be a forgery.

The commercial bias of the media is so pervasive that, on occasion, it lies behind clear instances of ideological bias. For example, MSNBC's primetime lineup of newscasts no doubt has a liberal bias. Nevertheless, as the *New York Times* reported, NBC's decision to target a liberal, relatively well-heeled audience was prompted by the ratings success of then-MSNBC anchorperson Keith Olbermann and by the prospective profits of competing successfully against Fox News's domination of the conservative audience.[4]

ASSIGNMENT

Study Reading 3.2.1, which includes sections of the "Report of the Independent Review Panel on the September 8, 2004, *60 Minutes Wednesday* Segment, 'For the Record,' Concerning President

---

[1] August 13, 2010: www.gallup.com/poll/142133/confidence-newspapers-news-remains-rarity.aspx
[2] Zogby Poll, March 14 2007, www.zogby.com/news/readnews.cfm?ID=1262
[3] PEW Research Center for People and the Press, September 13, 2009, http://people-press.org/report/543/
[4] Brian Stelter, "Seeking More Viewers, MSNBC Turns Left," August 22, 2008. p. C.3.

Bush's Air National Guard Service." The questions that follow the reading assess possible political and commercial bias in the Rather story.

READING 3.2.1
Report of the Independent Review Panel, by Dick Thornburgh and Louis D. Boccardi[5]

PART X. WHETHER THERE WAS A POLITICAL AGENDA DRIVING THE SEPTEMBER 8 SEGMENT

There has been widespread speculation in the media that the September 8 Segment was motivated, in whole or in part, by an anti-Bush political agenda. . . .

The question of whether a political agenda played any role in the airing of the Segment is one of the most subjective, and most difficult, that the Panel has sought to answer. The political agenda question was posed by the Panel directly to Dan Rather and his producer, Mary Mapes, who appear to have drawn the greatest attention in terms of possible political agendas. Both strongly denied that they brought any political bias to the Segment. The Panel recognizes that those who saw bias at work in the Segment are likely to sweep such denials aside. However, the Panel will not level allegations for which it cannot offer adequate proof.

The Panel does not find a basis to accuse those who investigated, produced, vetted or aired the Segment of having a political bias. The Panel does note, however, that on such a politically charged story, coming in the midst of a presidential campaign in which military service records had become an issue, there was a need for meticulous care to avoid any suggestion of an agenda at work. The Panel does not believe that the appropriate level of care to avoid the appearance of political motivation was used in connection with this story.

It should be noted that *60 Minutes Wednesday* was hardly alone in pursuing the story. Other mainstream media, including USA TODAY, The New York Times and The Associated Press, were pursuing the same story in what was clearly a competitive race to be first. In fact, USA TODAY on September 9 published a similar story relying on the same Killian documents, but has not been as criticized for its story as CBS News has been for the September 8 Segment. The Panel recognizes that some will see this widespread media attention not as evidence that *60 Minutes Wednesday* was not motivated by bias but instead proof that all of mainstream media has a liberal bias. That is a perception beyond the Panel's assignment. . . .

The Panel believes that additional factors in the production of the September 8 Segment rebut the notion that it was politically motivated. The most significant factors are discussed below.

The Panel asked Rather directly to comment on whether he was motivated in any way by a political animus in pursuing the September 8 Segment. He responded: "absolutely, unequivocally untrue." Rather related that over his long career, he has done tough stories on a number of Presidents, both Republican and Democrat, including: Lyndon Johnson and the Vietnam War; Richard Nixon and Watergate; Jimmy Carter and the Iran hostages; George H. W. Bush and Iran Contra; and Bill Clinton and Monica Lewinsky. With respect to the September 8 Segment, Rather said that he had full confidence in the people who put the story together and that he had no indication at the time that the documents were not authentic.

Mapes told the Panel that she was motivated by "proximity, not politics." Mapes has lived in Texas for 15 years and at least six of her thirty *60 Minutes Wednesday* stories before the September 8 Segment had a Texas nexus. The Panel was told by many at *60 Minutes Wednesday*

---

[5]Retrieved from http://wwwimage.cbsnews.com/htdocs/pdf/complete_report/CBS_Report.pdf.

and CBS News who worked with Mapes that she was motivated by reporting on a significant story and that they did not believe that political ideology became a part of her stories. Mapes stridently believed in both the authenticity of the documents and their content, and, indeed, told the Panel that she still does.

. . . The Panel finds no evidence that any of these individuals were motivated by political considerations.

PART XI. [EXCERPTS FROM] THE PANEL'S RECOMMENDATIONS

Competitive pressures are a fact of life in journalism and may impact the timing of a news story. The leadership of CBS News, however, should make clear to all personnel that competitive pressures cannot be allowed to prompt the airing of a story before it is ready. It would have been better to "lose" the story on the Killian documents to a competitor than to air it short of investigating and vetting to the highest standards of fairness and accuracy.

Source: Excerpt from Report of the Independent Review Panel by Dick Thornburgh and Louis D. Boccardi on the September 8, 2004, 60 Minutes Wednesday Segment "For the Record" concerning President Bush's Texas Air National Guard Service, January 5, 2005. Used by permission of CBS News Archives.

1. In one sentence, state the panel's conclusion on whether Rather's news report stemmed from an anti-Bush bias.

2. What evidence did the panel provide for its conclusion?

3. How did the panel respond to the charge that all the mainstream media are biased?

4. Do you find the panel's conclusion convincing and its evidence sufficient? Explain and support your answer.

5. What does the panel say about the role competitive pressures (commercial bias) played in CBS's decision to air the story?

EXERCISE 3.3   Are the News Media Doing Their Job? Hard and Soft News

INTRODUCTION

Media analysts and political scientists make distinctions between hard and soft news. *Hard news* covers significant international and national events. *Soft news* features human interest and celebrity stories. Soft news also includes "news you can use"; for example, stories about lifestyle issues, such as nutrition and exercise. Soft news is sometimes called *infotainment*—news that entertains rather than informs Americans about vital issues of the day. Indeed, infotainment has become so pervasive that candidates for president—and a one-time candidate for governor of California— have made use of entertainment shows to reach prospective voters. Witness Barack Obama on *The Tonight Show* or John McCain on *The Daily Show*. Young people aged 18 to 29 appear particularly to favor infotainment. According to one study, 21 percent said they prefer comedy outlets, such as *The Daily Show,* as their primary source of campaign information.[1] Other studies, however, show an ever-increasing use of the Internet for both hard and soft news, not only among young people, but among all age groups.[2] The Internet is likely to continue to increase as the primary source of both hard and soft news because of its accessibility and affordability. Its interactivity makes the Internet a less spectacle-driven source of news than television news; however, its lack of professional editorial control appears to be further blurring the boundaries between hard and soft news and between reliable and unreliable sources.

Because television provides sound, sight, and movement in "digestible," quick visuals and sound bites, it is more effective at delivering soft news than are newspapers. The Internet is a mixed bag: Blogs, for example, rely on the written word, but YouTube relies on videos that are often spectacular and that can easily be taken out of context. The upshot? Network television's news coverage is increasingly diluted—some would say contaminated—by matters that are entertaining and interesting but not necessarily newsworthy. Critics charge that news broadcasters are surrendering their traditional role—reporting and analyzing facts—to peddle entertainment. That transformation allegedly stems from the increased competition among the networks for ratings and profits. Indeed, many of the networks are now subsidiaries of entertainment corporations; for example, the Disney Corporation owns ABC, Viacom owns CBS, and Comcast owns NBC.

ASSIGNMENT

This assignment asks you to examine news coverage in the broadcast (television) and print (newspapers) media. If you don't have television, monitor the home page of television news websites. You can use any search engine to find the URL of the media source.

Over three weeknights, watch the evening news on three of the major television news sources (ABC, CBS, NBC, CNN, Fox News, MSNBC, or PBS NewsHour [not a commercial network]). As you watch, fill in the chart on the next page with the amount of time spent on each type of news. In the parentheses at the head of each column, identify the news networks you monitored. Apply the definitions of hard news and soft news from the first paragraph of the introduction to this exercise.

Based on the observations you recorded in the chart, answer the following questions.

1. Combining all three nights of observation, what percentage of total broadcast time (excluding commercials) did each network devote to hard news stories, both international and national?

Network 1: _____

Network 2: _____

Network 3: _____

---

[1] Melanie McFarland, "Young People Turning Comedy Shows into Serious News Source," *Seattle Post- Intelligencer,* January 22, 2004. The survey is by The Pew Research Center for the People and the Press.
[2] "Young People and News," A Report from the Joan Shorenstein Center on the Press, Politics and Public Policy, July 2007, http://www.hks.harvard.edu.

Network News Stories									
	News Network 1 ( )			News Network 2 ( )			News Network 3 ( )		
	Day1	Day 2	Day 3	Day1	Day2	Day 3	Day 1	Day 2	Day3
International hard news stories									
National hard news stories									
Total minutes of hard news									
Total minutes of soft news									
Total minutes of commercials									

2. Combining all three nights of observation, what percentage of total hard news broadcast time (excluding commercials) did each network devote to international news?

Network 1: _____

Network 2: _____

Network 3: _____

3. Did the networks follow up on hard news stories that had been aired the previous night? Did one network stand out for follow-up stories? If so, which one? What was the story?

_____

_____

_____

_____

_____

4. Which network newscast most consistently held your attention? Why did it hold your attention?

_____

_____

_____

_____

_____

Using the Internet, examine the home page for the *New York Times* (http://www.nytimes.com) and the home page of a newspaper from your hometown or your college town. (You can find the URL using any search engine.) Monitor the home pages of these two newspapers for three days during the week. Enter the topics of the news stories in the chart. In the parentheses at the head of the third column, write the name of the local newspaper you monitored.

Based on the observations recorded in the chart, answer the following questions.

Newspaper Stories			
	Day 1	**Day 2**	**Day 3**

New York Times

International hard news stories

National hard news stories

Soft news stories

Local Newpaper
(   )

International hard news stories

National hard news stories

Soft news stories

5. Did the *New York Times* or the local newspaper cover more hard news (international and national)?

_____

6. Did the *New York Times* or the local newspaper cover more international hard news?

_____

7. Based on your observations and analysis, write a paragraph explaining the respective advantages and disadvantages of newspaper and television news coverage.

_____

_____

_____

_____

_____

EXERCISE 3.4 Distinguishing Fact from Opinion in the Internet Age

INTRODUCTION

Many Americans take a dim view of their representatives in government, believing that politicians seek nothing more than power and perks and will say anything—even lie—to get elected. But how many citizens undertake the tough task of evaluating the accuracy of candidates' statements? The line between fact and opinion is not always clear, and drawing that line demands more knowledge and understanding of politics and public policy than many citizens have or want to have. Yet democracy hinges on an educated citizenry.

A *statement of fact* can be verified as true or refuted as false. In the social sciences, a statement of fact and truth are not necessarily the same. According to one social scientist, "Facts are not to be confused with Truth. A fact is only as good as the means of verification used to establish it, as well as the frame of reference within which it requires meaning. A great deal of science consists of using methodological advances to reverse, modify, or even falsify 'facts' . . . formerly verified."[1] A *statement of opinion* is based on personal values, ideology, or wishful prediction. With the passage of time, an opinion may turn out to be true, partially true, or false.

The Internet has made it ever more difficult to separate fact from opinion. While the abundance of information on the Internet has been a boon for democracy in all parts of the world, the prevalence of partisan spinning, ideological blogging, and rumor mongering is quickly blurring the distinction between fact and fiction. This blurring is made even more problematic because of a well-noted dilemma of the Internet Age: On one hand, Americans are so besieged with information that their minds numb to it; they absorb it without thinking about it. On the other hand, many Americans are only marginally attentive to politics and thus are not prone to seek clarification beyond what they happen to see or hear.

The assessment of the accuracy of Internet information has been made easier in recent years though a number of nonpartisan and, in some cases, nonprofit websites dedicated to separating fact from fiction, for example, politifact.com, FactCheck.org, and washingtonpost.com/blogs/fact-checker. These are excellent resources for citizens who want to be informed and who want to evaluate what they are told by reporters, bloggers, editorialists, government officials, interest group leaders, and leaders in the private sector. Exercise 3.4 asks you to do some fact checking of your own. We hope that fact checking will become a habit of citizenship.

WEB-BASED ASSIGNMENT

For the following questions, you'll locate statements from the transcripts of the presidential debates of 2008 between John McCain and Barack Obama and track down their accuracy on FactCheck.org. Most statements that candidates make about their positions on issues are statements of opinion, even when a candidate has abundant arguments and apparent evidence to support the position. For example, a candidate who says that the media are destroying family values—but who does not preface the statement with "I believe"—is misrepresenting a statement of opinion as a statement of fact. There is no body of evidence or standard of measurement by which that statement of opinion can be verified or refuted.

More often, statements are partial truths or truths out of context. One infamous example is a series of 1988 ads that George H. W. Bush ran against Michael Dukakis, the Democratic presidential candidate and then-governor of Massachusetts. The ads contained graphic scenes of a polluted Boston Harbor, complete with dead fish and signs warning people that the water was unfit for swimming. The ad meant to convey that the supposedly environment-friendly governor stood watch as Boston Harbor became more like a cesspool than a harbor. What was factual about the ad? Dukakis was governor and Boston Harbor was polluted. What was out of context and omitted from the ad? The pollution in Boston Harbor had preceded Dukakis's time in office by decades. The pollution of the harbor had actually decreased while Dukakis happened to be in office. Most important, the cleanup of Boston Harbor was largely a federal project, not a state project.

---

[1] Kenneth Hoover and Todd Donovan, *The Elements of Social Scientific Thinking*, 7th ed. (Boston: Bedford, St. Martin's, 2001), p. 132.

George H. W. Bush, who had been vice president for eight years, could more appropriately be assigned blame or praise for the condition of Boston Harbor than could Dukakis.

For the following questions, go to the site of the Commission on Presidential Debates for transcripts of the last three presidential debates, http://www.debates.org/index.php?page=debate-transcripts. Select one statement from McCain and one from Obama in each of the three debates.

Note: If you're completing this exercise after the debates for the 2012 presidential election, go to the website of the Commission on Presidential Debates: http://www.debates.org. There you can search for the transcripts for the 2012 debates. Substitute the 2012 Democratic and Republican presidential candidates for those already named in the table in question 1.

Now go to the FactCheck.org page of analysis for each of the three debates to track down the accuracy of the statements. Keep exploring debate statements until you find three that were fact-checked. If you're completing this exercise after the 2012 presidential election, go to FactCheck.org: http://www.factcheck.org. There you can search for the fact checking of the 2012 debates. Substitute the 2012 Democratic and Republican presidential candidates for those already named in the table in question 1.

Debate 1: http://www.factcheck.org/elections-2008/factchecking_debate_no_1.html

Debate 2: http://www.factcheck.org/elections-2008/factchecking_debate_no_2.html

Debate 3: http://www.factcheck.org/elections-2008/factchecking_debate_no_3.html

Web addresses sometimes change. If you can't locate a website, try an external search (e.g., Google) to find the website. Configurations within a website often change. If you can't find a particular link or article, for example, try an internal search of the website as well as an external search. Be resourceful! If you still can't find what you're searching for, move on to the next question.

1. Fill in the following table based on your fact checking. (If you run out of space, write on the lines below the table.)

	McCain	Obama
Statement Debate 1		
Accurate? Inaccurate? Partial Truth?		
Statement Debate 2		
Accurate? Inaccurate? Partial Truth?		
Statement Debate 3		
Accurate? Inaccurate? Partial Truth?		

Use these lines to complete any answers that don't fit in the table. Be sure to label the completed answers by candidate and debate number.

_____

_____

_____

_____

_____

2. In general, did you find one candidate was more accurate than the other? How so?

_____

_____

_____

3. In general, did you find that their statements were identifiable as either fact or opinion? Explain and provide a few examples.

_____

_____

_____

_____

_____

The following questions ask you to find three different political online sites. They can be traditional news sources, blogs, or editorials, whichever you prefer. Select one story on each site. Track down each story on one of the fact-checking websites already identified in this exercise. Fill out the following table. Keep exploring debate statements until you find three that were fact-checked.

Internet Site of Story	Summary of Story	How Accurate Is the Story?	Verification Website
1.			
2.			
3.			

4

Political Parties and Elections

EXERCISE 4.1   Presidential Elections: Are You Better Off Now Than You Were Four Years Ago?

INTRODUCTION

Voters without strong party ties and without strong ideologies— independent and moderate voters—often determine the outcome of presidential races. Whereas loyalist liberal Democrats and loyalist conservative Republicans routinely vote for their party's candidate, *swing voters* move between the two major parties' presidential candidates according to their assessment of the economy. In what's called *retrospective voting,* swing voters ask themselves the question Ronald Reagan posed to voters in 1980, in his race against Jimmy Carter, during a bad economy: "Are you better off now than you were four years ago?" In 1992, when the economy was in recession, Bill Clinton's advisers posted a large sign in the campaign headquarters: "It's the economy, stupid." The purpose? To remind Clinton to stay focused on the poor state of the economy, which voters—rightly or wrongly—blamed on the incumbent president, then George H. W. Bush. That strategy put Bill Clinton in the White House. The economic collapse in September of 2008 brought economic issues to the forefront and allowed candidate Obama to blame George W. Bush and, by implication, John McCain, also a Republican, for the policies that led to the economic devastation. In the midterm congressional elections of 2010, the economic issues typically associated with presidential campaigns dominated. With economic recovery being slow, continued high unemployment, and the president's approval ratings sliding ever downward, Obama and the Democrats suffered massive losses in Congress—with voters asking themselves, Are we better off than we were two years ago?

The economy has played a major role in the outcome of so many presidential races, beginning with Franklin Roosevelt's victory over Herbert Hoover during the Great Depression, because presidential candidates, appealing to the moderate and independent voters who usually determine the outcome of presidential elections, emphasize their determination to make us better off, even though no president has the power to fulfill such sweeping promises. There is little doubt that Obama's prospects for reelection in 2012 depend heavily on whether the economy continues to recover and whether that recovery reduces unemployment, thereby making Americans more confident about their economic prospects.

There are exceptions, of course, to the domination of economic issues. The presidential election of 2004 between George W. Bush and John Kerry was such an exception. The economy was in recovery after a recession in 2001–2002 (even though joblessness in some states remained relatively high). Whereas swing voters—moderates and independents—usually determine the outcome of a presidential election, their influence was diminished in 2004 because, in a close race like that in 2004, the rate at which party loyalists turn out to vote often decides the contest. Recognizing this, both parties invested heavily to mobilize their core supporters. President Bush's style and ideology polarized many voters into Bush and anti-Bush camps; thus, fewer voters than usual identified themselves as undecided—a common attribute of moderates and independents.

In the first presidential election after the events of 9/11 and the subsequent war on terrorism, many voters focused on national security issues. The prominence of the gay marriage issue and the presence of anti–gay marriage initiatives on eleven state ballots led to unusually high voter turnout among self-identified White Christian evangelicals, and an overwhelming majority of them voted for Bush. President Bush's endorsement of a constitutional amendment to prohibit gay marriage no doubt helped him among those voters. The gay marriage issue prompted many voters to embrace morality as the major issue in the campaign. So-called moral issues—like gay marriage, abortion, sexuality in the media, and secularism in public life—tend to favor Republican candidates.[1]

---

[1]See Curtis Gans, "President Bush, Mobilization Drives Propel Turnout to Post-1968 High; Kerry, Democratic Weaknesses Shown," Committee for the Study of the American Electorate, Press Release, November 4, 2004.

ASSIGNMENT

Questions 1 to 4, which follow the exit poll data in Tables 4.1.1 and 4.1.2, ask you to interpret the presidential elections of 2004 and 2008. An exit poll is a probability sample, taking into account population size and past voting history, of forty precincts in each state. They have a margin of error of ±3 percent.

TABLE 4.1.1 Exit Poll, Presidential Election of 2004*	Percentage of the Total Vote	Percentage Voting for Bush	Percentage Voting for Kerry
Party			
Democrat	37	10	89
Republican	37	93	7
Independent/Other	26	47	50
Ideology			
Liberal	21	13	86
Moderate	45	44	55
Conservative	33	83	16
Religion			
White evangelical/ born-again Christian	22	77	22
All others	78	42	57
Do you consider the war in Iraq			
Part of the war on terrorism?	54	80	19
Separate from the war on terrorism?	43	11	88
Issue that mattered most			
Moral values	22	80	18
Economy/jobs	20	18	80
Terrorism	19	86	14
Iraq	15	26	73
Health care	8	23	77
Taxes	5	57	43
Education	4	26	73
Who would you trust to handle terrorism?			
Only Kerry	31	1	99
Only Bush	48	97	3
Both of them	9	23	75
Neither of them	9	15	79
Family financial situation compared to four years ago			
Better today	31	79	20
Worse today	28	19	80
Same	39	48	50

*Does not include Ralph Nadar.

Source: Excerpts from Exit Poll, President-Decision 2004 from MSNBC. Copyright 2004 by MSNBC INTERACTIVE NEWS, LLC. Reproduced with permission of MSNBC INTERACTIVE NEWS, LLC via Copyright Clearance Center.

TABLE 4.1.2 Exit Poll, Presidential Election of 2008*	Percentage of the Total Vote	Percentage Voting for McCain	Percentage Voting for Obama
Party			
Democrat	39	10	89
Republican	32	90	9
Independent/other	29	44	52
Ideology			
Liberal	22	10	89
Moderate	44	39	60
Conservative	34	78	20
Religion			
White evangelical/ born-again Christian	26	74	24
All others	74	36	62
U.S. War in Iraq			
Approve	36	86	13
Disapprove	63	22	76
Issue that mattered most			
Energy	7	46	50
Iraq	10	39	59
Economy	63	44	53
Terrorism	9	86	13
Health care	9	26	73
Family financial situation compared to four years ago			
Better today	24	60	37
Worse today	28	19	80
Same	39	48	50
Was race of candidate a factor to you?			
Yes	9	46	53
No	90	56	52

*Does not include Ralph Nadar.

Source: Excerpts from Election Center 2008, Exit Polls, President. Copyright © 2008 Cable News Network. Turner Broadcasting System, Inc.

1. Consider voters' views of the economy. Review the category "Issue that mattered most" in 2004 and 2008.

   a. What percentage of voters responded that the economy mattered most to them?

      In 2004: _____

      In 2008: _____

   b. What percentage of those voters cast their ballot for the Democratic candidate (Kerry or Obama)?

      In 2004: _____

      In 2008: _____

Review the category "Family financial situation compared to four years ago" in 2004 and 2008.

    c. What percentage of voters responded that their family situation was worse than four years ago?

        In 2004: _____

        In 2008: _____

    d. What percentage of those voters cast their ballot for the Democratic candidate?

        In 2004: _____

        In 2008: _____

    e. What do the data you assembled in parts a–d tell you about the role of the economy in 2004 and 2008? Explain and support your answer.

    _____

    _____

    _____

    _____

    _____

2. Consider ideology and party loyalty in the electorate in 2004 and 2008. Review the "Ideology" category in 2004 and 2008.

    a. Do the data support the conclusion that voters were more divided into the liberal and conservative camps—with fewer moderates—in 2004 than in 2008? (Look at the "Percentage of the Total Vote" column to answer this question.) Explain and support your answer.

    _____

    _____

    _____

    b. Conservatives are likely to vote Republican, and liberals are likely to vote Democratic. Were conservatives more likely to vote for the Republican presidential candidate and liberals for the Democratic presidential candidate in 2004 or in 2008?

    _____

    _____

    _____

    c. Review the "Party" category in 2004 and 2008. Were self-proclaimed Democrats and self-proclaimed Republicans more likely to support their party's presidential candidate in 2004 or in 2008? Explain and support your answer.

    _____

    _____

    _____

    d. Which party's voters were more united behind its candidate in 2004 and 2008?

    _____

e. Compare and contrast how moderates and independents split their votes in 2004 and 2008.

_____

_____

_____

f. Do the data support the interpretation that moderate and independent voters, usually the decisive factor in a presidential election, were most decisive in 2004 or in 2008? Explain and support your answer.

_____

_____

_____

g. In light of your responses to parts a–f, do the data support the interpretation that the electorate was more ideologically polarized and exhibited more party loyalty in 2004 than in 2008? Explain and support your answer.

_____

_____

_____

3. Consider the interpretation that voters' perceptions of the candidates on those issues important to voters can determine the outcome of an election.

a. Look at the category, "Issues that mattered most," in 2004 and 2008. Compare and contrast the importance of terrorism as an issue in 2004 and 2008.

_____

_____

b. Republican presidential candidates are usually perceived as stronger than Democratic presidential candidates on national security issues. (See particularly the 2004 question, "Who would you trust to handle terrorism?) How did McCain fare among voters who thought that terrorism was an important issue in 2008? Comparing 2004 and 2008, do the data support the notion that, as the importance of national security issues declined, so did the prospects for the Republican candidate? Explain. (You might also want to take into account the questions about the war in Iraq in 2004 and 2008.)

_____

_____

_____

_____

4. Consider the interpretation that moral issues worked to Bush's advantage in 2004. Examine the "Issue that mattered most" category in 2004.

a. What percentage of voters thought that moral values mattered most in 2004? In 2008? What percentage of those voters supported Bush in 2004?

_____

b. What percentage of the voters identified themselves as White evangelical/born-again Christian in 2004 and 2008? What percentage favored Bush in 2004? What percentage favored Obama in 2008?

_____

c. Do the data support the contention that so-called moral issues helped to put Bush back in the White House in 2004? Support your answer.

_____

_____

_____

d. Which issue replaced moral values (and terrorism) in 2008 as the most important? Do the exit polls support the argument of this exercise that the economy—particularly a bad economy—is the most important factor in deciding presidential elections? Explain and support your answer.

_____

_____

_____

_____

_____

e. Was candidate Obama's race an important factor in the outcome of the election? Explain and support your answer.

_____

_____

_____

Figures 4.1.1 and 4.1.2 refer to question 5 on the next page.

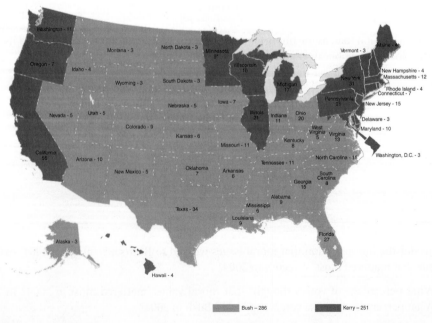

Bush – 286   Kerry – 251

FIGURE 4.1.1 Electoral Vote Map 2004. _Source:_ Michael Gastner, Cosma Shalizi, and Mark Newman, University of Michigan.

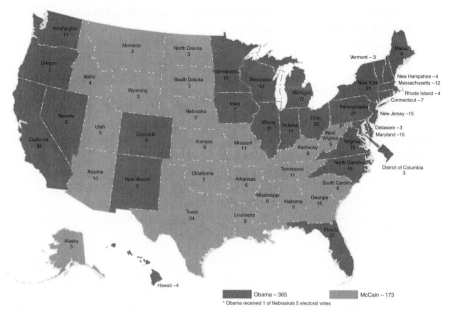

FIGURE 4.1.2   Electoral Vote Map 2008. *Source:* Michael Gastner, Cosma Shalizi, and Mark Newman, University of Michigan.

5. On the maps in Figure 4.1.1 (Bush–Kerry, 2004) and Figure 4.1.2 (McCain–Obama, 2008), states won by the Democratic presidential candidates (Kerry and Obama) are black. Those won by the Republican presidential candidates (Bush and McCain) are gray. The questions that follow are based on the figures.

  a. Which states did the Republican candidate win in both 2004 and 2008 (the so-called red states because they are usually colored red on electoral vote maps)?

  _____

  _____

  _____

  _____

  _____

  b. What characteristics are shared by the states (region, size of electoral vote, and the like) that supported Bush in both elections?

  _____

  _____

  _____

  c. Which states did the Democratic candidates win in both 2004 and 2008 (the so-called blue states because they are usually colored blue on electoral vote maps)?

  _____

  _____

  _____

  _____

  _____

d. What characteristics are shared by the states (region, size of electoral vote, and the like) that supported the Democratic candidates?

_____

_____

_____

e. Which states did Obama win in 2008 that Kerry lost in 2004? Which states did McCain win in 2008 that Bush lost in 2004?

_____

_____

_____

_____

f. *Web-Based Question.* If you were the Republican Party chair, would you be confident about that party's prospects in future presidential elections? Why or why not? Consider your answer by examining the competitiveness of the popular vote by state. For the popular vote totals state by state, go to the website of National Archives and Records Administration. For 2004, go to http://www.archives.gov/federal-register/electoral-college/2004/popular_vote.html. For 2008, go to http://www.archives.gov/federal-register/electoral-college/2008/popular-vote.html.

Web addresses sometimes change. If you can't locate a website, try an external search (e.g., Google) to find the website. Configurations within a website often change. If you can't find a particular link or article, for example, try an internal search of the website as well as. an external search. Be resourceful! If you still can't find what you're searching for, move on to the next question.

_____

_____

_____

_____

g. *Web-Based Question.* If you were the Democratic Party chair, would you be confident about that party's prospects in future presidential elections? Why or why not? Consider your answer by examining the competitiveness of the popular vote by state. For the popular vote totals state by state, go to the website of National Archives and Records Administration. For 2004, go to http://www.archives.gov/federal-register/electoral-college/2004/popular_vote.html. For 2008, go to http://www.archives.gov/federal-register/electoral-college/2008/popular-vote.html.

_____

_____

_____

_____

EXERCISE 4.2   Gerrymandering

INTRODUCTION

Legislative districts come in many shapes, from the compact and ordinary to the distended and bizarre. Describing a legislative district forged in the shape of a salamander, the editor of the *Boston Centinel* in 1811 coined the term *gerrymander*. The governor of Massachusetts who approved the salamander-shaped district was Elbridge Gerry. Since then, Gerry's name (linked with the last two syllables of the word *salamander*) has been used to describe the drawing of exotically shaped legislative districts designed to yield political advantage for political parties or incumbents.

Representation in the House is population based: States are awarded seats according to the relative size of their populations. The framers of the Constitution recognized that state populations would change and that the distribution of seats in the House would have to be adjusted accordingly. The Constitution requires that the reapportionment—the reallocation—of seats in the House take place every ten years based on the results of the federal census. The addition or subtraction of one or more of a state's seats in the House usually requires redrawing the boundaries of all the House districts in the state because, in 1964, the Supreme Court ruled that the equal protection clause of the Fourteenth Amendment requires that legislative districts be roughly equal in population—the standard of "one-person, one-vote."[1] (See Exercise 6.4, Legislative Apportionment.)

The task of redistricting has traditionally been carried out by a state's legislature, subject to the approval of its governor. If a state's legislators and governor cannot agree on a redistricting plan, the task reverts to the courts or a commission. As of 2005, there were twenty-one states that located the final authority for redistricting in some body other than the state legislature and governor. Oklahoma's redistricting commission, for example, consists of the state attorney general, the superintendent of public instruction, and the state treasurer. The redistricting boards and commissions of other states have much more complicated membership criteria.[2]

State legislators are keenly aware that redistricting is inherently political, easily turned to the advantage of a particular political party or interest, or to incumbents generally. In drawing new legislative districts, geographic coherence, demographic similarity, and fairness are often subordinated to politics. Although some redistricting schemes may be more egregiously political than others, no one can dodge the fact that grouping voters in legislative districts necessarily works to the advantage of some and to the disadvantage of others.

Those disadvantaged by redistricting often go to court. The round of redistricting that followed the 2000 census triggered over 150 lawsuits in at least forty states, according to the National Conference of State Legislators. Redistricting litigation focuses on three questions:

- How much variation in population between districts is permissible?
- Can states redistrict more often than once at the beginning of the decade?
- Does partisan gerrymandering violate the equal protection clause of the Constitution?

The Supreme Court remains reluctant to become entangled in the thicket of *political* redistricting, ruling that the matter is best left to the citizens and their elected representatives. Recent decisions indicate that the Court remains split on two important points: whether claims against political gerrymandering fall under the Court's jurisdiction, and what standards the Court would use to adjudicate those claims.[3] No gerrymander has yet been struck down by the Court solely on the grounds that it gives an unconstitutional political advantage to one party at the expense of another. The Court has ruled, however, against *racial* gerrymanders that dilute the power of minorities and ruled against the creation of districts with voting majorities of racial or ethnic minorities when race or ethnicity was the deciding factor in drawing the district lines.

With the courts unwilling or unable to address the political advantage derived from gerrymandering, citizens in a number of states have taken the matter into their own hands. In California, for example, gerrymandering resulted in a lock on power and position by incumbents

---

[1] *Wesberry v. Sanders; Reynolds v. Sims.*
[2] Details on the various state redistricting boards and commissions, and other information about redistricting, can be found on the website of the National Conference of State Legislatures at www.ncsl.org.
[3] *Davis v. Bandemer*, (1986); *Vieth v. Jubelirer* (2004).

that many voters there found obscene. Of the fifty-three House seats and 100 seats in the state legislature that were up for grabs in California in 2004, not even one changed party hands. To cite another example, California's twenty-second House district was so securely gerrymandered to the advantage of Republicans after the 2000 census that the Republican incumbent faced no challenger at all in the elections of 2004, 2008, and 2010. In response to incumbents' lock on power, California voters retaliated with the initiative process, a feature of California's state constitution that allows citizens to place proposed laws (in the form of propositions) on the ballot, bypassing the state legislature. In 2008, California voters approved Proposition 11, which stripped the state legislature and the governor of their authority to draw election districts for the state Senate, Assembly, and Board of Equalization, and vested the power instead in a newly established fourteen-member citizens' commission. California voters struck again in 2010 with Proposition 20, which gave the new citizens' commission the power to draw the districts for California's fifty-three members of the House, too.

ASSIGNMENT

To better understand the politics of gerrymandering, examine the model in Figure 4.2.1. This hypothetical state has four districts labeled A, B, C, and D. There are twenty-five voters in each district, for a total of 100 voters. The political party affiliation of each voter is indicated as R for Republican and D for Democrat. This hypothetical state is entitled to four seats in the national legislature. Figure 4.2.1 shows one method of dividing the state into its four legislative districts. The method seems *nonpartisan*, undertaken without regard for the interest of political parties or incumbents. The state has been divided into four quadrants, each a square that is equal in population. The districts appear to be neutral and impartial, drawn solely on the basis of simple geometry.

In answering the questions below, assume the following: *Republicans (R) and Democrats (D) vote by party affiliation; they never cross party lines; and they never vote for minor-party candidates.* Voting behavior in the real world, of course, is much less certain and much more complicated, but simplifying voting behavior in this way should make the politics of gerrymandering easier to grasp.

1. a. Under the districting plan in Figure 4.2.1, what percentage of the state's seats does the Republican Party command?

_____

b. What percentage of the state's seats does the Democratic Party command?

_____

```
      D   D   R   R   R | R   R   D   R   D
      D   D   R   R   R | R   R   R   D   D
  A   D   D   R   R   R | R   R   D   D   D  B
      D   D   R   R   R | R   R   D   R   R
      R   D   R   R   R | D   R   D   R   R
     ─────────────────────────────────────
      R   D   D   D   D | D   D   D   D   R
      R   R   D   D   D | D   D   R   D   R
  C   R   R   R   R   D | R   D   D   R   D  D
      R   D   R   D   D | R   D   R   R   D
      R   R   D   R   D | D   R   R   R   R
```

FIGURE 4.2.1   A Hypothetical State.

2. Under the districting plan in Figure 4.2.1, how does each party's share of the state's seats compare with the percentage of Republican and Democratic voters in the state? In other words, is each party's share of the state's seats roughly proportional to its share of voters in the state? Explain and support your answer.

_____

_____

_____

3. Under the districting plan in Figure 4.2.1, which party's hold on its seats is more secure? Explain and support your answer by specifying the margin by which each party holds its seats. Use whole numbers—not percentages. Think about it this way: Republicans hold district A by a margin of x number of seats over and above the number of Democrats in district A, and so on.

_____

_____

_____

4. Under the districting plan in Figure 4.2.1, in which two districts is the incumbent most secure? Explain and support your answer by specifying the incumbent's margin of control or advantage in those two districts. Use whole numbers—not percentages.

_____

_____

_____

5. a. _The Bipartisan Gerrymander: Advantage for the Incumbents_. Figure 4.2.2 shows the same distribution of voters as in Figure 4.2.1. Gerrymander the state to give a greater margin of protection or advantage to the two Republican and two Democratic incumbents who hold the seats under the districting plan in Figure 4.2.1. In other words, alter the district boundaries so that the Republican incumbents in districts A and B and the Democratic incumbents in districts C and D can count on a greater margin of victory on election day. The objective of a bipartisan gerrymander is to increase the electoral security of those already in office—the incumbents. A bipartisan gerrymander might result when Republicans and Democrats hold a roughly equal

D	D	R	R	R	R	R	D	R	D
D	D	R	R	R	R	R	R	D	D
D	D	R	R	R	R	R	D	D	D
D	D	R	R	R	R	R	D	R	R
R	D	R	R	R	D	R	D	R	R
R	D	D	D	D	D	D	D	D	R
R	R	D	D	D	D	D	R	D	R
R	R	R	R	D	R	D	D	R	D
R	D	R	D	D	R	D	R	R	D
R	R	D	R	D	D	R	R	R	R

FIGURE 4.2.2 The Bipartisan Gerrymander: Advantage for the Incumbents.

number of seats in a state legislature, denying either party the power to increase the number of legislative districts it controls. In drawing the boundaries of the new legislative districts, be sure that each district contains twenty-five voters and that each district is continuous (unbroken) in shape. Label your new districts A, B, C, and D.

b. Fill in the chart below with the former margin of victory and the new margin of victory for each incumbent. Use whole numbers—not percentages.

District	Former Margin of Victory	New Margin of Victory
A	_____	_____
B	_____	_____
C	_____	_____
D	_____	_____

6. a. *The Partisan Gerrymander: Advantage for the Republicans.* Figure 4.2.3 shows the same distribution of voters as in Figure 4.2.1. Gerrymander the state to give the Republican Party the maximum possible number of the state's four seats. A partisan gerrymander that increased the number of Republican districts might result from Republicans having control of both houses of a state legislature and the state's governorship as well. In drawing the boundaries of the new legislative districts, be sure that each district contains twenty-five voters and that each district is continuous (unbroken) in shape. Label your new districts A, B, C, and D.

D	D	R	R	R	R	R	D	R	D
D	D	R	R	R	R	R	R	D	D
D	D	R	R	R	R	R	D	D	D
D	D	R	R	R	R	R	D	R	R
R	D	R	R	R	D	R	D	R	R
R	D	D	D	D	D	D	D	D	R
R	R	D	D	D	D	D	R	D	R
R	R	R	R	D	R	D	D	R	D
R	D	R	D	D	R	D	R	R	D
R	R	D	R	D	D	R	R	R	R

FIGURE 4.2.3   The Partisan Gerrymander: Advantage for the Republicans.

b. According to your redistricting, what is the maximum number of seats you can award to the Republican Party?

_____

c. How does the Republican Party's share of the state's seats compare with the percentage of Republican voters in the state? Explain and support your answer by contrasting the Republican Party's percentage of the seats in the state with its percentage of voters in the state.

_____

_____

_____

7. a. *The Partisan Gerrymander: Advantage for the Democrats*. Figure 4.2.4 shows the same distribution of voters as in Figure 4.2.1. Gerrymander the state to give the Democratic Party the maximum possible number of the state's four seats. A partisan gerrymander that increased the number of Democratic districts might result from Democrats having control of both houses of a state legislature and the state's governorship as well. In drawing the boundaries of the new legislative districts, be sure that each district contains twenty-five voters and that each district is continuous (unbroken) in shape.

D	D	R	R	R	R	R	D	R	D
D	D	R	R	R	R	R	R	D	D
D	D	R	R	R	R	R	D	D	D
D	D	R	R	R	R	R	D	R	R
R	D	R	R	R	D	R	D	R	R
R	D	D	D	D	D	D	D	D	R
R	R	D	D	D	D	D	R	D	R
R	R	R	R	D	R	D	D	R	D
R	D	R	D	D	R	D	R	R	D
R	R	D	R	D	D	R	R	R	R

FIGURE 4.2.4 The Partisan Gerrymander: Advantage for the Democrats.

b. According to your redistricting, what is the maximum number of seats that you can award to the Democratic Party?

___

c. How does the Democratic Party's share of the state's seats compare with the percentage of Democratic voters in the state? Explain and support your answer by contrasting the Democratic Party's percentage of the seats in the state with its percentage of voters in the state.

___

8. Explain how you accomplished the gerrymander in question 7. In your explanation, demonstrate that you are thinking about political advantage and party interest. This requires more than just repeating or rephrasing the directions in question 7. *Exactly how* did you advance the power of Democrats at the expense of Republicans?

___

EXERCISE 4.3   To Vote or Not to Vote?

INTRODUCTION

Voting has always been a problem for American democracy, and it remains so today. The original (unamended) Constitution and the Bill of Rights did not explicitly confer on any U.S. citizen the right to vote.[1] For *most* of the republic's history, *most* Americans could not vote. A succession of battles for the right to vote eventually made universal suffrage the law. Yet recent elections continue to prove how difficult it remains for many citizens to cast their ballots unimpeded by dysfunctional electoral machinery and outright efforts to suppress voting.[2] But most problematic for U.S. democracy is the choice made by many citizens *not* to vote.

The electoral system and the voting process confound many Americans. That's partly because state and local governments have wide discretion in conducting elections. The nation's election machinery is so decentralized, for example, that the supervisor of elections in Palm Beach County, Florida, Theresa LePore, decided on her own authority to experiment with a new ballot format in the 2000 election. That many voters couldn't fathom the so-called "butterfly ballot"—and consequently miscast their votes for Pat Buchanan instead of for Al Gore—made news around the world and helped put George Bush in the White House in 2001. Within the federal limits explained later in this exercise, state governments have authority to establish voter eligibility requirements, voter registration procedures, and how and when voters will cast their ballots. The variation among these state electoral systems is striking—a testament to the vitality of federalism, in the view of some. Others see the diversity as federalism run amok—the root of confusion and unfairness in national elections.

State government restrictions on voter eligibility—formal and informal—long barred a broad swath of the population, particularly the poor, minorities, and women, from casting ballots. Amendments to the Constitution, Supreme Court decisions, and federal legislation slowly overcame state restrictions, expanding and securing the franchise for almost all. The Fifteenth Amendment, the Nineteenth Amendment, *Smith v. Allwright,*[3] the Voting Rights Act of 1965, and the Twenty-Sixth Amendment were milestones in the battle for universal suffrage. Today, all citizens 18 years of age and older are eligible to vote, with three general exceptions: those who fail to meet state residency requirements, convicted felons, and the mentally incompetent.[4] In the 1970 extension of the Voting Rights Act, the national government limited states to a maximum thirty-day residency requirement. But the federal government has not yet restricted the right of states to deny the franchise to convicted felons and the mentally incompetent.

Although eligibility barriers have come down, voting registration remains a hurdle for many citizens. In the United States, the burden of registration rests entirely on the citizenry. Other democracies place the burden on government. According to one critic of the U.S. system: "Every other democracy acknowledges an obligation on the part of the state to assemble the list of registered voters, either by imposing a duty to register to vote or by taking responsibility for assembling the lists. If Great Britain, Canada, France, and Germany assume the task of assembling lists of eligible voters, why shouldn't the United States adopt similar policies?"[5]

The federal government, in 1973, directed the states to facilitate voter registration. The so-called motor voter law required states to make voting registration available at selected state and local government offices and by mail. But many states did not fully fund or comply with the motor voter law. The Department of Justice responded by taking many states to court to secure their compliance. For the most part, however, state registration processes and requirements remain beyond the reach of the federal government and continue to vary significantly by state, posing differing degrees of difficulty to prospective voters.

---

[1]The right to vote is implicit, for example, in the Constitution's guarantee that every state will have a republican form of government and in the Constitution's references to the election of representatives, senators, and the president.

[2]See, for example, "The Long Shadow of Jim Crow: Voter Intimidation and Suppression in American Today" and "The New Face of Jim Crow: Voter Suppression in America" at www.pfaw.org.

[3]In April 1944, the Supreme Court decided by an 8–1 majority that all-white primary elections in the South had the practical effect of disfranchising African American voters in the general election.

[4]Information about the varied state restrictions on voting by felons is at www.felonvoting.procon.org. Two states allow felons to vote while the felons are incarcerated.

[5]Burt Neuborne, "Reclaiming Democracy," *The American Prospect*, Volume 12, Issue 5, March 12–March 26, 2001.

There is a dizzying array of variation among states in how they handle other aspects of their elections. Voter identification requirements, for example, continue to be hotly contested in state legislatures and in the courts. What constitutes acceptable identification and how election officials handle voters without acceptable identification varies from state to state. In Alabama, for example, a hunting or fishing license is acceptable identification. In Arizona, an Indian census card will suffice. In Florida, your retirement center identification is allowed. No state turns away from the polls a voter without acceptable identification—all states provide some recourse for those voters.

States also differ in how they handle absentee and early voting. All states offer some version of absentee voting; some permit "no excuse" absentee voting, while others impose restrictions. In 2010, two-thirds of the states offered early voting, generally during a period of ten to fourteen days prior to the election. Voters in these states may cast their ballots at government offices and in some cases even in grocery stores or shopping malls.[6]

Despite efforts by many states to increase turnout by making it easier to vote, many citizens decide to sit at home on election day. All sorts of factors are involved. Some people have experienced or heard of crowded and inconvenient polling places, voting machinery that doesn't work, incorrect registration rolls, or efforts to intimidate voters. Other potential voters stay at home because candidates failed to connect with them, negative campaigning turned them off, or favored issues were not addressed. Finally, some of those registered find themselves genuinely unable to get to the polls; others find ways to justify and rationalize their absence.

ASSIGNMENT: PART A, VOTER TURNOUT

The voting rate is a quantitative measurement of the extent to which U.S. citizens turn out to vote in elections, and it is often viewed as a key indicator of the health and vitality of U.S. democracy. A higher voting rate would seem to indicate that citizens embrace their democracy, making it more viable and secure. A very low voting rate, on the other hand, might cause one to wonder whether the lack of participation signals a desire by citizens to move to a political system where power derives from a source other than the vote of citizens, such as a dictatorship.

The voting rate can be calculated on different bases and reported in various ways. Some of these methods are explored in questions 1 to 3, which are based on Table 4.3.1.

1. The column in Table 4.3.1 labeled "Voting Age Population (VAP)" specifies the number of citizens who are 18 years of age or older. The next column specifies the percentage of the VAP who are *not* citizens.

  a. What's the voting rate of California's VAP? To make this calculation, divide the total number who voted in California (Turnout—that's the last column in the table) by California's VAP.

State	**Voting Age Population (VAP)**	**Percentage of Noncitizens in VAP**	**Total Ineligible Felons**	**Voting Eligible Population (VEP)**	**Turnout***
U.S. Total	235,809,266	8.3	3,148,613	218,054,301	89,099,476
California	28,018,834	17.5	231,652	22,822,532	10,095,485
Texas	18,350,170	13.7	436,250	15,407,666	4,979,870

TABLE 4.3.1 Voting Age and Voting Eligible Populations in the 2010 Election

*California and Texas calculate turnout based on the number of votes cast for governor.

Source: Michael P. McDonald, 2011, "2010 General Election Turnout Rates" United States Elections Project. Date accessed April 2011. Used by permission of Michael P. McDonald.

[6]Information on voter identification requirements, absentee and early voting, and other aspects of elections is available from the National Conference of State Legislatures at www.ncsl.org.

b. The number of noncitizens in a state's population affects the measurement and reporting of the voting rate because noncitizens are ineligible to vote. California has the highest percentage of noncitizens in its VAP: 17.5 percent, or 4,903,295. The number of the VAP in California who are citizens is 23,115,539. What's the voting rate of California's VAP who are citizens? To make this calculation, divide the total number who voted (turnout) by California's VAP who are citizens.

_____

c. What's the voting rate of the VAP in Texas who are citizens?   15 036 196.71

_____

2. The number of a state's felons, who are ineligible to vote in many states, may also affect the measurement and reporting of the voting rate. Texas, for example, has the largest number of felons ineligible to vote. The column labeled "Voting Eligible Population (VEP)" excludes not only noncitizens but also felons who are ineligible to vote. What's the voting rate of the VEP in Texas?

_____

3. In California, 17,285,833 citizens were registered to vote at the time of the 2010 election.

a. What was the voting rate of registered voters in California?

_____

b. What was the voting rate of the VEP in California?

_____

c. One of the measurements here provides a much more accurate picture of the health and vitality of U.S. democracy than the other. Which is it—the voting rate of registered voters or the voting rate of eligible voters? Explain and support your answer.

_____

_____

_____

_____

_____

Questions 4 and 5 are based on Table 4.3.2.

4. Table 4.3.2 indicates a 23.9-point difference between the percentage of 18- to 24-year-olds who reported voting and the percentage of 65- to 74-year-olds who reported voting. Let's call this the turnout gap. The 2008 turnout gap between younger and older Americans was _unusually low_ because of two factors: It was a presidential election year, and Democratic candidate Barack Obama energized many younger voters to go to the polls. By contrast, the turnout gap in the 2004 presidential election was 26.6 points. In the 2006 off-year election when the presidency was not up for grabs, the turnout gap was an astonishing 42.2 points.

a. What's the turnout gap (in percentage points) between those earning less than $20,000 annually and those earning $100,000 and over?

_____

b. What's the turnout gap (in percentage points) between those who have not finished high school and those with a bachelor's degree?

_____

TABLE 4.3.2	Reported Rates of Voting by Selected Characteristics, 2008*
Characteristic	**Reported Voted Percent**
Age	
18 to 24 years	48.5
25 to 34 years	57.0
35 to 44 years	62.8
45 to 54 years	67.4
55 to 64 years	71.5
65 to 74 years	72.4
75 and older	67.8
Marital Status	
Married	69.9
Widowed	61.6
Divorced	59.0
Separated	53.5
Never married	53.5
Educational Attainment	
Less than high school graduate	39.4
High school graduate of GED	54.9
Some college or associate's degree	68.0
Bachelor's degree	77.0
Advanced degree	82.7
Annual Family Income	
Total family members	65.5
Less than $20,000	51.9
$20,000–$29,999	56.3
$30,000–$39,999	62.2
$40,000–$49,999	64.7
$50,000–$74,999	70.9
$75,000–$99,999	76.4
$100,000 and over	91.8
Income not reported	49.0
Employment Status	
In the civilian labor force	65.2
Employed	65.9
Unemployed	54.7
Not in the labor force	60.3
Duration of Residence	
Less than 1 year	57.0
1 to 2 years	65.3
3 to 4 years	72.6
5 years or longer	77.8
Not reported	6.5
Region	
Northeast	62.9
Midwest	66.3

(continued)

TABLE 4.3.2	Reported Rates of Voting by Selected Characteristics, 2008 (continued)
Characteristic	**Reported Voted Percent**
South	62.6
West	63.3
Veteran Status	
Total population	63.6
Veteran	70.9
Nonveteran	62.8
Tenure	
Owner	67.8
Renter	51.6

Source: U.S. Census Bureau, Voting and Registration in the Election of November 2008, Population Characteristics, Issues May 2010.

*The data in Tables 4.3.2 and 4.3.3 come from the Census Bureau's Current Population Survey. Voters do not disclose to election officials, of course, information about their income, education, or any other characteristic, when casting their ballots. Consequently, exit polls and surveys are the only means of identifying the characteristics of voters. The Current Population Survey is rigorous, includes a large sample, and is conducted within two weeks of the election. Many of those surveyed (perhaps 10 percent) are reluctant to admit that they declined to do their civic duty and falsely report having voted. This makes it impossible to know exactly how many voters, for example, fall within a particular income bracket or any of the other selected characteristics in Table 4.3.2. The 2008 election is the most recent one for which this type of Census Bureau data were available at the time of publication.

c. The 2008 turnout gap is the greatest for which characteristic, age, income, or education?

_____

5. Which characteristics—other than age, income, and education—specified in Table 4.3.2 help account for the lower voter turnout of those age 18 to 24 years? In other words, which characteristics associated with low rates of voting might disproportionately affect and depress the turnout of those 18 to 24 years of age?

_____

_____

_____

Questions 6 to 9 are based on Table 4.3.3.

6. a. Which reason for not voting has the largest percentage point gap between 18- to 24-year-olds and those 65 years of age and over?

_____

b. What's that percentage point gap?

_____

TABLE 4.3.3 Reasons for Not Voting by Age: November 2008

Percentage Distribution of Reasons for Not Voting

Characteristic	Illness or Disability	Out of Town	Forgot to Vote	Not Interested	Too Busy, Conflicting Schedule	Transportation Problems	Did Not Like Candidates or Campaign Issues	Registration Problems	Bad Weather Conditions	Inconvenient Polling Place	Other Reason	Don't Know Or Refused
Age												
18 to 24 years	3.2	14.2	4.5	12.1	21.0	2.4	8.0	9.0	0.2	2.6	11.6	11.2
25 to 44 years	6.8	8.4	2.8	14.2	24.3	1.4	12.7	7.3	0.1	3.0	11.7	7.2
45 to 64 years	14.8	8.3	1.8	15.2	14.9	3.4	16.5	4.3	0.1	2.6	12.5	5.8
65 years and over	45.3	5.1	1.3	9.9	3.0	4.5	12.5	2.6	0.8	2.3	8.0	4.6
	42.1	9.1	3.2	2.2	1.8	2.1	4.5	6.4	0.6	0.3	3.0	6.6

Source: U.S. Census Bureau, Current Population Survey, November 2008, Table 12, Reasons for Not Voting by Selected Characteristics.

7. a. Which reason had the second largest percentage point gap between 18- to 24-years-olds and those 65 years of age and over?

_____

b. What's that percentage point gap?

_____

8. Which age cohort (group) appears to be most forgetful?

_____

9. According to the responses in Table 4.3.3, which age group found "registration problems" to be most difficult?

_____

ASSIGNMENT: PART B, THE YOUTH VOTE

The age qualification for voting has traditionally been 21 years, set by state governments. During World War II, many citizens felt that, if 18- to 20-year-olds could be drafted and die in combat, they should be able to vote, too. In 1943, Georgia lowered its voting age to 18; Kentucky followed suit—but not until 1955. When Alaska and Hawaii became states in the late 1950s, their constitutions had voting ages of 19 and 20, respectively.

The discrepancy between the draft age and the voting age arose again during the Vietnam War. One provision of the Voting Rights Act of 1970 established a voting age of 18 in all federal, state, and local elections. Several states objected to the national government overriding the traditional state prerogative of regulating the conduct of state and local elections. In 1970, in _Oregon v. Mitchell_, the Supreme Court ruled that Congress had the authority to set the voting age _only_ in elections for Congress and the presidency. The daunting prospect of having voting age requirements vary by state _and_ by the type of election prompted Congress to propose, and the states to ratify, the Twenty-Sixth Amendment, which states that "the rights of citizens of the United States, who are eighteen years of age or older, to vote shall not be abridged by the United States or by any state on account of age."

Given a political climate in the 1960s charged by the antiwar, civil rights, women's, and environmental movements, many observers expected America's newly enfranchised youth to storm the polls in the election of 1972. They did not. Only 50 percent of the newly enfranchised 18- to 20-year-olds turned out to vote in 1972, and the youth voting rate declined precipitously after that election. According to Census Bureau figures, only 40 percent of 18- to 24-year-olds reported voting in the 1980 election, and only 32 percent reported voting in the 2000 election.

To answer questions 1 to 6, go to http://www.civicyouth.org/new-census-data-confirm-increase-in-youth-voter-turnout-in-2008-election/. Under the title of the article, click on the link that says: "The fact sheet on youth voter turnout and trends in 2008 and a 50-state break-down can be downloaded here (PDF)." This takes you to a report titled "The Youth Vote in 2008," by Emily Hoban Kirby and Kei Kawashima-Ginsberg, updated August 17, 2009. This report is published by the Center for Information and Research on Civic Learning and Engagement (CIRCLE) at www.civicyouth.org.

Web addresses sometimes change. If you can't locate a website, try an external search (e.g., Google) to find the website. Configurations within a website often change. If you can't find a particular link or article, for example, try an internal search of the website as well as. an external search. Be resourceful! If you still can't find what you're searching for, move on to the next question.

1. According to the report, what are the three ways to measure the turnout of young voters?

a. Method 1: _____

_____

b. Method 2: _____

_____

c. Method 3: _____

_____

d. The three methods display roughly the same trend regarding the turnout of young voters. What is it?

_____

_____

_____

2. What is the percentage point gender gap between the voting rate of men and women in the 18–29 age bracket?

_____

3. Between the 2000 and 2008 elections, how did the turnout rate for African American youth change?

_____

_____

_____

4. In the 2008 election, how much more likely to vote were young people with college experience compared to those without college experience?

_____

5. a. In the 2008 election, for those in the 18–29 age bracket, which state had the highest turnout rate? What's that number?

_____

b. Which state had the lowest turnout rate? What's that number?

_____

6. a. Which state had the greatest difference between the youth and adult turnout rates? What's the percentage point gap?

_____

b. What's the national average percentage point gap?

_____

For questions 7 and 8, search the Web for "Ensuring the Rights of College Students to Vote," Statement before the Committee on House Administration, Sujatha Jahagirdar, Program Director, Student PIRGs New Voters Project, September 25, 2008. Study the statement and answer questions 7 and 8.

7. a. In your view, which barrier to student voting is the most significant? Explain and support your answer.

_____

_____

_____

_____

_____

b. In your view, what should be done to remove this barrier?

_____

_____

_____

_____

8. In your view, which barrier most clearly seems to have behind it an intent to suppress student voting? Explain and support your answer.

_____

_____

_____

_____

_____

EXERCISE 4.4   Alternative Voting Systems

INTRODUCTION

Nothing matters more in an election than the rules under which votes are cast and counted. Americans learned this lesson in the contested presidential election of 2000, when the candidate who came in second in the popular vote won the Oval Office. Of course, the presidential election is governed by the Electoral College whose web of rules and procedures prevailed over the popular will. In most elections in the United States, ballots are cast and counted according to the rules of the plurality voting system (explained later in this exercise). Most Americans take the plurality system for granted, even though few other democracies employ it and even though a number of viable alternatives to it exist.

Our examination of alternative voting systems will consider these questions: Does the system fairly and accurately gauge popular preferences? Which interests and viewpoints does a particular system reward, and which does it penalize? How does a system of casting and counting ballots shape citizens' views of the political system?

ASSIGNMENT

Described here are several different voting systems. Study each system and answer the questions that follow.

The Plurality Voting System In a plurality voting system, the candidate who receives the most votes wins. A plurality is different from a simple majority. To win a simple majority, a candidate must receive 50 percent of the total votes cast plus one more. In a plurality system, there is no minimum number of votes necessary to win.

Candidates from minor parties—the Libertarian Party or the Green Party, for example—find it difficult to win political office in the United States because of the interplay between the plurality voting system and *single-member districts*. In U.S. elections, voters in a congressional district, state legislative district, or other electoral districts usually elect just one official. The system is known as *winner-take-all, single-member district* because the winner of the election takes possession of the sole public office being contested in the election. There is no prize for the runners-up: The candidate with the most votes wins it all.[1] Winners are almost always members of the two major parties, Democrat or Republican, which monopolize political power in the United States. The two-party monopoly dates to the beginning of the republic and continues to shape the expectations and voting behavior of citizens and also the electoral strategies of candidates.

1. Go to the website of FairVote, The Center for Voting and Democracy, at http://www.fairvote.org/. Click on Who We Are and read the Overview. Then go to http://archive.fairvote.org/?page=168 and read the Frequently Asked Questions. Finally, go to http://archive.fairvote.org/?page=2337 and read the article "The Case for Proportional Representation," by Robert Richie and Steven Hill. Focus on the introduction to the article and the section titled What's the Problem. In the space below, briefly summarize the problems that FairVote identifies with the two-party monopoly and the winner-take-all system.

Web addresses sometimes change. If you can't locate a website, try an external search (e.g., Google) to find the website. Configurations within a website often change. If you can't find a particular link or article, for example, try an internal search of the website as well as. an external search. Be resourceful! If you still can't find what you're searching for, move on to the next question.

_____

_____

_____

_____

[1]The only exceptions are runoff elections in some primaries. We discuss those elections below.

_____

_____

_____

2. Explain how the combination of winner-take-all and the plurality voting system works against third-party candidates and discourages citizens from voting for those candidates.

_____

_____

_____

_____

_____

_____

The Runoff System The runoff system described here is used in primary elections in nine southern states. Under the rules in a runoff system election, a candidate must win a simple majority of the popular vote to win the party's nomination. If no candidate wins a simple majority in the first primary election, the top two finishers compete in a second primary, a _runoff primary,_ which again is decided by a simple majority vote.

3. Complete the table below by specifying the percentage of the popular vote each candidate would need to receive in the first primary election to produce a runoff election between candidates A and B, and then the percentage of the popular vote candidate A would need to win the runoff election. (Many percentage figures will produce the result you are seeking.)

First Primary Election	
Candidates	**Percentage of Vote Needed to Produce a Runoff Election**
A. Republican Party	_____
B. Republican Party	_____
C. Republican Party	_____
D. Republican Party	_____

Runoff Primary Election	
Candidates	**Percentage of Vote Needed to Win the Nomination**
A. Republican Party	_____
B. Republican Party	_____

4. Under which system, plurality or runoff, would a minority candidate—for example, an African American—have a greater chance of winning? Explain and support your answer. (Remember that the runoff is used in party primaries, so there is no two-party monopoly.)

_____

_____

_____

_____

_____

_____

_____

The Approval Voting System Under the approval voting system, voters may choose to cast one vote for as many or as few candidates on the ballot that they find acceptable. A voter may even choose to cast no votes at all. The requirement for winning the election could be plurality or simple majority (with the contingency of a runoff election). The United Nations, by the way, uses this system to select its secretary-general.

5. Consider these five candidates running on the ballot for a seat in your state legislature:

   Candidate A: Democrat, liberal, prochoice

   Candidate B: Democrat, moderate, prochoice

   Candidate C: Republican, moderate, prochoice

   Candidate D: Republican, moderate, prolife

   Candidate E: Republican, conservative, prolife

Consider the position of an independent voter strongly in favor of abortion rights (prochoice) and moderate to conservative on most other issues. For which candidates would this voter cast her or his votes under the approval voting system? Explain your answer.

_____

_____

_____

_____

_____

6. What type of candidate would the approval voting system tend to favor—one that is broadly acceptable to the electorate or one that attracts deep and enthusiastic support from a narrow segment of the electorate? Explain your answer by citing specific features of the approval voting system.

_____

_____

_____

_____

_____

7. Would the approval voting system tend to make it more or less difficult for minority group candidates such as African Americans to win office? Explain your answer.

_____

_____

_____

_____

_____

The Cumulative Voting System   Under the cumulative voting system, citizens can cast as many votes as there are candidates in the race, distributing the votes in any way they choose. For example, if there are six candidates on the ballot, a voter can cast all six votes for a strongly favored candidate, or one or more votes to any other candidates the voter favors. Here, too, candidates may win with a plurality or with a simple majority (and a contingency runoff election). Cumulative voting was adopted in 1987 by the cities of Alamogordo, New Mexico, and Peoria, Illinois, to meet court-imposed requirements regarding minority representation in municipal elections.

8. Consider the following candidates on the ballot:

Candidate A: Democrat, left-wing liberal, white, female

Candidate B: Democrat, liberal, white, female

Candidate C: Democrat, moderate, black, female

Candidate D: Republican, moderate, white, male

Candidate E: Republican, conservative, black, male

Candidate F: Republican, right-wing conservative, white, male

How would a lifelong left-wing liberal Democrat, active in the party and favoring liberal and feminist causes, most likely cast his or her six votes? Explain and support your answer.

_____

_____

_____

_____

_____

9. What type of candidate would the cumulative system tend to favor—one that is broadly acceptable to the electorate or one that attracts deep and enthusiastic support from a narrow segment of the electorate? Explain your answer by citing specific features of the approval voting system.

_____

_____

_____

_____

10. Would the cumulative voting system tend to make it more or less difficult for minority group candidates such as African Americans to win office? Explain your answer.

_____

_____

_____

_____

_____

The Transferable-Vote System   This is the most complex of the voting systems examined here, but some mathematicians maintain that it accounts most accurately for voters' preferences and that it, of all voting systems, is most likely to end in the election of a consensus candidate. The Associated Students of the University of California at Berkeley and the Tasmanian House of Assembly both use this system to elect their officers. Under the transferable-vote system, voters rank each candidate, assigning the number 1 to the candidate they favor most strongly, the number 2 to the next most favored candidate, and so on. An initial tally is made to determine how many number 1 rankings each candidate received. The candidate receiving the fewest is eliminated from the contest, and the number 1 rankings he or she received are transferred to the candidates those voters ranked number 2. This process of eliminating the candidate with the fewest number 1 rankings and distributing those votes to the voters' number 2 choice is repeated until all candidates but one have been eliminated. That candidate is the winner.

11. Put yourself in the position of a voter who is strongly committed to the Green Party and the principles it stands for. In your election district for the House of Representatives, only about 5 percent of registered voters are members of the Green Party. Democrats, Republicans, and independents each make up about 30 percent of the registered voters. The remaining 5 percent is distributed among other minority parties. Because of the two-party monopoly, there is no chance that a Green Party candidate will win a seat in the House either under the plurality election system or under the transferable-vote system. Given that situation, which of those two systems would you, as a voter strongly committed to the Green Party, prefer to participate under and why?

_____

_____

_____

_____

_____

12. Make one argument against the transferable-vote system.

_____

_____

_____

_____

_____

Proportional Representation The voting systems examined in this exercise are mostly used in candidate-based, single-district, winner-take-all elections. By contrast, many nations employ political party–based systems, multimember election districts, and proportional representation. In these systems, each party fields a slate (list) of candidates, and voters cast their ballots for the party they prefer. Seats in the legislature are awarded to each party according to the percentage of votes the party captures in the election. The party then elevates the appropriate number of candidates from its slate to seats in the legislature. Typically, parties that receive just a small percentage of the vote (e.g., less than 6 percent) are not awarded seats in the legislature. Under the proportional representation system, one party often is unable to capture an outright majority of the seats in the legislature. Coalitions between parties must then be formed to achieve the majority needed to control the legislature and, hence, to govern.

13. Fill in the right-hand column of the table below by allocating the 100 seats in this hypothetical parliament on a proportional basis—in other words, according to the percentage of the vote each party received. Assume that parties that win less than 6 percent of the vote receive no seats in the legislature.

Party	Percentage of Vote	Seats in Parliament (of 100)
A	38	_____
B	26	_____
C	20	_____
D	9	_____
E	4	_____
F	3	_____

14. Identify the possible coalitions of parties that would achieve majority control of Parliament.

_____

_____

15. Return to the FairVote article, "The Case for Proportional Representation." Study the section titled Why PR? and the subsections titled The Majority Argument and Other Reasons for PR.

   a. Which argument in favor of proportional representation do you find most persuasive and why?

   _____

   _____

   _____

   _____

   _____

   b. Which argument do you find least persuasive and why?

   _____

   _____

   _____

   _____

16. Which of the six voting systems examined in this exercise do you think is best? Explain and support your position.

_____

_____

_____

_____

_____

_____

5

Interest Groups

EXERCISE 5.1   AARP Versus Generations X and Y: Mismatched Interest Group Power

INTRODUCTION

Many citizens magnify their political power by joining or forming interest groups. Many others—for lack of knowledge, resources, or motivation—decline to do so. Interest group membership, like the voting rate, varies according to factors such as age, education, and economic position. The interests of Americans over age 50, for example, are represented muscularly—some would say notoriously—by AARP. Formerly called the American Association of Retired Persons, now it's known simply as AARP to acknowledge that many members are not retired. In fact, AARP recruits members as young as 50, who ordinarily have at least twelve to fifteen working years until retirement.

Because elected officials and the media often equate an interest group's power with the size of its membership, numbers count. AARP's membership of about 40 million is daunting—far surpassing that of any other public interest group. By comparison, the National Rifle Association (NRA) boasts a membership of about 4 million. Although its membership is a mere fraction of the AARP's, the NRA has the advantage of near unanimity among its members on the group's central issue: protecting a citizen's right to own firearms unimpeded by government regulation. Because AARP's objective of advancing the quality of life for older Americans is quite broad, its members often part company on just how to achieve that objective.

In 2003, AARP's leadership was reminded of the perils of taking policy positions for a membership that is notably diverse. AARP surprised its traditional Democratic allies in Congress and many of its members by backing President George W. Bush's proposal for a Medicare prescription drug benefit. Two components of the president's proposal had long been opposed by AARP: an experiment with limited privatization of the drug benefit and a means test requiring wealthy recipients to pay a bigger share of their premium. AARP members reacted by burning their membership cards outside the group's headquarters in Washington, DC, and demanding that AARP chief William Novelli be fired from his $420,000-a-year job. Eighty-five House Democrats expressed their outrage by announcing that they would resign from AARP or refuse to join in the future. One Florida resident interviewed by the *New York Times* said, "I'm going to resign from AARP. Its support of this drug plan tipped the balance. They're more sympathetic to the big drug and insurance companies than to ordinary seniors who want a simple solution."[1]

AARP experienced another mini-rebellion of its members in the summer of 2009 over its support for overhauling the nation's health-care system. During one six-week period, over 50,000 AARP members left the organization. An interest group called American Seniors Association (ASA), which bills itself as a conservative alternative to the AARP, made a bid for the defecting AARP members by urging them to tear up their AARP membership cards and send them to ASA to get a two-year membership at half price. Jim Dau, a spokesperson for AARP, said that "with a membership this big, there will be differences of opinion with our advocacy positions. But history has borne out that many came back. We want to earn them back."[2] One North Carolina AARP member told a reporter: "I do not want Obamacare or socialized medicine. The AARP talks out of both sides of their mouth. They say they don't support it but Obama says they do support his plan. They support other policies that have nothing to do with seniors, and I don't want my money supporting causes I don't agree with."[3]

---

[1] Robert Pear, "Florida Elderly Feel Let Down by Medicare Drug Benefit," *New York Times*, November 30, 2003.

[2] Katharine, Q. Seelye, "A Mini-Mutiny at AARP Over Health Care," *The New York Times*, August 18, 2009.

[3] Karen McMahan, "AARP Losing Members Over Health Care Debate," *Carolina Journal Online*, October 5, 2009.

AARP is usually categorized as a public—as opposed to a private—interest group. But the distinction between the two types of interest groups is not always clear. Generally, public interest groups advocate for broad political and social causes as opposed to seeking narrow material benefits for their members—the purpose of private interest groups such as the American Farm Bureau Federation, for example. AARP claims its mission is to enhance "the quality of life for all as we age," which would seem to anchor it securely in the public interest camp. Yet AARP also provides particular financial benefits to its members and makes money doing so. The American Automobile Association (AAA)—whose approximately 45-million-strong membership trumps AARP's—is generally considered a private interest group because it provides emergency and other road services to members.[4] Few AAA members are aware that the group lobbies against environmental, auto safety, and public transportation initiatives.[5]

How effectively interest groups deploy their resources and how genuinely they serve the interests of their members are controversial matters—particularly in the case of AARP. Dale Van Atta, a trenchant critic of AARP and author of *Trust Betrayed: Inside the AARP*, argues that government policymakers and journalists have overestimated the power of AARP and that other seniors' organizations are more effective at lobbying Congress.[6] Van Atta and other AARP critics skewer the organization as a money-making machine run by fat cats that often works against the interests of its members. Yet despite its critics, AARP remains widely perceived as the voice of the elderly and the mother of all interest groups.

A striking disparity in power and influence exists between AARP and groups that have struggled for years to organize and advocate for Americans in their twenties and thirties—a demographic group usually referred to as Generation X and Generation Y, respectively.[7] One recent effort to organize young adults for advocacy—on social security and other issues—flowered and died quickly. The 2030 Center was founded in 1997 to advocate for the economic interests of young adults, but it emphasized the need to bridge the generation gap on difficult issues such as Social Security reform. The group's name referred to Americans in their twenties and thirties as well as to the year 2030, a demographic benchmark when the leading edge of Generation X will begin claiming its Social Security retirement benefits. In 1999, the 2030 Center commissioned a poll of Generation X members; it purported to show that "an antagonistic political battle between older people, baby boomers, and young people is largely a myth."[8] Among other accomplishments, the group published a manual for strengthening Social Security for young workers, testified before congressional committees, and received significant media attention. The 2030 Center folded sometime in 2002.

A more recent example of interest group organizing younger Americans is Students for Saving Social Security (S4). The group was founded on the cheap in 2005 by Jonathan Swanson, a Yale University graduate, and Patrick Wetherille, who graduated from Georgetown University. Its budget never exceeded about $250,000 per year. By contrast, AARP reported total revenue in 2010 of over $1 billion—that's about 4,000 times the size of the S4 budget. And AARP spent over $20 million on lobbying in 2010, according to the Center for Responsive Politics.

S4's founding coincided with a national debate on President George W. Bush's plan to partially privatize Social Security by allowing Americans to set up individual investment accounts and fund them with some of the taxes otherwise paid to Social Security. Students for Saving Social Security advocated allowing Americans to divert even more of their Social Security taxes into individual accounts than Bush proposed. S4 characterized itself as a nonpartisan organization with the purpose of educating and mobilizing young Americans to address what the group believed was "the coming crisis in Social Security." Members of S4 received national coverage for their efforts to

---

[4]*Public Interest Group Profiles, 2005–2006* (CQ Press, 2004) lists AARP as a public interest group, but not the AAA.

[5]Ken Silverstein, "Smitten with a Club: Your AAA Dues Fuel Pollution and Sprawl," *Harpers Magazine*, May 2002.

[6]Dale Van Atta, *Trust Betrayed: Inside the AARP* (Washington, DC: Regnery Publishing, 1998). The organizations Van Atta cites as being more effective than AARP are the National Committee to Preserve Social Security, the Seniors Coalition, and the National Council of Senior Citizens.

[7]Generation X is generally considered to include those born between 1965 and 1980. Generation Y encompasses those born between 1980 and 2000. The baby boom generation is generally considered to include those born between 1946 and 1965.

[8]Americans for Generational Equity (AGE), founded in 1985, was the first organization to promote the notion of "future intergenerational conflict." Christopher Cuomo argued in 1997 that the divide between the young and old was a myth promoted by conservatives who sought to weaken Social Security. See "The Generation Gambit: The Right's Imaginary Rift Between Young and Old," Fairness & Accuracy in Reporting (FAIR), March/April 1997, at http://www.fair.org/index .php?page=1379.

win over candidates in the New Hampshire presidential primary in 2008.[9] One S4 staff member crossed the state on foot dressed as an ostrich; others rode around the state in their Ostrich Mobile—a beat-up GMC Suburban painted with political slogans. Why the ostrich theme? To prevent presidential candidates from sticking their heads in the sand on Social Security. (You can view a video of S4 members in their ostrich costumes in front of the White House at http://www .youtube.com/profile?user=Ostrichgirl.) In addition to receiving national news coverage, S4 was praised by former vice president Dick Cheney and former majority leader of the House, Richard K. Armey, among others. S4's grassroots organizing efforts managed to build a membership base of over 11,000 with over 300 college chapters. The group folded in late 2009.

The disparity in power and influence between interest groups representing seniors and those representing Generations X and Y will be apparent as efforts to "fix" Social Security continue. The generational battle, however, is just one fault line in the contest over the future of Social Security, which in 2010 provided benefits to over 54 million Americans. Many other interest groups with a wide array of perspectives and concerns have also joined the political battle. One example is the Institute for Women's Policy Research (IWPR), which is concerned about "the economic security of women in retirement and the possible effects of Social Security privatization on women." IWPR notes that nearly 60 percent of Social Security beneficiaries are women.[10]

Most observers agree that Social Security requires substantive reform to meet its long-term obligations to future retirees. The fundamental problem is demographic. As the baby boom generation reaches retirement age, the number of retirees drawing Social Security benefits will increase; the number of workers paying into the system will decrease. For example, in 1940, the ratio of workers paying into Social Security to retirees drawing benefits was 42 to 1, meaning that far more workers were paying into the system than were receiving benefits. By 2009, the ratio had dropped to 3 to 1. By 2031, the ratio is projected to be 2.1 to 1. Also straining the system is the increasing longevity of retirees.[11]

AARP is quick to point out that it seeks a solution to the Social Security problem that is fair to younger generations as well as to seniors. Perhaps that's because AARP doesn't want to alienate the generations it will be recruiting from in the not-so-distant future. It might be a sobering prospect indeed for members of Generations X and Y to consider that the day they'll be eligible for membership in AARP is not that far away.

ASSIGNMENT

Questions 1 to 11 explore the structure and functions of AARP and its position on Social Security reform.

1. What characteristics of those over age 50 make older Americans more effective interest group members than those of Generations X and Y? In other words, why have efforts to organize older Americans been so much more successful than efforts to organize members of Generations X and Y?

_____

_____

_____

_____

2. Web-Based Question. Take a few minutes and explore AARP's website at www.aarp.org. Generally speaking, does the website give more emphasis to services and benefits for AARP members or to the group's work on political advocacy and its positions on public issues?

---

[9]Brody Mullins, "To Get Attention in New Hampshire, Dress as an Ostrich," *Wall Street Journal*, January 8, 2008.

[10]http://womenandsocialsecurity.org/Women_Social_Security/about.htm.

[11]A brief and accessible introduction to the history of Social Security and the challenges the system faces can be found at www.ssa.gov/history/brief.html.

Web addresses sometimes change. If you can't locate a website, try an external search (e.g., Google) to find the website. Configurations within a website often change. If you can't find a particular link or article, for example, try an internal search of the website as well as an external search. Be resourceful! If you still can't find what you're searching for, move on to the next question.

_____

_____

To answer questions 3 to 8, click on "About AARP" on AARP's homepage. (In 2011, the link to "About AARP" was located in the bottom left-hand corner of the homepage, so you may need to look around.)

3. What does AARP claim its mission to be?

_____

_____

_____

4. Who does AARP claim to represent?

_____

_____

5. How does AARP finance its operations?

_____

_____

_____

6. How does AARP communicate with its members?

_____

_____

_____

7. How does AARP develop its policy positions? Look for the link titled "Our Policies." This will take you to a page titled "Where We Stand."

_____

_____

_____

_____

_____

_____

8. What advocacy efforts does AARP undertake?

_____

_____

_____

9. To answer questions 9a and 9b, you'll need a basic understanding of how Social Security works. Begin by using a search engine to locate the Social Security Administration's publication "Fast Facts and Figures about Social Security." Study the sections titled How Social Security Is Financed, Social Security's Demographic Challenge, and The Long-Run Financial Outlook. There are many other resources available on the Web to help you understand Social Security.

  a. What did you learn about Social Security that you didn't already know?

  _____

  _____

  _____

  b. What is one unanswered question you have about Social Security?

  _____

  _____

  _____

   Return to the AARP page titled "Our Policies" and locate the link to a document called "The Policy Book: AARP's Public Policies." Find the chapter on "Retirement Income," and read the section titled "AARP Principles for Social Security Solvency." Examine these principles from the point of view of an activist member of Students for Saving Social Security. Recall that, in the view of S4 members, Social Security is headed for a crisis. Here's more from S4 activists to help you understand their viewpoint:

> _We advocate the following on college campuses across the country:_
> **_Allowing younger workers the option to save at least 4 percent of their payroll taxes in a personal account._**
> _According to the Social Security Trustees, today's young workers can expect no more than 75 percent of promised benefits. Young people should have a choice: those who want to remain in the current system can do so, while those who want to dedicate a portion of their contributions to a personal account should have that option. If structured properly, personal accounts would provide a generationally equitable solution to make up for the expected benefit cuts that likely lie ahead._
> _Other benefits of giving workers the right to control some of their own retirement money include increased national savings and financial literacy as well as the widespread accrual of inheritable wealth. Personal accounts would give workers the right of property to a portion of their Social Security benefits, a right which the Supreme Court has ruled does not extend to taxes paid under the current system._

10. What do you think would be S4's critique of the "AARP Principles for Social Security Solvency"? In other words, what would S4 object to in the AARP principles and why?

_____

_____

_____

_____

_____

_____

_____

11. Return to the chapter on "Retirement Income" in the AARP Policy Book, study the section titled "Replacing a Portion of Social Security Benefits with Individual Accounts."
List five reasons why the AARP opposes individual accounts.

_____

_____

_____

_____

_____

_____

_____

_____

Questions 12 to 15 are based on Reading 5.1.1, an excerpt from "A Management Study of the Communications of the American Association of Retired Persons."

CASE 5.1.1
A Management Study of the Communications of the American Association of Retired Persons[12]

In a study of the American Association of Retired Persons, management consultant group Chester Burger & Co. found an organization divided. They encountered a staff that was confused about the composition of AARP's increasingly diverse membership. Originally established specifically to serve the needs of the retired, it had broadened its reach to include "the affluent, the needy, retired people, those still working, the mature, the old, the old old, the feeble elderly, active seniors, etc."

The management consultants found that staff members of AARP disagreed about the very purpose of the organization. One group within AARP supported an internally focused service-to-members approach while another supported an outwardly focused advocacy orientation that would use the organization's size and breadth to promote policies favorable to the retired and soon to be retired.

A service-oriented organization would refrain from taking positions that might spark disagreement among current members and inhibit recruitment of new members. An organization with a public policy orientation might risk offending some members from time to time in order to have an influence on the public debate over issues of importance to older members of society.

The management consultant study concluded that this debate within the group over "membership demographics" created "destructive static between these two opposing views of AARP's mission."

[12]Conducted by outside consultants, Chester Burger & Co., Inc., September 1985. The study is cited in Dale Van Atta, *Trust Betrayed: Inside the AARP* (Washington, DC: Regnery Publishing, 1998), p. 117.

12. How does the management study describe the diversity of AARP's membership?

_____

_____

_____

_____

_____

13. According to the management study, what conflict exists within AARP as the organization tries to grapple with the diversity of its "membership demographics"?

_____

_____

_____

_____

_____

14. What's ultimately at stake for AARP if advocacy undermines membership growth and the sale of services?

_____

_____

15. If you were the executive director of AARP, would you side with the service or advocacy faction? Explain and support your position.

_____

_____

_____

_____

_____

EXERCISE 5.2   Earmarks and Pork: Can We Live Without Them?

INTRODUCTION

Members of Congress are often accused of bringing federal dollars home to benefit their districts or states at the expense of the national interest. The common term for this use of federal funds was once *pork-barrel spending,* implying that the projects are wasteful and serve mainly to enhance the representative's reelection prospects. Today the more common language for special projects for districts and states is a more neutral sounding term, *earmarks.* Pork-barrel spending and earmarks are, for all intents and purposes, synonymous, but earmarks, despite the neutral terminology, have become even more controversial than good old-fashioned pork-barrel spending. The controversy arose from the congressional practice, beginning in the 1990s, of allowing representatives to target federal funding for pet projects with little oversight and accountability. Representatives were able, anonymously, to include spending for their project in an appropriations bill, and they were able to bypass congressional hearings, collaborative bill writing, and floor debate. Old-fashioned pork—before earmarks—had to be scrutinized by peers, and members of Congress had to identify their sponsorship of the expenditure publicly.

Presidents are among the loudest critics of Congress' penchant for pork. A president's national constituency and budget perspective often places the president above the narrow constituencies clamoring for federal dollars. (Remember that members of Congress are elected by district or state constituents, so it's not surprising that their perspective is different than the president's.) Both George W. Bush and Barack Obama issued executive orders that prohibited federal agencies from honoring so-called soft earmarks. Soft earmarks occur when members of Congress apply informal pressure on agencies to spend discretionary funds on pet projects. Federal agencies find the pressure difficult to resist because of their fear of congressional budgetary retaliation if the pressure is resisted. The effectiveness of the Bush and Obama executive orders is difficult to gauge because soft earmarks are informal and because of the complexity of keeping track of executive branch spending. But even presidents are not above playing politics with pork. They tend to be more enthusiastic about cutting pork-barrel spending in districts and states controlled by the other party than in those controlled by their own party.

Congress often prevails in battles with the president over pork-barrel spending. Why? Two factors are particularly important in explaining how representatives protect their slice of the pork. First, Congress has control over appropriations, and members can use their positions on key committees and subcommittees to protect special interests. Special interests in the representative's district or state support those members of Congress at election time. Second, even though members of Congress frequently have no direct stake in any other member's earmarks, they'll often let the earmark go unchallenged in order to ensure that their own earmarks go unchallenged.

Despite the odds stacked against major reform of earmarks, the Tea Party Movement, its congressional allies, and the news media's increased attentiveness to earmarks worked to effect reforms. Beginning in 2006, Congress moved to make earmarks transparent; for example, Congress required the Office of Management and Budget (OMB) to post earmarks on a publicly accessible website: http://earmarks.omb.gov/earmarks-public/.[1] In the budget-cutting frenzy of 2011, the chairs of the Appropriations Committee in the House and the Finance Committee in the Senate announced a two-year moratorium on earmarks. (The chairs had been two of the most frequent users of earmarks in the past.[2])

What are the prospects that earmark reform will become permanent? Skeptics point out that Congress has a history of going back to business as usual once political pressure and the concerns of the moment abate. Congressional members of both parties publicly aired their reservations about the moratorium. They claimed that a variety of legitimate interests in their districts and states still expect federal dollars to flow to worthy projects. (Lyndon Johnson, when he was in Congress, used to justify his special attention to his constituents' interests by quoting an old Texas

---

[1]Other earmark reforms can be found at SourceWatch.org, http://www.sourcewatch.org/index.php?title=Earmarks.

[2]Taxpayers for Common Sense, *TCS FY2010 Earmark Analysis,* on the TCS website, http://www.taxpayers.org. The chairs were Representative Harold Rogers (Republican, Kentucky) and Senator Daniel Inouye (Democrat, Hawaii).

saying, "You dance with the ones who brung you.") Many Americans, who tell pollsters that they favor earmark reform, might be expected to change their minds if ending earmarks means a loss of jobs or services that depend on federal funding. What might seem a wasteful project in someone else's district is often perceived as a worthy project in one's own district. We might also expect to see the increased use of soft earmarks as a way to circumvent the moratorium.

WEB-BASED ASSIGNMENT

Any organization that claims to represent the interests of all taxpayers should be suspect: Could all taxpayers possibly agree about where their taxes should be spent and about what fair taxation requires? Many organizations that claim to represent taxpayers are, in fact, highly partisan, with an ideological axe to grind. One noteworthy exception is Taxpayers for Common Sense (TCS), at http://www.taxpayers.org/.

Web addresses sometimes change. If you can't locate a website, try an external search (e.g., Google) to find the website. Configurations within a website often change. If you can't find a particular link or article, for example, try an internal search of the website as well as an external search. Be resourceful!

The purpose of TCS is stated on its home page, "Taxpayers for Common Sense is an independent and nonpartisan voice for taxpayers working to increase transparency and expose and eliminate wasteful and corrupt subsidies, earmarks, and corporate welfare." Note that subsidies and so-called corporate welfare—not only earmarks—are included in TCS's efforts to increase congressional transparency. Too many taxpayers' organizations scrutinize specific expenditures for pet projects, but they don't include ongoing subsidies and tax breaks to farmers and corporations. For example, a Tea Party member of Congress, Representative Stephen Fincher (Republican, Tennessee), elected in 2010 on a promise to slash federal spending to address out-of-control deficits, received over $3 million in agricultural subsidies between 1995 and 2009, and General Electric Company paid $0 in federal taxes in 2010, the result of a variety of tax breaks and loopholes.[3] In this part of the assignment, you will explore the TCS website.

1. On the TCS home page, click on "About Us." Explore the links on that page from "Mission" to "Advisory Board." Do you find any evidence of a significant partisan tilt toward the Republican or Democratic Party, or toward conservative or liberal ideology, in this taxpayers' group? Does TCS disclose its sources of funding? Explain and support your answer.

_____

_____

_____

2. On the TCS home page, click on the box, "TCS Recommended Cuts." Scroll down and find the "five simple principles" that guide TCS's recommended cuts. What are they?

_____

_____

_____

_____

_____

3. Continue to scroll down to "Areas Identified for Cuts." What are three of the areas? Summarize TCS's rationale for cuts in each area. Complete the table below.

---

[3]ABC World News, March 31, 2011, http://abcnews.go.com/Politics/tea-party-hypocrisy-lawmakers-tea-party-ties-government/story?id=13259014; David Kocieniewski, "GE Strategies Let It Avoid Taxes Altogether," *New York Times*, March 24, 2011, p. A1.

Number	Area of Recommended Cut	Rationale for Cut
1.		
2.		
3.		

4. Click on one of the three areas you selected for question 3. What are two specific programs for which TCS recommends budget cuts. What kinds of interest groups might be expected to oppose those cuts? Complete the table below.

Number	Targeted Program	Possible Opposing Interest Groups
1.		
2.		

5. During the 2004 presidential campaign, John McCain frequently cited Alaska's "Bridge to Nowhere," as an example of wasteful pork-barrel spending. (This led to some controversy over whether his running mate, then-governor of Alaska, Sarah Palin, had supported the project.) Because of media attention to the Bridge to Nowhere, it was not funded. Go back to the page titled "TCS Recommended Cuts." On the left side of the page, you'll see "Search by Tag." Pull down the search menu to "B." Look for the tag, "Bridge to Nowhere," and click on it. Scroll down until you find, "Golden Fleece: $190 Million Bridge to Nowhere." Click on the link. On that page, you will find the link, "Read the full TCS write-up: (June 12, 2003)." Click on this link, and read the TCS account. Then answer to the following questions.

a. Summarize the story of the Bridge to Nowhere.

_____
_____
_____
_____
_____

b. How well does the story illustrate the paradox of pork, that what might seem a wasteful project in someone else's state or district is often perceived as a worthy project in one's own state or district? Explain and support your response.

_____
_____
_____
_____

c. What reasons does TCS provide for exposing and opposing this project?

_____

_____

_____

_____

_____

d. Suppose you were part of the timber industry in or around Ketchikan, or that you ran a business that depended on the economic health of the timber industry. How would you feel about building the Bridge to Nowhere?

_____

_____

_____

In this part of the assignment, you will use the Office of Management and Budget's Earmarks website (mentioned in the Introduction to this exercise) at http://earmarks.omb.gov/earmarks-public/.

6. According to the OMB, what is the purpose of the website?

_____

_____

7. According to the OMB, what are the limitations of the earmark database?

_____

_____

8. Go to the search engine: "Search Earmark's Full Text." Use the search term of your home town or county, including the state abbreviation. Then complete the table below. If you cannot find enough earmarks with your town or county, add the college or university you are attending.

Number	Describe Project	Is it pork? Is it a worthy project? Briefly explain.
1.		
2.		
3.		

EXERCISE 5.3   Whither Campaign Finance Reform?

INTRODUCTION

Time and again, efforts to regulate cash flowing into federal election campaigns have foundered. Reforms have been enacted, only to be circumvented by the latest loophole or by judicial review. Campaign finance regulations have so far been unable to check the powerful attraction between private wealth and candidates running for office.

Reacting to the discovery of vast amounts of illegal money in Richard Nixon's reelection campaign of 1972, Congress in 1974 amended the Federal Election Campaign Reform Act to establish for the first time public funding of presidential election campaigns. In presidential primary elections, the new system provided federal matching funds for candidates who limit themselves to private individual contributions of $250 or less. Those contributions are then matched dollar for dollar from the Presidential Election Campaign Fund. The new system also provided public funding for the major parties' presidential candidates in the general election (and some qualifying minor parties). Candidates who accept public funding cannot take private contributions during the general election.

The decision to accept federal matching funds in the primary election or public funding in the general election is made by each presidential candidate. Until 2008, major-party candidates accepted general election funds, knowing that their campaigns would be supplemented by money funneled through the loopholes discussed in this exercise. Barack Obama, despite his previous support for campaign finance reform, was the first major-party candidate to decline federal general election funds, believing that he could raise more money, through a variety of innovative fundraising methods, than the presidential election fund could provide. Obama's advisers rationalized the decision by announcing that Obama's campaign was not going to "unilaterally disarm" against John McCain, who had accepted federal funds. Obama's campaign ended up raising a record $750 million. Its goal in 2012 is $1 billion. Most political observers believe that Obama's decision to reject federal funding spells the end of campaign funding for major-party candidates. Prospective candidates now know what Obama accomplished; they are not likely to "unilaterally disarm" either.

The use of federal matching funds during primaries also appears to be on its way out. Until 2000, most major-party candidates for their parties' nominations accepted these funds. George W. Bush, however, refused matching funds in 2000 and 2004 because he knew that he could raise more money on his own, and he did—$60 and $240 million, respectively. John Kerry also refused primary matching funds, having raised slightly less than Bush for the 2004 primaries. By 2008, all of the competitive contending candidates for their parties' nominations refused federal matching funds, with the exception of John Edwards, who later withdrew from the campaign. With the apparent de facto end of public financing of presidential elections, the floodgates of campaign cash have opened for private donors and presidential candidates.

What is the rationale for publicly financed presidential campaigns? The less candidates rely on soliciting funds from rich donors and special interests, the more responsive and accountable they are to the American people in general. Congress, in 1974, also placed limits on the amount that individuals, political action committees (PACs), and political parties can contribute directly to candidates in congressional campaigns. The purpose of these limits was to curtail the influence of wealthy donors and special interest groups.

Federal election reforms adversely affected the interests of many individuals and organizations. They responded by contesting the provisions of the new law and searching for loopholes in the language of the legislation. In 1976, in *Buckley v. Valeo,* the U.S. Supreme Court handed opponents of the new legislation a significant victory by ruling that political campaign contributions in some cases are protected speech under the First Amendment. That decision led to the proliferation of independent spending campaigns, in which individuals and groups can spend unrestricted amounts on *behalf* of candidates for federal office.[1] Data about independent spending campaigns will be part of your assignment for this exercise.

---

[1] The law requires unions and corporations to set up separate campaign organizations, known as political action committees (PACs), to contribute directly to or run campaigns on behalf of federal candidates. There are limits on *direct* contributions to candidates' campaigns, but PACs may spend as much as they like *on behalf of* federal candidates. Donations to PACs must be voluntary and solicited from employees, union members, or the public at large.

Even more significant was the Supreme Court decision in *Citizens United v. FEC* (2009), in which the Court, with its typical 5–4 conservative majority versus liberal minority split, ruled unconstitutional a significant provision of the Bipartisan Campaign Reform Act of 2002. The act, jointly sponsored by John McCain (Republican, Arizona) and Russ Feingold (Democrat, Wisconsin), had prohibited corporations and unions from using funds *from their own treasuries* to run campaigns on behalf of federal candidates. The Supreme Court ruled that corporations and unions had the full protection of the First Amendment's freedom of speech clause and therefore Congress could not place limits on legitimate corporate political activities. That decision will further open the floodgates of cash in federal elections and spells the end of a century of campaign reform legislation.[2] With the public attentive to seemingly more pressing issues, like the economy, and with the current majority on the Supreme Court hostile to government regulation of campaign finance, it appears unlikely that the effects of big money on U.S. elections and government will be addressed anytime soon.

ASSIGNMENT

Questions 1 and 2 are based on Table 5.3.1, which lists the top ten independent spending groups in the 2008 presidential election. Independent spending groups are allowed unrestricted fundraising and spending, but they may not coordinate their campaigns with the candidates' campaigns.

1. *Web-Based Question.*

   a. What percentage of the total expenditures of the top ten groups was spent on behalf of Obama, and what percentage was spent on behalf of Bush? You can determine the leaning of each group by going to the opensecrets.org website at http://www.opensecrets.org/527s/527cmtes.php?level=N&cycle=2008. Pull down the "election cycle" menu to 2008. Pull down the "view by" menu to Top 50. (Remember that you'll be working with only the top ten.) Click on the title of each of the top ten groups. Click on the group name again, and you'll find an "overview" of the group. There you will also find the "viewpoint" of the group. (You can assume that liberal groups ran campaigns on behalf of Obama and that conservative groups ran campaigns on behalf of McCain.)

   Web addresses sometimes change. If you can't locate a website, try an external search (e.g., Google) to find the website. Configurations within a website often change. If you can't find a particular link or article, for example, try an internal search of the website as well as an external search. Be resourceful! If you still can't find what you're searching for, move on to the next question.

TABLE 5.3.1   Top Ten Independent Spending Groups, 2008 Presidential Election

Committee	Total Receipts	Expenditures
Service Employees International Union	$27,432,667	$27,839,177
America Votes	$25,959,173	$24,491,324
American Solutions Winning the Future	$22,722,547	$22,966,088
EMILY's List	$13,659,555	$12,910,515
The Fund for America	$12,142,046	$12,142,044
GOPAC	$9,322,764	$9,407,146
Patriot Majority Fund	$8,266,627	$8,108,121
College Republican National Committee	$6,956,285	$7,537,976
RightChange.com	$6,736,563	$5,578,187
Citizens United	$6,477,080	$6,016,215

Source: "2008 Outside Spending, by Groups", Center for Responsive Politics (opensecrets.org). Used by permission of Center for Responsive Politics.

[2]In a case from Arizona (*Arizona Free Enterprise v. Bennett*, 2011), the Supreme Court struck down a public financing law in that state. See Adam Liptak, "Justices Review Arizona Law on Campaign Financing, Justices Strike Down Arizona Campaign Finance Law" *New York Times*, June 28, 2011, p. A15.

Obama percentage: _____

McCain percentage: _____

b. The last group in the top ten is Citizens United. That's the group that brought the suit against the Federal Elections Commission for enforcing the prohibition against corporations using funds from their own treasury for campaigns for or against federal candidates. Go back to the "overview" page for the group. (See question 1a.) Find out more about the group by clicking on the tabs to the right of "overview" ("contributors"; "expenditures"). Summarize what you found. Does the information you found help you to understand why Citizens United and groups like it might oppose restrictions on corporate funds in federal elections? Explain.

_____

_____

_____

_____

_____

2. Consider the Supreme Court decisions in *Buckley v. Valeo* and *Citizens United v. FEC*, both of which are described in the introduction to this exercise. Why is it unlikely that a bill banning independent spending campaigns by the organizations like those in Table 5.3.1, corporations, and unions, would end up accomplishing its objective?

_____

_____

_____

Questions 3 to 6 are based on Table 5.3.2, which shows total fundraising, expenditures, and sources of funding, by political party, for the 2008 national elections. Remember that this table does not include unregulated independent spending organizations' receipts and expenditures.

TABLE 5.3.2 Campaign Finances by Party, 2008*

Party	Total Raised	Total Spent	Total Cash on Hand	Total from PACs	Total from Individuals
House of Representatives					
All	$978,434,442	$938,040,528	$194,725,380	$323,006,171	$531,471,223
Democrats	$532,748,892	$490,401,278	$126,416,998	$195,302,068	$287,486,880
Republicans	$441,072,470	$443,377,745	$68,106,454	$127,409,084	$241,098,963
Senate					
All	$410,433,764	$418,618,638	$40,826,445	$80,948,287	$270,676,022
Democrats	$216,535,692	$217,319,894	$26,643,772	$34,989,737	$148,497,530
Republicans	$193,315,741	$200,716,241	$14,171,292	$45,949,304	$121,808,652
President					
All	$1,812,970,610	$1,759,227,339	$52,358,377	$5,739,318	$1,391,192,476
Democrats	$1,150,260,720	$1,122,584,286	$24,696,276	$2,983,002	$968,762,379
Republicans	$656,298,931	$630,350,412	$27,500,295	$2,748,049	$417,307,576

*Includes primaries elections and the general election.

Source: Center for Responsive Politics (opensecrets.org). Used by permission of Center for Responsive Politics.

3. a. What was the total amount of money raised and spent by the two major parties in 2008?

_____

b. What percentage of the total did the Democrats raise? What percentage did the Republicans raise?

Democrats' percentage:_____

Republicans' percentage:_____

c. What percentage of the total raised in 2008 was for the presidential race (both parties)?

_____

d. What percentage of the total in questions 3c did the Democrats/Obama raise?

_____

e. What explains the discrepancy between Republicans and Democrats in funds raised in the presidential race? (The answer lies in the introduction to this exercise.)

_____

_____

f. Were individuals or PACs more important to the parties' fundraising efforts?

_____

4. In 2004, Kerry, the Democrat, raised a total of approximately $281 million. Bush raised about $264 million. What was the total increase in the two major parties' presidential fundraising from 2004 to 2008? (You have the presidential total from 2008 in Table 5.3.2)

_____

5. In 2004, both Kerry and Bush received approximately $74 million in public financing for the general election. In 2008, McCain received approximately $84 million in public financing. Did Obama make the strategically correct decision in turning down public financing? In your opinion, did he make the ethically correct decision, especially in light of his earlier support for campaign finance reform and public financing? Explain and support your answer.

_____

_____

_____

_____

_____

6. Those who favor sweeping campaign finance reform typically support public financing of all federal campaigns. They believe that candidates who are supported by citizens in general would be less apt to favor major donors who helped them to win office. Those who oppose public financing argue that it artificially evens the odds between competing candidates. They prefer a free-market approach: The candidates should be able to show their mettle by raising as much as they can within legal limits, as long as candidates are required to disclose their contributors' names to the public. Assuming that all loopholes could be closed, including those in independent spending, and that candidates would have no choice but to accept public funding, would you support public funding of all federal campaigns (presidential and congressional races)? Explain and support your position. (Consider using a Web search engine to find other arguments for and against public financing.)

_____

_____

_____

_____

_____

6

Congress

EXERCISE 6.1 What Is the Proper Role of a Congressional Representative?

INTRODUCTION

Lawmakers must grapple with how to exercise the legislative power vested in them by citizens in their district or state. Should congressional representatives vote the will of their constituents? Or should representatives vote what they believe to be right, regardless of public opinion?

The *delegate model* of legislative representation is most consistent with the definition of democracy—rule by the people. According to this model, representatives look to their constituents for instruction on what issues to promote and, ultimately, on how to vote. Under the delegate model, representatives stand in place of their constituents and do their bidding.

The delegate model of representation raises several difficult issues. Should representatives be bound only by the will of those who voted for them, or are they duty-bound to consider the opinions of constituents who voted for other candidates? To what extent should campaign contributions—which come from a narrow segment of the constituency—be factored into representatives' decisions? Should representatives actively seek out constituent opinion, or should they rely only on input that reaches them through e-mails and phone calls? Should representatives be bound by the opinions and interests of their constituency on all issues or only on those that most directly affect the state or district? Should representatives be more responsive to constituents who have strong convictions on a particular issue rather than the so-called silent majority (those who do not voice their opinions)? These dilemmas of democratic politics complicate the delegate model of representation.

The *trustee model* of representation is less consistent with the definition of democracy. Not surprisingly, most of the framers of the Constitution, distrustful of democracy because of its tendency to majority tyranny, believed that representatives must act as filters for the passions and interests of their constituents. According to this model, representatives must transcend the short-term particular interests of their constituency and advocate for the long-term comprehensive interests of the nation. To make the trustee model more compatible with democracy, its advocates concede two points. First, representatives must remain accountable to their constituents on election day; that is, representatives who depart from constituent opinion must be prepared to be voted out of office. Second, representatives must attempt to educate their constituents and to convince them that their respective representative's positions are correct.

The trustee model also raises difficult issues. Does the representative really know what's best for her constituents better than they do? What motivates representatives under the trustee model? Is it the genuine conviction that the representative is championing what's best for her constituents or the nation? Or might the representative be responding to interest group pressure from outside the representative's state or district?

In practice, the dilemmas posed by the delegate and trustee models of representation are tempered by two realities. First, most voters cast their ballot for someone who represents their political, cultural, and economic interests. Second, many constituents don't know much about the particular bills their representatives vote on, or even how their representative voted. Even so, elected officials know all too well that an attentive group of constituents, by publicizing a vote it objects to, can make that vote a major issue in the next election.

ASSIGNMENT

1. Assume that a coalition of environmental interest groups—worried about global warming—has succeeded in bringing to the floor of the House a bill that would significantly tighten emission standards on automobiles. Many major automobile companies and their suppliers have factories in Michigan. Would a member of the House from a district in Michigan be more likely to follow the delegate or trustee model of representation in deciding how to vote on this bill? Explain and support your answer.

_____

_____

_____

_____

_____

2. In her campaign for election to the House, a candidate we'll call Betty Aquidneck, signed a pledge stating that if elected, she'd serve only three terms. Her support for term limits attracted many votes, garnered a generous campaign contribution from the interest group Term Limits Inc., and was instrumental in her victory. Aquidneck had never held political office before. She taught high school government and civics for twenty-five years before seeking election to the House. The centerpiece of her high school courses was the need to restore honesty and credibility to government. Eventually, her students and friends convinced Aquidneck to take her convictions out of the classroom and put them to the test in the House. Aquidneck's tireless focus on restoring honesty and credibility to government proved very popular with her constituents, who reelected her twice. Now at the end of her third term, Aquidneck must decide whether to honor her pledge to serve only three terms. Polls show that 65 percent of the voters in her district are demanding that she disregard the pledge and run for a fourth term.

    a. Make an argument that Aquidneck should follow the delegate model in making her decision.

_____

_____

_____

_____

_____

    b. Make an argument that Aquidneck should follow the trustee model in making her decision.

_____

_____

_____

_____

_____

3. Nebraska shares many of the characteristics of other midwestern states. Agriculture provides a significant portion of the state's income, even though fewer than 10 percent of its workers are employed in agriculture; the population is overwhelmingly white (Nebraska has a far lower percentage of minorities than the nation as a whole); and about a third of the state's population can be classified as rural.

a. On a vote to renew U.S. economic and military aid to Israel, would a U.S. senator from Nebraska be more likely to follow the delegate model or the trustee model? Explain and support your answer.

_____

_____

_____

_____

_____

b. A senator from Nebraska will vote on a bill to expand agricultural trade with North Korea—a nation that is developing nuclear weapons and may be supporting the proliferation of nuclear weapons. The senator has long been a staunch opponent of nuclear proliferation and a strong supporter of the war on terrorism.

Make an argument that the senator should follow the delegate model in casting his vote.

_____

_____

_____

_____

_____

Make an argument that the senator should follow the trustee model in casting his vote.

_____

_____

_____

_____

_____

4. Oregon is a state with vast acreage of old-growth forests. The economy of the state depends on the lumber industry. But tourism is important to the state's economy, too, and Oregon has a strong environmental movement. Would a U.S. senator representing Oregon be more likely follow the delegate model or the trustee model in voting on a bill to ban cutting old-growth forests? Explain and support your answer.

_____

_____

_____

_____

_____

5. In deciding whether to follow the delegate or trustee model of representation, a senator considers many factors, such as public opinion, party politics, the demographic and economic characteristics of the state, and the senator's own political ideology and personal values, among

others. For each issue listed here, identify factors that would be likely to cause a senator to adopt the delegate and the trustee models of representation. The answer to the first question has been completed for you.

a. Foreign policy

Delegate model: A senator would adopt the delegate model if the public in his or her state would be particularly attentive to some controversial foreign policy issues, for example, the war in Afghanistan.

Trustee model: A senator would turn to the trustee model if the public was not engaged or informed on a particular foreign policy issue, for example, the terms of a trade agreement between the United States and the nations of Central and South America.

b. Gay marriage

Delegate model: _____

_____

_____

_____

Trustee model: _____

_____

_____

_____

c. Federal highway construction funds

Delegate model: _____

_____

_____

_____

Trustee model: _____

_____

_____

_____

d. Social Security

Delegate model: _____

_____

_____

_____

_____

Trustee model: _____

_____

_____

_____

_____

6. a. *Web-Based Question.*   What is the number of your congressional district, and what is the name of your representative in the House of Representatives? (You can locate your representative by zip code at http://www.house.gov/house/MemberWWW_by_State.shtml.)

Web addresses sometimes change. If you can't locate a website, try an external search (e.g., Google) to find the website. Configurations within a website often change. If you can't find a particular link or article, for example, try an internal search of the website as well as an external search. Be resourceful!

_____

b. Identify an issue on which your representative would likely vote according to the delegate model of representation and an issue on which he or she would likely follow the trustee model. To do this, you'll need to know something about your representative and the characteristics of your congressional district. You can learn about your representative from his or her congressional home page at http://clerk.house.gov/members/index.html. Biographical details and information on how groups rate members of Congress are available at www.vote-smart.org. You need to conduct a search for your representative. Explain and support your answer.

Delegate model: _____

_____

_____

_____

_____

Trustee model: _____

_____

_____

_____

_____

EXERCISE 6.2 Why We Hate Congress but Love Our Member of Congress

INTRODUCTION

Incumbents seeking reelection to the House of Representatives almost always win. The astonishing reelection rate of these incumbents highlights the paradoxical voting behavior of many Americans: Voters may hate Congress, but they love their individual member of Congress.

Polls consistently find that the public holds Congress in lower esteem than any other government institution, but no matter: Voters continue to reelect their representatives in Congress. Since 1945, on average, 90 percent of House members seeking reelection won, and about 80 percent of U.S. senators were reelected.[1] Even in 1994, in the midterm election that gave Republicans control of both houses of Congress for the first time since 1954—and that was interpreted by many as an anti-incumbent election—slightly more than 90 percent of House members who ran for reelection won. And an extraordinary number won with 60 percent or more of the vote—for our purposes, the definition of a noncompetitive election. In 2004, the reelection rate for members of the House was 98.5 percent!

Republicans again took control of the House from Democrats in the 2010 election by playing up widespread popular dissatisfaction with many of President Barack Obama's initiatives—particularly health care reform. Obama acknowledged in a press conference after the election that his party has received a "shellacking" from the voters. Obama explained that "we were in such a hurry to get things done that we didn't change how things got done. And I think that frustrated people."

Primary among the advantages House incumbents hold over challengers is a legislative district drawn—redistricted or gerrymandered—to include friendly voters. Redistricting does not apply to the U.S. Senate because the boundaries of the states are set and representation in the Senate isn't population based. But in House and state legislative races, gerrymandering is an incumbent's best friend. Other advantages of incumbency include commanding more media attention than challengers, greater name recognition, superior fundraising, and the ability to deliver projects to the district and service to individual constituents.

In the early 1990s, several states attempted to restore competition to their elections by imposing term limits on their members in the U.S. House of Representatives and Senate, but the Supreme Court declared those limits unconstitutional.[2] Term limits for state government officeholders, however, have had a better survival rate. Since 1990, twenty-one states have imposed term limits on state legislators. Those limits were overturned by the courts or repealed by the legislature in six states, leaving term limits on the books in fifteen states in 2010. The result is dramatic: In 2010, a total of 380 state legislators were turned out of office because they had served the maximum number of terms allowed.[3]

---

[1] See Susan Welch et al., *Understanding American Government*, 6th ed. (Belmont, CA: Wadsworth, 2001), p. 285 and Figure 3.

[2] *U.S. Term Limits, Inc., v. Thornton* (1995).

[3] Information on term limits is available from the National Conference of State Legislatures at www.ncsl.

ASSIGNMENT

Questions 1 to 4 are based on Table 6.2.1.

TABLE 6.2.1	The 2010 House and Senate Elections	
	House	**Senate**
Number of races	435	34*
Number of open races (where incumbent did not seek reelection)	45	10
Number of incumbents seeking reelection who lost to challengers in the primary or general election[†]	58	4
Number of incumbents who won with more than 60 percent of the vote	237	10
Number of open races where the winner's margin was more than 60 percent of the vote	21	4

* Three special Senate elections are not included in this number.

[†] Incumbent Senator Lisa Murkowski lost the primary election, but she won the general election with the write-in vote. She is not included here as one of the four senators who lost to challengers. Four House incumbents lost their primary elections and are included here among the 58 House incumbents who lost.

1. What were the reelection rates for House and Senate incumbents in 2010? In other words, what percentage of incumbents in the House and Senate were reelected in 2010? Here's some help to get you started in calculating the reelection rate for House incumbents. Begin with the total number of seats in the House, 435. Because you're calculating the reelection rate for House *incumbents*, you'll need to subtract the number of open seats in the election. You'll also need to subtract the number of incumbents who were defeated. The resulting figure is the number of incumbents who won. Now calculate the reelection rate for House incumbents.

    a. House reelection rate: _____

    b. Senate reelection rate: _____

2. a. A New York Times/CBS News poll conducted during the third week of October 2010 asked this question: "Do you think the representative in Congress from your district has performed his or her job well enough to deserve re-election, or do you think it's time to give a new person a chance?" Fifty-nine percent of those responding to the poll answered that it was time for a new person. Thirty-one percent answered that their representative deserved reelection. Nine percent answered that it depends or didn't know. If voters in the November 2010 election had cast their ballots in the nation's 435 House races according to the responses to the poll question, what would the reelection rate for members of the House have been?

_____

    b. What might help account for the disconnect between the hypothetical reelection rate for the House based on the poll responses you calculated in question 2a and the actual reelection rate you calculated in question 1a? In formulating your answer, consider another question posed in the poll: "Did you vote for U.S. House of Representatives in the elections held in 2006, did something prevent you from voting, or did you choose not to vote for U.S. House of Representatives in 2006?" Fifty-one percent answered that they had voted in the 2006 House election; 41 percent answered that they had not voted; 8 percent didn't know.

_____

_____

_____

3. In what percentage of the 2010 House and Senate races where incumbents won was the margin of victory over 60 percent? Explain how you made the calculation.

a. House races: _____

b. Senate races: _____

c. How you made the calculation: _____

_____

_____

4. In what percentage of the 2010 open races in the House and Senate was the margin of victory over 60 percent? Explain how you made the calculation.

a. House races: _____

b. Senate races: _____

c. How you made the calculation: _____

_____

_____

5. What conclusion can you draw by comparing the percentage of House and Senate races where the incumbent's margin of victory was over 60 percent with the percentage of open races in the House and Senate where margin of victory was over 60 percent?

_____

_____

_____

_____

_____

6. It is widely recognized that monopoly domination of any sector of the economy by one or more corporations is not in the best interest of citizens. That's why Congress has enacted antitrust and other laws supporting the principle that private sector competition helps keep businesses accountable to consumers. If consumers don't like a particular product for whatever reason, they can vote with their dollars by taking their business elsewhere. Use this free-market analogy to identify and explain the problem that the reelection rate for members of Congress poses to representative democracy in the United States today.

_____

_____

_____

_____

_____

_____

_____

_____

_____

Use Table 6.2.2 to answer question 7.

7. a. Use your answer to question 1 and the data in Table 6.2.2 to calculate the percentage point gap between the 2010 reelection rate for members of the House and the percentage of Americans who have a great deal or quite a lot of confidence in Congress as an institution. What is that percentage point gap?

_____

TABLE 6.2.2 Public Confidence in U.S Institutions

Question: "Now I am going to read you a list of institutions in American Society. Please tell me how much confidence you have in each one—a great deal, quite a lot, some, or very little?" (All answers in the table are given in percentages.)

	A Great Deal/ Quite a Lot	Some	Very Little	None (Volunteered)	No Opinion
The military	76	18	4	1	1
Small business	66	26	6	*	1
The police	59	27	12	1	1
The church or organized religion	48	30	18	2	2
The medical system	40	38	20	1	1
The presidency	36	26	31	6	1
The U.S. Supreme Court	36	43	16	2	3
The public schools	34	39	23	1	2
The criminal justice system	27	44	24	3	1
Newspapers	25	41	29	4	2
Banks	23	45	28	2	1
Television news	22	41	32	4	1
Organized labor	20	41	33	3	4
Health maintenance organizations (HMOs)	19	43	28	4	5
Big business	19	42	35	3	1
Congress	11	37	45	5	2

Source: "Congress Ranks Last in Confidence in Institutions", The Gallup Poll, July 8–10, 2010. Copyright © 2011 Gallup, Inc. All rights reserved. Used by permission of the Gallup Organization.

b. Does that percentage point gap support or refute the notion that Americans hate Congress but love their own representatives in Congress?

_____

8. _Web-Based Question._ To explore the fundraising advantage of incumbents, go to www .opensecrets.org. Click on "Congressional Races" and select your state. That takes you to a list of congressional candidates and their spending in the last election.

Web addresses sometimes change. If you can't locate a website, try an external search (e.g., Google) to find the website. Configurations within a website often change. If you can't find a particular link or article, for example, try an internal search of the website as well as an external search. Be resourceful! If you still can't find what you're searching for, move on to the next question.

a. Look at the spending gap between the incumbent and the challenger in each House race for the state you selected. In what percentage of the races did the incumbent raise more money than the challenger?

_____

_____

b. In what percentage of the races did the incumbent raise at least twice as much money as the challenger?

_____

_____

c. Look next at the race for the congressional district where you reside. (If you don't know your district, go to www.opensecrets.org and enter your zip code.) Assuming that an incumbent was running in your district, did the incumbent raise more money than the challenger? If so, how much more?

_____

_____

In 1992, California voters passed Proposition 164, which limited the number of terms California's delegation in Congress could serve. Three years later, in _U.S. Term Limits, Inc., v. Thornton,_ the Supreme Court declared that any attempt to impose term limits by state legislative action (with or without the initiative) was unconstitutional. Arguments for and against Proposition 164 are reproduced in Reading 6.2.1. Study the arguments and then answer question 8, which follows the reading.

READING 6.2.1
Argument in Favor of and Against California Proposition 164

Argument in Favor of California Proposition 164[4]

> _Everybody is running for their own survival. The first priority of a member is to stay in office._
> —Sixteen-year California Representative Leon Panetta quoted inUSA Today,April 28, 1992.

Our founding fathers would be shocked at the abuses and attitudes of Congress today. While their policies were sending a record number of Californians to the unemployment line, members of the House voted themselves $40,000 in pay raises and Senate members received $27,600. Each one of them now earns more than $129,000 a year. And most of them will be eligible for million-dollar tax-subsidized pensions.

_____

[4]_Source:_ Voters' pamphlet, California general election, November 1992.

Our professional politicians in California's delegation have already given us a $4 trillion dollar national debt, a 9.5 percent California unemployment rate, 500,000 lost California jobs, banking and postal scandals, and the largest tax increase in U.S. history.

Incumbent politicians have rigged the system to ensure their reelection. The longer they are in Washington, the less our career representatives care about us. And the record shows that it's the long-term incumbents who are most likely to be caught in scandals.

California voters launched a national drive for term limits when we passed Proposition 140 in 1990. Term limits are an even better idea for Congress in 1992.

Proposition 164 will put term limits on California's Congress members. The terms of the president, the governor, and the California legislature are already limited; it's time to limit congressional terms, too.

Proposition 164 will:

- *Increase California's clout in Congress.* Proposition 164 begins to break up the "good ol' boy" seniority system in Congress, which rewards tenure, not accomplishment, and allows small states enormous power in Congress. With the largest delegation in the country, California's 54 representatives can work hard for California, instead of taking a backseat to politicians from Mississippi and West Virginia.
- *Give power back to the people of California.* Our representatives will be reminded they are public servants—not masters—who can serve for a definite time and then return home to *live under the laws they made.*
- *Reinvigorate Congress with new blood and new ideas* to tackle the tough problems facing our nation today.
- *Reintroduce courage and honesty* among our representatives by *weakening the hold of special interests, lobbyists, and bureaucracy* on Congress. Proposition 164 will force our representatives to face facts, come clean on problems, and propose bold new solutions.
- *Protect your right to vote and give you a real choice of candidates.* Incumbents dominate elections with free mail, huge staffs, free travel, and PAC funding. Term limits will open elections to competition, and Proposition 164's special write-in provision will allow voters to reelect exceptional representatives even if their terms have expired.

The dream of our founding fathers has not failed; the careerist politicians we've elected *have* failed. They put their own careers and multimillion dollar retirements ahead of the needs of California and the nation.

Proposition 164 will end political cronyism and reward merit, giving us a congressional delegation that will solve problems, not add to them.

Argument Against California Proposition 164

No matter how you feel about term limits, vote *no* on Proposition 164. It's not about term limits or congressional reform; it's about destroying California's clout in Congress.

Proposition 164 will cost California thousands of jobs, weaken our environmental protections, and shift greater burdens onto the backs of California taxpayers.

Proposition 164 only affects *California's own* members of Congress. It does not apply term limits to *all* members of Congress.

What's so bad about that? The answer is that California *competes* with other states for federal dollars—and we are sending more money to Washington than we get back in federal dollars for California. Proposition 164 means we will pay hundreds of billions of dollars in federal taxes and get less and less in return.

Powerful members of Congress decide how those federal dollars are spent. How do they get to be powerful? They stay a long time in Congress. It's called the seniority system. If California limits our terms while Texas, Florida, and New York don't limit theirs, Californians will lose. Our clout in Congress will go to other states, and they will grab more of the hard-earned dollars California taxpayers send to Washington.

We need strong California representation to get help for our struggling economy. What happens if we are devastated by another earthquake or similar disaster? We need congressional members on the major committees to see that we get help. With California-only term limits, we will end up with a delegation of low-ranking members who can't fight for our state against the powerful interests from other states.

Hundreds of thousands of jobs are at stake as cutbacks continue. Who will fight to protect those jobs for California? The Texans, New Yorkers and Floridians will be there for their states. Where will California be?

The governor's office and the [California state] legislature agree that we need to fight for more federal help to pay for the immigrant load on California. If we don't get federal help, California taxpayers must bear a greater burden. Proposition 164 means those federal dollars will go to other states.

This year we will be electing both U.S. senators and all California members of Congress. If we don't like the job incumbents are doing we can vote them out of office. Proposition 164 removes members of Congress without a vote of the people, whether or not they are doing a good job.

To quote the *Sacramento Bee*: "Seniority still counts for a lot in Washington, and if California members of the House are limited to only three two-year terms, and its U.S. senators to only two six-year terms, the state will have doomed itself to be permanently represented by a bunch of back benchers."

With 54 members in Congress—the most in the country—we should have the strongest delegation fighting for California in Washington. Proposition 164 ensures that we have one of the weakest. Keep California strong. Vote *no* on Proposition 164.

Source: California Ballot Pamphlet, General Election, November 3, 1992. This material is reprinted here with permission of the California Secretary of State for illustrative purposes only.

9. a. Identify what you think are the three most persuasive arguments on each side of the debate over Proposition 164.

In favor of the proposition: _____

Against the proposition: _____

_____

_____

_____

_____

_____

b. How would you have voted? Explain and support your position.

_____

_____

_____

_____

_____

EXERCISE 6.3   Blacks in Congress

INTRODUCTION

Like every other minority group in the United States, blacks always have been underrepresented in Congress. The political strength of blacks in the national legislature has never been proportional to the number of African Americans in the general population.

For several reasons, minority groups have long sought to increase their political power in Congress to match as closely as possible their presence in the general population. Proportional representation would boost the ability of minorities to shape the national agenda and address issues of concern, as well as allow minorities in Congress to function as role models, thus validating and encouraging the aspirations of others.

For African Americans, several obstacles stand in the way of proportional representation in Congress. Efforts to suppress black voting by intimidation and other means remain widespread.[1] Minority candidates face more than their share of difficulty raising campaign funds. And blacks running for office have to grapple with the segment of white voters who shun African American candidates because of their race.

Representation for African Americans in Congress—let alone proportional representation—never crossed the minds of the framers of the Constitution. Rather, their concern was to strike bargains with the slave states in the South to enable the creation of the new government. Toward that end, key provisions of the Constitution sanctioned and protected the South's system of human bondage. No African American would sit in the U.S. Congress until slavery was destroyed in the Civil War.

Black Representation in the House

Our examination of the struggle of African Americans to capture and hold political power in the House begins with the position of blacks in the South.[2] Before the Civil War, the vast majority of African Americans in the South (about 95 percent on the eve of the Civil War) were slaves; they were defined as property, not citizens, and therefore could not vote or hold public office.

In 1867, after the North's victory in the Civil War, Republicans in Congress passed the Reconstruction Acts, laws mandating the use of federal power to establish and protect the voting rights of the freed slaves. That application of federal power in the South on behalf of blacks, combined with the determination of newly enfranchised blacks to vote, sent Joseph Rainey to the House in 1870. He was the first African American to take a seat there.[3] Rainey was born a slave in South Carolina, but his father later purchased the family's freedom. To avoid being drafted to work for the Confederate Army during the Civil War, Rainey escaped to the West Indies. He returned to South Carolina at the end of the war and held several political positions before being elected to the House. He was reelected four times.

Between 1870 and 1877, thirteen other blacks from southern states served in the House. Together, those fourteen men served a total of twenty-one terms. But those striking gains, the product of the application of federal military force in the South, were short-lived. The commitment of whites in the North to the political equality of blacks in the South had always been weak and uncertain, and in 1877 the national government abandoned its effort to protect the freed slaves. Whites in the South, free to reestablish the traditional racial hierarchy, stripped blacks of their voting rights by wielding the literacy test, the poll tax, and the white primary. The disfranchisement of African Americans, combined with violence, economic intimidation, and Jim Crow segregation,[4] kept any other blacks in the South from winning a seat in Congress until well into the twentieth century.

---

[1]See, for example, "The Long Shadow of Jim Crow: Voter Intimidation and Suppression in America Today" and "The New Face of Jim Crow: Voter Suppression in America" at www.pfaw.org.

[2]In this exercise, the South consists of the eleven states of the Confederacy: Alabama, Arkansas, Florida, Georgia, Louisiana, Mississippi, North Carolina, South Carolina, Tennessee, Texas, and Virginia.

[3]Rainey won a special election in 1870 to fill a vacant seat in the House. He took his seat on December 12, 1870. He joined the members of the Forty-First Congress, who had been elected in 1868 and were already in session. The Forty-First Congress had convened in December 1869. Jefferson Long, the second black to take a seat in the House, was also elected in 1870 in a special election. He took his seat on December 22, 1870.

[4]The history of Jim Crow segregation is described at www.jimcrowhistory.org.

Paradoxically, African Americans in the North had to wait much longer than southern blacks to capture their first seat in the House. From the time the Constitution was adopted until the ratification of the Fifteenth Amendment in 1870, determining who could vote was strictly a state's right to decide. Northern states had a mixed record on black voting: Some allowed blacks to vote; others didn't. Even in northern states where blacks were allowed to vote, African Americans were not elected to the House. Blacks were a tiny fraction of the northern population and there were never enough black voters in any given House district to elect an African American.

That situation changed beginning around 1900, when many blacks fled the South to escape disfranchisement, economic deprivation, and racial violence—particularly a surge in the number of lynchings. These North-bound blacks laid the groundwork for the return of African Americans to the House. Gathering in congressional districts in Chicago, New York, and Detroit, northern blacks captured their first seat in the House in 1928 with the election of Oscar De Priest, a Republican representing a district on the South Side of Chicago. De Priest served three terms in the House. He was defeated in 1934 by Arthur Mitchell, the first black Democrat elected to the House.

Blacks in the South waited almost 100 years before the federal government again used its power to protect their voting rights. The Voting Rights Act of 1965 authorized the president to send federal officials to the South to ensure that blacks could vote without interference. President Lyndon Johnson aggressively enforced the new legislation. In 1965, for example, only 6 percent of the blacks eligible to vote in Mississippi were registered; by 1968, that rate had increased to 44 percent. The first blacks from the South to return to the House as a result of the renewed federal commitment to protect African American political equality were Barbara Jordan from Texas and Andrew Young from Georgia, both Democrats and both elected in 1972.

Black Representation in the Senate

The underrepresentation of blacks in the U.S. Senate has been staggering. With the adjournment of the 111th Congress late in 2010, the Senate was 222 years old. Blacks have been represented in the Senate during just thirty-one of those years, and at no time have African Americans occupied more than one seat in the Senate.

Hiram Revels was the first African American to serve in the Senate. He was born in North Carolina in 1827 to parents who were free blacks, which made him free, too. After a career in the ministry, Revels settled in Mississippi and was elected to the state legislature in 1869. The Mississippi legislature chose Revels in 1870 to fill one of the state's two vacant seats in the Senate. Revels served in the Senate from February 1870 until March 1871.[5]

Blanche Bruce, a Republican like Revels, was the second African American to serve in the Senate. Bruce held many local political offices in Mississippi, including registrar of voters and sheriff, and established himself as a wealthy cotton farmer. In 1874, the Mississippi legislature sent Bruce to the Senate, where he served just one term. He was the first black to serve a full term and the only former slave to serve.

Edward Brooke, the third black to serve in the Senate, was the first elected by popular vote and the first to represent a northern state. Brooke served with distinction in World War II and pursued a career in law before winning election as the attorney general of Massachusetts in 1962. In 1966, he won election to the Senate as a Republican and served two terms.

Carol Moseley-Braun is the only black woman and the first black Democrat to serve in the Senate. Moseley-Braun served in the Illinois legislature for ten years before winning a seat in the Senate in 1992 by defeating a white opponent. In that election, Moseley-Braun received 95 percent of the black vote and 48 percent of the white. She failed in her bid for reelection in 1998, attracting 93 percent of the African American vote but only 36 percent of the white vote. Her challenger in that election, Republican Peter Fitzgerald, who was white, capitalized on the fundraising scandals and other controversies that plagued Moseley-Braun and outspent her 2 to 1 in the campaign.

---

[5]Both of Mississippi's U.S. Senate seats had been empty since 1861, when Jefferson Davis and Albert Brown walked out of the Senate to signal Mississippi's secession from the Union. Those seats, and other southern seats, remained vacant for the duration of the Civil War and well into the period of Reconstruction. Congress required that the southern states ratify the Fourteenth Amendment and, in some cases, the Fifteenth Amendment as a condition of readmission to the Union and to filling their vacant seats in the Senate. While the Senate seats of the southern states were vacant, the six-year term carried by all seats in the Senate continued to run. The term for the seat Revels won was 1864–1870, which explains why Revels served just one year in the Senate.

Fitzgerald declined to seek a second term in 2004. Barack Obama won the Democratic Party's nomination to run for the open seat. Obama had served in the Illinois legislature since 1997 and was viewed by many as a rising star in the Democratic Party. The Republican nominee, Jack Ryan, who was white, withdrew prior to the election because of allegations that he had pressured his wife to accompany him to sex clubs. Several prominent Illinois Republicans declined to take up the race against Obama. With nowhere to turn, the Republican Party settled on Alan Keyes, an outspokenly conservative African American who asserted during the campaign that Jesus Christ would not vote for Obama.

For the first time, two African Americans faced each other in a race for a seat in the U.S. Senate. Obama routed Keyes, receiving over 70 percent of the votes cast. According to one exit poll, nine out of ten black voters and seven out of ten white voters backed Obama, who became the fifth African American to take a seat in the Senate.

Obama was elected the forty-fourth president of the United States on November 4, 2008, and shortly thereafter resigned from his seat in the Senate. Illinois governor Rod Blagojevich then appointed Democrat Roland Burris, an African American, as Obama's replacement. Shortly after naming Burris as Illinois's junior senator, Blagojevich was impeached and removed from office by the Illinois state legislature because of evidence that he had attempted to sell the Senate seat. Federal prosecutors later charged Blagojevich with sixteen felony counts, including extortion, conspiracy, and racketeering. Questions regarding how much Burris knew about Blagojevich's efforts to profit from his appointment power caused the Chicago *Tribune* to call on Burris to resign. He refused. But because of the controversy, Burris declined to run for reelection in 2010.

Of the 100 U.S. Senators sworn into office on January 5, 2011, to serve in the 112th Congress, none were African American.

ASSIGNMENT

Black representation in Congress has fluctuated dramatically since the Civil War. Blacks have, at times, achieved significant representation in the House and Senate, only to see those gains erode or vanish. Before answering questions 1 to 6, study Figures 6.3.1 and 6.3.2. These depictions of the African American struggle for proportional representation in the House will assist you in answering the questions.

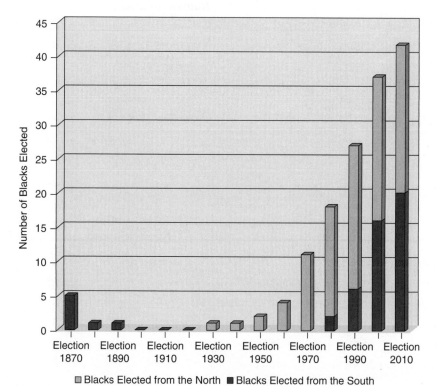

FIGURE 6.3.1   Black Representation in the House by Region

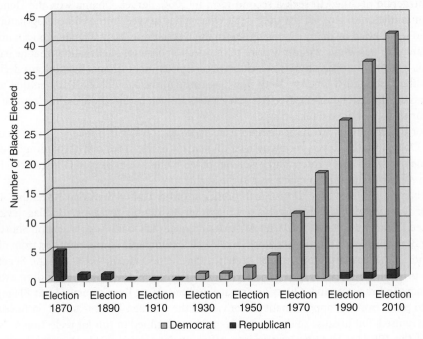

FIGURE 6.3.2 Black Representation in the House by Political Party Affiliation

1. Use the data in Table 6.3.1 to complete the chart titled Blacks in the House of Representatives. Notice that the data in Table 6.3.1 are grouped to correlate with the periods in the left-hand column of the chart. Your objective is to develop a quantitative measure of how the political power of blacks in the House has fluctuated since the Civil War.

TABLE 6.3.1	Blacks in the House of Representatives				
Election	**Congress***	**Size of House**	**Number of Blacks Elected**	**Party**	**Region**
1870*	41st	241	2	R	S
1870**	42d	241	5	R	S
1872	43d	292	7	R	S
1874	44th	292	7	R	S
1876	45th	292	3	R	S
1878	46th	292	0		
1880	47th	292	1	R	S
1882	48th	325	2	R	S
1884	49th	325	2	R	S
1886	50th	325	0		
1888	51st	325	3	R	S
1890	52d	325	1	R	S
1892	53d	356	1	R	S
1894	54th	356	1	R	S
1896	55th	356	1	R	S
1898	56th	356	1	R	S
1900	57th	356	0		

(Continued)

TABLE 6.3.1 Blacks in the House of Representatives (*Continued*)

Election	Congress*	Size of House	Number of Blacks Elected	Party	Region
1902	58th	386	0		
1904	59th	386	0		
1906	60th	386	0		
1908	61st	386	0		
1910	62d	386	0		
1912	63d	435	0		
1914	64th	435	0		
1916	65th	435	0		
1918	66th	435	0		
1920	67th	435	0		
1922	68th	435	0		
1924	69th	435	0		
1926	70th	435	0		
1928	71st	435	1	R	N
1930	72d	435	1	R	N
1932	73d	435	1	R	N
1934	74th	435	1	D	N
1936	75th	435	1	D	N
1938	76th	435	1	D	N
1940	77th	435	1	D	N
1942	78th	435	1	D	N
1944	79th	435	2	D	N
1946	80th	435	2	D	N
1948	81st	435	2	D	N
1950	82d	435	2	D	N
1952	83d	435	2	D	N
1954	84th	435	3	D	N
1956	85th	435	4	D	N
1958	86th	435	4	D	N
1960	87th	437[†]	4	D	N
1962	88th	435	5	D	N
1964	89th	435	6	D	N
1966	90th	435	6	D	N
1968	91st	435	10	D	N
1970	92d	435	11	D	N
1972	93d	435	16	D	2S 14N
1974	94th	435	16	D	3S 13N
1976	95th	435	16	D	3S 13N
1978	96th	435	17	D	2S 15N
1980	97th	435	18	D	2S 16N

(*Continued*)

TABLE 6.3.1	Blacks in the House of Representatives (*Continued*)				
Election	Congress*	Size of House	Number of Blacks Elected	Party	Region
1982	98th	435	21	D	2S 19N
1984	99th	435	20	D	2S 18N
1986	100th	435	22	D	4S 18N
1988	101st	435	24	D	5S 19N
1990	102d	453	27	1R 26D	6S 21N
1992	103d	435	39	1R 38D	18S 21N
1994	104th	435	41	2R 39D	17S 24N
1996	105th	435	39	1R 38D	16S 23N
1998	106th	435	35	1R 34D	16S 21N
2000	107th	435	37	1R 36D	16S 21N
2002	108th	435	37	0R 37D	17S 20N
2004	109th	435	40	0R 40D	18S 22N
2006	110th	435	40	0R 40D	17S 23N
2008	111th	435	39	0R 39D	16S 23N
2010	112th	435	42	2R 40D	19S 23N

Key: R = Republican; D = Democrat; S = southern state; N = nonsouthern state.

*Special election.

**Regular election.

†To accommodate the admission of Alaska and Hawaii in 1959, the size of the House was increased temporarily to provide each of the new states with one seat. The size of the House returned to 435 after the apportionment based on the 1960 census.

Source: Data come primarily from U.S. Senate, *Biographical Directory of the United States Congress, 1774–1989*, doc. 100–34 (Washington, D.C.: Joint Committee on Printing, 1989).

a. To fill in the chart column labeled Terms of Service in the House, use the data on the size of the House provided in the third column of Table 6.3.1. (The size of the House is the number of seats in the House, which is the same as the number of terms of service in the House.) For each period specified in the left-hand column of the chart, calculate the total number of terms of service in the House and enter your results.

   Sessions of Congress run for two years and are numbered sequentially. The 112th Congress, for example, was elected in November 2010 and was seated in January 2011. All 435 House terms in the 112th Congress expire when that Congress adjourns sometime late in 2012. Since the 63rd Congress (1913–1915), the number of seats in the House has been 435. For example, in the 91st to 111th Congresses (1969–2010), the total number of House terms was 9,135 (21 Congresses multiplied by 435 seats in each Congress).

   We've given you a head start in filling in the chart by entering the calculations for the 91st to 111th Congresses, as well as those for the 112th Congress. In making the calculations for the other periods, remember to factor in changes in the size of the House. The dates in Table 6.3.1 are important. But when making the required calculations, you must rely on *the sessions of Congress* specified by number in the second column of Table 6.3.1.

b. For each period in the left-hand column of the chart, determine the number of House terms served by blacks. You can find this information in the fourth column of Table 6.3.1. For each period, total the number of black representatives elected, then fill in the chart column labeled Number of House Terms That Blacks Served.

c. For each period in the left-hand column of the chart, calculate the percentage of House terms blacks served and enter your results in the chart column labeled Percentage of House Terms That Blacks Served. To make the calculation, divide the number of terms that blacks served by the number of terms of service in the House for each period. The resulting figure is the percentage of total House terms blacks served during that period.

Congress and Period*	Terms of Service in the House	Number of House Terms That Blacks Served	Percentage of House Terms That Blacks Served	Blacks as a Percentage of Total National Population[†]
Chart: Blacks in the House of Representatives				
41st–44th, 1869–1877	_____	_____	_____	13
45th–56th, 1877–1901	_____	_____	_____	11–13
57th–70th, 1901–1929	_____	_____	_____	10–11
71st–90th, 1929–1968	_____	_____	_____	10–11
91st–111th, 1969–2010	9,135	567	6.2	11–13
112th, 2011–2012	435	42	9.6	13

*Prior to the ratification of the Twentieth Amendment in 1933, Congress typically convened in December of the year *following* its election. The 44th Congress, for example, elected in 1874 did not convene until December 1875. Prior to the ratification of the Twentieth Amendment, Congress also typically did not adjourn until early in the year *following* the election of a new Congress. So, for example, the 44th and 45th Congresses were both in session at different times in 1877: the outgoing 44th Congress early in the year and the incoming 45th Congress in December. Since the ratification of the Twentieth Amendment, the incoming Congress convenes on January 3 following the November election, and the outgoing Congress usually adjourns before the election of the new Congress.

[†]According to Census Bureau figures, the black percentage of the nation's population has ranged from about 10 to 13 percent since the Civil War. This reported variation has less to do with actual changes in the black population than it does with the Census Bureau's methodology. For the purposes of this assignment, we assume that the nation's black population has remained at approximately 13 percent. The geographic distribution of African Americans, however, has changed dramatically.

Again, the calculations for the 91st to 111th Congresses, as well as those for the 112th Congress, have been completed for you.

That figure is useful for two reasons. First, it indicates how the political power of blacks in the House has changed since the Civil War. Second, we can compare that figure with the percentage of blacks in the total population to determine the extent to which black political strength in the House approximates the presence of blacks in the general population.

Looking at the percentage of total terms blacks served in the House is a more accurate measure of black political power than just counting the number of black representatives during a given period, a figure that does not capture multiple terms. For example, between 1928 and 1944, a period that includes the 71st to 78th Congresses, two blacks were elected to the House: De Priest and Mitchell. But to say that two blacks served during this period is hardly an accurate measure of black representation because De Priest served three terms and Mitchell served four. Looking only at the number of black members who served in the House over a period of multiple Congresses thus understates the extent of black representation.

2. From 1869 to 1877, the national government used force to protect black voting rights in the South. How did black representation in the House during that period compare with the succeeding period, 1877 to 1901, when the power of the national government had been withdrawn? To make the comparison, cite the quantitative measure of black political strength you developed filling in the chart, specifically, the column labeled Percentage of House Terms That Blacks Served.

_____

_____

_____

_____

_____

3. How did black representation in the House from 1929 to 1968 compare with the percentage of blacks in the total population? To make the comparison, cite the quantitative measure of black political strength that you developed filling in the chart, specifically, the column labeled Percentage of House Terms That Blacks Served.

_____

_____

_____

_____

_____

4. Table 6.3.1 indicates that no blacks were returned to the House by the elections of 1878 or 1886. Consequently, no blacks served in the House during the 46th and 50th Congresses. There have been two other periods since the Constitution was ratified when no African Americans—from the North or South—served in the House. Identify the beginning and ending dates of those periods.

Period 1: _____

Period 2: _____

5. Many believe that minority representation in Congress should approximate a minority's presence in the general population. In the 112th Congress, how far are blacks from achieving that goal? That is, how many more blacks would have had to have been elected to the House in 2010 to make black representation there commensurate with the proportion of blacks in the general population? To make the calculation, multiply the number of seats in the House by the percentage of African Americans in the general population (435×0.13). Next, subtract from that figure the number of blacks serving in the House in the 112th Congress.

_____

_____

6. a. For the elections of 1968 to 2010, what number of terms would blacks have had to serve in the U.S. Senate to achieve black representation commensurate with the proportion of blacks in general population? To find that figure, multiply the number of elections held during the period (one every two years) by the number of senators elected every two years (33.3).[6] The product is the total number of available Senate seats during the period. Next, multiply that figure by the approximate percentage (0.13) of blacks in the total population over the period.

_____

    b. Describe (using numbers) how far away African Americans were from achieving proportional representation during the period from 1968 to 2010. In other words, what's the gap between your answer to question 6a. and the number of Senate terms blacks were actually elected to during the period?

_____

_____

7. Table 6.3.2 specifies the racial composition of the population of Illinois and of each of its nineteen congressional (House) districts. Examine the column labeled Black or African American.

---

[6]Obviously we don't elect fractions of senators—although some critics of the Senate might assert otherwise. For election purposes, senators are divided into three classes as required by Article I, Section 3 of the Constitution. Senate Class III, consisting of 34 members, was elected in 2010. Senate Class I, consisting of 33 members, will be elected in 2012. Senate Class II, also consisting of 33 members, will be elected in 2014, and so on. Rather than laboring to apply this class system to the period from 1968 to 2010, we use the average number of 33.3 senators elected every two years.

TABLE 6.3.2 Illinois Congressional Districts, 110th Congress, by Race

	Total Population	White	Black or African-American	American Indian and Alaska Native	Asian	Native Hawaiian and Other Pacific Islander	Some Other Race	Two or More Races	Hispanic or Latino (of any race)	White Alone, Not Hispanic or Latino
Illinois	12,419,293	73.5	15.1	0.2	3.4	0	5.8	1.9	12.3	67.8
Congressional District										
District 1	653,647	29.5	65.5	0.2	1.4	0	2	1.4	4.8	27.3
District 2	653,647	29.7	62.4	0.2	0.6	0	5.3	1.8	10.4	25.6
District 3	653,647	77.9	5.9	0.3	2.9	0	10.3	2.7	21.3	68.2
District 4	653,647	46.5	4.3	0.7	1.8	0.1	42.1	4.5	74.5	18.4
District 5	653,647	77.5	2.3	0.3	6.5	0.1	9.8	3.5	23	65.9
District 6	653,647	82.3	2.7	0.2	8.1	0	4.6	2	12.5	75.3
District 7	653,647	29.8	62	0.2	3.9	0	2.6	1.5	5.8	27.3
District 8	653,647	84.4	3.3	0.2	5.7	0	4.5	1.8	10.8	78.8
District 9	653,647	68.5	10.9	0.3	12.4	0.1	4.6	3.3	11.5	62.5
District 10	653,647	81.2	5.4	0.2	5.9	0	5.5	1.7	12.3	75.2
District 11	653,647	87	7.8	0.2	0.8	0	2.8	1.3	6.7	83.7
District 12	653,647	80.6	16.4	0.3	0.8	0	0.7	1.2	1.8	79.7
District 13	653,647	84.9	5	0.1	6.6	0	1.8	1.5	5.5	81.6
District 14	653,647	83.4	4.7	0.3	1.8	0	7.9	1.9	18.5	74
District 15	653,647	89.5	5.7	0.2	2.3	0	1	1.2	2.2	88.5
District 16	653,647	88.9	5.4	0.2	1.3	0	2.7	1.4	6.5	85.7
District 17	653,647	89	7.2	0.2	0.6	0	1.6	1.3	3.7	87.3
District 18	653,647	90.8	6.5	0.2	0.9	0	0.6	1	1.5	90
District 19	653,647	94.6	3.5	0.2	0.5	0	0.4	0.8	1.1	94

Percent of Total Population

Source: U.S. Census Bureau, 110th Congressional District Summary File (100-Percent), Matrix P8.

a. In which of Illinois' congressional districts is the black population greater than 60%?

_____

b. How does the distribution of the black population within a state such as Illinois help explain why far more blacks have been elected to the House of Representatives than to the U.S. Senate? Explain and support your answer.

_____

_____

_____

_____

_____

EXERCISE 6.4   Legislative Apportionment

INTRODUCTION

Fair and effective representation for all citizens must be the basic aim of legislative apportionment. That's what the Supreme Court ruled in its *Reynolds v. Sims* decision in 1964.

Legislative apportionment is the process by which seats in a legislature are allocated to groups of citizens within legislative districts. The most fair and effective way to distribute those seats and establish legislative districts isn't always clear, and that's why legislative apportionment has been a politically charged issue. Bitter disputes over which citizens would get the seats, the votes, and hence the power in Congress and in the state legislatures have often marked U.S. history.

Two of these disputes nearly derailed the Constitutional Convention. States with smaller populations demanded, as their price for joining the union, that they receive the same number of seats in the national legislature as states with much larger populations. That impasse was resolved by the Great Compromise. Whites in the South demanded, as their terms for joining the union, that slaves be counted for the purpose of determining how many seats in the House each southern state would be allocated. That dispute was finessed by the Three-Fifths Compromise, an agreement between the North and the South to count three-fifths of the slaves in apportioning the House. After the destruction of slavery during the Civil War and the Fourteenth Amendment's guarantee that the freed slaves were indeed citizens, all African Americans were counted when the House was apportioned.

The Three-Fifths Compromise is history. But the terms of the Great Compromise still define the two strikingly different systems of representation in Congress today. In the House, representation is based on population: Seats are allocated to states in proportion to each state's share of the nation's population. The Constitution requires the national government to conduct a census every ten years and reallocate the 435 seats in the House among the fifty states to account for changes in the population of the states. Based on the 2010 census, each of the nation's 435 House districts was drawn to contain about 700,000 people. (That's the approximate number you get by dividing the nation's total 2010 census population by the 435 seats in the House.) Because the population of House districts is equal, and because each district has one representative and one vote, the political power of citizens in the House is roughly equal, regardless of the state in which they live.[1]

In contrast to the population-based system in the House, representation in the U.S. Senate is based on each state as a whole entity. The Constitution awards representation in the Senate equally to each state—two seats per state—regardless of a state's population. In effect, the Constitution treats states as privileged political and geographic units entitled to an equal and fixed amount of political power simply because they exist as states. In 2010, the approximately 550,000 citizens of Wyoming had the same number of votes in the Senate as the approximately 37 million citizens of California.[2]

In deference to the principle of federalism, the framers of the Constitution did not prescribe a system of representation for the state legislatures. The result is that states have employed a number of different structures. California's experience with legislative apportionment highlights many difficult political questions surrounding the allocation of seats in a state legislature.

In 1849, California's first state constitution established a bicameral (two-house) legislature consisting of a state assembly and a state senate. It specified that "representation shall be apportioned according to population." In 1879, California's second constitution added the requirement that state assembly and state senate districts be "as nearly equal in population" as possible. This meant that seats in both chambers of California's state legislature were apportioned equally among the citizens of the state—a population-based system of representation.

Until the 1880s, northern California had the overwhelming majority of the state's citizens, and hence most of the political power in the state legislature. By the 1920s, the shift in political

---

[1]Because the total population of a state is unlikely to be evenly divisible by the population that the census establishes for House districts, the number of persons per representative can never be precisely equal. As noted in the exercise, the 2010 census established a population of about 700,000 for House districts. States that had fewer than 700,000 people received more than their fair share of political power because the Constitution requires that every state have at least one seat in the House. States with populations greater than 700,000 (or any multiple of 700,000) but less than the number required for an additional seat in the House received less than their fair share of power. More details on apportionment can be found at www.census.gov/population/www/censusdata/apportionment/history.html.

[2]The population numbers here are taken from the 2010 census.

power to southern California was well under way. The rapidly growing urban population in southern California required that more seats in the state legislature be allocated to this region. Northern and rural interests perceived correctly that population-based apportionment worked against them, and they feared being overwhelmed by the growing political power of urban centers in the south. To preserve the power of rural interests and voters in the north, groups such as the California Farm Bureau Federation sponsored Proposition 28, a ballot initiative to amend the state constitution. Approved by voters in November 1926, Proposition 28 fundamentally restructured apportionment by eliminating population-based representation in the state senate. (The assembly remained population based.) The new basis for representation in the California state senate mirrored that in the U.S. Senate: The state's counties would hold the same privileged position that states occupy in the U.S. Senate. California's counties, because they were discrete geographic and political units, were assigned an equal and fixed amount of legislative power in the state senate—one vote per county—regardless of the county's population.

There was one problem: The size of the state senate was set by California's constitution at forty seats, and there were fifty-eight counties in the state. The difficulty was solved by awarding one seat in the state senate to each of the more populous counties and grouping together the less populous counties—but only up to a maximum of three counties per senate district. As Table 6.4.1 makes clear, twenty-seven state senate districts exactly matched the boundaries of a single county. Thirteen state senate districts were made up of either two or three counties grouped together. In 1964, in *Reynolds v. Sims*, the Supreme Court declared that population parity, not geography, must be the basis for allocating seats in state legislatures. That decision struck down the system of county-based representation in the California state senate that had been created by Proposition 28. By 1966, to comply with the Court's ruling, California had again returned to a population-based system of representation in its state senate.

ASSIGNMENT

Questions 1 to 4 explore the link between legislative apportionment and political advantage, and the Supreme Court's verdict in 1964 on apportionment in state legislatures.

1. According to the 2010 census, the fifteen smallest states (by population) in the nation are Alaska, Delaware, Hawaii, Idaho, Maine, Montana, Nebraska, New Hampshire, New Mexico, North Dakota, Rhode Island, South Dakota, Vermont, West Virginia, and Wyoming. Each of these fifteen states has from one to three members in the House of Representatives. Together, they have a total of twenty-six members in the House. Because there are 435 members in the House, these fifteen states have 5.9 percent of the seats in the House. The 5.9 percent figure is reached by dividing the number of seats these fifteen states have by the total number of seats in the House.

    a. According to the 2010 census, the nation's population for the purpose of apportioning the House was 309,183,463.[3] The population of the fifteen smallest states was 17,720,159. What percentage of the nation's total population do these fifteen states have? To make the calculation, simply divide the population of the fifteen smallest states by the total population of the nation.

_____

    b. Is the voting strength of these fifteen states in the House proportional to their share of the nation's population?

_____

2. a. Turning to the U.S. Senate, how many votes do the fifteen smallest states (by population) together have in the Senate?

_____

    b. It's clear that the voting strength of these fifteen states in the Senate is *not* proportional to their share of the nation's population. To make the voting strength of the fifteen states proportional

---

[3]This is the total apportionment population. The populations of the District of Columbia, Puerto Rico, and the U.S. island areas are excluded from the apportionment population because they do not have voting seats in the U.S. House of Representatives.

to their share of the nation's population, how many Senate seats in total would you assign to these fifteen states?

---

3. The four states with the largest populations in the nation are California, Florida, New York, and Texas. Together, these four states have a total of 143 members in the House, or 33 percent of the seats in the House.

  a. Again, the nation's total population according to the 2010 census was 309,183,463. The total population of the four largest states was 100,932,235. What percentage of the nation's total population do these four states have?

---

  b. Is the voting strength of these four states in the House proportional to their share of the nation's population?

---

4. a. Turning again to the U.S. Senate, how many votes do the four most populous states together have in the Senate?

---

  b. It's clear that the voting strength of these four states in the Senate is *not* proportional to their share of the nation's population. To make the voting strength of these four states proportional to their share of the nation's population, how many Senate seats in total would you assign to these four states?

Table 6.4.1 lists the population numbers and geographic sizes of the California state senate districts established in 1961 under the system of county-based representation. Use the information in the table to answer questions 5 to 7, which explore disparities in representation in the California state senate in the 1960s prior to the *Reynolds v. Sims* Supreme Court decision.

TABLE 6.4.1	Population and Area of California State Senate Districts Established in 1961		
District	**Counties**	**Population Numbers, 1960**	**Area, Square Miles**
1st	Modoc, Lassen, Plumas	33,525	11,209
2nd	Del Norte, Siskiyou	50,656	7,315
3rd	Humboldt	104,892	3,573
4th	Mendocino, Lake	64,845	4,763
5th	Trinity, Shasta	69,174	6,989
6th	Butte	82,030	1,663
7th	Sierra, Nevada, Placer	80,156	3,360
8th	Colusa, Glenn, Tehama	54,625	5,446
9th	El Dorado, Amador	39,380	2,307
10th	Yuba, Sutter	67,239	1,244
11th	Napa, Yolo	131,617	1,792
12th	Sonoma	147,375	1,579
13th	Marin	146,820	520
14th	San Francisco	740,316	45
15th	Solano	134,597	827

(*Continued*)

TABLE 6.4.1	Population and Area of California State Senate Districts Established in 1961 (*Continued*)		
District	**Counties**	**Population Numbers, 1960**	**Area, Square Miles**
16th	Alameda	908,209	733
17th	Contra Costa	409,030	734
18th	Santa Clara	642,315	1,302
19th	Sacramento	502,778	983
20th	San Joaquin	249,989	1,409
21st	San Mateo	444,387	454
22nd	Stanislaus	157,294	1,500
23rd	Santa Cruz, San Benito	99,615	1,835
24th	Madera, Merced	130,914	2,144
25th	Monterey	198,351	3,324
26th	Calaveras, Mariposa, Tuolumne	29,757	4,756
27th	Kings	49,954	1,395
28th	Alpine, Inyo, Mono	14,294	13,842
29th	San Luis Obispo	81,044	3,316
30th	Fresno	365,945	5,964
31st	Santa Barbara	168,962	2,738
32nd	Tulare	168,403	4,838
33rd	Ventura	199,138	1,851
34th	Kern	291,984	8,152
35th	Orange	703,925	782
36th	San Bernardino	503,591	20,131
37th	Riverside	306,191	7,177
38th	Los Angeles	6,038,771	4,060
39th	Imperial	72,105	4,284
40th	San Diego	1,033,011	4,255
Total California state population		15,717,204	

Source: Adapted from Legislative Sourcebook: The California Legislature and Reapportionment, 1849–1965 (Assembly of the State of California, 1965). Used by permission of California State Assembly.

5. a. Which California state senate district had the lowest population?

_____

b. Which district had the highest population?

_____

c. What is the ratio of population variance between the two districts? To answer this question, divide the smaller population figure into the larger one and express the result as a ratio, such as 30 to 1.

_____

6. The population variance you identified in question 5 is a measure of the disparity in voting power between individual citizens in the two state senate districts. How many times greater is the weight of a vote cast by a citizen in the smallest district than the weight of one cast by a voter in the largest district?

_____

7. According to the 1960 census, California's total population was 15,717,204. The twenty-one state senate districts with the smallest populations had a combined population of 1,684,614.

    a. What percentage of California's total population lived in the twenty-one smallest state senate districts?

_____

    b. What percentage of the total votes in the California state senate did the twenty-one smallest districts have?

_____

    c. What is your assessment of the distribution of political power in California's state senate in the early 1960s?

_____

_____

_____

_____

_____

       Excerpts from the Supreme Court's decision, *Reynolds v. Sims*, are included as Reading 6.4.1. In the *Reynolds* case, the plaintiffs argued that the apportionment of the Alabama state legislature deprived citizens of their rights under the equal protection clause of the Fourteenth Amendment. Disparities among districts in population and political power were widespread in state legislatures across the nation in 1964, when the Supreme Court issued its decision. In the Alabama state senate, population variance ratios were as high as 40 to 1. Study Reading 6.4.1, and then answer questions 8 to 11.

READING 6.4.1
Excerpts from *Reynolds v. Sims*, 377 U.S. 533 (1964)

Chief Justice Warren delivered the opinion of the Court.

      Legislators represent people, not trees or acres. Legislators are elected by voters, not farms or cities or economic interests. As long as ours is a representative form of government, and our legislatures are those instruments of government elected directly by and directly representative of the people, the right to elect legislators in a free and unimpaired fashion is a bedrock of our political system. It could hardly be gainsaid that a constitutional claim had been asserted by an allegation that certain otherwise qualified voters had been entirely prohibited from voting for members of their state legislature. And, if a State should provide that the votes of citizens in one part of the State should be given two times, or five times, or 10 times the weight of votes of citizens in another part of the State, it could hardly be contended that the right to vote of those residing in the disfavored areas had not been effectively diluted. It would appear extraordinary to suggest that a State could be constitutionally permitted to enact a law providing that certain of the State's voters could vote two, five, or 10 times for their legislative representatives, while voters living elsewhere could vote only once. And it is inconceivable that a state law to the effect that, in counting votes for legislators, the votes of citizens in one part of the State would be multiplied by two, five, or 10, while the votes of persons in another area would be counted only at face value, could be constitutionally sustainable. Of course, the effect of . . . state legislative districting schemes which give the same number of representatives to unequal numbers of constituents is identical. . . . Overweighting and overvaluation of the votes of those living here has the certain effect of dilution and undervaluation of the votes of those living there. The resulting discrimination against those individual voters living in disfavored areas is easily demonstrable mathematically. Their right to vote is simply not the same right to vote as that of those living in a favored part of the State. Two, five, or 10 of them must vote before the effect of their voting is equivalent to that of their favored neighbor. Weighting the votes of citizens differently, by any method or means, merely because of where they happen to reside, hardly seems justifiable. . . .

State legislatures are, historically, the fountainhead of representative government in this country. A number of them have their roots in colonial times, and substantially antedate the creation of our Nation and our Federal Government. In fact, the first formal stirrings of American political independence are to be found, in large part, in the views and actions of several of the colonial legislative bodies. With the birth of our National Government, and the adoption and ratification of the Federal Constitution, state legislatures retained a most important place in our Nation's governmental structure. But representative government is in essence self-government through the medium of elected representatives of the people, and each and every citizen has an inalienable right to full and effective participation in the political processes of his State's legislative bodies. Most citizens can achieve this participation only as qualified voters through the election of legislators to represent them. Full and effective participation by all citizens in state government requires, therefore, that each citizen have an equally effective voice in the election of members of his state legislature. Modern and viable state government needs, and the Constitution demands, no less.

Logically, in a society ostensibly grounded on representative government, it would seem reasonable that a majority of the people of a State could elect a majority of that State's legislators. To conclude differently, and to sanction minority control of state legislative bodies, would appear to deny majority rights in a way that far surpasses any possible denial of minority rights that might otherwise be thought to result. Since legislatures are responsible for enacting laws by which all citizens are to be governed, they should be bodies which are collectively responsive to the popular will. And the concept of equal protection has been traditionally viewed as requiring the uniform treatment of persons standing in the same relation to the governmental action questioned or challenged. With respect to the allocation of legislative representation, all voters, as citizens of a State, stand in the same relation regardless of where they live. Any suggested criteria for the differentiation of citizens are insufficient to justify any discrimination, as to the weight of their votes, unless relevant to the permissible purposes of legislative apportionment. Since the achieving of fair and effective representation for all citizens . . . is concededly the basic aim of legislative apportionment, we conclude that the Equal Protection Clause guarantees the opportunity for equal participation by all voters in the election of state legislators. Diluting the weight of votes because of place of residence impairs basic constitutional rights under the Fourteenth Amendment just as much as invidious discriminations based upon factors such as race . . . or economic status. . . . Our constitutional system amply provides for the protection of minorities by means other than giving them majority control of state legislatures. And the democratic ideals of equality and majority rule, which have served this Nation so well in the past, are hardly of any less significance for the present and the future. . . .

To the extent that a citizen's right to vote is debased, he is that much less a citizen. The fact that an individual lives here or there is not a legitimate reason for overweighting or diluting the efficacy of his vote. The complexions of societies and civilizations change, often with amazing rapidity. A nation once primarily rural in character becomes predominantly urban. Representation schemes once fair and equitable become archaic and outdated. But the basic principle of representative government remains, and must remain, unchanged—the weight of a citizen's vote cannot be made to depend on where he lives. Population is, of necessity, the starting point for consideration and the controlling criterion for judgment in legislative apportionment controversies. . . . A citizen, a qualified voter, is no more nor [sic] no less so because he lives in the city or on the farm. This is the clear and strong command of our Constitution's Equal Protection Clause. This is an essential part of the concept of a government of laws and not men. This is at the heart of Lincoln's vision of "government of the people, by the people, [and] for the people." The Equal Protection Clause demands no less than substantially equal state legislative representation for all citizens, of all places as well as of all races.

   We hold that, as a basic constitutional standard, the Equal Protection Clause requires that the seats in both houses of a bicameral state legislature must be apportioned on a population basis. Simply stated, an individual's right to vote for state legislators is unconstitutionally impaired when its weight is in a substantial fashion diluted when compared with votes of citizens living in other parts of the State.

8. Identify and explain the reasons for the Court's ruling against geographic-based apportionment.

_____

_____

_____

_____

_____

_____

_____

9. Assume that it is 1964, and that you've been charged with bringing the California state senate into compliance with the Supreme Court's ruling in _Reynolds v. Sims._ Begin your restructuring of the system of representation by capping the number of seats in the state senate at forty. Explain the process you would use to allocate the forty seats in the state senate to California's 15,717,204 citizens to comply with the Court's ruling.

_____

_____

_____

_____

_____

_____

10. The system of representation in the U.S. Senate—two votes per state—clearly violates the one-person, one-vote standard established by the Court in _Reynolds v. Sims._ What explains why the unequal and undemocratic system of state-based representation in the U.S. Senate persists, even after the _Reynolds v. Sims_ decision?

_____

_____

_____

_____

_____

11. What would be required to make representation in the U.S. Senate conform to the Supreme Court's one-person, one-vote standard?

_____

_____

_____

7

The Presidency

EXERCISE 7.1   The Electoral College

INTRODUCTION

The 2000 and 2004 presidential elections demonstrated that the Electoral College is no mere historical curiosity. Close observers of presidential elections have long noted the power of the Electoral College to shape the strategy of presidential campaigns. But who foresaw that the Electoral College vote in the 2000 election would produce a constitutional crisis and install in the Oval Office the candidate who received fewer popular votes?

The 2004 election again focused the nation's attention on the system the Constitution prescribes for electing the president. George W. Bush won a second term by capturing the majority of the Electoral College vote—and the majority of the popular vote, too. But if just 1 percent of Ohio voters had reversed themselves, John Kerry would have won the electoral vote (with one vote to spare) and been seated in the Oval Office, with about 3 million fewer votes than his opponent.

The process for electing the president is set forth in Article II, Section 1 of the Constitution, but key elements of the system developed in the years following the Constitutional Convention of 1787. In fact, the term *electoral college* does not appear in the Constitution and did not become the official designation for the body until 1845.[1] The Electoral College has been transformed over the past 200 years but without an overarching plan or philosophy to guide its evolution. To many observers, it is a peculiar, even bizarre system for electing the person who will occupy the most powerful office on the planet. One scholar described the Electoral College as "perhaps the world's most important governmental body that has neither meetings nor choices."[2]

How did the Electoral College come into being? The delegates at the Constitutional Convention of 1787 considered four ways to choose a president: by direct popular election, through Congress, through the state legislatures, or through intermediate electors. Direct popular election was ruled out because the vast majority of delegates wanted to restrain—not expand—democracy. They believed that popular elections would arouse the passions and self-interest of the people, destabilize the new government, undermine the public interest, and put demagogues in power. Democracy was so suspect in the framers' minds that only the House was given to the citizens to elect directly, and even there, state laws restricted the franchise to adult, white, male property holders. Election of the president by Congress was rejected because the delegates feared it might compromise the independence of the executive branch. The delegates also rejected election by the state legislatures because they feared it might make the president beholden to the states and undermine the authority of the newly established central government.

For want of a better option, the delegates settled on vesting the power to choose the president in intermediate electors. Because the Electoral College was a compromise negotiated among many, it's difficult to say precisely what the framers expected from the institution. But this much seems clear: They intended that the electors would select the president independent of public opinion. The framers assumed the electors would be educated and propertied men of talent and character, men who would be better able than the people at large to judge the qualifications of presidential candidates.

The electors have never been as insulated from public opinion, however, as the framers wanted. In the first presidential election, in 1789, four states held direct popular elections to choose their electors. In other states, the state legislatures picked

---

[1] See *Presidential Elections, 1789–1992* (Washington, DC: Congressional Quarterly Press, 1995) for comprehensive information on the history and functions of the Electoral College.

[2] Frank J. Sorauf, *Party Politics in America* (Boston: Little, Brown, 1984), p. 304.

the electors. As political parties developed and strengthened in the late 1790s, they began to offer voters slates of electors pledged to cast their ballots for the party's presidential and vice presidential candidates. The development of political parties essentially committed the electors to cast their ballots according to the popular will within their respective states. At the same time, direct popular election of electors spread widely and rapidly. By the election of 1836, South Carolina was the only state holding out against direct popular election of its electors: The South Carolina state legislature continued to pick the state's electors through the election of 1860. Since the Civil War, the direct popular election of electors has been almost completely universal and has, for the most part, bound electors to the public will—precisely what the framers wanted to avoid.

In the Constitution, the framers allocated Electoral College votes to the states by formula. Every state receives as many electoral votes as it has members in Congress. California, for example, has fifty-three seats in the House and two seats in the Senate, netting it fifty-five electoral votes. The Twenty-Third Amendment, ratified in 1961, awarded three electoral votes to the citizens of Washington, DC, bringing the total number of electoral votes to 538 (435 House seats plus 100 seats in the Senate plus three for the nation's capital).[3]

To win the presidency, a candidate must capture an absolute majority of the 538 Electoral College votes. That magic number is 270. If no presidential candidate wins 270 votes, the Constitution requires a contingency election in the House of Representatives. The House chooses from among the three candidates who received the most electoral votes. In the House, each state gets one vote. According to House rules, that vote is cast by the majority of the state's delegation in the House. The winner of the presidency must receive a majority of the fifty votes cast by the state delegations. The election of 1824, the last election to be decided in the House, is the best example of this constitutional provision in play. In that election, no candidate received a majority of the Electoral College vote or, for that matter, a majority of the popular vote. Andrew Jackson had the most electoral votes and the most popular votes, John Quincy Adams was the runner-up in the electoral and popular vote, and William Crawford came in third. The House considered the three candidates and chose Adams as president. The Constitution does not require that the House choose the candidate with the most electoral or the most popular votes.

If no candidate for the vice presidency reaches the requisite 270 Electoral College votes, the U.S. Senate chooses the vice president from the two candidates who have the most electoral votes. Each senator casts one vote, and a majority of the whole number of senators is required. Again, the Constitution does not require that the Senate select the candidate with the most electoral or the most popular votes.

Three elements of the Electoral College are essential to understanding how candidates win the presidency. First, the Electoral College is state centered. The general election for president is actually fifty separate state elections and one in Washington, DC, held on the same day. The national popular vote total is constitutionally irrelevant: All that counts is the popular vote total in each state. Winning in all states except Maine and Nebraska requires a plurality of the statewide popular vote.[4] That's the second key element of the Electoral College: Candidates do not need a majority of the popular vote in a state to win—only more popular votes than any other candidate. The third feature is winner-take-all. A state's electoral votes are not divided among the candidates according to the proportion of the popular vote they win. All of a state's electoral votes go to the candidate who wins a plurality of the popular vote in the state. Winner-take-all is not required by the Constitution, but all states except Maine and Nebraska have implemented it.

Interposed between the voters in a presidential election and the candidates seeking the presidency are the members of the Electoral College. Some states make this explicit by printing the names of the Electoral College members on the ballot under the name of the candidate to whom they are pledged. That would prove impractical, of course, in a large state like California, where fifty-five electors would be named for each presidential candidate on the ballot.

How are electors chosen? How do they carry out their responsibility? The system for choosing electors varies from state to state and from party to party. Generally speaking, state party organizations

[3]The District of Columbia was awarded the same number of votes as the number of seats in Congress it would be entitled to if it were a state.

[4]Both Maine and Nebraska award their Electoral College votes according to what's called the *district system,* one electoral vote to each congressional district in the state. The candidate with a plurality of the popular vote in the district wins that electoral vote. Two electoral votes in each state—those that represent the states' Senate seats—are awarded to the plurality winner of the statewide popular vote.

choose people to serve as electors based on their demonstrated loyalty and service to the party. Before the general election, each state party organization names a number of electors equal to the state's number of electoral votes. Each party's list of electors is called its *slate of electors*. The electors pledge to support the presidential and vice presidential candidates of the party. At this stage, the people named on each party's slate are only potential voting members of the Electoral College. Whether they will cast an Electoral College ballot depends on the results of the popular vote in their state.

On the first Monday after the second Wednesday in December, the electors pledged to the candidate who won the popular vote in each state go their state capitals, where each elector casts one vote for president and one vote for vice president. Their voting is public; in the 2000 election, it was carried live by C-SPAN and CNN. On January 6, the sitting vice president presides over the official counting of the Electoral College votes before a joint session of Congress.

The electors are not obligated by the Constitution or by federal law to cast their votes for the candidate to whom they pledged their support. Electors who break ranks with their party are called *faithless electors*. The practice is not common, and no presidential election has turned on it. Still, many states have passed laws attempting to bind electors to their pledges. Whether those laws are enforceable has yet to be determined. In 1992, presidential candidate Ross Perot tried to bind the electors pledged to him by requiring them to sign notarized oaths promising allegiance. Perot worried more than the major-party candidates about faithless electors because his campaign had to recruit potential electors from the ranks of campaign volunteers who had only a short history of commitment to him.

ASSIGNMENT

Figure 7.1.1 on the next page shows how the Electoral College worked in the 2008 election in California. This diagram should help you understand the Electoral College and answer the questions below. Another resource is the National Archives and Records Administration's Electoral College website at http://www.archives.gov/federal-register/electoral-college/.

1. State party organizations choose people as electors because of their demonstrated loyalty to the party. Even so, some electors fail to cast their electoral votes as pledged. In 1956, W. F. Turner, an Alabama elector pledged to Democratic presidential candidate Adlai Stevenson, cast his vote for a local judge. (Who knows? Maybe they were fishing buddies.) In the 2000 election, Barbara Lett-Simmons, an elector from Washington, DC, pledged to Al Gore, cast a blank ballot to protest the fact that the District of Columbia has no vote in Congress. What do you think could happen between the general election in November and the casting of electoral votes in December that might lead the electors to install as president the candidate everyone thought had lost the election? Think of an event so significant that it would break the ties of the electors' party loyalty.

_____

_____

_____

_____

_____

2. In setting up the Electoral College, the framers made a mistake. They assigned each elector two votes but did not require the electors, when casting their two votes, to specify whether they were voting for a candidate to be president or vice president. When the votes were tallied, the candidate with a majority became president and the runner-up became vice president. The framers apparently didn't anticipate that a president elected under this system might have as his vice president his opponent in the election. That is exactly what happened in the election of 1796, when John Adams, a Federalist, became president and Thomas Jefferson, a Democratic Republican, became vice president. The Twelfth Amendment (1804) eliminated this politically difficult possibility by requiring that electors cast separate ballots for president and vice president.

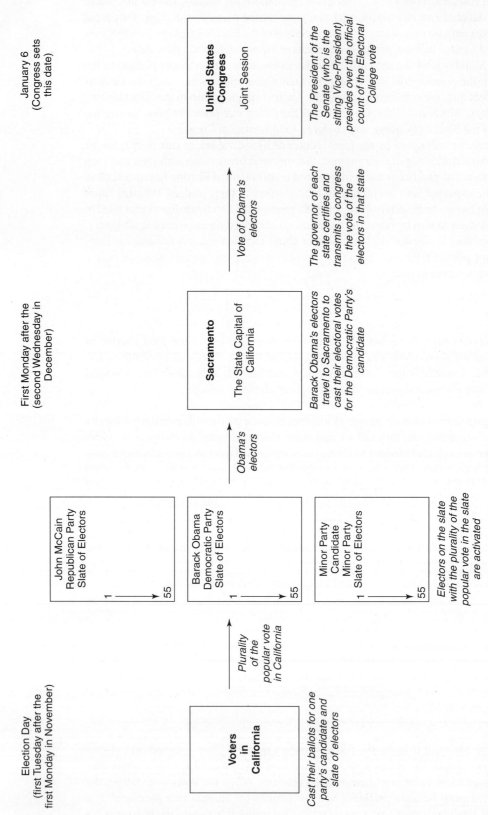

Election Day
(first Tuesday after the
first Monday in November)

First Monday after the
(second Wednesday in
December)

January 6
(Congress sets
this date)

**Voters
in
California**

*Cast their ballots for one
party's candidate and
slate of electors*

*Plurality
of the
popular vote
in California*

John McCain
Republican Party
Slate of Electors

1 → 55

Barack Obama
Democratic Party
Slate of Electors

1 → 55

Minor Party
Candidate
Minor Party
Slate of Electors

1 → 55

*Electors on the slate
with the plurality of the
popular vote in the slate
are activated*

*Obama's
electors*

Sacramento

The State Capital of
California

*Barack Obama's electors
travel to Sacramento to
cast their electoral votes
for the Democratic Party's
candidate*

*Vote of Obama's
electors*

**United States
Congress**

Joint Session

*The President of the
Senate (who is the
sitting Vice-President)
presides over the official
count of the Electoral
College vote*

FIGURE 7.1.1 How the Electoral College Works: The 2008 Election in California

150

But the possibility remains that the electoral vote could install a president from one party and a vice president from another. Explain a sequence of events that would be required to produce that result. Begin with a situation where the candidates for president and vice president each receive fewer than 270 electoral votes, the Democratic Party has a significant majority in the House, and the Republican Party has a significant majority in the Senate.

_____

_____

_____

_____

_____

_____

_____

3. In the 1980 presidential election, forty-one electoral votes were at stake in New York. Ronald Reagan, the Republican Party candidate, received 2,893,831 popular votes statewide, or 46.7 percent of the popular vote. Jimmy Carter, the Democratic Party candidate, received 2,728,372 popular votes in the state, or 44.0 percent of the popular vote. John Anderson was the Independent Party candidate; he received 467,801 popular votes, or 7.5 percent of the popular vote.

   a. According to the rules for awarding Electoral College votes, how were New York's forty-one electoral votes allocated to the candidates?

      Reagan: _____

      Carter: _____

      Anderson: _____

   b. Suppose you knew nothing about the rules for awarding electoral votes and had no access to the popular vote totals in this election. What does the distribution of electoral votes among the three candidates seem to indicate about each candidate's popular support in New York state?

      _____

      _____

      _____

4. Table 7.1.1 on the next page shows the popular vote by state in the 1976 presidential election. Jimmy Carter won a slim majority of the popular vote nationwide and 297 electoral votes. Gerald Ford received 240 electoral votes. Notice that one electoral vote is missing. Mike Padden, an elector in Washington state pledged to Ford, cast his electoral vote for Ronald Reagan. (This faithless elector wished to express his displeasure with the fact that Ford had beat out Reagan for the Republican Party's presidential nomination.)

   Relatively small changes in the popular vote in 1976 could have given Ford the White House. For example, take 5,559 popular votes in Ohio—about one-tenth of 1 percent of the total votes cast in the state—and move them out of Carter's column and into Ford's. Then give Ford 3,687 of Carter's popular votes in Hawaii, about 1 percent of the total votes cast there.

   a. What are the new electoral vote totals?

      Carter: _____

      Ford: _____

TABLE 7.1.1 Popular and Electoral College Votes, Presidential Election 1976

State	Total Popular Vote	Jimmy Carter (D)			Gerald Ford (R)		
		Popular Vote	Percentage of Total Popular Vote	Electoral College Vote	Popular Vote	Percentage of Total Popular Vote	Electoral College Vote
Alabama	1,182,850	659,170	55.7	9	504,070	42.6	
Alaska	123,574	44,058	35.7		71,555	57.9	3
Arizona	742,719	295,602	39.8		418,642	56.4	6
Arkansas	767,535	498,604	65.0	6	267,903	34.9	
California	7,867,117	3,742,284	47.86		3,882,244	49.4	45
Colorado	1,081,554	460,353	42.6		584,367	54.0	7
Connecticut	1,381,526	647,895	46.9		719,261	52.1	8
Delaware	235,834	122,596	52.0	3	109,831	46.6	
DC	168,830	137,818	81.6	3	27,873	16.5	
Florida	3,150,631	1,636,000	51.9	17	1,469,531	46.6	
Georgia	1,467,458	979,409	66.74	12	483,743	33.0	
Hawaii	291,301	147,375	50.6	4	140,003	48.0	
Idaho	344,071	126,549	36.8		204,151	59.3	4
Illinois	4,718,914	2,271,295	48.1		2,364,269	50.1	26
Indiana	2,220,362	1,014,714	45.7		1,183,958	53.3	13
Iowa	1,279,306	619,931	48.5		632,863	49.5	8
Kansas	957,845	430,421	44.9		502,752	52.5	7
Kentucky	1,167,142	615,717	52.8	9	531,852	45.6	
Louisiana	1,278,439	661,365	51.7	10	587,446	46.0	
Maine	483,216	232,279	48.1		236,320	48.9	4
Maryland	1,439,897	759,612	52.8	10	672,661	46.7	
Massachusetts	2,547,558	1,429,475	56.1	14	1,030,276	40.5	
Michigan	3,653,749	1,696,714	46.4		1,893,742	51.8	21
Minnesota	1,949,931	1,070,440	54.9	10	819,395	42.0	
Mississippi	769,361	381,309	49.6	7	366,846	47.7	
Missouri	1,953,600	998,387	51.1	12	927,443	47.5	
Montana	328,734	149,259	45.4		173,703	52.8	4
Nebraska	607,668	233,692	38.5		359,705	59.2	5
Nevada	201,876	92,479	45.8		101,273	50.2	3
New Hampshire	339,618	147,635	43.5		185,935	54.8	4
New Jersey	3,014,472	1,444,653	47.9		1,509,688	50.1	17
New Mexico	418,409	201,148	48.1		211,419	50.5	4
New York	6,534,170	3,389,558	51.9	41	3,100,791	47.5	
North Carolina	1,678,914	927,365	55.2	13	741,960	44.2	
North Dakota	297,188	136,078	45.8		153,470	51.6	3
Ohio	4,111,873	2,011,621	48.9	25	2,000,505	48.7	
Oklahoma	1,092,251	532,442	48.8		545,708	50.0	8

(Continued)

TABLE 7.1.1 Popular and Electoral College Votes, Presidential Election 1976 (*Continued*)

| State | Total Popular Vote | Jimmy Carter (D) | | | | Gerald Ford (R) | | |
		Popular Vote	Percentage of Total Popular Vote	Electoral College Vote	Popular Vote	Percentage of Total Popular Vote	Electoral College Vote
Oregon	1,029,876	490,407	47.6		492,120	47.8	6
Pennsylvania	4,620,787	2,328,677	50.4	27	2,205,604	47.7	
Rhode Island	411,170	227,636	55.4	4	181,249	44.1	
South Carolina	802,583	450,807	56.2	8	346,149	43.1	
South Dakota	300,678	147,068	48.9		151,505	50.4	4
Tennessee	1,476,345	825,879	55.9	10	633,969	42.9	
Texas	4,071,884	2,082,319	51.1	26	1,953,300	48.0	
Utah	541,198	182,110	33.7		337,908	62.4	4
Vermont	187,765	80,954	43.1		102,085	54.4	3
Virginia	1,697,094	813,896	48.0		836,554	49.3	12
Washington	1,555,534	717,323	46.1		777,732	50.0	8
West Virginia	750,964	435,914	58.1	6	314,760	41.9	
Wisconsin	2,104,175	1,040,232	49.4	11	1,004,987	47.8	
Wyoming	156,343	62,239	39.8		92,717	59.3	3
Totals	81,555,889	40,830,763	50.1	297	39,147,793	48.0	240

Note: The votes received by minor-party candidates are not noted.

Source: Dave Leip's Atlas of U.S. Presidential Elections, "Past Presidential Election Results," at www.uselectionatlas.org. Used by permission of Dave Leip.

b. Who is president based on the new Electoral College vote? Why?

_____

_____

_____

c. Where would this election be decided and which candidates have a chance to win the presidency? Explain and support your answer.

_____

_____

_____

_____

5. Table 7.1.2 shows the popular vote by state in the 2000 presidential election. Al Gore won a plurality of the popular vote nationwide. George W. Bush lost the popular vote to Gore but managed to win 271 electoral votes—one more than he needed to be president. If just 269 of Bush's popular votes in Florida had gone to Gore, Gore would have been president.

TABLE 7.1.2 Popular and Electoral College Votes, Presidential Election 2000

State	Total Popular Vote	George W. Bush (R)			Al Gore (D)		
		Popular Vote	Percentage of Total Popular Vote	Electoral College Vote	Popular Vote	Percentage of Total Popular Vote	Electoral College Vote
Alabama	1,666,272	941,173	56.5	9	692,611	41.6	
Alaska	285,560	167,398	58.6	3	79,004	27.7	
Arizona	1,532,016	781,652	51.0	8	685,341	44.7	
Arkansas	921,781	472,940	51.3	6	422,768	45.9	
California	10,965,856	4,567,429	41.7		5,861,203	53.5	54
Colorado	1,741,368	883,748	50.8	8	738,227	42.4	
Connecticut	1,459,525	561,094	38.4		816,015	56.0	8
Delaware	327,622	137,288	41.9		180,068	55.0	3
DC	201,894	18,073	9.0		171,923	85.2	2*
Florida	5,963,110	2,912,790	48.9	25	2,912,253	48.8	
Georgia	2,596,804	1,419,720	54.7	13	1,116,230	43.0	
Hawaii	367,951	137,845	37.5		205,286	55.8	4
Idaho	501,621	336,937	67.2	4	138,637	27.6	
Illinois	4,742,123	2,019,421	42.6		2,589,026	54.6	22
Indiana	2,199,302	1,245,836	56.7	12	901,980	41.0	
Iowa	1,315,563	634,373	48.2		638,517	48.5	7
Kansas	1,072,216	622,332	58.0	6	399,276	37.2	
Kentucky	1,544,187	872,492	56.5	8	638,898	41.4	
Louisiana	1,765,656	927,871	52.6	9	792,344	44.9	
Maine	651,817	286,616	44.0		319,951	49.1	4
Maryland	2,025,480	813,797	40.2		1,145,782	56.6	10
Massachusetts	2,702,984	878,502	32.5		1,616,487	59.8	12
Michigan	4,232,711	1,953,139	46.1		2,170,418	51.3	18
Minnesota	2,438,685	1,109,659	45.5		1,168,266	47.9	10
Mississippi	994,184	572,844	57.6	7	404,614	40.7	
Missouri	2,359,892	1,189,924	50.4	11	1,111,138	47.1	
Montana	410,997	240,178	58.4	3	137,126	33.4	
Nebraska	697,019	433,862	62.3	5	231,780	33.3	
Nevada	608,970	301,575	49.5	4	279,978	46.0	
New Hampshire	569,081	273,559	48.1	4	266,348	46.8	
New Jersey	3,187,226	1,284,173	40.3		1,788,850	56.1	15
New Mexico	598,605	286,417	47.9		286,783	47.9	5
New York	6,821,999	2,403,374	35.2		4,107,697	60.2	33
North Carolina	2,911,262	1,631,163	56.0	14	1,257,692	43.2	
North Dakota	288,256	174,852	60.7	3	95,284	33.1	
Ohio	4,701,998	2,350,363	50.0	21	2,183,628	46.4	
Oklahoma	1,234,229	744,337	60.3	8	474,276	38.4	

(Continued)

TABLE 7.1.2 Popular and Electoral College Votes, Presidential Election 2000 (*Continued*)

State	Total Popular Vote	George W. Bush (R)			Al Gore (D)		
		Popular Vote	Percentage of Total Popular Vote	Electoral College Vote	Popular Vote	Percentage of Total Popular Vote	Electoral College Vote
Oregon	1,533,968	713,577	46.5		720,342	47.0	7
Pennsylvania	4,913,119	2,281,127	46.4		2,485,967	50.6	23
Rhode Island	409,112	130,555	31.9		249,508	61.0	4
South Carolina	1,382,717	785,937	56.8	8	565,561	40.9	
South Dakota	316,269	190,700	60.3	3	118,804	37.6	
Tennessee	2,076,181	1,061,949	51.2	11	981,720	47.3	
Texas	6,407,637	3,799,639	59.3	32	2,433,746	38.0	
Utah	770,754	515,096	66.8	5	203,053	26.3	
Vermont	294,308	119,775	40.7		149,022	50.6	3
Virginia	2,739,447	1,437,490	52.5	13	1,217,290	44.4	
Washington	2,487,433	1,108,864	44.6		1,247,652	50.2	11
West Virginia	648,124	336,475	51.9	5	295,497	45.6	
Wisconsin	2,598,607	1,237,279	47.6		1,242,987	47.8	11
Wyoming	218,351	147,947	67.8	3	60,481	27.7	
Totals	105,401,849	50,455,156	47.9	271	50,997,335	48.4	266

Note: The votes received by minor-party candidates are not noted.

*One Gore elector in Washington, D.C., abstained from voting.

Source: Dave Leip's Atlas of U.S. Presidential Elections, "Past Presidential Election Results," at www.uselectionatlas.org. Used by permission of Dave Leip.

a. In what other state besides Florida did Bush have the smallest margin of victory in the popular vote total?

b. What is the minimum number of popular votes that, if shifted from Bush's column to Gore's, would have made Gore the winner of this state's electoral votes?

c. Would winning this state's electoral votes have made Gore president?

6. Political science professors have long cautioned that in some future presidential election, the winner of the popular vote would not be president. The 2000 election has given those instructors new credibility in the eyes of their students. Even so, it remains difficult for many students to understand how a candidate who loses the nationwide popular vote can win a majority of the Electoral College vote. The answer, of course, is that the winner-take-all feature of the Electoral College distorts the popular vote instead of taking an accurate account of it.

Careful analysis of the simplified two-state election below should reveal why, in the elections of 1888 and 2000, the winners of the popular vote did not win the Oval Office. Apply the rules of the Electoral College when answering the following questions.

- State X has fifteen electoral votes. The Republican candidate received 255,000 popular votes; the Democratic candidate received 250,000 popular votes.
- State Y has five electoral votes. The Republican candidate received 50,000 popular votes; the Democratic candidate received 150,000 popular votes.

    a. Which candidate won the popular vote?

    _____

    b. Which candidate won a majority of the electoral vote?

    _____

    c. To understand the reversal of the popular and Electoral College votes, look for patterns in the popular vote totals within each state and also between the two states. Think about it this way. The Republican candidate in state X won a big prize in the Electoral College vote by winning narrowly in the popular vote. The Democratic candidate in state Y won a small prize in the Electoral College vote by capturing a very wide margin of popular votes. Explain in your own words why the winner of the popular vote did not win the Electoral College vote.

    _____

    _____

    _____

    _____

    _____

    _____

    _____

7. The mechanics of the Electoral College are peculiar. Presidential campaigns must take careful account of those peculiarities and shape their electoral strategies around them. An _electoral strategy_ is the plan a campaign follows to allocate its limited resources—the candidate's time and money, for example. Continuous polling to measure a candidate's competitiveness in particular states helps the campaign decide which states to target and how to allocate campaign resources among those states.

    a. Look at Table 7.1.3 on the next page, which reflects the reapportionment of the House of Representatives based on the 2010 census. What is the minimum number of states a candidate would need to win to capture the White House? Remember that the number of a state's electoral votes equals the number of its representatives in the House plus its two Senate seats.

    _____

    b. No candidate today could win the 270 electoral votes required to be president by investing _all_ the campaign's resources _exclusively_ in the states you identified in question 7a. Why?

    _____

    _____

    _____

    _____

| TABLE 7.1.3 | Population and Representation in the House by State, 2010 Census Data | |

State	Population	Number of Representatives in the House
Alabama	4,802,982	7
Alaska	721,523	1
Arizona	6,412,700	9
Arkansas	2,926,229	4
California	37,341,989	53
Colorado	5,044,930	7
Connecticut	3,581,628	5
Delaware	900,877	1
Florida	18,900,773	27
Georgia	9,727,566	14
Hawaii	1,366,862	2
Idaho	1,573,499	2
Illinois	12,864,380	18
Indiana	6,501,582	9
Iowa	3,053,787	4
Kansas	2,863,813	4
Kentucky	4,350,606	6
Louisiana	4,553,962	6
Maine	1,333,074	2
Maryland	5,789,929	8
Massachusetts	6,559,644	9
Michigan	9,911,626	14
Minnesota	5,314,879	8
Mississippi	2,978,240	4
Missouri	6,011,478	8
Montana	994,416	1
Nebraska	1,831,825	3
Nevada	2,709,432	4
New Hampshire	1,321,445	2
New Jersey	8,807,501	12
New Mexico	2,067,273	3
New York	19,421,055	27
North Carolina	9,565,781	13
North Dakota	675,905	1
Ohio	11,568,495	16
Oklahoma	3,764,882	5
Oregon	3,848,606	5
Pennsylvania	12,734,905	18

(Continued)

TABLE 7.1.3	Population and Representation in the House by State, 2010 Census Data (*Continued*)

State	Population	Number of Representatives in the House
Rhode Island	1,055,247	2
South Carolina	4,645,975	7
South Dakota	819,761	1
Tennessee	6,375,431	9
Texas	25,268,418	36
Utah	2,770,765	4
Vermont	630,337	1
Virginia	8,037,736	11
Washington	6,753,369	10
West Virginia	1,859,815	3
Wisconsin	5,698,230	8
Wyoming	568,300	1
Total*	309,183,463	435

*This is the total 2010 apportionment population. The populations of the District of Columbia, Puerto Rico, and the U.S. island areas are excluded from the apportionment population because they do not have voting members in the House of Representatives.

8. Research carried out by Barack Obama's campaign in the months leading up to the 2008 presidential election showed conclusively—barring some unforeseeable event—that whatever resources he might commit to the state, Obama had no chance of winning the popular vote in Texas on November 9. Obama's research was confirmed by independent public opinion polls, one of which showed Obama trailing John McCain by 19 percentage points in early October. There was precedent: No Democratic Party presidential nominee had won Texas's electoral votes since Jimmy Carter in 1976.

Assume the role of chief campaign adviser to Barack Obama during the 2008 presidential election. Recognizing that Obama is likely to meet defeat at the hands of voters in this solidly Republican state, would you direct a substantial amount of the campaign's resources to Texas in the month before the election in an attempt to improve Obama's position? Cite specific features of the Electoral College to explain and support your reasoning.

_____

_____

_____

_____

_____

_____

_____

9. Dispense with the Electoral College. Assume that the president is directly elected by a plurality of the popular vote nationwide. Under this system, every popular vote counts, whatever a candidate's prospects of winning a plurality of the popular vote in any particular state.

Consider again the situation posed in question 8. Under the direct election system, would you direct a substantial amount of the campaign's resources to Texas in the month before the election in an attempt to improve Obama's position? Explain and support your answer.

_____

_____

_____

_____

_____

10. Return to the Electoral College system for electing the president and assume that you are managing Barack Obama's campaign in California. Early in October, about a month before the election, your polls show Obama with 60 percent support in the state and John McCain with 36 percent. This is no surprise: California has voted Democratic in every presidential election since 1992. At a meeting on October 10, the campaign's director of political advertising announces that he has developed and tested a series of television advertisements designed to boost Obama's standing in California over the next three weeks. He claims that the ads will increase Obama's lead to 70 percent by the day of the election, reducing McCain's standing to 28 percent. The ads will cost $5 million. Assume that the polling projections are accurate, that the campaign can afford the $5 million expenditure, and that you have it on good authority that McCain will not be presenting you with any surprises in California before the election. Should you authorize the $5 million expenditure for the ads? Cite specific features of the Electoral College to explain and support your reasoning.

_____

_____

_____

_____

_____

_____

_____

11. Dispense again with the Electoral College and assume that the president is directly elected by a plurality of the popular vote nationwide. Should you authorize the $5 million expenditure described in question 10? Explain and support your answer.

_____

_____

_____

_____

_____

12. Many advocates of Electoral College reform argue that the winner-take-all system for awarding electoral votes should be replaced by a *proportional system* that would allocate electoral votes to candidates according to the percentage of the popular vote received in each state. For example, proportional awarding in California in the 2000 election would have netted George W. Bush twenty-three electoral votes and Al Gore twenty-nine. California's other two electoral votes would have gone to minor-party candidates. What effect would proportional awarding have on the aspects of presidential elections identified in the following situations? Explain and support your answers.

    a. On the prospects of minor-party candidates:

_____

_____

_____

_____

_____

    b. On the extent to which candidates target and contest states such as California and Texas:

_____

_____

_____

_____

_____

    c. On the likelihood that no candidate receives a majority of the Electoral College vote and that the election has to be decided by the House:

_____

_____

_____

_____

13. Public opinion polls consistently show that 70 percent or more of Americans believe that the presidential candidate receiving the most popular votes nationwide should win the presidency. A nationwide popular election for president has not been established because it has been widely assumed that a constitutional amendment would be required to eliminate the Electoral College. The National Popular Vote bill seeks to establish the popular election of the president without a constitutional amendment. Go to www.nationalpopularvote.com, click on "Explanation," and read the one-page description of the National Popular Vote bill. Next click on "FAQ" and read "What is 'The Agreement Among the States to Elect the President by National Popular Vote' and How Would It Work?"

    Web addresses sometimes change. If you can't locate a website, try an external search (e.g., Google) to find the website. Configurations within a website often change. If you can't find a particular link or article, for example, try an internal search of the website as well as an external search. Be resourceful! If you still can't find what you're searching for, move on to the next question.

    a. Summarize the National Popular Vote bill and explain how it would work.

_____

_____

_____

_____

_____

_____

_____

b. How would the National Popular Vote bill change current Electoral College–based campaign strategies that emphasize the importance of competitive (swing) states?

_____

_____

_____

_____

_____

c. Click on "Answering Myths" and read "4.1 MYTH: Faithless presidential electors would be a problem under the National Popular Vote compact." California has voted for the Democratic candidate in every presidential election since 1992. Assume that the National Popular Vote bill is enacted and in place for the 2016 presidential election. Also assume that the Democratic presidential candidate in 2016 receives a plurality of the popular vote in California and that the Republican candidate receives a plurality of the popular vote nationwide. Explain how California would cast its 55 electoral votes under the system established by the National Popular Vote bill.

_____

_____

_____

_____

_____

EXERCISE 7.2   Evaluating Presidential Performance

INTRODUCTION

No one in the world is evaluated as searchingly, as frequently, or by so many as the president of the United States. A sitting president is scrutinized twenty-four hours a day. The product of all that scrutiny is public opinion, a fickle commodity at best. President Lyndon Johnson's approval rating, for example, was as high as 76 percent in his first year in office, but it later fell to 39 percent—dragged down by the widespread perception that the war in Vietnam had become a quagmire. And the scrutiny doesn't end when a president leaves office: Historians and political scientists are at the ready to dissect a former president's every action and decision for centuries to come.

All presidents attempt to shape current and future assessments of their performance. Early in his first term, President Bill Clinton met in the Oval Office with Richard Reeves, an author and historian who had published a study of John Kennedy's presidency.[1] Clinton discussed with Reeves the components of presidential greatness, presumably with the purpose of improving Clinton's own performance. To cement Kennedy's place in history, members of his family and his inner circle of advisers worked diligently after the assassination to perpetuate a number of myths about the Kennedy presidency. Richard Nixon, after resigning from office in disgrace, authored several books that he hoped would rehabilitate his reputation and encourage the public and scholars alike to see him as a great statesman.

People's perceptions of presidential performance are shaped by their expectations, which increased dramatically in the twentieth century. Before about 1900, the national government played an insignificant role in the daily lives of most Americans: Local and state governments provided the few services that governments rendered. It simply would not have occurred to most Americans to look to the president as the source of their prosperity and security.

Public expectations began to grow as Presidents Theodore Roosevelt, William Taft, and Woodrow Wilson led the national government to take on new responsibilities to ensure the nation's welfare. Roosevelt's crusades against abuses by the meat-packing and drug industries, for example, captured the imagination of many Americans and began to reshape their view of the presidency. But no president did more to inflate public expectations than Franklin D. Roosevelt (FDR), who promised that under his leadership the national government would restore security and stability to Americans mired in the Great Depression. Through his skillful use of press conferences and fireside chats broadcast on radio, FDR personalized the presidency and taught the nation to expect a great deal more from the office and its occupant.

In time, inflated by the rhetoric of politicians and the constant glare of the media, public expectations of presidents became unrealistically high. It may be comforting to think that presidents can take the reins of power and dispatch the nation's problems with the stroke of an executive order. But presidential power is much more constrained than that—limited by separation of powers, checks and balances, federalism, public opinion, and many other factors. An electorate that expects the president to work miracles is always going to be disappointed.

We expect public opinion of presidential performance to change day to day. Scholars' evaluations of presidential leadership also change, albeit more slowly. Early studies of President Herbert Hoover, for example, portrayed him as a rigid ideologue who was overwhelmed by the economic collapse in 1929 and incapable of making a credible response to the subsequent crisis. In the 1970s, historians began to reexamine Hoover's performance in office.[2] Today, many scholars credit Hoover with making a vigorous, if insufficient, response to the crisis. Those scholars acknowledge the constraints Hoover faced and the unprecedented use he made of the tools available to him. What accounts for the change in thinking? The passing of time yielded historical perspective and judgment. Until the 1970s, scholars seemed unable to evaluate Hoover without comparing him with his successor, FDR. Roosevelt's unprecedented use of the national government—not to mention his personality, his charm,

---

[1]*President Kennedy: Profile of Power* (New York: Simon & Schuster, 1993).

[2]For example, see Joan Hoff Wilson, *Herbert Hoover: Forgotten Progressive* (Boston: Little, Brown, 1975).

and his charisma—obscured Hoover's innovative response to the economic crisis. Only decades after Hoover left office were historians able to bring him out from Roosevelt's shadow and judge him on his own merits.

For scholars evaluating presidential performance, time yields not only perspective and judgment but also a more complete record—something essential to informed assessment. Executive branch departments and agencies, particularly the State Department and the Central Intelligence Agency (CIA), are notoriously slow in declassifying documents. But as the documentary record is filled in, new information may lead scholars to reassess presidential performance. In the 1990s, for example, the Kennedy and Johnson presidential libraries released tape recordings these presidents secretly made in the Oval Office. Diligent historians have performed the difficult task of transcribing the tapes.[3] In Kennedy's case, the tapes reveal the president's skill and luck in negotiating the Cuban missile crisis and bringing the world back from the brink of nuclear destruction. In Johnson's case, the tapes point to the president's desperate search for a politically acceptable alternative to the mounting escalation of the war in Vietnam.

Political scientists, historians, and journalists have long debated which criteria to employ in assessing presidential performance, how to weigh those criteria to produce a balanced evaluation, and how to rank a president in relation to other presidents. The modern version of presidential assessment was pioneered in 1948, in a study by Arthur Schlesinger Sr. His son, Arthur Schlesinger Jr., produced a similar study in 1996.[4] More recently, in 2000 and in 2009, C-SPAN surveyed 65 historians and presidential experts, asking them to evaluate the presidents in a number of categories: public persuasion, crisis leadership, economic management, moral authority, international relations, administrative skills, relations with Congress, vision/agenda setting, pursuit of equal justice for all, and performance within the context of his times.

ASSIGNMENT

Table 7.2.1 on next page shows data from the 2009 C-SPAN survey and places the presidents since Abraham Lincoln in historical context. Questions 1 to 3 are based on the table.

1. List the presidents who served during periods when the level of crisis or challenge was low and who attained a near-great or great ranking.

2. What is the highest ranking achieved by a president who served when the level of crisis or challenge was low?

3. What connection exists between the crises or challenges a president faces in office and the possibility of his achieving near-great or great status?

[3]Ernest R. May and Philip D. Zelikow, *The Kennedy Tapes: Inside the White House During the Cuban Missile Crisis* (Cambridge, MA: Harvard University Press, 1997); and Michael R. Beschloss, *Reaching for Glory: Lyndon Johnson's Secret White House Tapes, 1964–1965* (New York: Simon & Schuster, 2001).
[4]"The Ultimate Approval Rating," *New York Times Magazine,* December 16, 1996, p. 46.

TABLE 7.2.1   Rankings of Presidential Performance, 1860–2008

Term of Office	Important Issues or Events	Level of Crisis or Challenge	President	Ranking: C-SPAN Survey 2009	General Assessment
1861–1865	Civil War	Extreme	Lincoln	1	Great
1865–1868	Reconstruction	High	Andrew Johnson	41	Failure
1869–1876	Reconstruction	Moderate	Grant	23	Average
1877-1896	Industrialization, urbanization	Low	Hayes	33	Below average
	Westward expansion	Low	Garfield*	28	
		Low	Arthur	32	Below average
		Low	Cleveland	21	Average
		Low	Harrison	30	Below average
1897–1901	Spanish-American War	High	McKinley	16	Above average
1901–1908	Reform, foreign policy	High	Theodore Roosevelt	4	Near great
1909–1912	Reform	Moderate	Taft	24	Average
1913–1920	Reform, World War I	Extreme	Wilson	9	Near great
1921–1923	Economic expansion	Low	Harding	38	Failure
1923–1928	Economic expansion	Low	Coolidge	26	Average
1929–1932	Economic depression	High	Hoover	34	Below average
1933–1945	Great Depression, World War II	Extreme	Franklin D. Roosevelt	3	Great
1945–1952	Cold war, demobilization, Korean War	High	Truman	5	Near great
1953–1960	Cold war, economic expansion	Moderate	Eisenhower	8	Near great
1961–1963	Cold war, civil rights	High	Kennedy	6	Near great
1963–1968	Vietnam War, civil rights, Great Society	Very High	Lyndon Johnson	11	Above average
1969–1974	Vietnam War, Watergate	Very High	Nixon	27	Below average
1974–1976	Cold war	Moderate	Ford	22	Average
1977–1980	Economic recession, energy crisis	Moderate	Carter	25	Average
1981–1988	Cold war	Moderate	Reagan	10	Near great
1989–1992	Gulf war, economic recession	Moderate	George H. W. Bush	18	Above average
1993–2000	Foreign policy, impeachment	Moderate	Clinton	15	Average
2001–2008	9/11 terrorist attack, Wars in Afghanistan and Iraq	Very high	George W. Bush	36	Failure

*James A. Garfield, elected in 1880, was shot several months into his term by an angry office seeker and died two months later. Garfield served as president for a little over six months. The early death of this president makes him difficult to evaluate and rank.

4. Read the essay by Michael Kinsley, "The Power of One."[5] (You can find the essay on the Web.) In Kinsley's view, what is the most important component of presidential leadership? Cite language from the essay to support your answer.

_____

_____

_____

5. Read the essay by Benjamin Schwarz, "Bush Fibbed, and That Might Be OK."[6] (You can find the essay on the Web.) In Schwarz's view, what is the most important component of presidential leadership? Cite language from the essay to support your answer.

_____

_____

_____

6. The emergence of any single document or piece of information bearing on a president's performance is unlikely to alter scholars' assessment of that president decisively. Of course, we can imagine exceptions to that general rule. For example, almost since the day the Japanese attacked Pearl Harbor (December 7, 1941), some have accused President Franklin D. Roosevelt of knowing in advance that the attack was coming and purposely leaving the nation vulnerable so that he could galvanize public opinion behind his objective: to join the world war on the side of the Allies and to defeat Hitler. A clear majority of Americans did not want to enter the war, and Roosevelt, so the argument goes, recognized that only an attack by a foreign power against U.S. territory and citizens—2,400 people died at Pearl Harbor—would shake the public from its isolationist stupor.

Most scholars agree that the charges against Roosevelt are contradicted by the documentary record and are unlikely ever to be substantiated. But suppose the scholars are mistaken; suppose the charges are proved true. In your view, how would the revelation that Roosevelt had prior knowledge of the attack on Pearl Harbor affect scholars' assessment of his presidency?

This question is not as simple as it seems at first glance. One author who believes Roosevelt did know about the attack in advance argues that the president was right to sacrifice Pearl Harbor to achieve a greater good: the defeat of Hitler.[7] Address this author's argument in your answer. Explain and support your position.

_____

_____

_____

_____

_____

_____

_____

_____

[5]_Los Angeles Times,_ April 14, 2003.

[6]_Los Angeles Times,_ October 30, 2003.

[7]Robert B. Stinnett, _Day of Deceit: The Truth about FDR and Pearl Harbor_ (New York: Free Press, 2000). David Kahn published a devastating critique of Stinnett's book in the _New York Review of Books,_ November 2, 2000.

Questions 7 to 10 are based on the 2009 C-SPAN Survey of Presidential Leadership, which you'll find at www.americanpresidents.org. Notice that you can examine the total scores and overall ranking for each president as well as select from the list of individual leadership characteristics such as public persuasion and crisis leadership.

Web addresses sometimes change. If you can't locate a website, try an external search (e.g., Google) to find the website. Configurations within a website often change. If you can't find a particular link or article, for example, try an internal search of the website as well as an external search. Be resourceful! If you still can't find what you're searching for, move on to the next question.

7. Click on the list of historians and presidential experts who participated in the survey. Choose one and conduct a Web search to find his or her qualifications. For example, does this participant hold a position at a major university? Have they published any studies that would qualify them to participate in the survey? Write the results of your search here.

_____

_____

_____

_____

_____

8. a. Click on Index. Select Lyndon Johnson. According to the 2009 Category Ranking, in which two categories was Johnson ranked as the second greatest president?

_____

_____

b. In which category is Johnson ranked lowest? What is the number of his ranking in relation to the other presidents?

_____

c. What is the numeric gap between Johnson's highest and lowest rankings?

_____

d. Search the Web for information on Johnson's political career and on his accomplishments and failures as president that would help explain why he is ranked so high in two categories and so low in the other.

_____

_____

_____

_____

_____

_____

9. Select two other presidents of your choice. Identify the two presidents, specify the category in which each achieved the highest and lowest ranking under the 2009 Category Ranking, specify the number of his ranking in relation to other presidents, and calculate the numeric gap between the highest and lowest rankings.

a. President 1:

Highest category and number for that ranking: _____

_____

Lowest category and number for that ranking: _____

_____

Numeric gap between highest and lowest ranking: _____

b. President 2:

Highest category and number for that ranking: _____

_____

Lowest category and number for that ranking: _____

_____

Numeric gap between highest and lowest ranking: _____

c. Was the numeric gap between either of your presidents' highest and lowest scores as great as the gap for Johnson's?

_____

10. a. One of the individual leadership categories in the C-Span survey is moral authority. What is moral authority? Search the Web and write a definition here that you think applies to political leaders.

_____

_____

_____

_____

_____

b. According to the 2009 category ranking on moral authority how are Bill Clinton and John Kennedy ranked in relation to other presidents?

Clinton's numeric ranking: _____

Kennedy's numeric ranking: _____

c. Clinton is known to have had oral sex with an intern in the White House. Kennedy is known to have had sex with a number of women other than his wife in the White House. Can you think of one or more reasons why Kennedy's ranking on moral authority would be so much higher than Clinton's?

_____

_____

_____

_____

_____

11. In February 2010, the Gallup poll asked over 1,000 adults nationwide this question: "Who do you regard as the greatest United States president?" Respondents to the poll ranked the top seven presidents as follows:

1. Ronald Reagan
2. Abraham Lincoln
3. Bill Clinton
4. John Kennedy
5. George Washington
6. Franklin Roosevelt
7. Barack Obama

Compare the public's ranking of the top seven presidents with the ranking by historians and presidential experts in the C-Span survey using the 2009 Category Ranking.

a. What's the numeric gap between Reagan's ranking in the Gallop poll and his ranking in the C-Span survey?

_____

b. For which of the top seven presidents in the Gallop poll is the gap with the C-Span survey the greatest? Can you think of any factors that might account for such a large gap?

_____

_____

_____

_____

_____

EXERCISE 7.3   The Power of the Sword

INTRODUCTION

Presidents today own the power of the sword. Constitutional checks and balances have repeatedly proven too frail to restrain the war-making power of the executive branch. An order from the commander-in-chief alone will expend the nation's treasure in combat, spill its citizens' blood on foreign battlefields, inflict the pinpoint destruction of a terrorist safe house, or annihilate the world in a nuclear holocaust. Presidents have wielded this awesome power with mixed results. President Harry Truman's war in Korea, for example, is generally thought to have advanced national security; President Lyndon Johnson's war in Vietnam, by consensus opinion, undermined it.

The framers of the Constitution did not anticipate the concentration of nearly unchecked war-making power in the president's hands. Delegates at the Constitutional Convention took for granted that the power of the sword would be divided between the legislative and executive branches. Vesting all war power in the legislature, as the Articles of Confederation did, would dull the new government's ability to respond decisively to foreign threats. Vesting the power exclusively in the executive, as the English did, risked the president embarking unilaterally on misguided military adventures abroad. The delegates, then, awarded Congress the power to "declare war" and the president the power of "Commander in Chief." But each branch's war powers are wider than these narrow phrases suggest. In Article I, Section 8, the Constitution confers on Congress the power to provide for the common defense of the nation, to raise and support an army and navy, and to fund military operations. Article II, Section 1 grants broad "executive power" to the president, suggesting to some that he would lead in determining matters of peace and war. In addition, the president's oath of office binds him to "defend the Constitution of the United States."

Just how the two branches would share the war power had to be worked out in practice. One issue to be determined: the extent of executive authority absent a declaration of war from Congress. By commanding military force short of war to protect national security, the nation's first presidents offered an expansive definition of executive war power. President George Washington sent troops to fight Native Americans in the Battle of Fallen Timbers and his own citizens in the Whiskey Rebellion. There was no declaration of war from Congress in either case. In response to French raids on U.S. shipping in the West Indies, President John Adams waged an undeclared naval war against France from 1798 to 1800, with some engagements as far afield as the Indian Ocean and the Mediterranean Sea. President Thomas Jefferson fought the First Barbary War from 1801 to 1805, dispatching U.S. warships to the Mediterranean with orders to destroy the Barbary pirates' vessels and blockade Tripoli. Because Congress did not declare war against France or the Barbary pirates, neither Adams nor Jefferson exercised their commander-in-chief power under a declaration of war by Congress. Both presidents, however, did request and receive congressional authorization for the military operations they conducted. During the republic's history, presidents have employed armed force abroad over 300 times.[1]

The legislative branch has exercised its war power less frequently. Congress declared war for the first time in 1812 against the British, the second declaration came in 1846 against Mexico, and the third came in 1898 against Spain. World Wars I and II were the only declarations of war in the twentieth century, and there have been none since. Neither did Congress advance an expansive interpretation of its war power. The legislature might have claimed that the power to *authorize* war entailed the power to *prosecute* it, even to determine a war's aims, scope, pace, and the deployment of troops. But Congress has generally left these matters to the commander-in-chief. Why?

The legislature is inherently maladapted—institutionally and politically—to make war. Congress's bicameral division, its size, the diversity of its members' views, and its generally reactive posture make it a poor competitor with the energy and vigor of a singular commander-in-chief. In the post–World War II era, Congress's lack of instantaneous access to classified information gathered by executive branch agencies and the development of intercontinental ballistic missiles have constrained the legislature. Who besides the president could decide—in only

---

[1]For a list and brief description of the use of armed force abroad, see Congressional Research Service, "Instances of Use of United States Armed Forces Abroad, 1798–2009," January 2010, at opencrs.com/document/RL32170/.

minutes—whether to launch U.S. nuclear weapons? In addition, the imperative of political self-preservation has tempered Congress's desire to take the nation to war. Military debacles yank down the public approval ratings of government officeholders and institutions. From the legislative perspective, it is better to let the president take the fall. Finally, consider this: What if the House and Senate voted a declaration of war and the commander-in-chief refused to lead the charge? A troubling prospect indeed.

More often than declaring war, Congress has enacted so-called conditional resolutions that authorize the president to use armed force, subject to some specified limitation. Conditional resolutions do not delegate the legislature's power to the executive, but rather provide Congress's assent to military actions that the commander-in-chief undertakes on his own constitutional authority.

When Iraq invaded and occupied Kuwait in 1990, President George H. W. Bush requested a congressional resolution supporting the use of force to implement United Nations Security Council demands that Iraq withdraw. Congress complied, but it imposed this condition: Prior to using military force, the president must report that he had exhausted all diplomatic and other peaceful means to achieve compliance with UN resolutions.

After the September 11, 2001, attacks on the World Trade Center and the Pentagon, Congress passed a resolution authorizing the president

> to use all necessary and appropriate force against those nations, organizations, or persons he determines planned, authorized, committed, or aided the terrorist attacks that occurred on September 11, 2001, or harbored such organizations or persons, in order to prevent any future acts of international terrorism against the United States by such nations, organizations, or persons.

Note that this resolution does not contain the type of conditional clause found in the 1990 resolution and that its authorization of military action against unspecified "organizations or persons" is sweeping and unprecedented.

In the summer of 2002, President George W. Bush began to move toward a second war with Iraq, arguing that its possession of weapons of mass destruction posed a threat to the United States. In October, Congress authorized the president to use military force against Iraq, but only after he determined that measures short of war would not protect the United States, and that the use of force was consistent with the war on terrorism.[2]

Among conditional resolutions, the Tonkin Gulf Resolution of 1964 is notorious.[3] President Lyndon Johnson informed the nation on August 4, 1964, that North Vietnamese patrol boats in the Gulf of Tonkin had twice attacked U.S. destroyers on routine patrol there. The next day, Johnson asked Congress to go on record supporting in advance whatever military response he deemed necessary. The resolution stated that "Congress approves and supports the determination of the President, as Commander-in-Chief, to take all necessary measures to repel any armed attack against the Forces of the United States and to prevent further aggression." No conditions were imposed. The vote in the House was 416–0 and in the Senate 82–2. By 1967, Johnson had committed over 500,000 troops to the war in Vietnam. Many members of Congress regretted signing this so-called blank check, which they came to believe had allowed Johnson to escalate the conflict far beyond what anyone anticipated in 1964. But much "postgame" congressional criticism of the Tonkin Gulf Resolution was mere political posturing; after all, Congress annually funded every step of the escalation and, by the end of the war, approved drafting over 2.7 million Americans to fight in Vietnam.

In 1968, Senator William Fulbright, Chair of the Senate Foreign Relations Committee, held hearings on the Gulf of Tonkin incident, which established that Johnson had misrepresented the

[2]The 1991 resolution was titled "Authorization of Use of Military Force Against Iraq Resolution." The vote in the House was 250–183; in the Senate, it was 52–47. The 2001 resolution was called "Authorization for Use of Military Force." The vote in the House was 420–1; in the Senate, it was 98–0. The 2002 resolution was titled "Authorization for Use of Military Force Against Iraq Resolution of 2002." The vote in the House was 296–133; in the Senate, it was 77–23.

[3]For an analysis of the War Powers Resolution (WPR), including a list and brief description of presidents' use of armed force since 1973, see Congressional Research Service, "The War Powers Resolution: After Thirty-Six Years," April 2010, at opencrs.com/document/R41199/2010-04-22/.

event and had deceived Congress.[4] The war in Vietnam was so unpopular by 1968 that Johnson declined to seek his own party's nomination to run in the November election. Winning that election and taking office in January 1969, President Richard Nixon continued to wage war, even after Congress repealed the Tonkin Gulf Resolution in 1971. By January 1973, when the United States signed a cease-fire agreement with North Vietnam, 20,553 Americans had died under Nixon's prosecution of the conflict. The total number of Americans killed in the war was about 58,000.

In November 1973, Congress overrode Nixon's veto and passed into law the War Powers Resolution (WPR). (An excerpt from the law is provided as Reading 7.3.3.) Supporters claimed that the WPR would rein in the president's runaway war making, in their view the cause of the debacle in Vietnam. Opponents, including every president since the enactment of the WPR, claimed that the law was a brazenly unconstitutional infringement on the power of the commander-in-chief. Today, some view the WPR as a principled—if unsuccessful—effort by Congress to recapture the war power it had ceded to the executive; others see the WPR as a device to absolve Congress further from political responsibility for military failures.

Whatever the intent and motives of the supporters of the WPR, today the United States is vulnerable to attacks that the framers of the Constitution could not have anticipated. Perhaps more than any other factor, the impress of this vulnerability on the nation's psyche helps explain why Americans accept the president's exercise of sweeping war-making power. Yet for many the matter remains troubling. By escaping the constitutional restraint that war-making power be shared with the legislature, it has effectively become the president's alone—the most potent in his arsenal of powers and a foundation of the modern presidency. This concentration of the war-making power in the presidency has eroded the system of checks and balances by which the framers intended to thwart tyranny. The war on terrorism has energized debate on how the power of the sword should properly be shared between the legislative and executive branches. Whether the fight against terrorism leads to a rebalancing of the war power or to even greater concentration in the commander-in-chief remains to be seen.

ASSIGNMENT

1. Examine the chart titled "Categorizing and Quantifying the Use of Armed Force Abroad" on the next page. For each period specified in the left-hand column, calculate the average number of times *per year* that the United States deployed armed force abroad. To make the calculation, divide the number of times armed force was deployed abroad during each period by the number of years in the period. The calculation for the first period, 1788–Civil War, is 65 divided by 78 equals 0.8 times per year. Enter your calculations in the chart's third column.

2. For each period specified in the left-hand column of the chart, calculate the ratio of unilateral presidential deployment of armed force abroad to deployments authorized by Congress. We'll call this the presidential dominance ratio. To make the calculation, divide the number of unilateral presidential deployments by the number of deployments authorized by Congress for each period. The calculation for the first period, 1788–Civil War, is 65 divided by 6 equals 10.8 (round up to 11), for a ratio of 11:1, meaning that the president unilaterally deployed armed force abroad eleven times for every one time that Congress authorized it. Enter your calculations in the chart's right-hand column.

The data in the chart indicate a steady increase since 1788 in the number of military deployments per year, almost all stemming from unilateral presidential action. In *quantitative* terms, the president's use of the war power has far outstripped that of Congress. But the data in the chart don't tell us anything about the *qualitative* aspect of unilateral presidential deployments. In assessing the gravitation of war powers into the president's hands, one wants to investigate not merely the frequency of the president's use of armed force but also how the purpose and nature of presidential military deployments have changed over time. For example, if one were to find that

---

[4]The hearings determined, among other things, that the USS *Maddox* was not on routine patrol, but rather on an intelligence mission to some extent coordinated with covert South Vietnamese patrol boat raids against North Vietnamese coastal installations. Scholars continue to debate whether the second attack by the North Vietnamese against the *Maddox* and the *C. Turner Joy* on August 4 actually occurred. (The first attack on August 2 against the *Maddox* is well documented.) For a major study of the incidents, which concludes that the second attack did not occur, see Edwin E. Moise, *Tonkin Gulf and the Escalation of the Vietnam War* (Chapel Hill: University of North Carolina Press, 1996).

Chart: Categorizing and Quantifying the Use of Armed Force Abroad

Period (and Length)	Total Number of Times Armed Force Deployed Abroad	Average Number of Deployments per Year	Number of Declarations of War by Congress	Number of Conditional Use of Force Resolutions Passed by Congress*	Number of Unilateral Presidential Deployments	Presidential Dominance Ratio
1788–Civil War (78 years)	65	0.8	2	4	59	11:1
1866–Spanish-American War (34 years)	34	1	1	0	33	34:1
1899–World War II (47 years)	69	1.5	8†	0	61	9:1
1946–Second Iraq War (through 2009, 64 years)	163	2.5	0	7	156	23:1

*Congressional Research Service, "Declarations of War and Authorizations for the Use of Military Force: Historical Background and Legal Implications," March, 2007, at opencrs.com/document/RL31133/.

†During World War I, Congress voted separate declarations of war against Germany and Austria-Hungary in 1917. During World War II, Congress voted separate declarations of war against Japan, Germany, and Italy (in 1941), and against Bulgaria, Hungary, and Romania (in 1942).

174

early in the republic's history, presidential deployments of armed force tended to be long, costly, drawn-out affairs, and that today—in contrast—presidential war making tends to be quick and surgical, then one might be less alarmed by the executive's monopoly of the war power. Examine Reading 7.3.1. This reading describes five unilateral presidential deployments of armed force from the period before the Civil War and five examples from the period after World War II. Questions 3 and 4 ask you to compare and contrast the different examples.

READING 7.3.1
Descriptions of Unilateral Presidential Military Deployments of American Troops[5]

Five examples of deployments from the pre–Civil War period:

1813–1814, **Marguesas Islands.** U.S. forces built a fort on the island of Nukahiva to protect three prize ships that had been captured from the British.

1818, **Oregon.** The USS *Ontario,* dispatched from Washington, landed at the Columbia River and in August took possession of Oregon territory. Britain had conceded sovereignty, but Russia and Spain asserted claims to the area.

1843, November 29 to December 16, **Africa.** Four U.S. vessels demonstrated and landed various parties (one of 200 marines and sailors) to discourage piracy and the slave trade along the Ivory Coast and to punish attacks by the residents on U.S. sailors and shipping.

1854, July 9 to 15, **Nicaragua.** Naval forces bombarded and burned San Juan del Norte (Greytown) to avenge an insult to the U.S. minister to Nicaragua.

1858, January 2 to 27, **Uruguay.** Forces from two U.S. warships landed to protect U.S. property during a revolution in Montevideo.

Five examples of deployments from the post–World War II period:

1948, **Berlin.** After the Soviet Union established a land blockade of the U.S., British, and French sectors of the city of Berlin on June 24, 1948, President Harry Truman ordered the military to supply the city by air. A number of allies joined the United States in this effort. From June 1948 to May 1949—when the blockade was lifted—the Berlin airlift delivered over 1.5 million tons of supplies to the 2.5 million citizens of West Berlin.

1950–1953, **Korea.** In response to the North Korean invasion of South Korea, President Truman ordered U.S. air, naval, and ground forces into action against North Korea. Fourteen other United Nations members sent military units into action. U.S. forces deployed in Korea exceeded 300,000 during the last year of the conflict. Over 36,600 U.S. military were killed in action. Truman's commitment of military forces was by far the largest to date without a declaration of war from Congress. The deployment was sanctioned, however, by United Nations resolutions.

1962, **Cuba.** In mid-October, President John Kennedy was informed of Soviet efforts to station nuclear armed missiles in Cuba. In response, Kennedy ordered the U.S. Navy to enforce a "quarantine" preventing further shipments of Soviet military equipment to Cuba. Kennedy ordered that Soviet ships defying the quarantine be attacked. Kennedy's "quarantine" was in fact a naval blockade. Kennedy called it a quarantine because, according to international law, a blockade was an act of war. After very high-stakes negotiations, Soviet Premier Nikita Khrushchev agreed to withdraw the missiles.

---

[5]Some of these examples are taken from Congressional Research Service, "Instances of Use of United States Armed Forces Abroad, 1798-2009," January 2010, at opencrs.com/document/RL32170/ and from Congressional Research Service, "The War Powers Resolution: After Thirty-Six Years," April 2010, at opencrs.com/document/R41199/2010-04-22/.

1988, **Panama.** In mid-March and April 1988, during a period of instability in Panama and as pressure grew for Panamanian military leader General Manuel Noriega to resign, the United States sent 1,000 troops to Panama to "further safeguard the canal, U.S. lives, property and interests in the area." The forces supplemented 10,000 U.S. military personnel already in Panama.

1999, **Bosnia.** On January 19, 1999, by letter, President Clinton notified Congress that, "consistent with the War Powers Resolution" and pursuant to his authority as commander-in-chief, he was continuing to authorize the use of combat-equipped U.S. armed force in Bosnia and other states in the region to participate in and support the NATO-led Stabilization Force. He noted that U.S. SFOR military personnel totaled about 6,900, with about 2,300 U.S. military personnel deployed to Hungary, Croatia, Italy, and other regional states. Also, some 350 U.S. military personnel remain deployed in the former Yugoslav Republic of Macedonia as part of the UN Preventative Deployment Force.

3. How does the purpose or objective of unilateral presidential military deployments prior to the Civil War differ from those following World War II?

_____

_____

_____

_____

_____

4. How does the amount of military force applied by the president prior to the Civil War differ from that applied after World War II?

_____

_____

_____

Questions 5 to 10 are based on Reading 7.3.2, which includes excerpts from the WPR.

READING 7.3.2
Excerpts from the War Powers Resolution

Public Law 93-148, passed over President's veto November 7, 1973

JOINT RESOLUTION Concerning the war powers of Congress and the President.

Resolved by the Senate and House of Representatives of the United States of America in Congress assembled,

SHORT TITLE

Section 1. This joint resolution may be cited as the "War Powers Resolution."

PURPOSE AND POLICY

Sec. 2. (a) It is the purpose of this joint resolution to fulfill the intent of the framers of the Constitution of the United States and insure that the collective judgment of both the Congress and the President will apply to the introduction of United States Armed Forces into hostilities, or into situations where imminent involvement in hostilities is clearly indicated by the circumstances, and to the continued use of such forces in hostilities or in such situations.

(b) Under article I, section 8, of the Constitution, it is specifically provided that the Congress shall have the power to make all laws necessary and proper for carrying into execution, not only its own powers but also all other powers vested by the Constitution in the Government of the United States, or in any department or officer thereof.

(c) The constitutional powers of the President as Commander-in-Chief to introduce United States Armed Forces into hostilities, or into situations where imminent involvement in hostilities is clearly indicated by the circumstances, are exercised only pursuant to (1) a declaration of war, (2) specific statutory authorization [meaning a law passed by Congress], or (3) a national emergency created by attack upon the United States, its territories or possessions, or its armed forces.

CONSULTATION

Sec. 3. The President in every possible instance shall consult with Congress before introducing United States Armed Forces into hostilities or into situations where imminent involvement in hostilities is clearly indicated by the circumstances, and after every such introduction shall consult regularly with the Congress until United States Armed Forces are no longer engaged in hostilities or have been removed from such situations.

REPORTING

Sec. 4. (a) In the absence of a declaration of war, in any case in which United States Armed Forces are introduced—

(1) into hostilities or into situations where imminent involvement in hostilities is clearly indicated by the circumstances;

(2) into the territory, airspace or waters of a foreign nation, while equipped for combat, except for deployments which relate solely to supply, replacement, repair, or training of such forces; or

(3) in numbers which substantially enlarge United States Armed Forces equipped for combat already located in a foreign nation;

the President shall submit within 48 hours to the Speaker of the House of Representatives and to the President pro tempore of the Senate a report, in writing, setting forth—

(A) the circumstances necessitating the introduction of United States Armed Forces;

(B) the constitutional and legislative authority under which such introduction took place; and

(C) the estimated scope and duration of the hostilities or involvement.

(b) The President shall provide such other information as the Congress may request in the fulfillment of its constitutional responsibilities with respect to committing the Nation to war and to the use of United States Armed Forces abroad.

(c) Whenever United States Armed Forces are introduced into hostilities or into any situation described in subsection (a) of this section, the President shall, so long as such armed forces continue to be engaged in such hostilities or situation, report to the Congress periodically on the status of such hostilities or situation as well as on the scope and duration of such hostilities or situation, but in no event shall he report to the Congress less often than once every six months.

CONGRESSIONAL ACTION

Sec. 5. (b) Within sixty calendar days after a report is submitted or is required to be submitted pursuant to section 4(a)(1), whichever is earlier, the President shall terminate any use of United States Armed Forces with respect to which such report was submitted (or required to be submitted), unless the Congress (1) has declared war or has enacted a specific authorization for such use of United States Armed Forces, (2) has extended by law such sixty-day period, or (3) is physically unable to meet as a result of an armed attack upon the United States. Such sixty-day period shall be extended for not more than an additional thirty days if the President determines and certifies to the Congress in writing that unavoidable military necessity respecting the safety of United States Armed Forces requires the continued use of such armed forces in the course of bringing about a prompt removal of such forces.

(c) Notwithstanding subsection (b), at any time that United States Armed Forces are engaged in hostilities outside the territory of the United States, its possessions and territories without a declaration of war or specific statutory authorization, such forces shall be removed by the President if the Congress so directs by concurrent resolution.

INTERPRETATION OF JOINT RESOLUTION

Sec. 8. (2) (c) For purposes of this joint resolution, the term "introduction of United States Armed Forces" includes the assignment of members of such armed forces to command, coordinate, participate in the movement of, or accompany the regular or irregular military forces of any foreign country or government when such military forces are engaged, or there exists an imminent threat that such forces will become engaged, in hostilities.

5. According to the WPR, the president's legal authority as commander-in-chief to introduce U.S. armed forces into hostilities, or situations where hostilities are imminent, can be exercised under only three conditions. What are they?

_____

_____

_____

_____

_____

6. What does the WPR require the president to do within forty-eight hours of introducing U.S. armed forces into hostilities or situations where hostilities are imminent?

_____

_____

_____

_____

_____

7. What does the WPR require the president to do within sixty calendar days of introducing U.S. armed forces into hostilities or situations where hostilities are imminent?

_____

_____

8. The WPR lists three conditions under which the president would *not* be required to take the action you identified in question 7. List the three exceptions here.

_____

_____

_____

_____

_____

_____

_____

9. Suppose that a cruise ship plying the Mediterranean, and carrying 1,500 Americans, is seized by militants who demand the immediate release of all accused terrorists in U.S. custody. The pirates immediately behead ten Americans and continue the beheadings at the rate of one every 15 minutes, with the butchery televised worldwide. The terrorists claim they will continue the beheadings until their demand is met or until all the American passengers are dead. Suppose also that Congress is not in session and that it would take the members of the House and Senate 24 hours to convene in special session after receiving the president's call to do so.

    a. Would it be legal for the president under the WPR to use the armed forces of the United States—for example, the Navy Seals—to rescue the hostages? Explain.

    _____

    _____

    _____

    _____

    _____

    b. What action should the president take? What would the political ramifications be?

    _____

    _____

    _____

    _____

    _____

    _____

10. Suppose that the president dispatches 10,000 Marines to kill 2,500 terrorists who have gathered from around the world in the jungles of a remote Philippine island. The president reports the action to Congress according to the requirements of the WPR. Congressional and public opinion is evenly divided between those denouncing the president's adventurism abroad and those praising his aggressive pursuit of terrorists. After sixty days of combat and 500 Marines killed, the president certifies to Congress under Section 5(b) of the WPR that he needs an additional thirty days to win the fight. He notifies Congress that he is sending 5,000 more troops. But at the end of that thirty-day extension (the ninetieth day of combat), an additional 700 Marines are dead. Public opinion remains divided.

The president is determined to proceed—based on intelligence he can't share—indicating that victory is attainable. A majority in Congress sees only a quagmire and, under Section 5(c) of the WPR, orders the president by concurrent resolution (which does not require the president's signature) to terminate hostilities immediately and remove all U.S. military forces from the Philippines. Congress also declares by concurrent resolution that the president is in violation of Sections 2(c) and 5(c) of the WPR and threatens to cut off funding for the military operation.

a. Did the president have legal authority under the WPR to order the Marines to attack the terrorists in the first place? Explain.

_____

_____

_____

_____

_____

b. What other act of Congress referred to in this exercise might give the president the authority to attack the terrorists?

_____

_____

_____

c. Suppose that the president continues to defy Congress's demands to withdraw the troops and that he escalates the conflict by introducing more Marines and increased firepower into the theater of combat. In that event, do you think Congress would follow through on its threat to cut off funding for troops in the field as a way to restrain the commander-in-chief? Explain and support your position.

_____

_____

_____

_____

_____

_____

_____

Questions 11 and 12 are based on Reading 7.3.3, which includes excerpts from the Report of the Senate Foreign Relations Committee on the War Powers Resolution (1972).

READING 7.3.3
Excerpts from the Report of the Senate Foreign Relations Committee on the War Powers Resolution, February 9, 1972

The purpose of the war powers bill . . . is to fulfill—not to alter, amend, or adjust—the intent of the framers of the United States Constitution in order to insure that the collective judgment of both the Congress and the President will be brought to bear in decisions involving the introduction of the Armed Forces of the United States in hostilities or in situations where imminent involvement in hostilities is indicated by circumstances. . . .

The essential purpose of the bill, therefore, is to reconfirm and to define with precision the constitutional authority of Congress to exercise its constitutional war powers with respect to "undeclared" wars and the way in which this authority relates to the constitutional responsibilities of the President as Commander-in-Chief. The bill is in no way intended to encroach upon, alter or detract from the constitutional powers of the President, in his capacity as Commander-in-Chief, to conduct hostilities authorized by Congress, to repel attacks or the imminent threat of attacks upon the United States or its armed forces, and to rescue endangered American citizens and nationals in foreign countries. . . .

The heart and core of the bill—the provision which will give substance and weight to the Congressional war power—is Section 5, which provides that the use of the armed forces under any of the emergency conditions spelled out in Section 3 shall not be sustained for a period beyond thirty days unless Congress adopts legislation specifically authorizing the continued use of the armed forces. The intended effect of Section 5 is to impose a prior and unalterable restriction on the emergency use of the armed forces by the President. Emergency use of the armed forces by the President—under Section 8—would be undertaken with full knowledge on his part that the operation could be continued beyond a thirty-day period only with the specific authorization of Congress. The President would thereby stand forewarned against any emergency use of the armed forces that did not conform with the law and that he did not feel confident would command the support of majorities of both Houses of Congress. . . .

The Committee concurs in the view expressed by Justice Harlan: that when checks and balances are disrupted in one area of our public policy, all others are affected, and so are the basic rights of the citizens. As Professor Alpheus Thomas Mason said in his testimony before the Committee, "Separation of powers in war making, constitutionally shared by Congress and the President, has all but vanished. The President is in complete, unqualified control." In the Committee's view, as in the view of the framers of the Constitution, "complete, unqualified control" in one area poses the danger, if not indeed the inevitability, of "complete, unqualified control" over all other areas of our national life. . . .

The Committee does not contest the need of "flexibility," nor of adaptability, in our political process in order to accommodate to modern conditions. . . . What the Committee does contest is that expansive view of Executive prerogative which holds that the President may use the armed forces at will, even in conditions falling short of a genuine national emergency, and that he may sustain that use for as long as he, and he alone, sees fit. Such unrestricted Presidential control of the armed forces is neither necessary or wise in our nuclear age, reconcilable with the Constitution, nor tolerable in a free society. . . .

The framers of the Constitution vested the war power in Congress not primarily because they felt confident that the legislature would necessarily exercise it more wisely but because they expected the legislature to exercise it more *sparingly* than it had been exercised by the Crown [meaning the King of England], or would be likely to be exercised by the President as the successor to the Crown. The framers, it would appear, were concerned with the way in which war would be initiated in making certain that it would not be initiated easily, capriciously, or often. . . .

11. According to the committee's report, what is the heart and core of the bill? What's the intended effect of this part of the bill? Cite specific language from the report in your answer.

_____

_____

_____

_____

_____

12. According to the committee's report, the Constitution's system of checks and balances, as it relates to war powers, is out of order. Explain. Cite specific language from the report in your answer.

_____

_____

_____

_____

_____

Questions 13 and 14 are based on Reading 7.3.4, an excerpt from President Richard Nixon's message on his veto of the WPR.

READING 7.3.4
President Richard Nixon's Veto of the War Powers Resolution

To the House of Representatives:

I hereby return without my approval House Joint Resolution 542—the War Powers Resolution. While I am in accord with the desire of the Congress to assert its proper role in the conduct of our foreign affairs, the restrictions which this resolution would impose upon the authority of the President are both unconstitutional and dangerous to the best interests of our Nation.

The proper roles of the Congress and the Executive in the conduct of foreign affairs have been debated since the founding of our country. Only recently, however, has there been a serious challenge to the wisdom of the Founding Fathers in choosing not to draw a precise and detailed line of demarcation between the foreign policy powers of the two branches.

The Founding Fathers understood the impossibility of foreseeing every contingency that might arise in this complex area. They acknowledged the need for flexibility in responding to changing circumstances. They recognized that foreign policy decisions must be made through close cooperation between the two branches and not through rigidly codified procedures.

These principles remain as valid today as they were when our Constitution was written. Yet House Joint Resolution 542 would violate those principles by defining the President's powers in ways which would strictly limit his constitutional authority.

Clearly Unconstitutional

House Joint Resolution 542 would attempt to take away, by a mere legislative act, authorities which the President has properly exercised under the Constitution for almost 200 years. One of its provisions would automatically cut off certain authorities after sixty days unless the Congress extended them. Another would allow the Congress to eliminate certain authorities merely by the passage of a concurrent resolution—an action which does not normally have the force of law, since it denies the President his constitutional role in approving legislation.

I believe that both these provisions are unconstitutional. The only way in which the constitutional powers of a branch of the Government can be altered is by amending the Constitution—and any attempt to make such alterations by legislation alone is clearly without force.

Undermining our Foreign Policy

While I firmly believe that a veto of House Joint Resolution 542 is warranted solely on constitutional grounds, I am also deeply disturbed by the practical consequences of this resolution. For it would seriously undermine this Nation's ability to act decisively and convincingly in times of international crisis. As a result, the confidence of our allies in our ability to assist them could be diminished and the respect of our adversaries for our deterrent posture could decline. A permanent and substantial element of unpredictability would be injected into the world's assessment of American behavior, further increasing the likelihood of miscalculation and war.

If this resolution had been in operation, America's effective response to a variety of challenges in recent years would have been vastly complicated or even made impossible. We may well have been unable to respond in the way we did during the Berlin crisis of 1961, the Cuban missile crisis of 1962, the Congo rescue operation in 1964, and the Jordanian crisis of 1970—to mention just a few examples. In addition, our recent actions to bring about a peaceful settlement of the hostilities in the Middle East would have been seriously impaired if this resolution had been in force.

While all the specific consequences of House Joint Resolution 542 cannot yet be predicted, it is clear that it would undercut the ability of the United States to act as an effective influence for peace. For example, the provision automatically cutting off certain authorities after 60 days unless they are extended by the Congress could work to prolong or intensify a crisis. Until the Congress suspended the deadline, there would be at least a chance of United States withdrawal and an adversary would be tempted therefore to postpone serious negotiations until the 60 days were up. Only after the Congress acted would there be a strong incentive for an adversary to negotiate. In addition, the very existence of a deadline could lead to an escalation of hostilities in order to achieve certain objectives before the 60 days expired.

The measure would jeopardize our role as a force for peace in other ways as well.

It would, for example, strike from the President's hand a wide range of important peace-keeping tools by eliminating his ability to exercise quiet diplomacy backed by subtle shifts in our military deployments. It would also cast into doubt authorities which Presidents have used to undertake certain humanitarian relief missions in conflict areas, to protect fishing boats from seizure, to deal with ship or aircraft hijackings, and to respond to threats of attack. . . . Finally, since the bill is somewhat vague as to when the 60 day rule would apply, it could lead to extreme confusion and dangerous disagreements concerning the prerogatives of the two branches, seriously damaging our ability to respond to international crises.

Failure to Require Positive Congressional Action

I am particularly disturbed by the fact that certain of the President's constitutional powers as Commander in Chief of the Armed Forces would terminate automatically under this resolution 60 days after they were invoked. No overt Congressional action would be required to cut off these powers—they would disappear automatically unless the Congress extended them. In effect, the Congress is here attempting to increase its policy-making role through a provision which requires it to take absolutely no action at all.

In my view, the proper way for the Congress to make known its will on such foreign policy questions is through a positive action, with full debate on the merits of the issue and with each member taking the responsibility of casting a yes or no vote after considering those merits. The authorization and appropriations process represents one of the ways in which such influence can be exercised. I do not, however, believe that the Congress can responsibly contribute its considered, collective judgment on such grave questions without full debate and without a yes or no vote. Yet this is precisely what the joint resolution would allow. It would give every future Congress the ability to handcuff every future President merely by doing nothing and sitting still. In my view, one cannot become a responsible partner unless one is prepared to take responsible action. . . .

RICHARD NIXON
The White House,
October 24, 1973

13. What argument does Nixon make to support his position that the WPR is unconstitutional? Cite specific language from Nixon's veto message to support your answer.

_____

_____

_____

_____

_____

_____

14. What argument does Nixon make to support his position that the WPR undermines the conduct of foreign policy? Cite specific language from Nixon's veto message to support your answer.

_____

_____

_____

_____

_____

_____

8

Bureaucracy and the Regulatory Process

EXERCISE 8.1   The Fourth Branch

INTRODUCTION

The title *chief executive* suggests that the president, in principle, commands and controls the executive branch of the national government. Many presidents have embraced Franklin Delano Roosevelt's view that "the Presidency was established as a single strong Chief Executive in which was vested the entire executive power of the National Government."[1] The framers of the Constitution, however, refused to confer that much power on the president. Instead, the framers divided jurisdiction over the executive branch between Congress and the president, and assigned to Congress a substantial role in executive branch affairs. For example, to staff the highest positions in the executive branch, the president must secure the consent of the Senate. Congress also has the power to create and reconfigure executive branch agencies and departments, and to direct and fund their operations through legislation.

In Article II, Section 1, the Constitution vests the executive power in the president. But nowhere does it bestow the title *chief executive* on the president, and it has very little to say about the president's management of the executive branch. There are only three direct references in the Constitution to the president's power over executive branch departments. The first allows the president to "require the Opinion in writing, of the principal Officer in each of the executive Departments, upon any Subject relating to the Duties of their respective Offices." The second gives the president the power to appoint, subject to Senate approval, executive branch officers. In the third reference, the president is admonished to "take Care that the Laws be faithfully executed."

In 1789, President George Washington carried out his responsibility as head of the executive branch by supervising about fifty civilian employees: the State Department had nine, the War Department had two, and the Treasury Department had thirty-nine. By the time of the Civil War, the federal bureaucracy had added a fourth cabinet department: the Department of Interior. By 1900, the number of civilian employees in the executive branch had gone up to about 240,000 and a fifth cabinet department had been added: the Department of Agriculture.

By the end of the twentieth century, the federal bureaucracy had become larger and more powerful than any nineteenth-century American could have imagined. Today, the executive branch consists of fifteen Cabinet departments and dozens of agencies, commissions, and government corporations. The Office of Personnel Management reported that 2,094,000 civilians worked for the federal government in 2009. This figure excludes Postal Service employees, which numbered 623,128 in 2009. (By way of comparison, the Census Bureau reported that the nation's 89,526 state and local governments employed a total of 16,600,000 full-time equivalent employees in 2009.)

The increasing size and complexity of the federal bureaucracy raise important questions about the president's ability to oversee it. What does it mean to be the chief executive of the federal government? Is it possible for the president to command and control, or even manage and supervise, the federal bureaucracy?

---

[1]Quoted in Richard M. Pious, *The American Presidency* (New York: Basic Books, 1979), p. 211.

ASSIGNMENT

1. *Web-Based Question.* Get acquainted with the federal bureaucracy by going to the "A–Z Index of U.S. Government Departments and Agencies" at http://www.usa.gov/Agencies/Federal/All_Agencies/index.shtml. Here, you'll find a listing of all the departments and agencies, and their various subunits, in the federal bureaucracy. For example, under the directory for the letter A, click on Arthritis and Musculoskeletal Coordinating Committee. This takes you to the website of the National Institute of Arthritis and Musculoskeletal and Skin Diseases (NIAMS). NIAMS is a subunit of the National Institutes of Health (NIH), which is an agency in the Department of Health and Human Services, one of the fifteen cabinet departments in the federal bureaucracy.

Web addresses sometimes change. If you can't locate a website, try an external search (e.g., Google) to find the website. Configurations within a website often change. If you can't find a particular link or article, for example, try an internal search of the website as well as an external search. Be resourceful! If you still can't find what you're searching for, move on to the next question.

a. Click on a few letters of the A–Z Index and estimate the total number of departments, agencies, and subunits of the federal bureaucracy.

_____

b. Use the Index to explore two links of your choice to agencies or subunits in the federal bureaucracy that you have not heard of before. Identify those agencies or subunits and the mission or purpose of each.

Subunit 1: _____

_____

_____

_____

Subunit 2: _____

_____

_____

_____

2. Examine the organization chart of the executive branch in Figure 8.1.1 on the next page. What do the vertical lines in the chart suggest about the president's position and authority in the executive branch?

_____

_____

_____

On Figure 8.1.1, locate the box that contains Executive Office of the President (EOP). The task of the EOP is to assist the president in formulating and implementing his policies. The EOP consists of about 2,000 employees divided among the various offices and councils within the EOP. The Office of Management and Budget (OMB) is the largest of these—with about 600 employees—and functions as the president's primary "watchdog" in attempting to ensure that the departments and agencies in the federal bureaucracy carry out the president's policies.

3. *Web-Based Question.* Go to the home page of the OMB and read about "The Mission and Structure of the Office of Management and Budget."

PRESIDENT

Vice President

Executive Office of the President
White House Office
Council on Environmental Quality
Office of Management and Budget
Office of Science and Technology Policy
Council of Economic Advisors
National Security Council
Office of the United States
Trade Representative
Office of Administration
Office of Policy Development

CABINET DEPARTMENTS								
Department of Agriculture	Department of Commerce	Department of Defense	Department of Education	Department of Energy	Department of Health and Human Services	Department of Housing and Urban Development		Department of Homeland Security
Department of the Interior	Department of Justice	Department of Labor	Department of State	Department of Transportation	Department of the Treasury	Department of Veterans Affairs		

INDEPENDENT ESTABLISHMENTS AND GOVERNMENT CORPORATIONS

ACTION
Administrative Conference of the U.S.
African Development Foundation
American Battle Monuments
  Commission
Appalachian Regional Commisssion
Board for International Broadcasting
Central Intelligence Agency
Commission on the Bicentennial of
  the United States Constitution
Commission on Civil Rights
Commission of Fine Arts
Commodity Futures Trading
  Commission
Consumer Product Safety
  Commission
Environmental Protection Agency
Equal Employment Opportunity
  Commission

Export-Import Bank of the U.S.
Farm Credit Administration
Federal Communications Commission
Federal Deposit Insurance Corporation
Federal Election Commision
Federal Emergency Management
  Agency
Federal Home Loan Bank Board
Federal Labor Relations Authority
Federal Maritime Commission
Federal Mediation and Conciliation
  Service
Federal Mine Safety and Health Review
  Commission
Federal Reserve System, Board of
  Governors of the
Federal Trade Commission
General Services Administration
Inter-American Foundation

Interstate Commerce Commission
Merit Systems Protection Board
National Aeronautics and Space
  Administration
National Archives and Records
  Administration
National Capital Planning Commission
National Credit Union Administration
National Foundation on the Arts and
  the Humanities
National Labor Relations Board
National Mediation Board
National Science Foundation
National Transportation Safety Board
Nuclear Regulatory Commission
Occupational Safety and Health Review
  Commission
Office of Personnel Management
Office of Special Counsel

Panama Canal Commisssion
Peace Corps
Pennsylvania Avenue
  Development Corporation
Postal Rate Commission
Railroad Retirement Board
Securities and Exchange
  Commission
Selective Service System
Small Business Administration
Tennessee Valley Authority
U.S. Arms Control and Disarmament
  Agency
U.S. Information Agency
U.S. International Development
  Cooperation Agency
U.S. International Trade
  Commission
U.S. Postal Service

FIGURE 8.1.1 Organization Chart of the Executive Branch of the United States

a. What is the mission of the OMB? Cite specific language from the OMB mission statement in your answer.

_____

_____

_____

_____

_____

b. What are the first two "critical processes" the OMB uses to carry out its mission?

_____

_____

_____

_____

_____

4. For the OMB to function successfully as the president's watchdog and assist him in overseeing the federal bureaucracy, OMB employees must be responsive to the president's policy preferences. To help attain a high level of responsiveness, the president fills the top positions in the OMB with appointees who share his policy preferences and who are presumably loyal to the president. Do you think that the president, with the help of these top officials in the OMB, would be able to direct, supervise, and manage the 600 employees in OMB effectively? Explain and support your answer.

If you're not sure how to approach this question, consider the position of the president of your college or university. Your president no doubt has several vice presidents, deans, and perhaps even directors who assist in carrying out the president's policies and supervising the university's employees. Find out how many employees work at your university and ask one of your professors or someone in your student government if they believe it is possible for an effective university president (and maybe yours is not!) to supervise—with assistance—that many employees.

_____

_____

_____

_____

_____

_____

_____

5. The federal bureaucracy consists of the departments and agencies in the two large lower boxes in Figure 8.1.1. They're labeled "Cabinet Departments" and "Independent Establishments and Government Corporations." Note that the federal bureaucracy is connected by a vertical line upward through the Executive Office of the President to the president himself. How and why would the president's ability to direct the federal bureaucracy differ from his ability to direct the OMB?

_____

_____

_____

_____

_____

6. Locate the U.S. Department of Agriculture (USDA) in Figure 8.1.1. In 2010, according to its Performance and Accountability Report, the USDA had "more than 100,000 employees deliver more than $188 billion to provide public services through USDA's more than 300 programs worldwide." How significant a component of the entire executive branch does the USDA appear to be? Explain your answer.

_____

_____

_____

_____

_____

7. Figure 8.1.2 on next page is an organization chart of the Department of Agriculture. Note that there are seven major subunits within the USDA, each headed by an undersecretary. Locate the Undersecretary for Natural Resources and Environment. Notice that the Forest Service is one of the agencies charged with overseeing natural resources and the environment. According to the organizational chart, how significant a component of the entire USDA does the Forest Service appear to be? Explain your answer.

_____

_____

_____

_____

_____

8. *Web-Based Question.* Go to the Forest Service's website at www.fs.fed.us. Click on "About Us" and then on "Meet the Forest Service." Read the material there to better understand the size, scope, and mission of the Forest Service.

a. How many acres of land does the Forest Service administer?

b. What is the title of the head of the Forest Service?

c. How many people work for the Forest Service?

d. The Forest Service is a large and important agency by any standard, yet it doesn't appear in Figure 8.1.1, the organization chart of the executive branch. What does the exclusion of the Forest Service from that chart indicate about the executive branch?

9. In the 1930s, when Franklin Delano Roosevelt was president, the federal bureaucracy was less than half its present size. Even so, Roosevelt made the following complaint:

> The Treasury is so large and far-flung and ingrained in its practices that I find it almost impossible to get the action and results I want—even with Henry [Morgenthau] there. But the Treasury is not to be compared with the State Department. You should go through the experience of trying to get any changes in the thinking, policy, and action of the career diplomats and then you'd know what a real problem was. But the Treasury and the State Department put together are nothing compared with the Na-a-vy. The admirals are really something to cope with—and I should know. To change anything in the Na-a-vy is like punching a feather bed. You punch it with your right and you punch it with your left until you are finally exhausted, and then you find the damn bed just as it was before you started punching.[2]

[2]Richard E. Neustadt, *Presidential Power: The Politics of Leadership from FDR to Carter* (New York: John Wiley and Sons, 1980), p. 33.

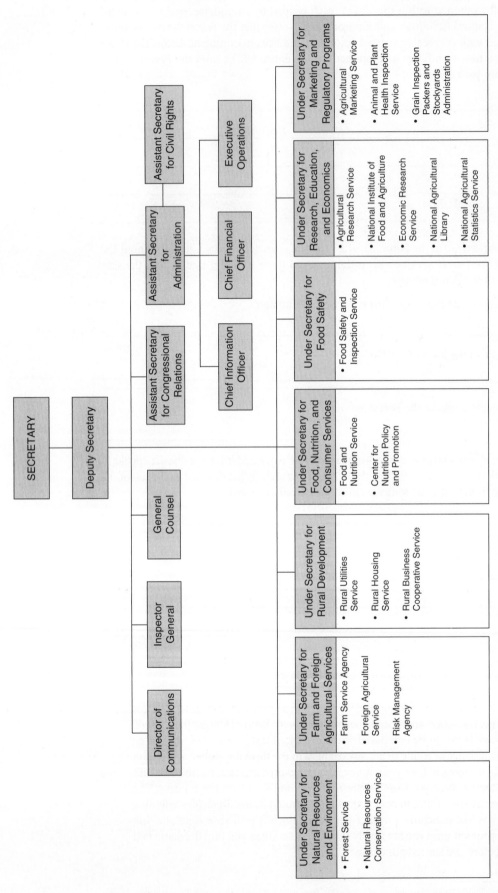

FIGURE 8.1.2 Organization Chart of the U.S. Department of Agriculture

In one sentence, using your own words, state the problem Roosevelt struggled with as head of the executive branch.

_____

_____

_____

10. During Richard Nixon's term in office, this celebrated outburst by the president was recorded for posterity on the taping system he had secretly installed in the Oval Office:

> We have no discipline in this bureaucracy. We never fire anybody. We never repri-
> mand anybody. We never demote anybody. We always promote the sons-of-bitches
> that kick us in the ass. . . . We are going to quit being a bunch of goddamn soft-headed
> managers. . . . When a bureaucrat deliberately thumbs his nose, we're going to get
> him. . . . The little boys over in [the State Department] particularly, that are against us
> [the Defense Department, the Department of Health, Education, and Welfare]—
> those three areas particularly. . . . There are many unpleasant places were civil service
> people can be sent. . . . When they don't produce in this administration, somebody's
> ass is kicked out. . . . Now, goddamn it, those are the bad guys—the guys down in the
> woodwork.[3]

a. What did Nixon likely mean by "the guys down in the woodwork"?

_____

_____

_____

b. Identify the problem in contemporary government that triggered Nixon's anger.

_____

_____

_____

11. In recent decades, many political scientists have come to think of the departments and agencies in the executive branch as a fourth branch of government. What evidence can you find in this exercise to support that characterization?

_____

_____

_____

_____

_____

_____

_____

[3]J. Anthony Lukas, _Nightmare: The Underside of the Nixon Years_ (New York: Viking Press, 1976), p. 18.

EXERCISE 8.2   The National Security State

INTRODUCTION

For most of their history, Americans have had to sacrifice comparatively little to maintain their national security. Much of the work was done for them by nature. Americans built their nation in one of the most secure regions of the world. Vast oceans to the east and west have insulated the country for most of its history, protecting it from conflict and turmoil in Europe and Asia and deterring would-be invaders from striking. U.S. national security has been bolstered as well by neighbors to the north and south that pose little threat to the United States.

That helps explain why many Americans long viewed large standing armed forces with suspicion. For American colonists, the instruments of royal tyranny and the abridgement of their liberties were the British army and navy. Consequently, Americans in the early years of the republic looked not to a national army to protect them but to their various state militias, whose importance was acknowledged in the Second Amendment to the Constitution. In 1787, the framers were careful to subordinate the military to civilian control and to vest two key powers in the hands of Congress instead of the executive: the power to raise armies and the power to declare war (Article I, Section 8). According to the Constitution, the president's role was limited to commanding the armies raised and authorized by Congress (see Exercise 7.3).

The confidence of Americans in the security of their nation was shattered by the Japanese attack on Pearl Harbor on December 7, 1941. The United States was no longer a natural fortress. Japanese aircraft carriers had crossed the Pacific undetected, penetrated U.S. defenses, and revealed that U.S. territory was vulnerable to foreign attack. Advances in military technology played a part in the Japanese attack; more threatening advances made during and after World War II would threaten U.S. national security during the cold war and into the twenty-first century.

In 1949, the Soviet Union exploded its first atomic bomb and later threatened the United States with its capacity to deliver atomic weapons on intercontinental bombers. That threat paled in comparison with the development of intercontinental ballistic missiles (ICBMs) as vehicles for delivering nuclear warheads. Because it was impossible to defend against incoming ICBMs, the United States was rendered utterly vulnerable to an attack by the Soviet Union. To limit its vulnerability, the United States adopted the doctrine of mutual assured destruction (MAD): A nuclear attack on the United States by the Soviet Union would trigger a massive nuclear counterattack by the United States. In a classic standoff, the Soviet Union made the same threat.

The Japanese attack on Pearl Harbor and the rise of the Soviet Union as a nuclear superpower led to the American conviction that projecting military power abroad was essential to achieving national security at home. Adversaries had to be contained overseas before they could carry their threat to American shores. Consequently, beginning in the late 1940s, the United States developed a series of military alliances with nations in strategic areas of the world. President George Washington, in his farewell address to the nation in 1796, had warned Americans of the dangers of permanent alliances with foreign powers. The nation heeded Washington's advice until 1949, when the United States joined its first peacetime military alliance—the North Atlantic Treaty Organization (NATO). For a nation so long averse to becoming entangled with foreign powers and so insistent on maintaining its freedom of action in foreign affairs, this was powerful evidence that Americans had embraced a new vision of national security.

National security state is the term scholars often use to describe the United States in the post–World War II era. A national security state is a nation permanently mobilized for war. That mobilization entails enormous social and economic costs to the nation, costs that Americans would never have accepted before World War II. The foundation of the national security state was laid in 1950, when President Harry Truman approved National Security Council Document 68 (NSC-68)—a blueprint for putting the nation on a permanent wartime footing and for obtaining public and congressional approval for the sacrifices that would be required, primary among them a vast increase in military spending and maintenance of large standing military forces. NSC-68's recommendations for massive increases in defense spending were controversial, and Truman at first was reluctant to accept them. But the outbreak of the Korean War in June 1950 made the case for constructing the national security state.

The precise costs of the national security state are difficult to determine. Obviously, national security requires the maintenance of large standing military forces as well as the departments and

agencies in the executive branch needed to sustain those forces. Other costs are less obvious. In the quest to develop and maintain a nuclear arsenal, the Departments of Energy and Defense contaminated vast swaths of land with nuclear and other wastes. The clean-up costs promise to run into the trillions of dollars. And there are more far-reaching costs, too. The public resources dedicated to the national security state remain unavailable for other uses, such as improving the nation's infrastructure, schools, and health-care system. In the interest of fighting the cold war—and now the war on terrorism—the national security state abridged the civil liberties and civil rights of many citizens. Sustaining the national security state undoubtedly entails other costs that have yet to be revealed.

Despite sustained investment in the national security state, the United States continues to grapple with its vulnerability. Efforts to defend the nation against ballistic missile and terrorist attacks are the latest in a long line of efforts to recover the sense of national security that Americans enjoyed before World War II. A terrorist attack on U.S. territory using chemical, biological, or nuclear weapons would pose an unprecedented challenge to the national security state. Since the end of World War II, the ability of the United States to deliver a punishing military attack has deterred conventional enemy nations from striking U.S. territory. But terrorists are an amorphous target largely beyond the president's reach, so they are unlikely to be deterred by military retaliation. Whether the national security state can manage to defend itself against this vulnerability remains to be seen.

ASSIGNMENT

Table 8.2.1 lists data on U.S. military spending from 1791 to 1950 by year or by period. When a period is shown—for example, 1850–1859, the expenditure noted is the yearly average for that period. Notice that the dollar amount of military spending for each year or period is in current dollars, which means that the figures have *not* been adjusted for inflation. A dollar spent on the military in 1820, for example, would have purchased substantially more goods or services than a dollar spent in 1920. But the spending figures in Table 8.2.1 do not compensate for that erosion in value.[1]

TABLE 8.2.1 U.S. Military Spending, 1791–1950, in Current Dollars		
Year or period	**Military Spending Per Year**	
1791–1799	2,013,000	
1800–1809	2,872,000	
1810	3,948,000	
1811	3,999,000	
1812	15,777,000	War of 1812 begins
1813	26,099,000	
1814	27,662,000	
1815	23,454,000	War of 1812 ends
1816	19,920,000	Demobilization
1817	11,319,000	
1818	8,577,000	
1819	10,350,000	
1820–1829	6,413,000	
1830–1839	12,041,000	
1840–1845	12,240,000	
1846	17,248,000	Mexican War begins

(Continued)

[1]Figures adjusted for inflation would allow more accurate comparisons of spending over time, but adjusted figures are not available for the years preceding 1945.

TABLE 8.2.1	U.S. Military Spending, 1791–1950, in Current Dollars (*Continued*)	
Year or period	**Military Spending Per Year**	
1847	46,207,000	
1848	34,910,000	Mexican War ends
1849	24,640,000	Demobilization
1850–1859	24,988,000	
1860	27,925,000	
1861	35,402,000	Civil War begins
1862	437,036,000	
1863	662,521,000	
1864	776,518,000	
1865	1,153,936,000	Civil War ends
1866	327,774,000	Demobilization
1867	126,258,000	
1868	149,023,000	
1869	98,503,000	
1870–1879	53,171,000	
1880–1889	51,756,000	
1890–1895	46,415,000	
1896	77,979,000	
1897	83,512,000	
1898	150,816,000	Spanish-American War
1899	293,783,000	Demobilization
1900	190,728,000	
1901	205,123,000	
1902	180,075,000	
1903–1915	291,294,000	
1916	337,030,000	
1917	617,574,000	U.S. enters World War I
1918	6,148,795,000	World War I ends
1919	11,011,387,000	Demobilization
1920	2,357,974,000	
1921	1,768,450,000	
1922	935,531,000	
1923	730,252,000	
1924–1935	768,382,000	
1936–1940	1,213,587,000	
1941	6,252,001,000	U.S. enters World War II
1942	22,905,097,000	

(Continued)

TABLE 8.2.1	U.S. Military Spending, 1791–1950, in Current Dollars (*Continued*)

Year or period	Military Spending Per Year	
1943	63,413,912,000	
1944	75,975,964,000	
1945	80,537,254,000	World War II ends
1946	40,184,000,000	Demobilization
1947	13,205,000,000	
1948	10,151,000,000	
1949	11,241,000,000	
1950	11,674,000,000	

Note: Current dollars have not been adjusted for inflation.

Source: Adapted from Census Bureau, *Historical Statistics of the United States* (Washington, D.C.: U.S. Government Printing Office, 1975).

1. Use the data in Table 8.2.1 to complete the chart titled Wars and Military Spending. Your objective is to compare the average annual military spending in the years immediately preceding and following each war. To determine the *prewar average,* calculate the approximate average annual military spending over the five years preceding the war. The *wartime high* figure is just that—the highest amount spent on defense in any year during the war. To determine the *postwar average,* calculate the approximate average annual military spending during the four or five years following the war. In your calculation of the postwar average, don't include the figure for the year immediately following the war, the year labeled *demobilization.* Military spending may remain at wartime levels for a brief period after the fighting has stopped, reflecting the costs of demobilizing the forces. Finally, in the right-hand column of the chart, note the ratio of prewar spending to postwar spending. Simply divide the prewar average into the postwar average, rounding that number to the nearest tenth. Notice that the ratio tells you how many times greater postwar spending was than prewar spending. We've given you a head start by entering the data in the chart for the War of 1812 and the Mexican War.

Chart: Wars and Military Spending

War	Prewar Average	Wartime High	Postwar Average	Prewar Average: Postwar Average
War of 1812	$3,300,000	$27,662,000	$11,000,000	1:3.3
Mexican War	$12,000,000	$46,000,000	$25,000,000	1:2.1
Spanish-American War	_____	_____	_____	_____
Civil War	_____	_____	_____	_____
World War I	_____	_____	_____	_____
World War II	_____	_____	_____	_____

2. How did the six wars listed in the chart affect the long-term pattern of military spending? Use data from the chart to support your answer.

_____
_____
_____
_____
_____

3. Look again at the chart. Did defense spending after any of the wars listed ever drop to the prewar spending average?

4. Table 8.2.2 shows annual military spending since 1945. When a period is shown, the expenditure noted is the yearly average for that period. The amounts in the table are in constant 2011 dollars: They have been adjusted for inflation. A dollar adjusted for inflation would purchase the same amount of military supplies or services in 1945 as it would in 2011. Figures that are adjusted for inflation allow us to make more accurate and meaningful comparisons over long periods of time because the otherwise distorting effect of inflation has been compensated for. From data in the table, describe briefly and in general terms the trend or pattern in annual military spending since the end of the Korean War.

TABLE 8.2.2	U.S. Military Spending, Fiscal Years 1945–2011, in Constant 2011 Dollars	
1945	$815,000,000,000	World War II ends
1946	407,200,000,000	Demobilization
1947	110,800,000,000	
1948	71,900,000,000	
1949	100,500,000,000	
1950	106,500,000,000	Korean War begins
1951	173,600,000,000	
1952	326,200,000,000	
1953	367,100,000,000	Korean War ends
1954	338,500,000,000	Demobilization
1955	291,300,000,000	
1956	282,600,000,000	
1957	291,100,000,000	
1958	291,200,000,000	
1959	300,400,000,000	
1960	291,300,000,000	
1961	296,100,000,000	
1962	309,000,000,000	
1963	311,300,000,000	
1964	315,500,000,000	
1965	286,500,000,000	Johnson escalates Vietnam War
1966	322,200,000,000	
1967	383,700,000,000	
1968	425,100,000,000	
1969	409,300,000,000	
1970	384,600,000,000	
1971	353,600,000,000	
1972	338,900,000,000	
1973	314,500,000,000	U.S. troops leave Vietnam
1974	303,700,000,000	
1975–1979	295,900,000,000	
1980–1989	430,200,000,000	

(*Continued*)

TABLE 8.2.2	U.S. Military Spending, Fiscal Years 1945–2011, in Constant 2011 Dollars (*Continued*)	
1990–1999	346,500,000,000	
2000	373,400,000,000	
2001	377,700,000,000	9/11 terrorist attacks; Afghanistan War
2002	424,900,000,000	
2003	483,400,000,000	Iraq War
2004	530,800,000,000	
2005	558,500,000,000	
2006	569,000,000,000	
2007	584,100,000,000	
2008	637,900,000,000	
2009	674,300,000,000	
2010	727,100,000,000	
2011	$749,700,000,000	

Note: These figures are adjusted for inflation.

Source: Todd Harrison, *Analysis of the FY 2011 Defense Budget* Table 4, p. 61. Used by permission of Center for Strategic and Budgetary Assessments.

5. a. Estimate the average annual military expenditure since the end of the Korean War for the years the United States was not fighting a major war. In other words, exclude from your estimate military spending during the years the United States was fighting wars in Vietnam, Afghanistan, and Iraq. This figure is the post–Korean War peacetime military spending average.

---

b. Compare military spending at the height of the Vietnam War in 1968 to the peacetime average of military spending after the Korean War. To do this, divide the estimate you made in question 5a by the amount of spending at the height of the Vietnam War. This figure represents peacetime military spending as a percentage of wartime military spending. Enter your percentage calculation here.

---

c. What does your comparison of peacetime to wartime military spending indicate about the monetary cost of maintaining the national security state—even when the nation is not at war?

---

6. The cold war between the United States and the Soviet Union ended in 1991 with the collapse of the Soviet Union. At the time, many observers predicted that the end of the cold war would bring a peace dividend, meaning that spending on the national security state would be reduced and the savings would be redirected to education, the environment, medical care, and even reducing taxes.

a. From the data in Table 8.2.2, calculate the average yearly military expenditures during the 1980s (when the cold war was under way), and the average yearly military expenditure during the 1990s (after the cold war had ended). What is the approximate average annual peace dividend the nation captured in the 1990s?

---

b. What percentage of yearly military spending in the 1980s does the annual peace dividend represent? To make the calculation, divide the average annual peace dividend by the average yearly military expenditure in the 1980s.

---

c. What factors might explain the relatively meager peace dividend?

_____

_____

_____

_____

_____

7. President Bush's budget for fiscal year 2003 called for a substantial increase in defense spending. The president's budget message to Congress opened with these lines: "Americans will never forget the murderous events of September 11, 2001. They are for us what Pearl Harbor was to an earlier generation of Americans: a terrible wrong and a call to action." There is some historical basis for the parallel that the president made. The Japanese attack on Pearl Harbor awakened Americans to an unanticipated vulnerability—surprise attack from abroad by a hostile nation-state. The terrorist attacks on September 11, 2001, awakened Americans to another vulnerability—surprise attack from within by organized terrorists directed from abroad.

In response to the Japanese attack on Pearl Harbor, U.S. defense spending increased dramatically to prosecute World War II and to build the national security state. Make the following calculations to see if spending on the national security state following the 9/11 terrorist attacks is likely to increase as radically as it did following the Japanese attack on Pearl Harbor.

a. Look again at the chart titled Wars and Military Spending. How many times greater, on average, was defense spending after World War II than defense spending before the war?

_____

b. Multiply the defense spending listed in Table 8.2.2 for 2000 by the factor you found in question 7a. This is the level that defense spending would have to reach to make the post-9/11 increase comparable to the post–Pearl Harbor increase. Write the product here.

_____

c. Total spending by the national government in 2003 was $2.1 trillion. Total spending in 2009 was $3.5 trillion. Do you think that the so-called war on terrorism will ever command an increase in defense spending proportionately as great as the increase required to maintain national security after the Japanese attack on Pearl Harbor? Explain and support your answer.

_____

_____

_____

_____

_____

8. To gauge the impact of the wars in Afghanistan and Iraq on military spending and the national security state, make the following calculations.

a. From Table 8.2.2, calculate the average annual military spending for the years 2002 to 2011.

_____

b. How does average annual military spending for the years 2002 to 2011—including the costs of the wars in Afghanistan and Iraq—compare with military spending in 1953 at the height of the Korean War, and with military spending in 1968 at the height of the Vietnam War?

Remember that you are working with figures adjusted for inflation, so a 1953 dollar, for example, has the same purchasing power as a 2011 dollar.

_____

_____

_____

_____

One study estimated that through 2011, Department of Defense military operations in Afghanistan and Iraq cost $1.1 trillion.[2] This amount does not include training and equipping Afghan and Iraqi security forces, foreign assistance and diplomatic activities, veterans' benefits, and other social and economic costs of the two wars.

c. From Table 8.2.2, add the total military spending from 2002 through 2011.

_____

d. Divide the cost of military operations in Afghanistan and Iraq from 2002 through 2011 by your answer to question 8c. The result is the percentage of total military spending from 2002 through 2011 owing to the cost of military operations alone in the wars in Afghanistan and Iraq.

_____

e. What percentage of total military spending during the period 2002 to 2011 was not devoted to fighting the wars in Afghanistan and Iraq?

_____

f. What does your answer to question 8e indicate about the cost of maintaining the national security state?

_____

_____

_____

[2]Stephen Daggett, _Cost of Major U.S. Wars,_ June 29, 2010, Congressional Research Service, RS22926.

EXERCISE 8.3 How Much Regulation Is Enough? How Much Is Too Much? A Case Study of Gene Therapy Protocols

INTRODUCTION

The dizzying pace of change in biotechnology has generated conflict between those who see the promise of medical cures and corporate profits, and those who fear the damage emerging technologies might inflict on the public. For federal regulators, the challenge is determining the right amount of regulation—rules that protect the general welfare without imposing undue delay on patients waiting for new treatments or undue costs on industry. For the American people, protection from hazardous therapies and medications is of paramount concern. For the biotechnology and pharmaceutical industries, the bottom line is profit. In recent years, the politics of regulation has become more contentious, pitting public interest groups against the deregulatory fervor of the Bush Administration and the resurgent Republicans in Congress after the 2010 midterm elections.

A case study in the pros and cons of government regulation of new medical technology is gene therapy: "Genes, which are carried on chromosomes, are the basic physical and functional units of heredity. . . . When genes are altered so that the encoded proteins are unable to carry out their normal functions, genetic disorders can result. Gene therapy is a technique for correcting defective genes responsible for disease development. Researchers may use one of several approaches for correcting faulty genes."[1]

The problem of determining how much regulation is enough in the field of gene therapy was brought to light by the death of an 18-year-old patient in 1999. Jesse Gelsinger had been undergoing gene therapy for a liver disease in a clinical trial at the University of Pennsylvania's Institute of Gene Therapy. (Many of the human subjects in clinical trials are suffering from life-threatening illnesses; the trials offer them their last hope of a cure.) Federal investigators later determined that the researchers had violated several federal regulations (see Reading 8.3.1).

Two government offices are responsible for monitoring gene therapy clinical trials. The Food and Drug Administration (FDA) is the primary watchdog; it tracks adverse reactions until the new therapy is approved. The second is the Recombinant DNA Advisory Committee (RAC) of the National Institutes of Health (NIH). The RAC was created to reassure Americans who are wary of genetic engineering; its role is primarily advisory, although it does approve the procedures for clinical trials. After the death of Jesse Gelsinger, the FDA and RAC proposed new rules for gene therapy protocols (see Reading 8.3.2).

Despite some optimism about gene therapy in the years after the Gelsinger incident, hopes were dashed again when "the FDA placed a temporary halt on all gene therapy trials using retroviral vectors in blood stem cells. The FDA took this action after it learned that a second child treated in a French gene therapy trial had developed a leukemia-like condition."[2] On February 28, 2003, the FDA's Biologics Response Modifiers Advisory Committee (now called Cell, Tissue, and Gene Therapies Advisory Committee) issued a report calling for new safeguards in the use of retroviruses in gene therapy.[3] Still, even with the new regulations in place, in July 2007, Jolee Mohr died at the University of Chicago Medical Center after undergoing a gene therapy protocol for rheumatoid arthritis, not an immediately life-threatening illness. The FDA temporarily halted the new gene therapy trials, but they were allowed to continue after the FDA's investigation found that Mohr's death was not linked to the therapy. Her husband was not happy with the regulatory ruling. He believed that the investigation was incomplete because the cause of her death had not been determined.

The debate about regulation of gene therapy continues to flare up. In 2007, the Inspector General of the Department of Health and Human Services issued a critical report of the FDA's lax regulation of clinical trials. FDA oversight of gene therapy clinical trials is "disorganized and underfinanced," according to the report.[4] On the other hand, Dr. Sally Satel, a psychiatrist, in an

---

[1] Doegenomes.com: http://www.ornl.gov/sci/techresources/Human_Genome/medicine/genetherapy.shtml.

[2] Doegenomes.com: http://www.ornl.gov/sci/techresources/Human_Genome/medicine/genetherapy.shtml.

[3] FDA regulations for gene therapy protocols are available at http://www.fda.gov/BiologicsBloodVaccines/GuidanceComplianceRegulatoryInformation/Guidances/CellularandGeneTherapy/ucm072957.htm

[4] Gardiner Harris, "Report Assails FDA Oversight of Clinical Trials, *New York Times,* September 28, 2007.

opinion piece for the *New York Times,* argues that the government's imposition of hundreds of regulations and the paperwork required for compliance with them have, if anything, been over-enforced to such an extent that the cost of conducting clinical trials has exceeded the medical benefits of the research.[5]

The good news is that, despite regulatory issues, a consensus is emerging that gene therapy has seen a number of successes in recent years, especially in the treatment of certain forms of leukemia.[6]

ASSIGNMENT

Study Readings 8.3.1 and 8.3.2 to answer the questions that follow.

READING 8.3.1
Human Gene Therapy: Harsh Lessons, High Hopes

In the ten years since [the] first genetic treatment on September 14, 1990, the hyperbole has exceeded the results. Worldwide, researchers launched more than 400 clinical trials to test gene therapy against a wide array of illnesses. Surprisingly, cancer has dominated the research. Even more surprising, little has worked.

"There was initially a great burst of enthusiasm that lasted three, four years where a couple of hundred trials got started all over the world," says W. French Anderson, now at the University of Southern California in Los Angeles. "Then we came to realize that nothing was really working at the clinical level."

Abbey S. Meyers, president of the National Organization for Rare Disorders Inc., an umbrella organization of patients' groups, is much more blunt. "We haven't even taken one baby step beyond that first clinical experiment," Meyers says. "It has hardly gotten anywhere. Over the last ten years, I have been very disappointed."

And then things got worse.

In September 1999, a patient died from a reaction to a gene therapy treatment at the University of Pennsylvania's Institute of Human Gene Therapy in Philadelphia. Jesse Gelsinger, an exuberant 18-year-old from Tucson, Arizona, suffered from a broken gene that causes one of those puzzling metabolic diseases of genetic medicine. An optimistic, altruistic Gelsinger went to Philadelphia to help advance the science that might eventually cure his type of illness. Instead, the experiment killed him.

In the aftermath of his death, there has been a flurry of activity to minimize the chance of future accidental deaths. The Food and Drug Administration, along with the National Institutes of Health, launched several investigations of the University of Pennsylvania studies and others. The inquiries provided disappointing news: Gene therapy researchers were not following all of the federal rules requiring them to report unexpected adverse events associated with the gene therapy trials; worse, some scientists were asking that problems not be made public. And then came the allegations that there were other unreported deaths attributed to genetic treatments, at least six in all.

"Probably the clearest evidence of the system not working is that only 35 to 37 of 970 serious adverse events from [a common type of gene therapy trial] were reported to the NIH" as required, says LeRoy Walters, the recently retired head of the Kennedy Institute of Ethics at Georgetown University and former chairman of NIH's Recombinant DNA Advisory Committee. "That is fewer than 5 percent of the serious adverse events."

The news hit the clinical trial community like a thunderclap. The consequences have been immediate and wide-ranging, and may threaten future research.

---

[5]"Clinical Trials Wrapped in Red Tape," August 7, 2009.
[6]Gina Kolata, "After Setbacks, Small Successes for Gene Therapy," *New York Times,* November 6, 2009.

"Participation in gene therapy trials is way down because the public is not sure what to make of this," says Philip Noguchi, M.D., director of the Cellular and Genetic Therapy Division in FDA's Center for Biologic Evaluation and Research (CBER). "They want to know what the government is doing to help restore the confidence in this field."

RESPONDING TO THE CRISIS

The federal government moved quickly to do just that. [The] FDA immediately shut down the trial in which Gelsinger had volunteered, and all clinical gene transfer trials at the University of Pennsylvania in January. The university went on to severely restrict the research of its once-high-flying gene therapy institute director James Wilson, M.D., announcing in May that all his work would be confined to animal and laboratory experiments and that he would be barred from conducting studies in people.

[The] FDA also suspended gene therapy trials at St. Elizabeth's Medical Center in Boston, a major teaching affiliate of Tufts University School of Medicine, which sought to use gene therapy to reverse heart disease, because scientists there failed to follow protocols and may have contributed to at least one patient death. FDA also temporarily suspended two liver cancer studies sponsored by the Schering-Plough Corporation because of technical similarities to the University of Pennsylvania study.

. . . [A]s nervousness spread through the field in the months after revelations about Gelsinger's death, some research groups voluntarily suspended gene therapy studies, including two experiments sponsored by the Cystic Fibrosis Foundation and studies at Beth Israel Deaconess Medical Center in Boston aimed at hemophilia. The scientists paused to review their studies and make sure they learned from the mistakes made at the University of Pennsylvania.

In March, the Department of Health and Human Services announced two initiatives by [the] FDA and NIH. The Gene Therapy Clinical Trial Monitoring Plan is designed to ratchet up the level of scrutiny with additional reporting requirements for study sponsors. A series of Gene Transfer Safety Symposia was designed to get researchers to talk to each other, to share their results about unexpected problems, and to make sure that everyone knows the rules.

In addition, [the] FDA launched random inspections of seventy clinical trials in more than two dozen gene therapy programs nationwide and instituted new reporting requirements. "We see the need to get the concept across that this is for keeps," says FDA's Noguchi. "You can be sloppy when you are dealing with a scientific paper, but you can't be sloppy when you are dealing with a human. Everything matters."

So far, the inspections only suggest that one other program appears to be in trouble, he says, but by the fall, "[w]e should be able to say accurately the state of the art of gene therapy and where it needs to improve."

Meanwhile, President Clinton announced more "new actions designed to ensure that individuals are adequately informed about the potential risks and benefits of participating in research . . . and steps designed to address the potential financial conflicts of interest faced by researchers." In addition, the President said in May, "We are also sending the Congress a new legislative proposal to authorize civil monetary penalties for researchers and institutions found to be in violation of regulations governing human clinical trials." If the legislation passes, [the] FDA will, for the first time for drugs and biologics, have the power to essentially fine researchers and their institutions, up to $250,000 and $1 million, respectively.

"This is a clear message," HHS [Health and Human Services] Secretary Donna E. Shalala, Ph.D., said in May, "that we intend to get serious." . . .

THE GELSINGER CASE

When Orkin and Motulsky [S.H. Orkin and A.G. Motulsky were two doctors who had been appointed to an FDA committee to review the efficacy of the NIH's investment in gene therapy trials] reported on the technical limitations of gene transfer techniques five years ago, they virtually predicted problems in the clinic. During that same December meeting at which Orkin and Motulsky made their disheartening report, the RAC approved the University of Pennsylvania gene therapy trial for ornithine transcarboxylase deficiency (OTCD). [The] FDA, too, allowed the study to proceed.

The treatment idea was fairly straightforward. OTCD occurs when a baby inherits a broken gene that prevents the liver from making an enzyme needed to break down ammonia. With the OTCD gene isolated, the University of Pennsylvania researchers packaged it in a replication-defective adenovirus. To reach the target cells in the liver, the Philadelphia scientists wanted to inject the adenovirus directly into the hepatic artery that leads to that organ. Some members of the NIH RAC objected, fearing that direct delivery to the liver was dangerous. Nonetheless, after a vigorous public discussion with the University of Pennsylvania researchers, the RAC voted for approval of the study.

At age 18, Jesse Gelsinger was in good health, but [he] was not truly a healthy teenager. He had a rare form of OTCD that appeared not to be linked to his parents, but the genetic defect arose spontaneously in his body after birth. During his youth, he had many episodes of hospitalization, including an incident just a year before the OTCD trial in which he nearly died from a coma induced by liver failure. But a strict diet that allowed only a few grams of protein per day and a pile of pills controlled his disease to the point where he appeared to be a normally active teenager. With the encouragement of his father, Paul Gelsinger, Jesse volunteered for the study, and when he was initially evaluated, his medical condition qualified him to participate.

Gelsinger received the experimental treatment in September 1999. Four days later, he was dead. No one is really sure exactly why the gene therapy treatment caused his death, but it appears that his immune system launched a raging attack on the adenovirus carrier. Then an overwhelming cascade of organ failures occurred, starting with jaundice, and progressing to a blood-clotting disorder, kidney failure, lung failure, and ultimately brain death.

In its investigation, [the] FDA found a series of serious deficiencies in the way that the University of Pennsylvania conducted the OTCD gene therapy trial, some more serious than others. For example, researchers entered Gelsinger into the trial as a substitute for another volunteer who dropped out, but Gelsinger's high ammonia levels at the time of the treatment should have excluded him from the study. Moreover, the university failed to immediately report that two patients had experienced serious side effects from the gene therapy, as required in the study design, and the deaths of monkeys given a similar treatment were never included in the informed consent discussion.

[The] FDA's discussions with the university remain ongoing.

Source: From Larry Thompson, "Human Gene Therapy: Harsh Lessons, High Hopes," *FDA Consumer Magazine*, September–October 2000: www.fda.gov/fdac/features/2000/500_gene.html

READING 8.3.2
Enhancing the Protection of Human Subjects in Gene Transfer Research at the NIH

PROTOCOL REVIEW

- Safety will be best protected if subjects are not enrolled in novel gene transfer trials until RAC [Recombinant DNA Advisory Committee] discussion has occurred and the investigator has responded to the RAC recommendations.
- The timing of review of gene transfer protocols by RAC, the local IRB [Institutional Review Board] and IBC [Institutional Biosafety Committee], and [the] FDA should be altered to ensure that RAC can function as an effective advisory committee to investigators, institutional IRBs and IBCs, and FDA.

- The requirement that the investigator obtain IRB approval prior to submission to OBA [Office of Biotechnology Activities]/RAC should be eliminated. This change would allow investigators to receive RAC input at an earlier stage of protocol development.
- IBC approval should be withheld until RAC review is complete. In the case of non-novel protocols, IBC approval can be granted as soon as the IBC is notified that the protocol has been deemed non-novel.
- In the case of novel protocols, IBC approval must be withheld until after RAC discussion and the investigator has responded to the review, thereby preventing the initiation of a trial prior to RAC review.
- RAC should complete its review and revision of the definition of "novel" gene transfer protocols and the process/mechanism for determining whether or not a protocol is "novel." Public comment and input should be solicited.
- To clarify the types of research that are subject to the NIH Guidelines, RAC should complete its review and revision of the definition of gene transfer research to ensure that all applicable and appropriate areas of research are subject to oversight and review.

SERIOUS ADVERSE EVENT REPORTING

- Public discussion of serious adverse events is an important component of the oversight process.
- NIH/OBA should continue to receive from investigators reports of serious adverse events. The Working Group acknowledged that [the] FDA is working on a proposed rule to make public some information regarding serious adverse events in gene transfer, and encourages the agency to move expeditiously in meeting this goal.
- Serious adverse events should not be considered trade secrets or proprietary, and must be reported to RAC.
- Data in aggregate made available to the public should be analyzed and interpreted.
- All reasonable measures must be taken to protect the privacy of the individual(s) who suffered the adverse event, without compromising the health of others in similar trials.
- A majority of the Working Group recommended that NIH and [the] FDA must work together to simplify, streamline, and harmonize reporting of serious adverse events. This includes clarification of the timing requirements for reporting specific types of serious adverse events.
- NIH should work with [the] FDA to expand and enhance education and outreach programs to investigators and sponsors conducting gene transfer research to inform them of their reporting obligations.
- NIH should explore ways for promoting the communication of serious adverse events to the relevant IBCs and IRBs.
- A standing body should be established to conduct ongoing analyses of adverse event data. This body should include basic scientists, clinicians, patient advocates, and ethicists. Additional ad hoc members can be appointed for their expertise on an as needed basis. This group would:
  —review all reports of adverse events,
  —analyze the data for trends,
  —develop a cumulative report that would be presented annually at a public RAC meeting and made available to the public, and
  —identify trends or even single events that may warrant further public discussion or federal action.

PROFESSIONAL AND PUBLIC EDUCATION

- NIH/OBA should target education efforts at specialty clinical centers where gene transfer studies are likely to be conducted or subjects recruited, such as CF [cystic fibrosis] centers or hemophilia clinics. In addition, OBA/RAC should produce a pamphlet or brochure on gene transfer research targeted to families and consumers and post such information on its website.
- In collaboration with [Office for Human Research Protections (OHRP)] and other relevant groups, OBA should continue its initiatives for a series of workshops for IRBs and IBCs on gene transfer research.

- OBA should work with OHRP to encourage IRB cooperation in ensuring that human subjects are not enrolled in gene transfer trials until RAC deems a protocol non-novel, or if novel, the protocol has completed the RAC review process.
- NIH should work with OHRP to encourage the inclusion of additional resource sites for information regarding participation in clinical trials in the informed consent form. For gene transfer clinical trials, this information should include a reference to the RAC review process and directions regarding how to obtain relevant information from OBA/RAC.

Source: Advisory Committee to the Director, Working Group on NIH Oversight of Clinical Gene Transfer Research, "Executive Summary," in *Enhancing the Protection of Human Subjects in Gene Transfer Research at the National Institutes of Health,* July 12, 2000: www.nih.gov/about/director/07122000.htm.

1. Which federal rules did the gene therapy researchers who treated Jesse Gelsinger violate?

_____

_____

_____

_____

_____

_____

_____

2. How did the FDA respond to the discovery of rule violations in gene therapy clinical trials?

_____

_____

_____

_____

_____

_____

_____

3. Jesse Gelsinger volunteered for gene therapy with the hope of curing his liver disease. Families like the Gelsingers, along with researchers and biotechnology companies, often argue that increased federal regulations—such as those proposed in Reading 8.3.2—impede scientific progress and unduly limit the number of clinical trials available to people who are critically ill. They also argue that the federal government overreacted to Jesse Gelsinger's death when the FDA and NIH closed down the University of Pennsylvania's clinical trials and then issued new regulations and guidelines. Others argue, however, that the public at large requires vigorous protection by governmental agencies that have the scientific expertise to assess the merits of new medical protocols and the independence to regulate researchers who have too much at stake in the success of their own protocols. Do you think the FDA and NIH regulatory response to the Gelsinger death was justified? Explain and support your answer.

_____

_____

_____

_____

_____

4. *Web-Based Question.* The controversy over government regulation is typically not about total regulation versus no regulation. Instead, it is more commonly about the quantity of regulation. Go to the FDA website at http://www.fda.gov/BiologicsBloodVaccines/CellularGeneTherapyProducts/default.htm. This website describes the regulatory offices that oversee cellular and gene therapy products and the rules governing this scientific and economic activity. Explore the website and some of the links on the site. Do you now agree or disagree with many research scientists and biotechnology companies that complain about government regulation and red tape? Explain and support your answer.

Web addresses sometimes change. If you can't locate a website, try an external search (e.g., Google) to find the website. Configurations within a website often change. If you can't find a particular link or article, for example, try an internal search of the website as well as an external search. Be resourceful!

_____

_____

_____

_____

_____

9

The Judiciary

EXERCISE 9.1 Establishing Judicial Review

INTRODUCTION

Wielding the power of judicial review, courts today routinely strike down as unconstitutional legislative and executive branch actions at the national, state, and local levels of government. For critics of the nation's courts, judicial review is antidemocratic: When politically unaccountable federal courts, for example, invalidate legislation passed by duly elected members of Congress and signed into law by the president of the United States, the will of the people is denied. For proponents, judicial review is an essential restraint on the will of the majority, and a safeguard of individual liberties and minority rights.

Dramatic controversies over the Supreme Court's exercise of judicial review punctuate U.S. history. Here are two examples. In 1857, in *Dred Scott v. Sanford*, the Court declared unconstitutional a federal law—the Missouri Compromise—banning slavery in the northern territories. The ruling inflamed northern opinion, discredited the Court in the eyes of many, and hurled the nation toward civil war. Senator John P. Hale of New Hampshire responded by introducing a resolution to abolish the Supreme Court! Disputes over judicial review flared again in the 1930s, when the Supreme Court declared unconstitutional many New Deal measures aimed at rescuing the nation from the depths of the Great Depression. President Franklin D. Roosevelt counterattacked by demanding that Congress enact legislation that would have created six new seats on the Court so that Roosevelt could fill them with justices who would affirm the constitutionality of his legislative program.

When the framers took up judicial review at the Constitutional Convention in Philadelphia in 1787, it proved less divisive; the vast majority of delegates supported the principle that the federal judiciary would be the final authority interpreting law and the Constitution.[1] Several clauses in the Constitution allude to judicial review, but the framers declined to spell out the power because it raised an unsettling question: Would judicial supremacy over *the text* of the Constitution entail a "judicial veto" over *the actions* of the legislative and executive branches? James Madison rejected such a broad notion of judicial supremacy, but other Constitution-makers claimed in their state ratifying conventions that the judicial check would indeed limit the national government. Alexander Hamilton, in *Federalist No. 78,* asserted that the Supreme Court must be vested with the power of judicial review, but that even so armed, it would remain the weakest of the branches.

The Supreme Court established its power to declare an act of Congress unconstitutional in *Marbury v. Madison* (1803) by ruling that Section 13 of the Judiciary Act of 1789—a federal law—was contradicted, and trumped, by the Constitution. At stake in the case: whether a Federalist Party appointee, William Marbury, would serve—or be denied—a five-year term as a justice of the peace on a Washington, DC, court. Few disputes reaching the Supreme Court have been substantively so insignificant, yet because of the participants' stature, the high political drama of the case, and the force of Chief Justice John Marshall's opinion, few cases have commanded as much attention from scholars and students.

In the election of 1800, for the first time, the Federalist Party lost control of Congress and the presidency. Federalists feared that the victorious Republican Party—led by Thomas Jefferson, the new president—would savage the young government and bring the nation to ruin. To preserve Federalist influence as a bastion against the Republican tide, the

---

[1]Henry J. Abraham, *The Judicial Process,* 7th ed. (New York: Oxford University Press, 1998), pp. 335–336.

outgoing Federalist president, John Adams, joined with the lame-duck[2] Federalist Congress to create fifty-nine new positions in the judiciary. Adams filled these posts with loyal Federalist Party judges, often referred to as "midnight appointments" to indicate the desperate and last-minute nature of Adams's gambit.

John Marshall, a Federalist and Adams's secretary of state, was responsible for certifying and delivering to the new appointees their judicial commissions, documents authorizing them to take their seats on the bench. Unfortunately for seventeen of the new appointees, Marshall was in a hurry. Adams had nominated, and the Federalist Congress had confirmed, Marshall as the new chief justice of the Supreme Court. In his rush to step down as secretary of state and take up his new post, Marshall left seventeen judicial commissions on his desk, undelivered. The new Republican president, Jefferson, found the commissions and ordered his secretary of state, James Madison, not to deliver them—thereby retaliating against the Federalist effort to pack the judiciary and thus setting the stage for a confrontation between the executive and judicial branches.

William Marbury and three other Adams appointees waiting to receive their commissions sued to force Madison to deliver the documents. They took their case directly to the Supreme Court and demanded that the Court issue an order, called a *writ of mandamus*, compelling Madison to carry out his duty as secretary of state. Because Marshall agreed to hear Marbury's case before any lower court had examined it, the Supreme Court exercised original jurisdiction.[3] (See Box 9.1.1 on original versus appellate jurisdiction.)

Presiding over the case spawned by his own negligence, Marshall appeared trapped. If he issued the writ, Madison would defy it. Having no way to physically compel Madison, Marshall and the Court would appear impotent. Declining to issue the writ, on the other hand, would appear a cowardly endorsement by default of Madison's dereliction of his duty as secretary of state.

Marshall extricated the Court from this dilemma by ruling that Section 13 of the Judiciary Act of 1789 had unconstitutionally bestowed on the Supreme Court a new power: to issue writs of mandamus—*under its original jurisdiction*—to public officials who failed to perform their official duties. Marshall argued that Section 13 expanded the original jurisdiction of the Supreme Court beyond that specified in the Constitution, and that when an act of Congress conflicts with the Constitution, that legislation must not be allowed to stand. Marshall's interpretation of the Constitution circumscribed Congress' power and expanded that of his own Court.

Today, no act of Congress or the president, or of state and local governments, is immune to judicial scrutiny. The bracing, panoramic scope of judicial review and the centralization of power in the nation's highest court would shock those who struggled, early in the republic's history, with defining the Court's power. However, the full potential of judicial review took time to develop. After *Marbury*, the Court waited over half a century before striking down another act of Congress. In the late nineteenth century, the Court exercised judicial review more frequently, but limited its reach mainly to the problem of state government regulation of private economic matters. In the twentieth century, and especially in the 1950s through the 1970s, the Court discarded restraint and vastly expanded its jurisdiction into the realms of civil rights and civil liberties, fundamentally reshaping U.S. society. Today's justices, and many observers of the Court, are divided over the wisdom of this course. Do the justices too often *make* law instead of *interpreting* law? Dissenting from the majority opinion in *Webster v. Reproductive Health Services* (1989), an abortion rights case, Justice Antonin Scalia wrote that the majority were needlessly prolonging "this

---

[2]Before the Twentieth Amendment was ratified in 1933, Congress would typically not adjourn until March of the year following the election. Because the new president was not sworn in until March, Adams had several months after his defeat to push legislation through the still-Federalist Congress.

[3]Many aspects of Marshall's decision and the events surrounding it remain disputed by scholars. A close examination of Section 13 of the Judiciary Act of 1789 indicates that it did not broaden the Court's original jurisdiction. Marshall may have recognized this because he did not even cite in his decision the language in Section 13 that he was declaring unconstitutional. Furthermore, Article III, Section 2 of the Constitution does not stipulate that the Court has original jurisdiction *only* in cases "affecting Ambassadors, other public Ministers and Consuls, and those in which a State shall be a Party." Scholars have pointed out that, because many members of the Congress that drafted and enacted the Judiciary Act of 1789 had been delegates to the Constitutional Convention, they probably would not have passed a law that conflicted with the Constitution. See, for example, "The 200th Anniversary of *Marbury v. Madison*: The Reasons We Should Still Care About the Decision, and the Lingering Questions It Left Behind," by Joel B. Grossman, at http://writ.news.findlaw.com/commentary/20030224_grossman.html.

Court's self-awarded sovereignty over a field where it has little proper business since the answers to most of the cruel questions posed are political and not judicial."

In the *Marbury* case, recognizing the comparative weakness of the Court, Marshall deftly avoided confrontations with the legislative and executive branches. By the late twentieth century, however, with its power handsomely enlarged, the Court stood as an equal and coordinate—not inferior—branch of the federal government. So confident were the justices in the power and position of the Court that they waged battle directly with President Richard Nixon. In *United States v. Nixon* (1974), the Court ordered Nixon to turn over secretly recorded tapes containing material politically fatal to him. The president yielded to the Court's order, affirming that the justices of the High Court were indeed the final arbiters of the Constitution—even in a direct confrontation with the chief executive.

BOX 9.1.1   Original Versus Appellate Jurisdiction of the United States Supreme Court

Original Jurisdiction

- The authority to hear cases before any other court does—these cases begin and end in the Supreme Court.
- Article III, Section 2 of the Constitution gives the Supreme Court original jurisdiction over "Cases affecting Ambassadors, other public Ministers and Consuls, and those in which a State shall be a party."
- Very few cases (one to five per year) come to the Supreme Court under its original jurisdiction, and most of these involve states suing each other over contested borders.
- Congress has no control over the Supreme Court's original jurisdiction because its original jurisdiction is specified in the Constitution.

Appellate Jurisdiction

- The authority to hear cases on appeal from the U.S. courts of appeal or from state supreme courts: These cases have been heard in other courts before reaching the Supreme Court.
- Article III, Section 2 of the Constitution provides that in all cases other than those that fall under the Supreme Court's original jurisdiction, "the Supreme Court shall have appellate Jurisdiction, both as to Law and Fact, with such Exceptions, and under such Regulations as the Congress shall make."
- Almost all of the cases decided by the Supreme Court (fewer than seventy-five per year recently) come to it on the basis of its appellate jurisdiction.
- Congress has control over the Supreme Court's appellate jurisdiction and may restrict that jurisdiction if it chooses, although such restriction has not happened since the Civil War.

ASSIGNMENT

Study Reading 9.1.1, an excerpt from *Marbury v. Madison,* and Reading 9.1.2, an excerpt from *Federalist No. 78,* and answer the questions that follow.

READING 9.1.1
Marbury v. Madison, 5 U.S. 137 (1803)

That the people have an original right to establish, for their future government, such principles as, in their opinion, shall most conduce to their own happiness, is the basis on which the whole American fabric has been erected. The exercise of this original right is a very great exertion; nor can it nor ought it to be frequently repeated. The principles, therefore, so established are deemed fundamental. And as the authority, from which they proceed, is supreme, and can seldom act, they are designed to be permanent.

This original and supreme will organizes the government, and assigns to different departments their respective powers. It may either stop here; or establish certain limits not to be transcended by those departments.

The government of the United States is of the latter description. The powers of the legislature are defined and limited; and that those limits may not be mistaken or forgotten, the constitution is written. To what purpose are powers limited, and to what purpose is that limitation committed to writing; if these limits may, at any time, be passed by those intended to be restrained? The distinction between a government with limited and unlimited powers is abolished, if those limits do not confine the persons on whom they are imposed, and if acts prohibited and acts allowed are of equal obligation. It is a proposition too plain to be contested, that the constitution controls any legislative act repugnant to it; or, that the legislature may alter the constitution by an ordinary act.

Between these alternatives there is no middle ground. The constitution is either a superior, paramount law, unchangeable by ordinary means, or it is on a level with ordinary legislative acts, and like other acts, is alterable when the legislature shall please to alter it.

If the former part of the alternative be true, then a legislative act contrary to the constitution is not law: if the latter part be truew, then written constitutions are absurd attempts, on the part of the people, to limit a power in its own nature illimitable.

Certainly all those who have framed written constitutions contemplate them as forming the fundamental and paramount law of the nation, and consequently the theory of every such government must be, that an act of the legislature repugnant to the constitution is void.

This theory is essentially attached to a written constitution, and is consequently to be considered by this court as one of the fundamental principles of our society. . . .

It is emphatically the province and duty of the judicial department to say what the law is. Those who apply the rule to particular cases, must of necessity expound and interpret that rule. If two laws conflict with each other, the courts must decide on the operation of each. So if a law be in opposition to the constitution: if both the law and the constitution apply to a particular case, so that the court must either decide that case conformably to the law, disregarding the constitution; or conformably to the constitution, disregarding the law: the court must determine which of these conflicting rules governs the case. This is of the very essence of judicial duty.

If then the courts are to regard the constitution; and the constitution is superior to any ordinary act of the legislature; the constitution, and not such ordinary act, must govern the case to which they both apply.

Those then who controvert the principle that the constitution is to be considered, in court, as a paramount law, are reduced to the necessity of maintaining that courts must close their eyes on the constitution, and see only the law.

This doctrine would subvert the very foundation of all written constitutions. It would declare that an act, which, according to the principles and theory of our government, is entirely void, is yet, in practice, completely obligatory. It would declare, that if the legislature shall do what is expressly forbidden, such act, notwithstanding the express prohibition, is in reality effectual. It would be giving to the legislature a practical and real omnipotence with the same breath which professes to restrict their powers within narrow limits. It is prescribing limits, and declaring that those limits may be passed at pleasure. . . .

It is also not entirely unworthy of observation, that in declaring what shall be the supreme law of the land, the constitution itself is first mentioned; and not the laws of the United States generally, but those only which shall be made in pursuance of the constitution, have that rank.

Thus, the particular phraseology of the constitution of the United States confirms and strengthens the principle, supposed to be essential to all written constitutions, that a law repugnant to the constitution is void, and that courts, as well as other departments, are bound by that instrument.

The rule [meaning the law] must be discharged.

READING 9.1.2
Alexander Hamilton, *Federalist No. 78*

. . . Whoever attentively considers the different departments of power must perceive, that, in a government in which they are separated from each other, the judiciary, from the nature of its functions, will always be the least dangerous to the political rights of the Constitution; because it will be least in a capacity to annoy or injure them. The Executive not only dispenses the honors, but holds the sword of the community. The legislature not only commands the purse, but prescribes the rules by which the duties and rights of every citizen are to be regulated. The judiciary, on the contrary, has no influence over either the sword or the purse; no direction either of the strength or of the wealth of the society; and can take no active resolution whatever. It may truly be said to have neither FORCE nor WILL, but merely judgment; and must ultimately depend upon the aid of the executive arm even for the efficacy of its judgments.

This simple view of the matter suggests several important consequences. It proves incontestably, that the judiciary is beyond comparison the weakest of the three departments of power; that it can never attack with success either of the other two; and that all possible care is requisite to enable it to defend itself against their attacks. It equally proves, that though individual oppression may now and then proceed from the courts of justice, the general liberty of the people can never be endangered from that quarter; I mean so long as the judiciary remains truly distinct from both the legislature and the Executive. For I agree, that "there is no liberty, if the power of judging be not separated from the legislative and executive powers."

And it proves, in the last place, that as liberty can have nothing to fear from the judiciary alone, but would have every thing to fear from its union with either of the other departments; that as all the effects of such a union must ensue from a dependence of the former on the latter, notwithstanding a nominal and apparent separation; that as, from the natural feebleness of the judiciary, it is in continual jeopardy of being overpowered, awed, or influenced by its co-ordinate branches; and that as nothing can contribute so much to its firmness and independence as permanency in office, this quality may therefore be justly regarded as an indispensable ingredient in its constitution, and, in a great measure, as the citadel of the public justice and the public security.

The complete independence of the courts of justice is peculiarly essential in a limited Constitution. By a limited Constitution, I understand one which contains certain specified exceptions to the legislative authority; such, for instance, as that it shall pass no bills of attainder, no ex post facto laws, and the like. Limitations of this kind can be preserved in practice no other way than through the medium of courts of justice, whose duty it must be to declare all acts contrary to the manifest tenor of the Constitution void. Without this, all the reservations of particular rights or privileges would amount to nothing.

Some perplexity respecting the rights of the courts to pronounce legislative acts void, because contrary to the Constitution, has arisen from an imagination that the doctrine would imply a superiority of the judiciary to the legislative power. It is urged that the authority which can declare the acts of another void, must necessarily be superior to the one whose acts may be declared void. As this doctrine is of great importance in all the American constitutions, a brief discussion of the ground on which it rests cannot be unacceptable.

There is no position which depends on clearer principles, than that every act of a delegated authority, contrary to the tenor of the commission under which it is exercised, is void. No legislative act, therefore, contrary to the Constitution, can be valid. To deny this, would be to affirm, that the deputy is greater than his principal; that the servant is above his master; that the representatives of the people are superior to the people themselves; that men acting by virtue of powers, may do not only what their powers do not authorize, but what they forbid.

If it be said that the legislative body are themselves the constitutional judges of their own powers, and that the construction they put upon them is conclusive upon the other departments, it may be answered, that this cannot be the natural presumption, where it is not to be collected from any particular provisions in the Constitution. It is not otherwise to be supposed, that the Constitution could intend to enable the representatives of the people to substitute their will to that of their constituents. It is far more rational to suppose, that the courts were designed to be an intermediate body between the people and the legislature, in order, among other things, to keep the latter within the limits assigned to their authority. The interpretation of the laws is the proper and peculiar province of the courts. A constitution is, in fact, and must be regarded by the judges, as a fundamental law. It therefore belongs to them to ascertain its meaning, as well as the meaning of any particular act proceeding from the legislative body. If there should happen to be an irreconcilable variance between the two, that which has the superior obligation and validity ought, of course, to be preferred; or, in other words, the Constitution ought to be preferred to the statute [meaning the law], the intention of the people to the intention of their agents. . . .

1. According to the excerpts from Marshall's ruling in Reading 9.1.1 and from Federalist No. 78 in Reading 9.1.2, if the Constitution says one thing and a law passed by Congress says another, which must give way? Explain by citing passages from each reading to support your answer.

_____

_____

_____

_____

_____

_____

_____

_____

_____

2. According to Marshall's ruling, the clause in Article III, Section 2 that specifies the original jurisdiction of the Court is restrictive—meaning that the types of original jurisdiction authorized are the only ones granted by the Constitution to the Court. But some scholars assert that Marshall and his colleagues misinterpreted the Constitution and that this clause in Article III, Section 2 does not necessarily preclude Congress from adding to the original jurisdiction of the Supreme Court. Examine carefully the following excerpt of Article III, Section 2:

> In all cases affecting Ambassadors, other public Ministers and Consuls, and those in which a State shall be a Party, the supreme Court shall have original jurisdiction. In all the other Cases before mentioned, the supreme Court shall have appellate Jurisdiction, both as to Law and Fact, with such Exceptions, and under such Regulations as the Congress shall make.

Do you think that Marshall has the stronger argument, or do his critics? Cite specific language— or the lack thereof—in the excerpt above to support your position.

_____

_____

_____

_____

_____

_____

_____

3. If you sided with Marshall in question 2, rewrite the passage in Article III, Section 2 to *expressly preclude* the Supreme Court from exercising original jurisdiction in cases other than those specified. If you sided with Marshall's critics in question 2, rewrite the passage in Article III, Section 2 to *expressly authorize* the Supreme Court to exercise original jurisdiction in cases other than those specified.

_____

_____

_____

_____

_____

_____

_____

4. In Readings 9.1.1 and 9.1.2, do Marshall and Hamilton suggest that judicial review is a narrow power that must be exercised cautiously, or is it a broad, unlimited power? Cite specific language—or the lack thereof—in each reading to support your answer.

_____

_____

_____

_____

_____

_____

_____

_____

5. In Reading 9.1.2, Hamilton argues that the courts are the weakest of the three departments of power (branches of government). How does Hamilton support his argument? Cite specific language in Reading 9.1.2 to support your answer.

_____

_____

_____

_____

_____

_____

_____

6. The threat that judicial review poses to the legislative and executive branches depends on the significance of the legislation the Court strikes down and on how frequently the Court exercises the power of judicial review. Consider the quantitative aspect of judicial review. Between 1803 and 1899, for example, the Court declared unconstitutional in whole or in part twenty-six acts of Congress. Between 1986 and its decision in *McConnell v. FEC* in 2003, the Court (presided over by Chief Justice William Rehnquist) declared unconstitutional in whole or in part forty acts of Congress.[4]

    a. Describe how the frequency with which the Court strikes down acts of Congress has changed.

_____

_____

_____

_____

_____

    b. Does the change you described in question 6.a support or undermine Hamilton's prediction that the judiciary would be the weakest of the three departments of power? Explain and support your answer.

_____

_____

_____

_____

_____

7. We take for granted today that the Supreme Court exclusively has the power to determine what is constitutional and what is not. But a judicial monopoly on constitutional interpretation was not inevitable. In Reading 9.1.3, President Thomas Jefferson suggested two alternative approaches to constitutional interpretation. Identify each approach and explain its strengths and weaknesses.

    a. Jefferson's first approach: _____

_____

_____

---

[4]http://supreme.justia.com/constitution/046-acts-of-congress-held-unconstitutional.html. Or conduct an Internet search for acts of Congress held unconstitutional in whole or in part by the Supreme Court of the United States.

_____

_____

_____

b. Jefferson's second approach:_____

_____

_____

_____

_____

READING 9.1.3
Thomas Jefferson to W. H. Torrance, Monticello, June 11, 1815

. . . [W]hether the judges are invested with exclusive authority to decide on the constitutional-ity of a law, has been heretofore a subject of consideration with me in the exercise of official duties. Certainly there is not a word in the constitution which has given that power to them more than to the executive or legislative branches. Questions of property, of character and of crime being ascribed to the judges, through a definite course of legal proceeding, laws involv-ing such questions belong, of course, to them; and as they decide on them ultimately and without appeal, they of course decide *for themselves*. The constitutional validity of the law or laws again prescribing executive action, and to be administered by that branch ultimately and without appeal, the executive must decide for *themselves* also, whether, under the constitution, they are valid or not. So also as to laws governing the proceedings of the legislature, that body must judge *for itself* the constitutionality of the law, and equally without appeal or control from its co-ordinate branches. And, in general, that branch which is to act ultimately, and without appeal, on any law, is the rightful expositor of the validity of the law, uncontrolled by the opinions of the other co-ordinate authorities. It may be said that contradictory decisions may arise in such case, and produce inconvenience. This is possible, and is a necessary failing in all human proceedings. Yet the prudence of the public functionaries, and authority of pub-lic opinion, will generally produce accommodation. . . . This is what I believe myself to be sound. But there is another opinion entertained by some men of such judgment and informa-tion as to lessen my confidence in my own. That is, that the legislature alone is the exclusive expounder of the sense of the constitution, in every part of it whatever. And they allege in its support, that this branch has authority to impeach and punish a member of either of the oth-ers acting contrary to its declaration of the sense of the constitution. It may indeed be an-swered, that an act may still be valid although the party is punished for it, right or wrong. However, this opinion which ascribes exclusive exposition to the legislature, merits respect for its safety, there being in the body of the nation a control over them, which, if expressed by re-jection on the subsequent exercise of their elective franchise, enlists public opinion against their exposition, and encourages a judge or executive on a future occasion to adhere to their former opinion. Between these two doctrines, every one has a right to choose, and I know of no third meriting any respect.

EXERCISE 9.2   Judicial Activism Versus Judicial Restraint: The Supreme Court and the Juvenile Death Penalty

INTRODUCTION

The debate between proponents of judicial activism and advocates of judicial restraint is as old as the republic. The debate centers on this question: What is the proper role of the federal courts, particularly the Supreme Court, in the U.S. constitutional system? The answer to this question cannot be found in the Constitution because the framers did not spell out the judicial powers. In fact, even judicial review—the extraordinary power of the federal courts to decide the constitutionality of legislative and executive branch actions—is missing from the Constitution. It was Chief Justice John Marshall, ruling in *Marbury v. Madison* (1803), who bestowed judicial review on the courts (see Exercise 9.1).

That decision sparked an early debate about the role of the Supreme Court, with detractors claiming that the Court had overreached itself in declaring an act of Congress unconstitutional and in claiming for itself a power that is nowhere specified in the Constitution. Controversy over the role of the Supreme Court in the constitutional system flared again in 1857, when the Court waded into the great controversy of the day: the question of slavery in the western territories. In *Scott v. Sanford* the Court ruled that slaves are not citizens of the United States under the provisions of the Constitution and went on to declare the Missouri Compromise unconstitutional. For the first time since *Marbury*, the Court exercised the power of judicial review, igniting a firestorm of controversy that propelled the nation toward civil war. It would take the Civil War and the Thirteenth and Fourteenth Amendments (ratified in 1865 and 1868, respectively) to fix what judicial activists had broken.

The debate between judicial activism and judicial restraint continues. The modern controversy can be traced to 1953, when President Dwight D. Eisenhower appointed Earl Warren chief justice of the Court. Under Warren's leadership, from 1953 to 1969, a solid majority of the Court initiated extraordinary changes in our understanding of constitutional liberties and rights, especially the fair trial rights of the accused and the equal protection rights of African Americans. And, for the first time, the Court ruled that a number of provisions of the Bill of Rights must be applied to protect citizens from the actions of state governments. The Court's activism inevitably generated a political reaction. Conservatives, who felt the Court was undermining law and order, called for Warren's impeachment. In 1968, presidential candidate Richard Nixon ran on a promise to appoint strict constructionists to the federal courts, by which he meant judges who would not read their own political agenda into the language of the Constitution and who generally would defer to the will of the people—or at least to the will of elected officials. Presidents Ronald Reagan, George H. W. Bush Sr., and George W. Bush repeated Nixon's pledge to appoint strict constructionists to the bench.

Behind the debate between judicial activism and judicial restraint is a lot of hypocrisy. Conservatives, for example, have bitterly criticized activist judges for establishing abortion and homosexual rights, but they are ready and willing to enlist federal judicial intervention in right-to-life cases. One such example was the much-publicized battle in 2005 between Terri Schiavo's parents and her husband over the removal of her life support. Liberals sharply criticize judges who yoke themselves to the framers' intent, but they are not beyond invoking judicial restraint when activist judges wield judicial power in favor of conservative political interests. An example was the Supreme Court's unprecedented decision, in *Bush v. Gore* (2000), to overrule the Florida courts and to put George W. Bush in the White House. Some judges and law professors may care about the tenets of activism and restraint, but the best predictor of the Supreme Court's justices' votes is political ideology, not judicial activism or restraint. Indeed, once a conservative majority emerged on the Supreme Court in the early 1990s, conservative voices became less concerned with judicial restraint and more concerned with the furtherance of the conservative ideological agenda, whereas liberals began to advocate for more restraint. President Obama, for example, has argued *against* judicial activism on several occasions and, during a State of the Union Address, criticized the conservative Supreme Court justices—some of whom were in attendance—for breaking with precedent in a recent decision striking down federal limits on corporate and union campaign spending.[1] One study found that Justices Scalia and Thomas, noted for their vociferous

---

[1]*Citizens U. Federal Elections Commission* (2010).

defense of judicial restraint, are actually more activist than the liberals on the Court.[2] Not surprisingly, most Americans' opinions—Supreme Court justices included—about what the Constitution means are more likely informed by their policy preferences than by their preference for a consistent method of constitutional interpretation. (See Box 9.2.1 for a summary of the differences between judicial activism and judicial restraint.)

BOX 9.2.1   Tenets of Judicial Activism and Judicial Restraint

Judicial Activism

- ***The Constitution is a living document.*** The Constitution's meaning is not fixed and therefore cannot always conform to the specific historical intentions of its authors. Indeed, on many constitutional matters, the intention of the framers cannot be discerned. The principles set forth in the Constitution are timeless, but the language of the document must be adapted to changing times and conditions. The framers used general and often ambiguous language to allow future generations of Americans to create their own politics. They did not intend for the Constitution to become a straitjacket. An activist judiciary plays an essential role in the process of adapting the Constitution to new political problems and dilemmas.
- ***A constitutional system ultimately depends on the federal courts to protect minority and individual rights.*** Elected officials need to be in sync with the majority to get reelected. It's not surprising, then, that they may neglect minority and individual rights. Because federal judges are appointed, not elected, and because they have life tenure, subject to impeachment and removal from office, they are less likely to succumb to the tyranny of the majority. In the long run, an activist judiciary, insulated from majority public opinion, is the branch of government that is most likely to protect minority and individual rights.

Judicial Restraint

- ***The job of judges is to apply the Constitution, not to rewrite it.*** Judges are obligated to interpret the Constitution with scrupulous regard for the meaning of its language and by adhering strictly to the intent of the framers. When judges go beyond these parameters, they inevitably and improperly substitute their own personal views and preferences for those specified in the Constitution. To interpret the Constitution correctly, judges must restrain themselves from acting as though they know better than the Constitution itself or the people who wrote it.
- ***Judges must defer to the elected representatives of the people and to the people themselves.*** Unless a law clearly violates specific language in the Constitution, democracy requires that judges defer to the elected representatives of the people. Judges cannot and should not protect the people from poorly conceived laws; in the spirit of democracy, the people themselves must act to correct laws that they find to be unwise. There is a manifest difference between bad public policy and unconstitutional public policy. Republican government will not long survive if the people look to the courts for redress rather than to themselves and to their elected representatives. In James Madison's words (in *Federalist No. 10*), "The ultimate repository of liberty is in the people."
- ***Judges should stick to precedent in deciding cases.*** A legal system requires continuity. Abrupt changes in the law, especially overturning precedent decisions, leads to chaos and to political challenges to judicial independence. Respecting precedent keeps judges honest; that is, it keeps them within the boundaries established by previous cases.

ASSIGNMENT

Reading 9.2.1, from the Court's decision in *Roper v. Simmons* (2005), illustrates the conflict between judicial activism and judicial restraint. In 1993, at the age of 17, Christopher Simmons and a friend broke into the home of St. Louis County resident, Shirley Cook, intending to rob her while she slept. Cook awoke and recognized Simmons. The two teenagers then bound Cook with duct tape and electrical wire and threw her from a bridge into the river below. Simmons had previously told friends he wanted to commit a murder and that as a juvenile he could get away with it.

At age 18, Simmons was tried, convicted, and sentenced to death under Missouri state law, which allowed the execution of those who committed certain crimes as juveniles. The Supreme

---

[2]Lori Ringhand, "Judicial Activism: An Empirical Examination of Voting Behavior on the Rehnquist Court," *Constitutional Commentary* (Spring 2007), pp. 43–102.

Court had ruled in *Stanford v. Kentucky* (1989) that state death penalty laws for juveniles were not in violation of the Eighth Amendment's prohibition against cruel and unusual punishment. Based on that U.S. Supreme Court ruling, the Missouri Supreme Court turned down Simmons's appeal. But in a precedent-setting case, in 2002 (*Atkins v. Virginia*), the Supreme Court ruled that capital punishment for the mentally retarded *did* violate the Eighth Amendment. Based on the Court's reasoning in that case, Simmons filed a writ of *habeas corpus* to the Missouri Supreme Court arguing that his conviction also violated the Eighth Amendment. The Missouri Supreme Court agreed. The state of Missouri then appealed to the U.S. Supreme Court, which, by a vote of 5–4, ruled that the death penalty as applied to juveniles was unconstitutional. At the time of the Court's ruling, nineteen states permitted the execution of juvenile convicted murderers, and seventy-two inmates were on death row in twelve states for murders they committed as juveniles. Since the decision in *Roper,* the Court has ruled, in *Graham v. Florida* (2010), that life imprisonment without possibility of parole for juvenile offenders was a violation of the Eighth Amendment. With the Court's rulings to place limits on punishment for juveniles, fewer states are now trying juvenile defendants in adult courts.[3]

Study Reading 9.2.1 and answer the questions that follow.

READING 9.2.1
From *Roper V. Simmons*, 543 U.S. 551 (2005)

From Justice Kennedy's Opinion of the Court:

The prohibition against "cruel and unusual punishments," like other expansive language in the Constitution, must be interpreted according to its text, by considering history, tradition, and precedent, and with due regard for its purpose and function in the constitutional design. To implement this framework we have established the propriety and affirmed the necessity of referring to "the evolving standards of decency that mark the progress of a maturing society" to determine which punishments are so disproportionate as to be cruel and unusual. . . . The inquiry into our society's evolving standards of decency did not end there. . . . Instead we returned to the rule, established in decisions predating Stanford, that "the Constitution contemplates that in the end our own judgment will be brought to bear on the question of the acceptability of the death penalty under the Eighth Amendment." . . .

A majority of States have rejected the imposition of the death penalty on juvenile offenders under 18, and we now hold this is required by the Eighth Amendment. . . .

Our determination that the death penalty is disproportionate punishment for offenders under 18 finds confirmation in the stark reality that the United States is the only country in the world that continues to give official sanction to the juvenile death penalty. This reality does not become controlling, for the task of interpreting the Eighth Amendment remains our responsibility. Yet . . . the Court has referred to the laws of other countries and to international authorities as instructive for its interpretation of the Eighth Amendment's prohibition of "cruel and unusual punishments." . . .

Over time, from one generation to the next, the Constitution has come to earn the high respect and even, as Madison dared to hope, the veneration of the American people. See *The Federalist* No. 49. The document sets forth, and rests upon, innovative principles original to the American experience, such as federalism; a proven balance in political mechanisms through separation of powers; specific guarantees for the accused in criminal cases; and broad provisions to secure individual freedom and preserve human dignity. These doctrines and guarantees are central to the American experience and remain essential to our present-day self-definition and national identity. Not the least of the reasons we honor the Constitution, then, is because we know it to be our own. It does not lessen our fidelity to the Constitution or

---

[3]Mosi Secret, "States Try Fewer Teenage Defendants in Adult Courts," *New York Times,* March 5, 2011.

our pride in its origins to acknowledge that the express affirmation of certain fundamental rights by other nations and peoples simply underscores the centrality of those same rights within our own heritage of freedom.

From Justice Scalia's Dissenting Opinion:

In urging approval of a constitution that gave life-tenured judges the power to nullify laws enacted by the people's representatives, Alexander Hamilton assured the citizens of New York that there was little risk in this, since "[t]he judiciary . . . ha[s] neither FORCE nor WILL but merely judgment." [*Federalist No. 78*] But Hamilton had in mind a traditional judiciary, "bound down by strict rules and precedents which serve to define and point out their duty in every particular case that comes before them." Bound down, indeed. What a mockery today's opinion makes of Hamilton's expectation, announcing the Court's conclusion that the meaning of our Constitution has changed over the past 15 years—not, mind you, that this Court's decision 15 years ago was *wrong*, but that the Constitution *has changed*. The Court reaches this implausible result by purporting to advert, not to the original meaning of the Eighth Amendment, but to "the evolving standards of decency," . . . of our national society. It then finds, on the flimsiest of grounds, that a national consensus which could not be perceived in our people's laws barely 15 years ago now solidly exists. Worse still, the Court says in so many words that what our people's laws say about the issue does not, in the last analysis, matter: "[I]n the end our own judgment will be brought to bear on the question of the acceptability of the death penalty under the Eighth Amendment." The Court thus proclaims itself sole arbiter of our Nation's moral standards—and in the course of discharging that awesome responsibility purports to take guidance from the views of foreign courts and legislatures. Because I do not believe that the meaning of our Eighth Amendment, any more than the meaning of other provisions of our Constitution, should be determined by the subjective views of five Members of this Court and like-minded foreigners, I dissent.

1. Based on your examination of Justice Kennedy's opinion of the Court, would you identify him as a practitioner of judicial activism or judicial restraint? Cite specific language in his concurring opinion to support your position.

_____

_____

_____

_____

_____

_____

_____

2. Justice Scalia did not vote with the majority; he justified his decision in a *dissenting opinion*. Based on your examination of Justice Scalia's opinion, would you identify him as a practitioner of judicial activism or judicial restraint? Cite specific language in his dissenting opinion to support your position.

_____

_____

_____

_____

_____

_____

_____

_____

3. In your view, should the Supreme Court justices factor into their decision on the juvenile death penalty today's standards of decency including how other nations handle the issue? Explain and support your position.

_____

_____

_____

_____

_____

4. In your view, what role should the Supreme Court play in the American political system? Should the justices practice judicial activism or judicial restraint? Explain and support your position.

_____

_____

_____

_____

_____

5. Reflect carefully and honestly on this question: Was the preference you expressed for judicial activism or judicial restraint in question 4 influenced by your personal view of whether the juvenile death penalty is right or wrong? Explain your answer.

_____

_____

_____

EXERCISE 9.3 What Role Should the Senate Play in Judicial Appointments?

INTRODUCTION

The power to determine who sits on the nation's highest courts has always been contested. Today, it is a bitter battleground between the political parties because federal judges are the final arbiters of what the Constitution means. Serving for life, they will leave their mark on the nation long after the president who nominated them and the senators who confirmed them are no longer in office.

Article 2, Section 2 of the Constitution specifies that the president "shall nominate, and by and with the Advice and Consent of the Senate, shall appoint . . . Judges of the Supreme Court, and all other Officers of the United States; whose Appointments are not herein otherwise provided for; and which shall be established by Law." (The appointment power was extended to all federal judgeships in the Federal Judiciary Act of 1789.) The president alone controls who is nominated to the federal courts; the Senate alone controls who is confirmed. To place a president's nominee on a federal court requires a simple majority vote (50 percent plus one vote) in the Senate. Although we often speak of the president's power to appoint federal judges, the Constitution divides that power between the president and the Senate.

The politics surrounding appointments to the federal judiciary—already contentious—were further polarized during George W. Bush's presidency. President Bush, a conservative determined to appoint conservative judges, confronted a Senate in which the minority Democratic Party (2002–2005) was equally determined to deny Bush his more controversial conservative nominees.

Because the Democrats were the minority party in the Senate in the 108th and 109th Congresses (2003 and 2005), they were unable to use the Senate Judiciary Committee to block Bush's nominees. Instead, Democrats resorted to a less commonly used procedure to block judicial nominations—the *filibuster*. The Republican majority in the Senate lacked the required number of votes (sixty) to shut down these Democratic filibusters—a procedure known as *cloture*.

Because the Constitution gives Congress the authority to "determine the Rules of its Proceedings" (Article I, Section 5), the majority leader of the Senate, Bill Frist (Republican, Tennessee), threatened in 2005 to change Senate rules to prohibit the filibuster of judicial nominations. Frist's threat became known as the "nuclear option" because it would compromise the Senate's tradition of unlimited debate and lead to war between Republicans and Democrats in the Senate at the expense of Bush's legislative agenda. Frist and most Senate Republicans argued that the president's judicial nominees are entitled to an up or down vote; Democrats argued that the filibuster was an important tradition in the Senate, especially as it protected minority rights. On May 23, 2005, moderate Democrats and moderate Republicans agreed to a compromise by which three of the president's filibustered nominees would be given up or down votes. Democrats, according to the agreement, would still be allowed to filibuster judicial nominees in "extraordinary circumstances." As of this writing (2011), Republicans, now in the minority in the Senate, have successfully used the threat of a filibuster to block several of President Obama's nominations to lower federal courts. The problem with achieving a consensus about an up or down vote on judicial nominees is the "whose ox is gored" dilemma: Neither party is willing to reform the rules regarding the use of the filibuster because the majority now might be the minority later. (See Box 9.3.1 for a summary account of the filibuster and cloture procedures in the Senate.)

With partisan passions over judicial appointments becoming more and more heated, U.S. government confronts a prominent constitutional controversy about the Senate's role in the judicial appointment process and the meaning of the phrase "by and with the advice and consent of the Senate."

> ### BOX 9.3.1 Filibuster and Cloture
>
> **Filibuster**
>
> - The filibuster is a procedural feature that highlights the Senate's tradition of unlimited debate.
> - Filibustering is the use of dilatory or obstructive tactics to block a measure by preventing it from coming to a vote.
> - The possibility of filibusters exists because Senate rules place few limits on senators' rights. A senator who seeks recognition usually has a right to the floor if no other senator is speaking, and then may speak for as long as he or she wishes. Today, the mere threat of a filibuster derails Senate action unless the majority has at least sixty votes.
>
> **Cloture**
>
> - Senate Rule XXII, known as the cloture rule, enables senators to terminate a filibuster.
> - Sixteen Senators initiate cloture by presenting a motion to end debate.
> - The Senate does not vote on the cloture motion until the second day after the motion is made. Three-fifths of the votes of all senators—that equals sixty votes—is required to invoke cloture.
>
> *Source:* Congressional Research Service, Library of Congress, "Filibusters and Clotures in the Senate," March 28, 2003: http://www.senate.gov/reference/resources/pdf/RL30360.pdf.

ASSIGNMENT

Reading 9.3.1 consists of some excerpts from the debates about advice and consent at the Constitutional Convention of 1787. Reading 9.3.2 includes selections from *The Federalist,* specifically Alexander Hamilton's explanation of the Senate's power of advice and consent. Judges and scholars still refer to the proceedings of the Constitutional Convention and *The Federalist* authors' arguments to interpret ambiguous language in the Constitution. Readings 9.3.3 and 9.3.4 bring the debate into the present. They are excerpts from testimony at a Senate hearing (108th Congress, May 6, 2003) on the role of the Senate in judicial appointments. Reading 9.3.3 is an argument for a relatively weak Senate role of advice and consent, whereas Reading 9.3.4 is an argument for a strong Senate role. The questions that follow the readings ask you to assess contrasting views on the meaning of "advice and consent."

> ## READING 9.3.1
> ### James Madison, *Debates at Federal Convention, 1787*
>
> **June 13, 1787**
>
> MR. MADISON [JAMES MADISON, DELEGATE FROM VIRGINIA]: [He] objected to an appt. by the whole Legislature. Many of them were incompetent Judges of the requisite qualifications. They were too much influenced by their partialities. The candidate who was present, who had displayed a talent for business in the legislative field, who had perhaps assisted ignorant members in business of their own, or of their Constituents, or used other winning means, would without any of the essential qualifications for an expositor of the laws prevail over a competitor not having these recommendations, but possessed of every necessary accomplishment. He proposed that the appointment should be made by the Senate, which as a less numerous & more select body, would be more competent judges, and which was sufficiently numerous to justify such a confidence in them.
>
> **July 21, 1787**
>
> COL. MASON [GEORGE MASON, DELEGATE FROM VIRGINIA]: Notwithstanding the form of the proposition by which the appointment seemed to be divided between the Executive & Senate, the appointment was substantially vested in the former alone. . . . He considered the appointment by the Executive as a dangerous prerogative. It might even give him an influence over the Judiciary department itself.

September 7, 1787

Col. Mason: He took occasion to express his dislike of any reference whatever of the power to make appointments to either branch of the Legislature. On the other hand he was averse to vest so dangerous a power in the President alone.

Mr. Hamilton [Alexander Hamilton, delegate from New York]: The nomination to offices will give great weight to the President. Here then is a mutual connection & influence, that will perpetuate the President, and aggrandize both him & the Senate.

READING 9.3.2
Excerpts from *The Federalist* on Advice and Consent

ALEXANDER HAMILTON, *FEDERALIST NO. 66*

It will be the office of the President to NOMINATE, and, with the advice and consent of the Senate, to APPOINT. There will, of course, be no exertion of CHOICE on the part of the Senate. They may defeat one choice of the Executive, and oblige him to make another; but they cannot themselves CHOOSE, they can only ratify or reject the choice of the President. They might even entertain a preference to some other person, at the very moment they were assenting to the one proposed, because there might be no positive ground of opposition to him; and they could not be sure, if they withheld their assent, that the subsequent nomination would fall upon their own favorite, or upon any other person in their estimation more meritorious than the one rejected. Thus it could hardly happen, that the majority of the Senate would feel any other complacency towards the object of an appointment than such as the appearances of merit might inspire, and the proofs of the want of it destroy.

ALEXANDER HAMILTON, *FEDERALIST NO. 76*

The sole and undivided responsibility of one man [the president] will naturally beget a livelier sense of duty and a more exact regard to reputation. He will, on this account, feel himself under stronger obligations, and more interested to investigate with care the qualities requisite to the stations to be filled, and to prefer with impartiality the persons who may have the fairest pretensions to them. He will have FEWER personal attachments to gratify, than a body of men who may each be supposed to have an equal number; and will be so much the less liable to be misled by the sentiments of friendship and of affection. A single well-directed man, by a single understanding, cannot be distracted and warped by that diversity of views, feelings, and interests, which frequently distract and warp the resolutions of a collective body. There is nothing so apt to agitate the passions of mankind as personal considerations whether they relate to ourselves or to others, who are to be the objects of our choice or preference. Hence, in every exercise of the power of appointing to offices, by an assembly of men, we must expect to see a full display of all the private and party likings and dislikes, partialities and antipathies, attachments and animosities, which are felt by those who compose the assembly. The choice which may at any time happen to be made under such circumstances, will of course be the result either of a victory gained by one party over the other, or of a compromise between the parties. In either case, the intrinsic merit of the candidate will be too often out of sight. In the first, the qualifications best adapted to uniting the suffrages of the party, will be more considered than those which fit the person for the station. In the last, the coalition will commonly turn upon some interested equivalent: "Give us the man we wish for this office, and you shall have the one you wish for that." This will be the usual condition of the bargain. And it will rarely happen that the advancement of the public service will be the primary object either of party victories or of party negotiations. . . .

But might not his nomination be overruled? I grant it might, yet this could only be to make place for another nomination by himself. The person ultimately appointed must be the object of his preference, though perhaps not in the first degree. It is also not very probable that his nomination would often be overruled. The Senate could not be tempted, by the preference they might feel to another, to reject the one proposed; because they could not assure themselves, that the person they might wish would be brought forward by a second or by any subsequent nomination. They could not even be certain, that a future nomination would present a candidate in any degree more acceptable to them; and as their dissent might cast a kind of stigma upon the individual rejected, and might have the appearance of a reflection upon the judgment of the chief magistrate, it is not likely that their sanction would often be refused, where there were not special and strong reasons for the refusal.

To what purpose then require the co-operation of the Senate? I answer, that the necessity of their concurrence would have a powerful, though, in general, a silent operation. It would be an excellent check upon a spirit of favoritism in the President, and would tend greatly to prevent the appointment of unfit characters from State prejudice, from family connection, from personal attachment, or from a view to popularity. In addition to this, it would be an efficacious source of stability in the administration.

ALEXANDER HAMILTON, *FEDERALIST NO. 77*

To this union of the Senate with the President, in the article of appointments, it has in some cases been suggested that it would serve to give the President an undue influence over the Senate, and in others that it would have an opposite tendency—a strong proof that neither suggestion is true. To state the first in its proper form is to refute it. It amounts to this: the President would have an improper influence over the Senate, because the Senate would have the power of restraining him. This is an absurdity in terms. It cannot admit of a doubt that the entire power of appointment would enable him much more effectually to establish a dangerous empire over that body than a mere power of nomination subject to their control.

Let us take a view of the converse of the proposition: "the Senate would influence the Executive." As I have had occasion to remark in several other instances, the indistinctness of the objection forbids a precise answer. In what manner is this influence to be exerted? In relation to what objects? The power of influencing a person, in the sense in which it is here used, must imply a power of conferring a benefit upon him. How could the Senate confer a benefit upon the President by the manner of employing their right of negative upon his nominations? If it be said they might sometimes gratify him by an acquiescence in a favorite choice, when public motives might dictate a different conduct, I answer that the instances in which the President could be personally interested in the result would be too few to admit of his being materially affected by the compliances of the Senate. Besides this, it is evident that the POWER which can originate the disposition of honors and emoluments is more likely to attract than to be attracted by the POWER which can merely obstruct their course. If by influencing the President be meant restraining him, this is precisely what must have been intended. And it has been shown that the restraint would be salutary, at the same time that it would not be such as to destroy a single advantage to be looked for from the uncontrolled agency of that magistrate. The right of nomination would produce all the good, without the ill. Upon a comparison of the plan for the appointment of the officers of the proposed government with that which is established by the constitution of this State, a decided preference must be given to the former. In that plan the power of nomination is unequivocally vested in the executive. And as there would be a necessity for submitting each nomination to the judgment of an entire branch of the legislature, the circumstances attending an appointment, from the mode of conducting it, would naturally become matters of notoriety, and the public would be at no loss to determine what part had been performed by the different actors. The blame of a bad nomination would fall upon the President singly and absolutely. The censure of rejecting a good one would lie entirely at the door of the Senate, aggravated by the consideration of their having counteracted the good intentions of the executive. If an ill appointment should be made, the executive, for nominating, and the Senate, for approving, would participate, though in different degrees, in the opprobrium and disgrace.

READING 9.3.3
Excerpts from the Testimony of Dr. John Eastman, Professor, Chapman University School of Law, Senate Hearings on Judicial Nominations and the Filibuster[1]

I. The Constitutional Structure of the Appointment Process Envisions a More Limited Role for the Senate than is Currently Claimed, and None for a Minority Faction of the Senate.

As is well known to this body, Article II of the Constitution provides that the President "shall nominate, and by and with the Advice and Consent of the Senate, shall appoint, . . . Judges of the Supreme Court" and of such inferior courts as Congress has ordained and established. This is one of the fundamental components of the separation of powers mechanism devised by our nation's founders to protect against governmental tyranny. By it, the Senate provides an important check on the power of the President, but it is only a check; recent claims that the advice and consent clause gives to the Senate a co-equal role in the appointment of federal judges simply are not grounded either in the Constitution's text or in the history and theory of the appointments process. Necessarily, the claim that such power exists in less than a majority of the Senate is even more problematic.

A. The Framers of the Constitution Assigned to the President the Pre-eminent Role in Appointing Judges.

1. The President Alone Has the Power to Nominate

Article II of the Constitution provides that the President "shall nominate, and by and with the Advice and Consent of the Senate, shall appoint . . . Judges of the su-preme [sic] Court [and such inferior courts as the Congress may from time to time ordain and establish]." As the text of the provision makes explicitly clear, the power to choose nominees—to "nominate"—is vested solely in the President, and the President also has the primary role to "appoint," albeit with the advice and consent of the entire Senate. The text of the clause itself thus demonstrates that the role envi-sioned for the Senate was a much more limited one than is currently being claimed by some, and it was, in any event, a role assigned to the entire Senate, not to a minor-ity faction. . . .

In *Federalist No. 76*, for example, Alexander Hamilton explained at length that "one man of discernment is better fitted to analyze and estimate the peculiar quali-ties adapted to particular offices, than a body of men of equal or perhaps even of superior discernment." . . .

Note the very limited role that the Senate serves in Hamilton's view—which, of course, echoes the views expressed at the Constitutional Convention by both those who defended and those who opposed giving the appointment power to the President. In the founders' view, the Senate acts as a brake on the President's ability to fill offices with his own friends and family members rather than qualified nomi-nees, but beyond that, the element of choice—the essence of the power to fill the office—belongs to the President alone. The Senate has the power to refuse nomi-nees, but in the Constitutional scheme it has no proper authority in picking the nominees—either through direct choice or through logrolling and deal-making of the kind that the modern filibuster encourages. . . .

2. The Framers Envisioned a Narrow Role for the Senate in the Confirmation Process.

Of course, there is more to the appointment power than the power to nominate, and the Senate unquestionably has a role to play in the confirmation phase of the

---

[1]Senate Hearing 108-227, "Judicial Nominations, Filibusters, and the Constitution, When a Majority Is Denied the Right to Consent," Subcommittee on the Constitution, Civil Rights, and Property Rights of the Senate Judiciary Committee, May 6, 2003: http://frwebgate.access.gpo.gov/cgi-bin/getdoc.cgi?dbname=108_senate_hearings&docid=f:90460.wais.

appointment process. But the role envisioned by the framers was as a check on improper appointments by the President, one that would not undermine the President's ultimate responsibility for the appointments he made. The Senate's confirmation power therefore acts only as a relatively minor check on the President's authority—it exists only to prevent the President from selecting a nominee who "does not possess due qualifications for office." Essentially, it exists to prevent the President from being swayed by nepotism or mere political opportunism. Assessing a candidate's "qualifications for office" arguably did not give the entire Senate grounds for imposing an ideological litmus [test] on the President's nominees, at least where the questioned ideology did not prevent a judge from fulfilling his oath of office. It necessarily did not give such a power to a small faction of the Senate, as has become the practice through the use of ideologically-grounded holds or filibusters.

READING 9.3.4
Excerpts from the Statement of Senator Ted Kennedy (Democrat, Massachusetts), Senate Hearings on Judicial Nominations and the Filibuster[2]

It is always interesting in a hearing such as this, as we are trying to find out where authority and responsibilities lie, to look back at the Constitutional Convention itself. In the Constitutional Convention, when it met in Philadelphia from late May until mid September in 1787, on May 29th the Convention began its work on the Constitution with the Virginia Plan introduced by Governor Randolph, which provided that a national judiciary be established or be chosen by the national legislature, and under this plan the President had no role at all, in the selection of judges. When this provision came before the Convention on June 5th, several members were concerned that having the whole legislature select judges was to [sic] unwieldy and James Wilson suggested an alternative proposal that the President be given the sole power to appoint judges. That idea had no support. Rutledge of South Carolina said that he was by no means disposed to grant so great a power to any single person. James Madison agreed that the legislature was too large a body, and stated that he was rather inclined to give the appointment power to the Senatorial Branch of the legislative group, "sufficiently stable and independent to provide deliberate judgments,"' were the words he used. A week later Madison offered a formal motion to give the Senate the sole power to appoint judges, and this motion was adopted without any objection whatsoever at the Constitutional Convention.

On June 19th the Convention formally adopted the working draft of the Constitution, and it gave the Senate the exclusive power to appoint the judges. July 18th the Convention reaffirmed its decision to grant the Senate its exclusive power. James Wilson again proposed judges be appointed by the Executive, and again his motion was defeated overwhelmingly. The issue was considered again on July 21st, and the Convention again agreed to the exclusive Senate appointment of judges. In a debate concerning the provision, George Mason called the idea of Executive appointment of Federal judges a dangerous precedent. Not until the final days of the Convention was the President given power to nominate the judges. So on September 4th, two weeks before the Convention's work was completed, the last important decision made by the founding fathers, the Committee proposed that the President should have a role in selecting judges. It stated the President shall "nominate, and by and with the advice and consent of the Senate, shall appoint the judges of the Supreme Court."' The debates make clear that while the President had the power to nominate, the Senate still had a central role. Governor [sic] Morris of Pennsylvania described the provision as giving the Senate the power to appoint the judges nominated to them by the President. And the Convention, having repeatedly rejected the proposals that would lodge exclusive power to select judges to the Executive Branch, could not possibly have intended to reduce the Senate to a rubber stamp role.

[2]Senate Hearing 108-227, "Judicial Nominations, Filibusters, and the Constitution, When a Majority Is Denied the Right to Consent," Subcommittee on the Constitution, Civil Rights, and Property Rights of the Senate Judiciary Committee, May 6, 2003: http://frwebgate.access.gpo.gov/cgi-bin/getdoc.cgi?dbname=108_senate_hearings&docid=f:90460.wais.

It is important that Americans understand what our founding fathers deliberated, what they believed, what they thought they were achieving with the power of the United States Senate not to be a rubber stamp for the presidency, and they also expected advice and consent. . . . We have had an amazing life experience for this country and when you review what the founding fathers had intended and expected and what the rules had shown, it is clear that it was the function of advice and consent. It was the involvement of the United States Senate in the consideration and voting of various nominees on it in this process, that has contributed to this experience. We should all take the time to review that, because it has been the experience in the United States when this process has worked. That is not the way it is working at the present time.

We would be failing our responsibilities if we were just to be a rubber stamp. We certainly have no obligation to ignore or suspend our long-standing rules and become a rubber stamp.

1. Based on Readings 9.3.1 to 9.3.4, identify three arguments that support a strong role for the Senate in its exercise of the power of advice and consent over judicial nominations, including arguments for the use of the filibuster. Cite the reading(s) from which each of your arguments is derived.

_____

_____

_____

_____

_____

_____

_____

_____

_____

_____

2. Based on Readings 9.3.1 to 9.3.4, identify three arguments that support a weak role for the Senate in its exercise of the power of advice and consent over judicial nominations, including arguments for prohibiting the filibuster. Cite the reading(s) from which each of your arguments is derived.

_____

_____

_____

_____

_____

_____

_____

_____

_____

_____

3. In your view, should senators be allowed to use the filibuster to block a president's judicial nominations to federal courts? Explain and support your position by citing specific passages in the readings.

_____

_____

_____

_____

_____

EXERCISE 9.4   Beating the Odds on Judicial Appointments

INTRODUCTION

When it comes to the exercise of judicial power, nothing counts more than who sits on the nation's highest court. Justices arrive on the Supreme Court with political views and positions on constitutional interpretation. Their personal experience and political bias affect how they decide cases involving volatile social issues like abortion—about which the Constitution has nothing direct to say. Liberal justices, for example, find in the Constitution a right to abortion; conservative justices do not find this right in the Constitution.

Presidents and their advisers calculate carefully in selecting a nominee to the Supreme Court, especially because a nominee will have life tenure and carry a president's legacy for years to come. Political considerations include whether the president is in his first term, thinking of reelection, or in his second term—and thus more free from interest group pressure and public opinion. Today, presidents often consider diversity—race, ethnicity, gender, religion. When Thurgood Marshall, the first African American appointed to the Court, retired in 1991, President George H. W. Bush continued African American representation by naming Clarence Thomas as Marshall's replacement. The president's support in the Senate must be calibrated institutionally because a majority vote is required to elevate the nominee to a life term. Given the rancor over judicial nominations that has persisted since the defeat of Robert Bork's nomination in 1987, the president must ask himself whether he has the stomach and political capital for the possibility of a bruising fight.

Presidents' policy considerations include finding a nominee who fits a particular ideological profile, although some presidents have been more insistent on an ideological litmus test than others. President George W. Bush stated that his ideal nominee would be another Antonin Scalia or Clarence Thomas—judges known for their conservative decisions. In addition to seeking a nominee to match the president's ideology and policy positions, the president must consider the aims of the varied constituencies in the president's coalition. In the case of the Republican Party, for example, conservative Christians expect a president's nominee to be soundly anti-abortion; the Chamber of Commerce and the National Association of Manufacturers are concerned about the nominee's record on government regulation.

Finally, the professional qualifications of nominees are assessed. Beginning in the Eisenhower Administration, presidents sought the advice of the American Bar Association's (ABA's) Standing Committee of Federal Judiciary before making judicial nominations. The committee rates judicial candidates as "well qualified," "qualified," or "not qualified." A unanimous rating of "well qualified" for President Bill Clinton's nominees, Ruth Bader Ginsburg and Stephen Breyer, for example, eased their Senate confirmation. But a unanimous ABA rating of "qualified"[1] (the highest rating available at the time) was of little help to Harrold G. Carswell, one of President Richard Nixon's nominees. Carswell had served only six months on the U.S. Court of Appeals prior to his nomination to the Supreme Court. Critics charged that his credentials were too thin to warrant a seat on the Court and that his record on civil rights was suspect. Carswell's confirmation prospects weren't advanced when the floor manager of the nomination, Senator Roman Hruska (Republican, Nebraska), endorsed Carswell's mediocrity: "Even if he is mediocre there are a lot of mediocre judges and people and lawyers. They are entitled to a little representation, aren't they, and a little chance?"[2] The Senate rejected Carswell's nomination by a vote of 51 to 45. President George W. Bush, in 2001, ended the traditional practice of consulting the ABA in advance of making federal judicial nominations. Bush's action stemmed from Republican criticism that the ABA was biased against conservative nominees and from the desire to bring conservative groups, such as the Federalist Society, into the evaluation of prospective nominees. In 2009, President Barack Obama asked the ABA to resume its traditional role of evaluating the qualifications of prospective nominees prior to the president making judicial nominations.

The Constitution's framers chose life tenure as the foundation of an independent judiciary to insulate justices from majority public opinion and the political considerations of elective

---

[1]Prior to voting on Carswell's rating, the ABA committee instituted a new system that rated the nominee as either "qualified" or "not qualified."

[2]Richard Harris, *Decision* (New York: E.P. Dutton, 1971), p. 110.

office.[3] For presidents, life tenure holds out the promise that an appointee will protect and extend the president's legacy long after the president himself has departed from the White House. William O. Douglas, one of President Franklin D. Roosevelt's appointments, served thirty-six years on the Supreme Court—clear into Gerald Ford's presidency. William H. Rehnquist carried President Richard M. Nixon's legacy across the presidencies of Ford, Carter, Reagan, Bush (George H. W.), Clinton, and into the presidency of George W. Bush.

Life tenure has proved a curse, however, for some presidents. Several Supreme Court justices have surprised the presidents who appointed them—and the senators who confirmed them—by recasting themselves under the cloak of life tenure. Nominees who were thought to be reliably liberal discovered themselves to be conservatives—and vice versa. Although presidents might view these transformations as betrayal, the view from the Court is different. Even a loyal ally of the president may be moved by institutional influences such as the traditional and fiercely guarded independence of the Court, the legal arguments of the justices and law clerks, and the respect often accorded to prior court rulings. At the end of his sixteen-year term as chief justice, Earl Warren stated that he did not "see how a man could be on the Court and not change his views substantially over a period of years . . . for change you must if you are to do your duty on the Supreme Court."[4]

After leaving office, former president Harry Truman observed that "packing the Supreme Court simply can't be done. . . . I've tried and it won't work. . . . Whenever you put a man on the Supreme Court he ceases to be your friend. I'm sure of that."[5] President Dwight D. Eisenhower agreed: His appointment of Chief Justice Earl Warren went notoriously awry. As governor of California, Warren helped Eisenhower secure the Republican Party's nomination at the 1952 convention. In return, Eisenhower promised Warren the first vacancy on the Court. After Chief Justice Fred Vinson died of a heart attack in 1953, Warren held Eisenhower to the promise. Warren's record as attorney general and governor of California indicated political compatibility with Eisenhower's brand of moderate Republicanism. As chief justice, however, Warren angered the president and conservatives across the nation by embracing judicial activism to advance individual rights and social justice in the areas of racial discrimination, criminal procedures, and personal privacy, to name a few. Indeed, less than a year after taking his seat on the bench, Warren brilliantly orchestrated a unanimous decision declaring unconstitutional state laws mandating racially segregated schools. *Brown v. Board of Education of Topeka* inflamed the South, alarmed conservatives in both parties, and helped launch a revolution in race relations.

After Eisenhower had left office and the extent of the Warren Court's revolution had become clear, Eisenhower often remarked that his biggest mistake was "the appointment of that dumb son of a bitch Earl Warren."[6]

To ensure that its Supreme Court appointments didn't backfire, the Reagan Administration screened its nominees for ideological compatibility more carefully and aggressively than any previous presidency. The process included thorough scrutiny of candidates' speeches, articles, and court opinions; day-long interviews with Department of Justice officials; and deliberations by the members of the White House Judicial Selection Committee to determine which candidates to recommend for the president's consideration. The interviews were particularly controversial. Some potential nominees cried foul at being asked directly about their view on issues such as abortion. After all, most judges consider it a violation of their impartiality and neutrality to commit to a position before they have considered the particulars of a case.

Political scientists continue to investigate and debate how recent presidents have fared in their efforts to use the judicial appointment power to protect and extend their legacies. The questions that follow examine a slice of that debate.

[3]The Constitution does not use the term *life tenure* but states that judges "shall hold their Offices during good Behavior." Federal court judges may be removed from office for violating the "good behavior" standard. The removal process is as follows: The House of Representatives must vote by simple majority to impeach the judge, who would then be tried in the Senate where a two-thirds vote is required to convict and remove the judge. The vice president presides over the trial in the Senate. In U.S. history, only one Supreme Court justice—Samuel Chase, in 1805—has been impeached. He was acquitted in the Senate.

[4]Anthony Lewis, "A Talk with Warren on Crime, the Court, the Country," *New York Times Magazine,* October 19, 1969, pp. 128–29.

[5]Lecture at Columbia University, New York City, April 28, 1959. Quoted in Henry J. Abraham, *The Judicial Process,* 7th ed. (New York: Oxford University Press, 1998), p. 79.

[6]Stephen E. Ambrose, *Eisenhower: The President* (New York: Simon & Schuster, 1984), p. 190.

ASSIGNMENT

The data in Table 9.4.1 indicate the conservatism and liberalism of nine recent presidents and their appointees to the Supreme Court. In the column titled "Ideology Score," the higher the number, the more conservative the president or Supreme Court justice. The lower the number, the more liberal the president or justice. This column also provides the average ideology score for all of a president's appointees.

TABLE 9.4.1	Measuring the Ideology of Presidents and Their Supreme Court Appointees*	
	Ideology Score	**Years of Service**
Dwight Eisenhower (R)	550	
Earl Warren	308	15
John M. Harlan II	628	16
William J. Brennan, Jr.	265	33
Charles E. Whittaker	673	5
Potter Stewart	555	22
Eisenhower Appointee Average	486	
John Kennedy (D)	200	
Byron White	556	31
Arthur J. Goldberg	248	3
Kennedy Appointee Average	402	
Lyndon Johnson (D)	275	
Abe Fortas	336	4
Thurgood Marshall	211	24
Johnson Appointee Average	274	
Richard Nixon (R)	710	
Warren E. Berger	735	17
Harry A. Blackmun	492	24
Lewis F. Powell, Jr.	677	16
William H. Rehnquist	815	15
Nixon Appointee Average	680	
Gerald Ford (R)	700	
John Paul Stevens	341	36
Ford Appointee Average	341	
Ronald Reagan (R)	800	
Sandra Day O'Connor	680	26
Antonin Scalia	757	(1986–)
Anthony M. Kennedy	647	(1988–)
Reagan Appointee Average	695	

(Continued)

TABLE 9.4.1	Measuring the Ideology of Presidents and Their Supreme Court Appointees* (*Continued*)		
		Ideology Score	**Years of Service**
George H. W. Bush (R)		760	
David H. Souter		374	10
Clarence Thomas		822	(1991–)
Bush (George H. W.) Appointee Average		598	
Bill Clinton (D)		250	
Ruth Bader Ginsberg		312	(1993–)
Stephen G. Bryer		372	(1994–)
Clinton Appointee Average		342	
George W. Bush (R)		740	
John G. Roberts		753	(2005–)
Samuel Alito		740	(2006–)
Bush (George W.) Appointee Average		747	

*The data on presidential ideology is adapted from "The Increasing Importance of Ideology in the Nomination and Confirmation of Supreme Court Justices," by Lee Epstein, Jeffrey A. Segal, and Chad Westerland, Drake Law Review, Volume 56, Spring 2008, p. 110. The data on Supreme Court Justice ideology is from "Rational Judicial Behavior: A Statistical Study," by William M. Landes and Richard A. Posner, John M. Olin Law & Economics Working Paper No. 404, The Law School, The University of Chicago, April 2008, available at: http://ssrn.com/abstract=1126403.

1. **a.** Which president is most conservative?

   b. Which president is most liberal?

   c. Which Supreme Court justice is most conservative?

   d. Which Supreme Court justice is most liberal?

2. The *presidential compatibility gap* is the point spread between the ranking of a president and those of a justice the president appointed. The higher the number, the more disappointed a president would likely be with the rulings of his appointee. The lower the number, the more satisfied a president would likely be.

   a. Look at the average ranking for each president's appointees. Which president has the lowest presidential compatibility gap?

   b. Which president has the highest presidential compatibility gap?

3. Which of Eisenhower's appointees is farthest away from Eisenhower's brand of conservatism? What's the presidential compatibility gap?

_____

_____

4. Which of Kennedy's appointees is farthest away from Kennedy's brand of liberalism? What's the presidential compatibility gap?

_____

_____

5. Which Republican presidents appointed justices who turned out to be more conservative than those presidents?

_____

_____

6. Which Democratic president appointed a justice who turned out to be more liberal than that president?

_____

_____

7. For which president and which appointee is the presidential compatibility gap the greatest? In other words, which president would be most disappointed in which of his appointees?

_____

_____

8. A president's disappointment with the rulings of an appointee who departed from the president's own brand of liberalism or conservatism would presumably be magnified the longer that appointee remained on the Court. In the case of Eisenhower, the nominee who's farthest from Eisenhower's brand of conservatism—Brennan—served longer than any of Eisenhower's other appointments. Identify three other presidents for which this was also a problem.

President 1: _____

Appointee and years of service: _____

Presidential compatibility gap: _____

President 2: _____

Appointee and years of service: _____

Presidential compatibility gap: _____

President 3: _____

Appointee and years of service: _____

Presidential compatibility gap: _____

9. Consider the following example of the complex factors that contribute to the presidential compatibility gap. Supreme Court Justice Lewis F. Powell Jr. retired in June 1987. President Ronald Reagan nominated Federal Appeals Court Judge Robert Bork to fill the vacancy. On October 23, 1987, the Senate defeated Bork's nomination by a vote of 58 to 42. At the time of Bork's defeat, the Democrats held fifty-five seats in the Senate; the Republicans held forty-five. Factors in Bork's defeat included the unprecedented mobilization of civil rights, labor, and women's organizations opposed to Bork's conservative political and legal views, as well as disarray in the Reagan Administration resulting from the Iran-Contra scandal and the consequent failure of the White House to fully mobilize conservative resources on Bork's behalf.

On October 29, 1987, less than a week after Bork's defeat, Reagan announced that he would nominate Federal Appeals Court Judge Douglas Howard Ginsburg to fill the still-vacant seat. Ginsburg, was forced to withdraw his nomination before Reagan formally submitted it to the

Senate, however, because of the disclosure that Ginsburg had smoked marijuana while a student and faculty member at Harvard Law School. The disclosure embarrassed Reagan, whose "just say no to drugs campaign" was in full swing at the time.

Consider Reagan's political position as he attempted for the third time to fill the seat vacated by Powell. Reagan was undoubtedly aware that only one other president in the twentieth century—Richard M. Nixon—had failed twice in a row to elevate his nominees to a vacant seat on the Court. If Reagan failed a third time, he would have the distinction of being the first president since the Civil War to do so.

How would you advise Reagan to proceed? Would you recommend that Reagan nominate again a conservative whose record indicates that he or she would practice the president's brand of conservatism? Or would you recommend that Reagan compromise his political principles and nominate a more moderate candidate who could attract enough Democratic votes to be confirmed? Explain and support your recommendation.

_____

_____

_____

_____

_____

_____

_____

Study Reading 9.4.1, excerpts from Reagan's news conference announcing his third nominee, and answer the questions that follow.

READING 9.4.1
Remarks Announcing the Nomination of Anthony M. Kennedy to Be an Associate Justice of the Supreme Court of the United States, November 11, 1987

The President: It's not just in fulfillment of my constitutional duty but with great pride and respect for his many years of public service, that I am today announcing my intention to nominate United States Circuit Judge Anthony Kennedy to be an Associate Justice of the Supreme Court. Judge Kennedy represents the best tradition of America's judiciary. . . .

During his 12 years on the Nation's second highest court, Judge Kennedy has participated in over 1400 decisions and authored over 400 opinions. He's a hard worker and, like Justice Powell, whom he will replace, he is known as a gentleman. He's popular with colleagues of all political persuasions. And I know that he seems to be popular with many Senators of varying political persuasions as well. . . .

Judge Kennedy is what many in recent weeks have referred to as a true conservative—one who believes that our constitutional system is one of enumerated powers—that it is we, the people who have granted certain rights to the Government, not the other way around. And that unless the Constitution grants a power to the Federal Government, or restricts a State's exercise of that power, it remains with the States or the people. . . .

Judge Kennedy has participated in hundreds of criminal law decisions during his tenure on the Ninth Circuit Court of Appeals. In that time he's earned a reputation as a courageous, tough, but fair jurist. He's known to his colleagues and to the lawyers who practiced before him as diligent, perceptive, and polite. The hallmark of Judge Kennedy's career has been devotion—devotion to his family, devotion to his community and his civic responsibility, and devotion to the law. He's played a major role in keeping our cities and neighborhoods safe from crime. He's that special kind of American who's always been there when we needed leadership. I'm certain he will be a leader on the Supreme Court.

The experience of the last several months has made all of us a bit wiser. I believe the mood and the time is now right for all Americans in this bicentennial year of the Constitution to join together in a bipartisan effort to fulfill our constitutional obligation of restoring the United States Supreme Court to full strength. By selecting Anthony M. Kennedy, a superbly qualified judge whose fitness for the high court has been remarked upon by leaders of the Senate in both parties, I have sought to ensure the success of that effort.

I look forward, and I know Judge Kennedy is looking forward, to prompt hearings conducted in the spirit of cooperation and bipartisanship. I'll do everything in my power as President to assist in that process. . . .

Q [QUESTION FROM REPORTER]: Mr. President, throughout this whole process, Senator Hatch says there have been a lot of gutless wonders in the White House. Do you know who they are, who he is referring to, why he would say such a thing since he is such a devoted conservative?

THE PRESIDENT: . . . [W]hen these ceremonies here this morning are over, I'm going to try to find out where he gets his information because, you know something, I haven't been able to find a gutless wonder in the whole place.

Q: Do you know why he was so upset?

THE PRESIDENT: I don't know. I don't know, unless he's been reading the paper too much.

Q: Mr. President, you said that Judge Kennedy is popular with people of all political persuasions. What happened to your plan to give the Senate the nominee that they would object to just as much as Judge Bork?

THE PRESIDENT: Maybe it's time that I did answer on that, where that was said and why—and it was humorously said. I was at a straight party organization affair, a dinner. And when I finished my remarks, which were partisan, a woman, down in front, member there, just called out above all the noise of the room, "What about Judge Bork?" And she got great applause for saying that. And then the questions came. Was I going to give in and try to please certain elements in the Senate? And I made that—intended to be facetious answer to her. And so, as I say, it was—sometimes you make a facetious remark and somebody takes it seriously and you wish you'd never said it, and that's one for me. . . .

Q: Did you cave into the liberals, Mr. President? Some conservatives are saying you caved into the liberals, appointing someone who can be confirmed, but not appointing someone who is going to turn the Court around.

THE PRESIDENT: When the day comes that I cave in to the liberals, I will be long gone from here. *[Laughter]*

Q: Judge Kennedy, did they ask you if you'd ever smoked marijuana?

Q: Did you ever smoke marijuana?

Q: Did they ask you?

JUDGE KENNEDY: They asked me that question, and the answer was no, firmly, no.

Q: Mr. President, do you think conservatives, sir, will back this nominee? You know, Senator Helms, at one point, is alleged to have said, "No way, Jose," to Judge Kennedy.

THE PRESIDENT: We'll find out about that in the coming days ahead. . . .

Note: The President spoke at 11:30 A.M. in the Briefing Room at the White House. Marlin Fitzwater was Assistant to the President for Press Relations.

Source: From http://www.reagan.utexas.edu/archives/speeches/1987/111187a.htm.

10. **a.** Did Reagan follow the recommendation you made in question 9?

b. How did Reagan describe Kennedy's political ideology?

c. What evidence do you find in Reagan's remarks that Kennedy was a compromise nominee—in other words, not the "true conservative" Reagan would have preferred?

d. What questions did reporters raise indicating that Kennedy was not a "true conservative"?

10

Civil Rights

EXERCISE 10.1 Mandating Racial Segregation by State Law

INTRODUCTION

Blacks liberated from slavery by the Civil War defined *freedom* in expansive terms, arguing that freedom necessarily includes the right to vote and hold political office, equality before the law, and the ownership of land. Many whites, North and South, defined *freedom* for blacks in the most narrow, restrictive terms, arguing that freedom is nothing more than the absence of slavery. The battle over the meaning of *freedom* for African Americans raged during the late nineteenth century, throughout the twentieth, and into the twenty-first as the United States continues its painful and drawn-out adjustment to the end of slavery.

In 1867, Congress, under the leadership of the Radical Republicans, passed the Reconstruction Acts, legislation that secured for the freed slaves the right to vote and a measure of legal equality. African Americans were elected to political office throughout the South, and in 1870, for the first time, took seats in the U.S. House of Representatives and Senate (see Exercise 6.3). Those gains were made possible by use of the North's military power on behalf of African Americans in the South. The commitment of most whites in the North to racial justice for the freed slaves had never been very strong, and in 1877 the North pulled its troops out of the South. Unencumbered, whites in the South reasserted supremacy by passing state laws to disfranchise and segregate blacks. African Americans were stripped of their voting rights by voter registration restrictions such as the literacy test, the poll tax, and the white primary. Jim Crow laws buttressed white supremacy by mandating the separation of whites and blacks in almost every public area of life. Blacks were forced by these state laws into separate and inferior schools, restrooms, parks, restaurants, hotels, trains, streetcars, swimming pools, and even cemeteries. White supremacists used violence and economic intimidation to maintain the color line. (For information on the Jim Crow system of segregation, including the origin of the term, go to jimcrowhistory.org.)

In 1890, the Louisiana state legislature required railroads to provide "equal but separate accommodations for the white and colored races" and prohibited travelers from riding in railcars designated for the other race. A group of civil rights advocates from New Orleans challenged the law in court. They received some support from railroad companies, which objected to the additional expense of providing separate cars for black and white passengers. The dispute eventually made its way to the Supreme Court in the case *Plessy v. Ferguson* (1896).

In 1909 blacks and whites, alarmed at the deteriorating position of African Americans, formed an interest group called the National Association for the Advancement of Colored People (NAACP). Its mission: to secure full rights of citizenship for black Americans. Beginning in the 1930s, the NAACP filed a series of lawsuits challenging the Jim Crow system of racial separation in the South. Those suits made some inroads against segregation in the areas of graduate education and interstate transportation, but progress was slow. The system of race-based segregation established in state laws across the South was firmly entrenched.

Beginning in the 1940s, the NAACP challenged segregation in public schools. One case, *Briggs v. Elliott* (1952), was initiated by black parents in Clarendon County, South Carolina, where the school board in the 1949–1950 term spent $43 per black child and $179 per white child. The Supreme Court consolidated *Briggs* with three other challenges to school segregation under the name of a case from Kansas, *Brown v. Board of Education of Topeka* (1954). The case was argued before the Court by Thurgood Marshall, the lead attorney for the NAACP's Legal and Educational Defense Fund, who was later appointed by President Lyndon Johnson to a seat on the Supreme Court. Earl Warren, the chief justice who engineered the Court's unanimous decision in *Brown*, had been appointed to the Court by President Dwight Eisenhower in 1953.

ASSIGNMENT

Study Reading 10.1.1, an excerpt from *Plessy v. Ferguson*, and Reading 10.1.2, an excerpt from *Brown v. Board of Education of Topeka*, and answer the questions that follow. In the *Plessy* case, Mr. Justice Brown delivered the *majority* opinion of the Court, which carried the force of law. Mr. Justice Harlan, the lone vote against the majority opinion, offered his written dissent—which did not carry the force of law. In the *Brown* case, Mr. Chief Justice Warren delivered the unanimous opinion of the Court.

READING 10.1.1
Plessy v. Ferguson, 163 U.S. 537 (1896)

Mr. Justice Brown delivered the opinion of the court

The constitutionality of this act is attacked upon the ground that it conflicts both with the thirteenth amendment of the constitution, abolishing slavery, and the fourteenth amendment, which prohibits certain restrictive legislation on the part of the states.

1. That it does not conflict with the thirteenth amendment, which abolished slavery and involuntary servitude, except a punishment for crime, is too clear for argument. . . .
2. . . . The object of the [fourteenth] amendment was undoubtedly to enforce the absolute equality of the two races before the law, but, in the nature of things, it could not have been intended to abolish distinctions based upon color, or to enforce social, as distinguished from political, equality, or a commingling of the two races upon terms unsatisfactory to either. Laws permitting, and even requiring, their separation, in places where they are liable to be brought into contact, do not necessarily imply the inferiority of either race to the other, and have been generally, if not universally, recognized as within the competency of the state legislatures in the exercise of their police power. The most common instance of this is connected with the establishment of separate schools for white and colored children, which have been held to be a valid exercise of the legislative power even by courts of states where the political rights of the colored race have been longest and most earnestly enforced. . . .

We think the enforced separation of the races, as applied to the internal commerce of the state, neither abridges the privileges or immunities of the colored man, deprives him of his property without due process of law, nor denies him the equal protection of the laws, within the meaning of the fourteenth amendment. . . .

In this connection, it is also suggested by the learned counsel for the plaintiff in error that the same argument that will justify the state legislature in requiring railways to provide separate accommodations for the two races will also authorize them to require separate cars to be provided for people whose hair is of a certain color, or who are aliens, or who belong to certain nationalities, or to enact laws requiring colored people to walk upon one side of the street, and white people upon the other, or requiring white men's houses to be painted white, and colored men's black, or their vehicles or business signs to be of different colors, upon the theory that one side of the street is as good as the other, or that a house or vehicle of one color is as good as one of another color. The reply to all this is that every exercise of the police power must be reasonable, and extend only to such laws as are enacted in good faith for the promotion of the public good, and not for the annoyance or oppression of a particular class. . . .

We consider the underlying fallacy of the plaintiff's argument to consist in the assumption that the enforced separation of the two races stamps the colored race with a badge of inferiority. If this be so, it is not by reason of anything found in the act, but solely because the colored race chooses to put that construction upon it. The argument necessarily assumes that if, as has been more than once the case, and is not unlikely to be so again, the colored race should become the dominant power in the state legislature, and should enact a law in precisely similar terms, it would thereby relegate the white race to an inferior position. We imagine that the white race, at least, would not acquiesce in this assumption. The argument also assumes that social prejudices may be overcome by legislation, and that equal rights cannot be secured to the negro except by an enforced commingling of the two races. We cannot accept this proposition. If the two races are to meet upon terms of social equality, it must be the result of natural affinities, a mutual appreciation of each other's merits, and a voluntary consent of individuals. . . . Legislation is powerless to eradicate racial instincts, or to abolish distinctions based upon physical differences, and the attempt to do so can only result in accentuating the difficulties of the present situation. If the civil and political rights of both races be equal, one cannot be inferior to the other civilly or politically. If one race be inferior to the other socially, the constitution of the United States cannot put them upon the same plane. . . .

Mr. Justice Harlan dissenting

In respect of civil rights, common to all citizens, the constitution of the United States does not, I think, permit any public authority to know the race of those entitled to be protected in the enjoyment of such rights. . . . Indeed, such legislation as that here in question is inconsistent not only with that equality of rights which pertains to citizenship, national and state, but with the personal liberty enjoyed by every one within the United States.

It was said in argument that the statute of Louisiana does not discriminate against either race, but prescribes a rule applicable alike to white and colored citizens. But this argument does not meet the difficulty. Every one knows that the statute in question had its origin in the purpose, not so much to exclude white persons from railroad cars occupied by blacks, as to exclude colored people from coaches occupied by or assigned to white persons. Railroad corporations of Louisiana did not make discrimination among whites in the matter of accommodation for travelers. The thing to accomplish was, under the guise of giving equal accommodation for whites and blacks, to compel the latter to keep to themselves while traveling in railroad passenger coaches. No one would be so wanting in candor as to assert the contrary. The fundamental objection, therefore, to the statute, is that it interferes with the personal freedom of citizens. . . . If a white man and a black man choose to occupy the same public conveyance on a public highway, it is their right to do so; and no government, proceeding alone on grounds of race, can prevent it without infringing the personal liberty of each.

It is one thing for railroad carriers to furnish, or to be required by law to furnish, equal accommodations for all whom they are under a legal duty to carry. It is quite another thing for government to forbid citizens of the white and black races from traveling in the same public conveyance, and to punish officers of railroad companies for permitting persons of the two races to occupy the same passenger coach. . . .

Our constitution is color-blind, and neither knows nor tolerates classes among citizens. In respect of civil rights, all citizens are equal before the law. The humblest is the peer of the most powerful. The law regards man as man, and takes no account of his surroundings or of his color when his civil rights as guaranteed by the supreme law of the land are involved. It is therefore to be regretted that this high tribunal, the final expositor of the fundamental law of the land, has reached the conclusion that it is competent for a state to regulate the enjoyment by citizens of their civil rights solely upon the basis of race. . . .

The destinies of the two races, in this country, are indissolubly linked together, and the interests of both require that the common government of all shall not permit the seeds of race hate to be planted under the sanction of law. What can more certainly arouse race hate, what more certainly create and perpetuate a feeling of distrust between these races, than state enactments which, in fact, proceed on the ground that colored citizens are so inferior and degraded that they cannot be allowed to sit in public coaches occupied by white citizens? That, as all will admit, is the real meaning of such legislation as was enacted in Louisiana. . . .

The arbitrary separation of citizens, on the basis of race, while they are on a public highway, is a badge of servitude wholly inconsistent with the civil freedom and the equality before the law established by the constitution. It cannot be justified upon any legal grounds.

READING 10.1.2
Brown v. Board of Education of Topeka, 347 U.S. 483 (1954)

Mr. Chief Justice Warren delivered the opinion of the Court

These cases come to us from the States of Kansas, South Carolina, Virginia, and Delaware. They are premised on different facts and different local conditions, but a common legal question justifies their consideration together in this consolidated opinion.

In each of the cases, minors of the Negro race, through their legal representatives, seek the aid of the courts in obtaining admission to the public schools of their community on a nonsegregated basis. In each instance, they had been denied admission to schools attended by white children under laws requiring or permitting segregation according to race. This segregation was alleged to deprive the plaintiffs of the equal protection of the laws under the Fourteenth Amendment. In each of the cases other than the Delaware case, a three-judge federal district court denied relief to the plaintiffs on the so-called "separate but equal" doctrine announced by this Court in *Plessy v. Ferguson.* Under that doctrine, equality of treatment is accorded when the races are provided substantially equal facilities, even though these facilities be separate. . . .

The plaintiffs contend that segregated public schools are not "equal" and cannot be made "equal," and that hence they are deprived of the equal protection of the laws. Because of the obvious importance of the question presented, the Court took jurisdiction. Argument was heard in the 1952 Term, and reargument was heard this Term on certain questions propounded by the Court.

Reargument was largely devoted to the circumstances surrounding the adoption of the Fourteenth Amendment in 1868. It covered exhaustively consideration of the Amendment in Congress, ratification by the states, then existing practices in racial segregation, and the views of proponents and opponents of the Amendment. This discussion and our own investigation convince us that, although these sources cast some light, it is not enough to resolve the problem with which we are faced. At best, they are inconclusive. The most avid proponents of the post-War Amendments undoubtedly intended them to remove all legal distinctions among "all persons born or naturalized in the United States." Their opponents, just as certainly, were antagonistic to both the letter and the spirit of the Amendments and wished them to have the most limited effect. What others in Congress and the state legislatures had in mind cannot be determined with any degree of certainty.

An additional reason for the inconclusive nature of the Amendment's history, with respect to segregated schools, is the status of public education at that time. In the South, the movement toward free common schools, supported by general taxation, had not yet taken hold. Education of white children was largely in the hands of private groups. Education of Negroes was almost nonexistent, and practically all of the race were illiterate. In fact, any education of Negroes was forbidden by law in some states. Today, in contrast, many Negroes have achieved outstanding success in the arts and sciences as well as in the business and professional world. It is true that public school education at the time of the Amendment had advanced further in the North, but the effect of the Amendment on Northern States was generally ignored in the congressional debates. Even in the North, the conditions of public education did not approximate those existing today. The curriculum was usually rudimentary; ungraded schools were common in rural areas; the school term was but three months a year in many states; and compulsory school attendance was virtually unknown. As a consequence, it is not surprising that there should be so little in the history of the Fourteenth Amendment relating to its intended effect on public education. . . .

In the instant cases, that question [of whether *Plessy v. Ferguson* should be held inapplicable to public education] is directly presented. Here . . . there are findings below that the Negro and white schools involved have been equalized, or are being equalized, with respect to buildings, curricula, qualifications and salaries of teachers, and other "tangible" factors. Our decision, therefore, cannot turn on merely a comparison of these tangible factors in the Negro and white schools involved in each of the cases. We must look instead to the effect of segregation itself on public education.

In approaching this problem, we cannot turn the clock back to 1868 when the Amendment was adopted, or even to 1896 when *Plessy v. Ferguson* was written. We must consider public education in the light of its full development and its present place in American life throughout the Nation. Only in this way can it be determined if segregation in public schools deprives these plaintiffs of the equal protection of the laws.

Today, education is perhaps the most important function of state and local governments. Compulsory school attendance laws and the great expenditures for education both demonstrate our recognition of the importance of education to our democratic society. It is required in the performance of our most basic public responsibilities, even service in the armed forces. It is the very foundation of good citizenship. Today it is a principal instrument in awakening the child to cultural values, in preparing him for later professional training, and in helping him to adjust normally to his environment. In these days, it is doubtful that any child may reasonably be expected to succeed in life if he is denied the opportunity of an education. Such an opportunity, where the state has undertaken to provide it, is a right which must be made available to all on equal terms.

We come then to the question presented: Does segregation of children in public schools solely on the basis of race, even though the physical facilities and other "tangible" factors may be equal, deprive the children of the minority group of equal educational opportunities? We believe that it does. . . .

To separate [children in grade and high schools] from others of similar age and qualifications solely because of their race generates a feeling of inferiority as to their status in the community that may affect their hearts and minds in a way unlikely ever to be undone. The effect of this separation on their educational opportunities was well stated by a finding in the Kansas case by a court which nevertheless felt compelled to rule against the Negro plaintiffs:

> Segregation of white and colored children in public schools has a detrimental effect upon the colored children. The impact is greater when it has the sanction of the law; for the policy of separating the races is usually interpreted as denoting the inferiority of the negro group. A sense of inferiority affects the motivation of a child to learn. Segregation with the sanction of law, therefore, has a tendency to [retard] the educational and mental development of negro children and to deprive them of some of the benefits they would receive in a racial[ly] integrated school system.

Whatever may have been the extent of psychological knowledge at the time of *Plessy v. Ferguson,* this finding is amply supported by modern authority. Any language in *Plessy v. Ferguson* contrary to this finding is rejected.

We conclude that in the field of public education the doctrine of "separate but equal" has no place. Separate educational facilities are inherently unequal. Therefore, we hold that the plaintiffs and others similarly situated for whom the actions have been brought are, by reason of the segregation complained of, deprived of the equal protection of the laws guaranteed by the Fourteenth Amendment. . . .

It is so ordered.

1. In one sentence, state the Supreme Court's decision in *Plessy v. Ferguson.*

_____

_____

_____

2. Identify what you think is the most important argument made by the majority to justify its decision in *Plessy.* Cite specific language from the majority opinion in explaining the argument you chose.

_____

_____

_____

_____

_____

_____

_____

3. Identify what you think is the most important argument made by Justice John Marshall Harlan in his dissent in *Plessy.* Cite specific language from his dissent in explaining the argument you chose.

_____

_____

_____

_____

_____

_____

_____

4. How does the majority opinion in *Plessy* differ from Justice Harlan's dissent on the important question of the Louisiana state legislature's *intent* in enacting the law that segregated railcars? Explain and support your answer by citing specific language from the majority opinion and the dissent.

_____

_____

_____

_____

_____

_____

_____

5. In one sentence, state the Supreme Court's decision in _Brown v. Board of Education of Topeka._

_____

_____

_____

6. Identify what you think is the most important argument made by the Supreme Court to justify its decision in _Brown._ Cite specific language from the Court's decision in explaining the argument you chose.

_____

_____

_____

_____

_____

_____

_____

7. Before _Brown_ reached the Supreme Court, many school districts in the South dramatically increased their spending on black schools, hoping to stop the Court from ruling that segregated schools are unconstitutional. The strategy didn't work: Despite an influx of funds, most black schools remained patently inferior to white schools. In 1954, for example, public funding per pupil for black schools in the South was only 60 percent of funding for white schools. But what if the strategy had worked? Suppose that southern whites had spent enough to make black schools the equivalent of white schools. Suppose that the defendants in _Brown_ were able to demonstrate conclusively to the justices on the Supreme Court that schools for African Americans across the South were in every tangible and measurable way equal to schools for whites. In the _Brown_ opinion, what do the justices say that indicates whether real equality between black and white schools would have altered their decision? Cite language from _Brown_ to support your answer.

_____

_____

_____

_____

_____

_____

_____

8. In the early 1950s, the judiciary was the only branch of the national government to act against segregation in the South. Both the executive and the legislative branches proved unable or unwilling to strike down the Jim Crow system. And when the Supreme Court ruled in *Brown*, its decision was vehemently opposed in the South. What features of the Court give it the freedom to make unpopular decisions? Cite specific language from Articles II and III of the Constitution in your answer.

_____

_____

_____

_____

_____

9. *Web-Based Question.* Search the Web for answers to the following questions. One useful site is the Civil Rights Project at UCLA.

    a. Over the last several years, have public schools become more or less integrated?

_____

    b. What factors help explain this trend?

_____

_____

_____

_____

_____

_____

10. *Web-Based Question.* Go to one of the many websites that examine the pros and cons of various current political issues. One useful site is procon.org. Examine the debate over this question: *Is desegregation in public schools still necessary to achieve racial equality?*

    a. What argument on the *yes* side do you find most persuasive and why?

_____

_____

_____

_____

_____

_____

    b. What argument on the *no* side do you find most persuasive and why?

_____

_____

_____

_____

_____

_____

EXERCISE 10.2   Same-Sex Marriage: The New Civil Right?

INTRODUCTION

The gay rights movement began with a riot in New York City in 1969, when city police raided the Stonewall Inn, a gay bar. At that time, it was illegal for people of the same gender to dance together. Since then, many have suggested parallels between the struggle for gay rights and the battles still being waged for the civil rights of ethnic and racial minorities and women.

The legal battle in the fight for gay rights tests the application of the Fourteenth Amendment's equal protection clause: "No state shall . . . deny to any person within its jurisdiction the equal protection of the laws." Even though many states and localities have protected gays and lesbians from employment and housing discrimination, and even though many cities and businesses have adopted policies that extend medical insurance and other benefits to those in same-sex domestic partnerships, gay and lesbian rights have not been protected by federal statute, nor has the U.S. Supreme Court included gays and lesbians as a protected class under the equal protection clause. In 2010, however, a Federal District Court in California struck down California's Proposition 8—which voters had passed in 2008 to amend that state's constitution to prohibit the recognition of same-sex marriage—on the grounds that it violated the Fourteenth Amendment. (As of this writing, that decision has been appealed to the U.S. Ninth Circuit Court of Appeals and may eventually be heard by the U.S. Supreme Court.)

The closest the Supreme Court has come to linking the equal protection clause and sexual orientation is in case *Romer v. Evans* (1996). In that case, the Court struck down Colorado's Amendment 2 (a voter initiative) because it singled out gays and lesbians as a class and denied them protection under Colorado's constitution. Ordinances protecting gays and lesbians from discrimination in cities like Denver, Boulder, and Aspen had been nullified under the Colorado initiative. The Court did not decide whether the Fourteenth Amendment protected gays and lesbians, but it ruled that no state could *a priori* exclude a class of people from such protection.

In *Lawrence v. Texas* (2003), the Supreme Court struck down antisodomy laws as an unconstitutional violation of the liberties included in the *due process clause* of the Fourteenth Amendment. The issue that commanded a majority vote of the Court was not discrimination against gays and lesbians, but rather the right to intimate sexual relations among consenting adults, whether heterosexual or homosexual (see Exercise 11.2). Justice Antonin Scalia, in a dissenting opinion, predicted with trepidation that the decision in *Lawrence* would eventually be used as a precedent to establish a right to same-sex marriage.

Some advocates of a civil right to same-sex marriage believe that the Civil Rights Act of 1964 and other federal statutes that prohibit discrimination based on sex should apply to discrimination against gays, lesbians, and transgendered people as well. Cass Sunstein, a professor of law at the University of Chicago (later serving in the Obama Administration), argues that discrimination against homosexuals is rooted in the fear that gay rights will undermine traditional male and female gender roles. Because homosexuals do not conform to those role expectations, they become the object of discrimination.[1]

The political controversy over same-sex marriage intensified in 1993, when the Hawaii Supreme Court ruled that denying gays and lesbians the right to marry violated the Hawaii constitution. (In 1998, Hawaii voters reversed that decision by ratifying an amendment to the state's constitution that defined marriage as a union between a man and a woman, but in 2010 the Hawaii legislature voted to recognize civil unions.) The 1993 decision by the Hawaii court engendered an outcry in state capitals and in Washington, DC. Some feared that states would be forced to recognize same-sex marriages under the full faith and credit clause of Article IV, Section 1 of the Constitution: "Full faith and credit shall be given in each state to the public acts, records, and judicial proceedings of every other state. And the Congress may by general laws prescribe the manner in which such acts, records, and proceedings shall be proved, and the effect thereof."

In response to demands from some groups and state governments, Congress passed the Defense of Marriage Act (DOMA) in 1996, which (1) granted states the authority to exempt themselves from same-sex marriages recognized by other states and (2) defined marriage as a union between a man and a woman under federal law. Forty-one states now ban recognition of

---

[1] Cass R. Sunstein, *Designing Democracy: What Constitutions Do* (New York: Oxford University Press, 2001).

same-sex marriages. Six states plus the District of Columbia recognize same-sex marriage, and three states recognize civil unions. Three states recognize same-sex marriages from other states, and seven states recognize varying degrees of spousal legal rights under "domestic partnership" laws.[2] In 2010, President Obama's Attorney General, Eric Holder, announced that the Justice Department would no longer support the constitutionality of DOMA in federal courts.

As the campaign for the presidency heated up late in 2004, President George W. Bush announced that he favored an amendment to the U.S. Constitution to define marriage as a union between a man and a woman. Presidential candidate John Kerry stated that he, too, opposed same-sex marriage but thought that the issue should be left up to each state—consistent with the constitutional principle of federalism. Exit polls from the 2004 presidential election suggested that the same-sex marriage issue helped Bush mobilize and win the support of the vast majority of conservative Christian voters, especially in the eleven states that had ballot measures prohibiting same-sex marriage (see Exercise 4.1).[3]

Congress remained short of the two-thirds majority in the House and Senate required to propose a constitutional amendment restricting the right to gay marriage. Even if Congress proposed such an amendment, three-fourths of the state legislatures would be required to ratify it. The framers of the Constitution made it exceedingly difficult to amend the Constitution; they did not want the "passions and prejudices" of the moment frozen into the nation's fundamental law. Only one constitutional amendment restricted, rather than enlarged, the realm of freedom for citizens: the Eighteenth, which ushered in prohibition. Not surprisingly, that's the only amendment that has been repealed (the Twenty-First Amendment).

The contemporary controversy over same-sex marriage is so heated because the prospect of same-sex marriage challenges deeply embedded moral and cultural norms. But all civil rights movements challenge long-held values. At one time, military leaders maintained that the integration of African Americans into the armed forces would undermine morale, just as they later maintained that openly gay men and women would undermine military morale. In 2010, Congress repealed the so-called don't ask, don't tell policy, which had mandated the discharge of soldiers found to be actively homosexual.

ASSIGNMENT

In the election of November 2008, Californians voted to amend the state constitution to define marriage as a union between men and women. The ballot measure, Proposition 8, passed with 52 percent of the vote. Reading 10.2.1 includes the language of the ballot measure, followed by arguments in favor and against, and with rebuttals to each. Study the reading and answer the questions that follow.

READING 10.2.1
California Proposition 8: Limit on Marriage Initiative Constitutional Amendment

PROPOSED LAW

Proposition 8

SECTION 1. Title
     This measure shall be known and may be cited as the "California Marriage Protection Act."

SECTION 2. Section 7.5 is added to Article I of the California Constitution, to read:

SECTION 7.5. Only marriage between a man and a woman is valid or recognized.

---

[2]Information about how states handle the issue of same-sex marriage can be found at the website of the National Conference of State Legislatures: http://www.ncsl.org.

[3]All eleven measures to prohibit same-sex marriage passed. Kerry won only one of those states, Oregon, in the presidential election.

Proposition 8   Eliminates right of same–sex couples to marry. Initiative constitutional amendment.

Argument in Favor of Proposition 8	Argument Against Proposition 8
Proposition 8 is simple and straightforward. It contains the same 14 words that were previously approved in 2000 by over 61% of California voters: "Only marriage between a man and a woman is valid or recognized in California."	OUR CALIFORNIA CONSTITUTION—the law of our land—SHOULD GUARANTEE THE SAME FREEDOMS AND RIGHTS TO EVERYONE—NO ONE group SHOULD be singled out to BE TREATED DIFFERENTLY.
Because four activist judges in San Francisco wrongly overturned the people's vote, we need to pass this measure as a constitutional amendment to RESTORE THE DEFINITION OF MARRIAGE as a man and a woman.	In fact, our nation was founded on the principle that all people should be treated equally. EQUAL PROTECTION UNDER THE LAW IS THE FOUNDATION OF AMERICAN SOCIETY.
Proposition 8 is about preserving marriage; *it's not an attack on the gay lifestyle.* Proposition 8 doesn't take away any rights or benefits of gay or lesbian domestic partnerships. Under California law, "domestic partners shall have the same rights, protections, and benefits" as married spouses. (Family Code § 297.5.) There are NO exceptions. Proposition 8 WILL NOT change this.	That's what this election is about—equality, freedom, and fairness, for all. Marriage is the institution that conveys dignity and respect to the lifetime commitment of any couple. PROPOSITION 8 WOULD DENY LESBIAN AND GAY COUPLES that same DIGNITY AND RESPECT. That's why Proposition 8 is wrong for California.
YES on Proposition 8 does three simple things: *It restores the definition of marriage* to what the vast majority of California voters already approved and human history has understood marriage to be.	Regardless of how you feel about this issue, the freedom to marry is fundamental to our society, just like the freedoms of religion and speech. PROPOSITION 8 MANDATES ONE SET OF RULES FOR GAY AND LESBIAN COUPLES AND ANOTHER SET FOR EVERYONE ELSE. That's just not fair. OUR LAWS SHOULD TREAT EVERYONE EQUALLY.
It overturns the outrageous decision of four activist Supreme Court judges who ignored the will of the people.	In fact, the government has no business telling people who can and cannot get married. Just like government has no business telling us what to read, watch on TV, or do in our private lives. We don't need Prop. 8; WE DON'T NEED MORE GOVERNMENT IN OUR LIVES.
It protects our children from being taught in public schools that "same-sex marriage" is the same as traditional marriage.	REGARDLESS OF HOW ANYONE FEELS ABOUT MARRIAGE FOR GAY AND LESBIAN COUPLES, PEOPLE SHOULD NOT BE SINGLED OUT FOR UNFAIR TREATMENT UNDER THE LAWS OF OUR STATE. Those committed and loving couples who want to accept the responsibility that comes with marriage should be treated like everyone else.
Proposition 8 protects marriage as an essential institution of society. While death, divorce, or other circumstances may prevent the ideal, the best situation for a child is to be raised by a married mother and father.	DOMESTIC PARTNERSHIPS ARE NOT MARRIAGE.
The narrow decision of the California Supreme Court isn't just about "live and let live." State law may require teachers to instruct children as young as kindergarteners about marriage. (Education Code § 51890.) If the gay marriage ruling is not overturned, TEACHERS COULD BE REQUIRED to teach young children there is *no difference* between gay marriage and traditional marriage.	When you're married and your spouse is sick or hurt, there is no confusion: you get into the ambulance or hospital room with no questions asked. IN EVERYDAY LIFE, AND ESPECIALLY IN EMERGENCY SITUATIONS, DOMESTIC PARTNERSHIPS ARE SIMPLY NOT ENOUGH. Only marriage provides the certainty and the security that people know they can count on in their times of greatest need.
We should not accept a court decision that may result in public schools teaching our kids that gay marriage is okay. That is an issue for parents to discuss with their children according to their own values and beliefs. *It shouldn't be forced on us against our will.*	EQUALITY UNDER THE LAW IS A FUNDAMENTAL CONSTITUTIONAL GUARANTEE. Prop. 8 separates one group of Californians from another and excludes them from enjoying the same rights as other loving couples.
Some will try to tell you that Proposition 8 takes away legal rights of gay domestic partnerships. That is false. Proposition 8 DOES NOT take away any of those rights and does not interfere with gays living the lifestyle they choose.	

Argument in Favor of Proposition 8	Argument Against Proposition 8
However, while gays have the right to their private lives, *they do not have the right to redefine marriage for everyone else.* CALIFORNIANS HAVE NEVER VOTED FOR SAME-SEX MARRIAGE. If gay activists want to legalize gay marriage, they should put it on the ballot. Instead, they have gone behind the backs of voters and convinced four activist judges in San Francisco to redefine marriage for the rest of society. That is the wrong approach. Voting YES on Proposition 8 RESTORES the definition of marriage that was approved by over 61% of voters. Voting YES overturns the decision of four activist judges. Voting YES *protects our children.* *Please vote YES on Proposition 8 to RESTORE the meaning of marriage.*	Forty-six years ago I married my college sweetheart, Julia. We raised three children—two boys and one girl. The boys are married, with children of their own. Our daughter, Liz, a lesbian, can now also be married—if she so chooses. All we have ever wanted for our daughter is that she be treated with the same dignity and respect as her brothers—with the same freedoms and responsibilities as every other Californian. My wife and I never treated our children differently, we never loved them any differently, and now the law doesn't treat them differently, either. Each of our children now has the same rights as the others, to choose the person to love, commit to, and to marry. Don't take away the equality, freedom, and fairness that everyone in California—straight, gay, or lesbian—deserves. Please join us in voting NO on Prop. 8.

Rebuttal to Argument in Favor of Proposition 8	Rebuttal to Argument Against Proposition 8

Don't be tricked by scare tactics.
   • PROP. 8 DOESN'T HAVE ANYTHING TO DO WITH SCHOOLS
There's NOT ONE WORD IN 8 ABOUT EDUCATION. In fact, local school districts and parents—not the state—develop health education programs for their schools.
NO CHILD CAN BE FORCED, AGAINST THE WILL OF THEIR PARENTS, TO BE TAUGHT ANYTHING about health and family issues. CALIFORNIA LAW PROHIBITS IT.
And NOTHING IN STATE LAW REQUIRES THE MENTION OF MARRIAGE IN KINDERGARTEN!
It's a smokescreen.
   • DOMESTIC PARTNERSHIPS and MARRIAGE AREN'T THE SAME.
CALIFORNIA STATUTES CLEARLY IDENTIFY NINE REAL DIFFERENCES BETWEEN MARRIAGE AND DOMESTIC PARTNERSHIPS. Only marriage provides the security that spouses provide one another—it's why people get married in the first place!
Think about it. Married couples depend on spouses when they're sick, hurt, or aging. They accompany them into ambulances or hospital rooms, and help make life-and-death decisions, with no questions asked. ONLY MARRIAGE ENDS THE CONFUSION AND GUARANTEES THE CERTAINTY COUPLES CAN COUNT ON IN TIMES OF GREATEST NEED.
Regardless of how you feel about this issue, we should guarantee the same fundamental freedoms to every Californian.
   • PROP. 8 TAKES AWAY THE RIGHTS OF GAY AND LESBIAN COUPLES AND TREATS THEM DIFFERENTLY UNDER THE LAW.
	Proposition 8 is about traditional marriage; it is not an attack on gay relationships. Under California law gay and lesbian domestic partnerships are treated equally; they already have the same rights as married couples. Proposition 8 does not change that.
	What Proposition 8 does is restore the meaning of marriage to what human history has understood it to be and over 61% of California voters approved just a few years ago.
	Your YES vote ensures that the will of the people is respected. It overturns the flawed legal reasoning of four judges in San Francisco who wrongly disregarded the people's vote, and ensures that gay marriage can be legalized only through a vote of the people.
	Your YES vote ensures that parents can teach their children about marriage according to their own values and beliefs without conflicting messages being forced on young children in public schools that gay marriage is okay.
	Your YES vote on Proposition 8 means that only marriage between a man and a woman will be valid or recognized in California, regardless of when or where performed. But Prop. 8 will NOT take away any other rights or benefits of gay couples.
	Gays and lesbians have the right to live the lifestyle they choose, but they do not have the right to redefine marriage for everyone else. Proposition 8 respects the rights of gays while still reaffirming traditional marriage.
	Please vote YES on Proposition 8 to RESTORE the definition of marriage that the voters already approved.

Argument in favor of proposition 8	Argument against proposition 8
	Equality under the law is one of the basic foundations of our society. Prop. 8 means one class of citizens can enjoy the dignity and responsibility of marriage, and another cannot. That's unfair. PROTECT FUNDAMENTAL FREEDOMS. SAY NO TO PROPOSITION 8.

Source: Official Voter Information Guide, California General Election, November 4, 2008. This material is reprinted here with permission of the California Secretary of State for illustrative purposes only.

1. Would you have voted for or against Proposition 8? Explain and support your answer by referring to the ballot arguments that you find most convincing.

_____

_____

_____

_____

_____

_____

_____

_____

_____

_____

2. If you would have voted *for* California Proposition 8, banning same-sex marriages, would you also have voted to ban civil unions? Explain and support your answer. (If you would have voted against Proposition 8, skip this question.)

_____

_____

_____

_____

_____

3. George W. Bush supported an amendment to the U.S. Constitution to define marriage as a union between a man and a woman. Some critics of such an amendment to the U.S. Constitution maintain that their opposition stems from their commitment to protect the traditional powers and prerogatives of state governments—not from support for same-sex marriage. They argue that the regulation of marriage is a reserved power of the states and that the federal government has no business telling the states who should or should not be granted marriage licenses. Do you think that the same-sex marriage/civil union issue should be left up to the states? Explain and support your position. (Your response should be consistent with your response to question 1.)

_____

_____

_____

_____

_____

In a much anticipated and widely publicized decision, Judge Walker, of the Federal District Court for Northern California, ruled that Proposition 8 violated the due process and equal protection clauses of the Fourteenth Amendment, and that the State of California had no rational interest in making or enforcing that law. Reading 10.2.2 includes excerpts from Judge Walker's opinion (*Perry v. Schwarzenegger* [2010]), in which he explains his finding that the proposition violated the equal protection clause of the U.S. Constitution. (Perry was the plaintiff, arguing that then-governor Arnold Schwarzenegger had violated her and her partner's constitutional rights in enforcing the law, that is, in not mandating the issuing of marriage licenses to same-sex couples.) Study the reading and answer the questions that follow.

READING 10.2.2
Excerpts from *Perry v. Schwarzenegger*

The Equal Protection Clause of the Fourteenth Amendment provides that no state shall "deny to any person within its jurisdiction the equal protection of the laws." . . .

. . . Plaintiffs challenge Proposition 8 as violating the Equal Protection Clause because Proposition 8 discriminates both on the basis of sex and on the basis of sexual orientation. Sexual orientation discrimination can take the form of sex discrimination. . . . Proposition 8 also operates to restrict Perry's choice of marital partner because of her sexual orientation; her desire to marry another woman arises only because she is a lesbian. The evidence at trial shows that gays and lesbians experience discrimination based on unfounded stereotypes and prejudices specific to sexual orientation. Gays and lesbians have historically been targeted for discrimination because of their sexual orientation. . . . As the case of Perry and the other plaintiffs illustrates, sex and sexual orientation are necessarily interrelated, as an individual's choice of romantic or intimate partner based on sex is a large part of what defines an individual's sexual orientation. Sexual orientation discrimination is thus a phenomenon distinct from, but related to, sex discrimination. . . . Those who would choose to marry someone of the same sex—— homosexuals—have had their right to marry eliminated by an amendment to the state constitution. . . . Having considered the evidence, the relationship between sex and sexual orientation and the fact that Proposition 8 eliminates a right only a gay man or a lesbian would exercise, the court determines that plaintiffs' equal protection claim is based on sexual orientation, but this claim is equivalent to a claim of discrimination based on sex.

. . . The Equal Protection Clause renders Proposition 8 unconstitutional under any standard of review. . . . The evidence presented at trial shows that gays and lesbians are the type of minority strict scrutiny was designed to protect, . . .where a group has experienced a "'history of purposeful unequal treatment' or been subjected to unique disabilities on the basis of stereotyped characteristics not truly indicative of their abilities."

. . . No evidence at trial illuminated distinctions among lesbians, gay men and heterosexuals amounting to "real and undeniable differences" that the government might need to take into account in legislating. The trial record shows that strict scrutiny is the appropriate standard of review to apply to legislative classifications based on sexual orientation. All classifications based on sexual orientation appear suspect, as the evidence shows that California would rarely, if ever, have a reason to categorize individuals based on their sexual orientation.

. . . Proposition 8 cannot withstand any level of scrutiny under the Equal Protection Clause, as excluding same-sex couples from marriage is simply not rationally related to a legitimate state interest. One example of a legitimate state interest in not issuing marriage licenses to a particular group might be a scarcity of marriage licenses or county officials to issue them. But marriage licenses in California are not a limited commodity, and the existence of 18,000 same-sex married couples in California shows that the state has the resources to allow both same-sex and opposite-sex couples to wed. . . .

The state must have an interest apart from the fact of the tradition itself. The evidence shows that the tradition of restricting an individual's choice of spouse based on gender does not rationally further a state interest despite its "ancient lineage." Instead, the evidence shows that the tradition of gender restrictions arose when spouses were legally required to adhere to specific gender roles. . . . Proposition 8 thus enshrines in the California Constitution a gender restriction that the evidence shows to be nothing more than an artifact of a foregone notion that men and women fulfill different roles in civic life. The tradition of restricting marriage to opposite-sex couples does not further any state interest. Rather, the evidence shows that Proposition 8 harms the state's interest in equality, because it mandates that men and women be treated differently based only on antiquated and discredited notions of gender. . . .

Tradition alone cannot legitimate this purported interest. Plaintiffs presented evidence showing conclusively that the state has no interest in preferring opposite-sex couples to same-sex couples or in preferring heterosexuality to homosexuality. Moreover, the state cannot have an interest in disadvantaging an unpopular minority group simply because the group is unpopular. . . .

4. On what basis does Judge Walker find that discrimination based on sexual orientation and discrimination based on sex are interrelated? (This is an important finding because discrimination based on sex was prohibited in the Civil Rights Act of 1964.)

_____

_____

_____

_____

_____

5. What reasons does Judge Walker provide for finding that Proposition 8 denies same-sex couples equal protection under the law?

_____

_____

_____

_____

_____

_____

_____

_____

In 1967, the Supreme Court, in _Loving v. Virginia_, decided that laws prohibiting interracial marriage (antimiscegenation laws) violated the Fourteenth Amendment to the Constitution. Reading 10.2.3 includes the language of the two Virginia statutes under which the Lovings, an interracial couple, were prosecuted and which the Supreme Court later nullified in the _Loving_ decision. Study the reading and then answer question 6.

READING 10.2.3
Virginia Antimiscegenation Statutes

The Lovings were convicted of violating 20–58 of the Virginia Code:

> "Leaving State to evade law. . . . If any white person and colored person shall go out of this State, for the purpose of being married, and with the intention of returning, and be married out of it, and afterwards return to and reside in it, cohabiting as man and wife, they shall be punished as provided in 20–59, and the marriage shall be governed by the same law as if it had been solemnized in this State. The fact of their cohabitation here as man and wife shall be evidence of their marriage."

Section 20–59, which defines the penalty for miscegenation, provides:

> "Punishment for marriage. . . . If any white person intermarry with a colored person, or any colored person intermarry with a white person, he shall be guilty of a felony and shall be punished by confinement in the penitentiary for not less than one nor more than five years."

6. Randall Kennedy, professor of law at Harvard University, makes the following analogy between laws that once banned interracial marriages and laws that now prohibit same-sex marriage: "The . . . significance of *Loving* today is that it helps to buttress the case for tolerating same-sex marriages. Just as many people once found trans-racial marriage to be a loathsome potentiality well-worth prohibiting, so, too, do many people find same-sex marriage to be an abomination. This frightened, reflexive reaction will likely dissipate in many of the same ways that antipathy to the idea of trans-racial marriage has dissipated."[4] Do you agree or disagree with Professor Kennedy that discrimination against same-sex marriage is analogous to antimiscegenation laws? Explain and support your position.

_____

_____

_____

_____

_____

[4]Randall Kennedy, *"Loving v. Virginia at 30,"* February 6, 1997. See SpeakOut.com: http://speakout.com/activism/opinions/3208-1.html.

EXERCISE 10.3   The Gender Wage Gap

INTRODUCTION

All paychecks are not created equal: Since 2000, women have earned about 75 cents for every dollar earned by men.[1]

Imbedded in the gender wage gap are difficult and contentious issues, such as the roles of men and women in society, undervaluing women's work, and even globalization. With the exception of agreement that the gender wage gap exists, there is little consensus about it. Is the gap narrowing? What causes the wage gap? What's to be done about it?

Most parties to the debate agree that the gender wage gap has a number of sources, among them:

- Differences in the age, education, skill, experience, job tenure, and marital status of men and women workers
- Social norms and expectations—for example, the notion that some occupations are "men's work" and others are "women's work"
- That traditional "women's work" (nursing, teaching, etc.) and the skills and training necessary to perform it are simply undervalued
- The different choices men and women make regarding family—for example, whether to marry, whether to have children, and how to share child-rearing responsibilities
- The proportions of men and women working part-time versus full-time
- The proportions of men and women workers who are unionized versus those who are not

Researchers who study the gender wage gap have attempted to control for the variables identified in this list using statistical analysis. Even so, a portion of the gap remains unaccounted for.[2] Many suspect that this unexplained portion of the gap stems from discrimination against women workers—discrimination that is illegal under federal law and court rulings.[3] There is no doubt that discrimination against women and minorities in pay and advancement exists in the workplace. Companies frequently settle gender-based wage discrimination lawsuits by admitting discriminatory practices, paying cash settlements, and changing their employment practices to match the law.[4]

One gender-based wage discrimination case captured national attention by making its way to the Supreme Court, whose decision against the plaintiff was later overturned by legislation passed by Congress. President Obama highlighted the issue by making that bill—the Lilly Ledbetter Fair Pay Act—the first he signed into law on January 29, 2009. Obama told Ledbetter's story over and over during his 2008 presidential campaign.

Lilly Ledbetter, who was 70 years old when Obama signed the law named after her, had worked as a supervisor at Goodyear Tire and Rubber's plant in Gadsden, Alabama, for almost twenty years. As her retirement neared, someone slipped her a salary schedule showing that her male coworkers were making more than she had been. Based on evidence presented at trial that her salary was as much as 40 percent below the lowest-paid male supervisor at the plant, a jury concluded that she had been the victim of illegal gender-based pay discrimination and awarded her $3 million in damages. That amount was later reduced to $300,000 because of the damage cap in Title VII of the Civil Rights Act of 1964.

At the Supreme Court, Goodyear argued that Ledbetter's claims were barred under the law because she did not file her charges within 180 days of receiving the first check for which she had been underpaid. Ledbetter argued that the 180-day statute of limitations runs from the date of

---

[1]Figures are available from the Census Bureau, The National Committee on Pay Equity, and The National Women's Law Center, among others.

[2]See, for example, "Women's Earnings: Work Patterns Partially Explain Difference between Men's and Women's Earnings," General Accounting Office Report, October 2003. The report is available at http://www.gao.gov/. Type in the search engine: GAO-04-35.

[3]Title VII of the Civil Rights Act of 1964 was the first federal legislation to address systematically race and gender discrimination in the workplace. In *Reed v. Reed* (1971), the Supreme Court ruled for the first time that statutory gender discrimination violated the equal protection clause of the Fourteenth Amendment.

[4]In 2010, the drug maker Novartis Pharmaceuticals Corporation settled a class-action lawsuit alleging gender discrimination in pay, promotions, and pregnancy-related matters for $175 million. In addition to the monetary settlement, Novartis agreed to change its employment practices that were in violation of Title VII of 1964.

any paycheck whose amount has been reduced by gender-based discrimination. The Court sided with Goodyear.

The Leadership Conference on Civil and Human Rights offered this critique of the Court's decision in *Ledbetter v. Goodyear Tire and Rubber Co.*: "The decision fails to protect most victims of pay discrimination because it ignores workplace reality. Very few employees have ready access to their colleagues' salaries, or to any other information which would clue them in to the fact that they are paid less than their peers. In the case of Lilly Ledbetter, the plaintiff in the Ledbetter case, she only found out about the discrimination against her when she received an anonymous note well after the discrimination had begun. As a result of the Ledbetter decision, employees who don't learn about paycheck discrimination until more than 180 days past the moment when the decision to pay them less is made will have no remedy."

Within a few weeks of the *Ledbetter* decision, the House Education and Labor Committee held a hearing to begin the lengthy legislative process that would be required to reverse the Court's decision. Congress eventually produced two versions of a bill to address the problem, but because of a Bush Administration promise to veto those bills, legislative action stalled until after Obama's election in 2008.

The Lilly Ledbetter Fair Pay Act of 2009 rebuked the Court by establishing, among other provisions, that it's an unlawful employment practice "when an individual is affected by application of a discriminatory compensation decision or other practice, including each time wages, benefits, or other compensation is paid, resulting in whole or in part from such a decision or other practice."

When President Obama signed the bill in the East Room of the White House, he said that "equal pay is by no means just a women's issue—it's a family issue. It's about parents who find themselves with less money for tuition and child care; couples who wind up with less to retire on; households where one breadwinner is paid less than she deserves; that's the difference between affording the mortgage—or not; between keeping the heat on, or paying the doctor bills—or not. And in this economy, when so many folks are already working harder for less and struggling to get by, the last thing they can afford is losing part of each month's paycheck to simple and plain discrimination."

Because the Supreme Court's decision against Ledbetter overturned the jury award of $300,000, Ledbetter received no monetary compensation for the gender wage discrimination she had suffered. At the signing ceremony with President Obama, she said that "Goodyear will never have to pay me what it cheated me out of. In fact, I will never see a cent from my case. But with the passage and the President's signature today, I have an even richer reward. I know that my daughter and granddaughters, and your daughters and granddaughters, will have a better deal. That's what makes this fight worth fighting. That's what made this a fight we had to win. And now with this win we will make a big difference in the real world."

ASSIGNMENT

Questions 1 to 6 are based on data from the Department of Labor in Table 10.3.1.

TABLE 10.3.1	Median Weekly Earnings of Full-Time Wage and Salary Workers by Detailed Occupation and Sex, 2010			
	Men		Women	
	Number of Workers (in Thousands)	Median Weekly Earnings	Number of Workers (in Thousands)	Median Weekly Earnings
Management Occupations				
Chief executives	769	2,217	265	1,598
Human resource managers	71	1,458	174	1,170
Food-service managers	308	769	290	626
Medical and health-service managers	138	1,510	356	1,163

(Continued)

TABLE 10.3.1	Median Weekly Earnings of Full-Time Wage and Salary Workers by Detailed Occupation and Sex, 2010 (Continued)			
	Men		**Women**	
	Number of Workers (in Thousands)	**Median Weekly Earnings**	**Number of Workers (in Thousands)**	**Median Weekly Earnings**
Professional Occupations				
Computer programmers	333	1,243	96	1,177
Counselors	154	780	363	818
Social workers	144	865	557	788
Lawyers	435	1,895	234	1,461
Elementary and middle school teachers	461	1,024	1,947	931
Pharmacists	97	1,930	88	1,605
Registered nurses	207	1,201	1,970	1,039
Service Occupations				
Police officers and sheriffs	608	992	96	772
Waiters and waitresses	287	450	538	381
Janitors and building cleaners	1,099	494	437	400
Sales and Office Occupations				
Real estate broker and sales agents	174	978	187	683
Insurance sales agents	158	973	184	649
Postal service mail carriers	198	952	94	897
Secretaries and administrative assistants	102	725	2,297	657
Production Occupations				
Bakers	74	435	72	406
Butchers	217	508	64	478
Sewing machine operators	33	n.d.*	92	410
Bus drivers	184	660	148	502
Driver/sales and truck drivers	2,307	691	79	492
Taxi drivers and chauffeurs	216	570	35	n.d.*
Construction Occupations				
Carpenters	659	624	10	n.d.*
Electricians	552	890	8	n.d.*
Highway maintenance workers	99	729	3	n.d.*
Installation, Repair, and Maintenance Occupations				
Aircraft mechanics and service technicians	126	986	4	n.d.*
Automotive service technicians and mechanics	585	680	11	n.d.*
Telecommunications line installers and repairers	137	873	12	n.d.*

*No data (n.d.) are shown where the number of workers in the occupation is less than 50,000.

1. Identify two occupations in which women are significantly overrepresented, meaning that the number of women in the occupation is much larger than the number of men.

_____

_____

2. Identify two occupations in which women are significantly underrepresented.

_____

_____

3. In how many of the occupations listed in Table 10.3.1 do the median weekly earnings of women exceed those of men?

_____

4. Identify an occupation in which the median weekly earnings of men and women are nearly equal.

_____

5. Identify an occupation in which the median weekly earnings of men and women are far from equal.

_____

6. The gender wage gap is the difference between the earnings of men and women in a given occupation or group of occupations.

   a. What is the weekly earnings gap between men and women lawyers?

   _____

   b. What would be the approximate yearly earnings gap between men and women lawyers?

   _____

The data in Table 10.3.1 indicate that women are often paid less than men for the same work. The data also illustrate the extent of gender segregation in the workforce. One study found that in male-dominated, low-skill occupations, the median weekly earnings were $553, while in female-dominated, low-skill occupations, the weekly earnings were $408—a wage gap of 26 percent. In comparable high-skilled occupations, the wage gap is 33 percent.[5] This is the problem of *comparative worth*: Occupations dominated by women pay less—and often a lot less—than occupations with comparable education and skill requirements dominated by men. Addressing the problem of comparative worth has proved controversial.

7. *Web-Based Question.* Search the Web for arguments for and against establishing comparable pay for comparable worth. One article on the pro side is "Comparable Pay for Comparable Worth—It's Time," by E. James Brennan of the Economic Research Institute. An article on the con side is "Why Comparable Worth Legislation Would Do More Harm Than Good," by Ann Bares of the Altura Consulting Group. Feel free to consult other articles available on the Web.

Web addresses sometimes change. If you can't locate a website, try an external search (e.g., Google) to find the website. Configurations within a website often change. If you can't find a particular link or article,

---

[5]"Separate and Not Equal? Gender Segregation in the Labor Market and the Gender Wage Gap," September 2010, Institute for Women's Policy Research.

for example, try an internal search of the website as well as an external search. Be resourceful! If you still can't find what you're searching for, move on to the next question.

a. In your view, what's the strongest argument in favor of comparable pay for comparable work? Explain your choice.

_____

_____

_____

_____

_____

_____

b. In your view, what's the strongest argument against comparable pay for comparable work? Explain your choice.

_____

_____

_____

_____

_____

_____

In April 2009, in an effort to address the gender wage gap, Senator Tom Harkin (Democrat, Iowa) and several Democratic cosponsors introduced the Fair Pay Act in the House and Senate. The introduction of the bill coincided with Equal Pay Day, an event coordinated by the National Committee on Pay Equity (NCPE), a coalition of labor unions, women's and civil rights organizations, and other associations and commissions. The NCPE was founded in 1979 with the purpose of eliminating gender- and race-based wage discrimination and achieving pay equity. In introducing the Fair Pay Act of 2009, Senator Harkin said: "In this day in age, there is no such thing as 'women's work' or 'men's work.' In nearly 10 million American households, the mother is the only breadwinner. These families have the same struggles to pay the rent or make mortgage payments, buy the groceries, cover the medical bills and save for a child's education. In these tough economic times, we need to simply make sure an honest day's work is rewarded. We must end wage discrimination and on Equal Pay Day, we can start by closing the pay gap and simply paying women fairly." Legislation similar to the Fair Pay Act of 2009 has been introduced in every Congress since 1994, but it has failed to pass. The Fair Pay Act of 2009 was no exception. The last major legislation passed by Congress on the issue of pay equity was the 1963 Pay Equity Act, signed into law by President John F. Kennedy. Questions 8 and 9 are based on Reading 10.3.1, an excerpt from the Fair Pay Act of 2009.

READING 10.3.1
Senate Bill 904: The Fair Pay Act of 2009

SEC. 2. FINDINGS

Congress finds the following:

   (1) Wage rate differentials exist between equivalent jobs segregated by sex, race, and national origin in Government employment and in industries engaged in commerce or in the production of goods for commerce.

   (2) The existence of such wage rate differentials—

   (A) depresses wages and living standards for employees necessary for their health and efficiency;

   (B) prevents the maximum utilization of the available labor resources;

   (C) tends to cause labor disputes, thereby burdening, affecting, and obstructing commerce;

   (D) burdens commerce and the free flow of goods in commerce; and

   (E) constitutes an unfair method of competition.

   (3) Discrimination in hiring and promotion has played a role in maintaining a segregated work force.

   (4) Many women and people of color work in occupations dominated by individuals of their same sex, race, and national origin.

   (5) (A) United States Census Bureau data shows that in 2007, women in the United States working full-time, year-round earned roughly 78 cents for every dollar earned by a man working full-time, year-round.

   (B) A 2003 study by the General Accountability Office found that even when accounting for key factors generally known to influence earnings such as race, marital status, age and number of children as well as hours worked and time out of the workforce, a 20 percent gap in pay remains which cannot be accounted for but may be partially explained by women make less who work in traditionally female dominated careers as well as other discrimination in the workplace.

   (6) Section 6(d) of the Fair Labor Standards Act of 1938 prohibits discrimination in compensation for 'equal work' on the basis of sex.

   (7) Artificial barriers to the elimination of discrimination in compensation based upon sex, race, and national origin continue to exist more than 4 decades after the passage of section 6(d) of the Fair Labor Standards Act of 1938, the Equal Pay Act of 1963, and the Civil Rights Act of 1964 (42 U.S.C. 2000a et seq.). Elimination of such barriers would have positive effects, including—

   (A) providing a solution to problems in the economy created by discrimination through wage rate differentials;

   (B) substantially reducing the number of working women and people of color earning low wages, thereby reducing the dependence on public assistance; and

   (C) promoting stable families by enabling working family members to earn a fair rate of pay.

SEC. 3. EQUAL PAY FOR EQUIVALENT JOBS

   (A) Amendment— Section 6 (29 U.S.C. 206) is amended by adding at the end the following:

   "(h)(1)(A) Except as provided in subparagraph (B), no employer having employees subject to any provision of this section shall discriminate, within any establishment in which such employees are employed, between employees on the basis of sex, race, or national origin by paying wages to employees in such establishment in a job that is dominated by employees of a particular sex, race, or national origin at a rate less than the rate at which the employer pays wages to employees in such establishment in another job that is dominated by employees of the opposite sex or of a different race or national origin, respectively, for work on equivalent jobs.

   (B) Nothing in subparagraph (A) shall prohibit the payment of different wage rates to employees where such payment is made pursuant to—

(i) a seniority system;

(ii) a merit system;

(iiii) a system that measures earnings by quantity or quality of production; or

(iv) a differential based on a bona fide factor other than sex, race, or national origin, such as education, training, or experience, except that this clause shall apply only if—

  (I) the employer demonstrates that—

    (aa) such factor—

      (AA) is job-related with respect to the position in question; or

      (BB) furthers a legitimate business purpose, except that this item shall not apply if the employee demonstrates that an alternative employment practice exists that would serve the same business purpose without producing such differential and that the employer has refused to adopt such alternative practice; and

    (bb) such factor was actually applied and used reasonably in light of the asserted justification; and

  (II) upon the employer succeeding under subclause (I), the employee fails to demonstrate that the differential produced by the reliance of the employer on such factor is itself the result of discrimination on the basis of sex, race, or national origin by the employer.

(C) The Equal Employment Opportunity Commission shall issue guidelines specifying criteria for determining whether a job is dominated by employees of a particular sex, race, or national origin for purposes of subparagraph (B)(iv). Such guidelines shall not include a list of such jobs.

(D) An employer who is paying a wage rate differential in violation of subparagraph (A) shall not, in order to comply with the provisions of such subparagraph, reduce the wage rate of any employee. . . .

8. Study Section 2 of the Fair Pay Act, "Findings."

a. In your view, which finding is most persuasive? Why do you think so?

_____

_____

_____

_____

_____

_____

_____

b. In your view, which finding is least persuasive? Why do you think so?

_____

_____

_____

_____

_____

_____

_____

9. Study Section 3 of the Fair Pay Act, "Equal Pay for Equivalent Jobs." Carefully examine the following sentence from Section 3, and particularly the use of the word *equivalent*: "no employer . . . shall discriminate . . . between employees on the basis of sex, race, or national origin by paying wages . . . in a job that is dominated by employees of a particular sex, race, or national origin at a rate less than the rate at which the employer pays wages to employees . . . in another job that is dominated by employees of the opposite sex or of a different race or national origin . . . for work on equivalent jobs."

    a. Identify and explain a significant objection that employers would likely raise to this provision of the proposed legislation.

_____

_____

_____

_____

_____

    b. Explain, in your own words, when the payment of different wage rates for men and women is permitted under the bill.

_____

_____

_____

_____

_____

10. *Web-Based Question.* On the Web, locate "Handling the Arguments Against Pay Equity," compiled by the National Committee on Pay Equity. Study the claims by opponents of pay equity and the responses to those claims by the National Committee on Pay Equity. Begin with Section 1: General Claims About the Wage Gap.

    a. In your view, for which claim against equal pay is the response in favor of equal pay *most* persuasive? Explain and support your answer.

_____

_____

_____

_____

_____

    b. In your view, for which claim against equal pay is the response in favor of equal pay *least* persuasive? Explain and support your answer.

_____

_____

_____

_____

_____

c. Moving to Section 2, Arguments Against Job Evaluation Systems, briefly summarize in your own words the response to the claim that different jobs dominated by women and men cannot be compared because it would be like comparing apples and oranges. Do you find the response convincing? Why or why not?

_____

_____

_____

_____

_____

_____

_____

d. Also in Section 2, summarize in your own words the response to the claim that it's reasonable for some men to be paid more because they have dangerous jobs or jobs that demand physical strength. Do you find the response convincing? Why or why not?

_____

_____

_____

_____

_____

_____

_____

e. Moving to Section 3, summarize in your own words the response to the claim that pay equity legislation will result in government wage setting. Do you find the response convincing? Why or why not?

_____

_____

_____

_____

_____

_____

_____

EXERCISE 10.4   The End of Affirmative Action?

INTRODUCTION

Affirmative action refers to government or private-sector programs in employment, higher education admissions, K–12 school placement, and government contracting that give preference to *underrepresented groups*—those that have suffered a pattern of historical disadvantage and discrimination. Underrepresented groups are those whose numbers in a public school, college, university, or place of employment are disproportionately low compared to their numbers in the general population that the institution or employer serves. Affirmative action initially focused on African Americans, but in time it was applied to members of other minority groups and women.

In 1965, President Lyndon B. Johnson issued Executive Order 11246, making affirmative action official government policy. Johnson believed that the Civil Rights Act (CRA) of 1964, which prohibited discrimination in employment, would be slow to achieve racial equality. That's because CRA placed the burden on individuals to prove discrimination and because discrimination in individual cases is difficult to prove. Therefore, Johnson decided that the federal government must make an affirmative effort to hire African Americans. The federal government later required affirmative action programs to be in place for businesses contracting with the government and for colleges and universities receiving federal aid. From there, affirmative action programs were adopted by the private sector, often voluntarily. (Many corporations became convinced that affirmative action was good business; the addition of women and minorities to the workplace enabled businesses to penetrate new markets.) Later, some public school districts adopted race as a factor to be considered in honoring intradistrict transfer requests to maintain the integration of public schools after court-ordered bussing ended.[1] Proponents of affirmative action assumed that as minority representation in colleges, universities, and the workplace increased, the need for affirmative action policies would disappear. This has happened in some cases; for example, women no longer receive preference in admission to law schools because they now make up about half of first-year law school students, but they continue to receive preference in many engineering programs, although some states have banned the use of affirmative action in public universities.

Affirmative action programs never enjoyed widespread support for several reasons. First, there had never been a legislative debate about them. Affirmative action was instituted by executive action—later passing court muster—so that the public was not adequately educated about the rationale for the programs. Second, many whites charged that they had become the victims of so-called reverse discrimination; that is, affirmative action discriminated against whites in the effort to remediate the effects of centuries of discrimination against blacks. Third, early affirmative action programs that set quotas for minority representation were vigorously contested. For example, a medical school might reserve a certain number of first-year slots exclusively for members of minority groups, in the process denying admission to what might have been, by traditional criteria, better-qualified white applicants. Even after the Supreme Court declared the use of quotas unconstitutional in most cases, opponents of affirmative action insisted that quotas were still in effect—under the guise of goals.

The U.S. Supreme Court first addressed affirmative action in 1978, in *Regents of the University of California v. Bakke*. Alan Bakke was twice rejected for admission to the University of California at Davis medical school. The university had reserved sixteen of the one hundred openings for applicants who were economically or educationally "disadvantaged." Because some minority applicants who were statistically less qualified were accepted under the special admissions program, Bakke charged that his equal protection rights under the Fourteenth Amendment had been violated. The Court agreed with Bakke. A majority of the justices held that quotas were unacceptable, although a plurality agreed that race and national origin could be considered as one of many criteria in the admissions process.

In 1996, California voters approved a ballot measure, the California Civil Rights Initiative (CCRI, Proposition 209), which abolished preferences for any individual or group on the basis

---

[1]The use of race as a tiebreaker in honoring transfer requests in public schools was barred by a deeply divided Supreme Court, in *Parents Involved in Community Schools v. Seattle School District No. 1*, 551 U.S. 701 (2007).

of race, sex, color, ethnicity, or national origin in public employment, public education, or public contracting. Proponents of the measure argued that thirty years of preferential programs had leveled the playing field, and that the programs were demeaning to minorities. Opponents countered that the programs had helped women and minorities overcome the effects of past and present discrimination and that the CCRI promoted racial divisiveness.[2] Voters in three states (Washington, Michigan, and Nebraska) have since passed similar initiatives. The Michigan initiative came in response to one of the Supreme Court decisions described in Readings 10.4.1 and 10.4.2.

ASSIGNMENT

Two precedent-setting affirmative action cases decided by the Supreme Court are *Gratz v. Bollinger* (2003) and *Grutter v. Bollinger* (2003). Both cases came from the University of Michigan—the first involving its undergraduate admissions affirmative action program and the second its law school admissions program. Readings 10.4.1 and 10.4.2 describe the affirmative action admissions programs at the University of Michigan Law School and the University of Michigan undergraduate school. Reading 10.4.3 outlines the criteria the Supreme Court uses in determining the constitutionality of affirmative action programs. Study the readings and answer the questions that follow.

READING 10.4.1
Description of Affirmative Action Program at the University of Michigan Law School (*Grutter* Case)

The University of Michigan Law School (Law School), one of the nation's top law schools, follows an official admissions policy that seeks to achieve student body diversity through compliance with *Regents of Univ. of Cal. v. Bakke,* 438 U.S. 265. Focusing on students' academic ability coupled with a flexible assessment of their talents, experiences, and potential, the policy requires admissions officials to evaluate each applicant based on all the information available in the file, including a personal statement, letters of recommendation, an essay describing how the applicant will contribute to Law School life and diversity, and the applicant's undergraduate grade point average (GPA) and Law School Admissions Test (LSAT) score. Officials must also look beyond grades and scores to so-called soft variables, such as recommenders' enthusiasm, the quality of the undergraduate institution and the applicant's essay, and the areas and difficulty of undergraduate course selection. The policy does not define diversity solely in terms of racial and ethnic status and does not restrict the types of diversity contributions eligible for "substantial weight," but it does reaffirm the Law School's commitment to diversity with special reference to the inclusion of African American, Hispanic, and Native American students, who otherwise might not be represented in the student body in meaningful numbers. By enrolling a "critical mass" of underrepresented minority students, the policy seeks to ensure their ability to contribute to the Law School's character and to the legal profession. When the Law School denied admission to petitioner Grutter, a white Michigan resident with a 3.8 GPA and 161 LSAT score, she filed this suit, alleging that respondents had discriminated against her on the basis of race in violation of the Fourteenth Amendment, Title VI of the Civil Rights Act of 1964, and 42 U.S.C. §1981; that she was rejected because the Law School uses race as a "predominant" factor, giving applicants belonging to certain minority groups a significantly greater chance of admission than students with similar credentials from disfavored racial groups; and that respondents had no compelling interest to justify that use of race.

Source: Grutter v. Bollinger, 539 U.S. 306(2003).

---

[2]A. G. Bloc, "Proposition 209: Affirmative Action," *California Journal,* September 1996, pp. 8–10.

READING 10.4.2
Description of Affirmative Action Program in the University of Michigan's Undergraduate Admissions (*Gratz* Case)

Petitioner Gratz and Hamacher, both of whom are Michigan residents and Caucasian, applied for admission to the University of Michigan's (University) College of Literature, Science, and the Arts (LSA) in 1995 and 1997, respectively. Although the LSA considered Gratz to be well qualified and Hamacher to be within the qualified range, both were denied early admission and were ultimately denied admission. To promote consistency in the review of the many applications received, the University's Office of Undergraduate Admissions (OUA) uses written guidelines for each academic year. The guidelines have changed a number of times during the period relevant to this litigation. The OUA considers a number of factors in making admissions decisions, including high school grades, standardized test scores, high school quality, curriculum strength, geography, alumni relationships, leadership, and race. During all relevant periods, the University has considered African Americans, Hispanics, and Native Americans to be "underrepresented minorities," and it is undisputed that the University admits virtually every qualified applicant from these groups. The current guidelines use a selection method under which every applicant from an underrepresented racial or ethnic minority group is automatically awarded 20 points of the 100 needed to guarantee admission.

Petitioners filed this class action alleging that the University's use of racial preferences in undergraduate admissions violated the equal protection clause of the Fourteenth Amendment, Title VI of the Civil Rights Act of 1964, and 42 U.S.C. §1981. They sought compensatory and punitive damages for past violations, declaratory relief finding that respondents violated their rights to nondiscriminatory treatment, an injunction prohibiting respondents from continuing to discriminate on the basis of race, and an order requiring the LSA to offer Hamacher admission as a transfer student.

Source: Gratz v. Bollinger, 539 U.S. 244(2003).

READING 10.4.3
Criteria the Supreme Court Uses to Determine the Constitutionality of Affirmative Action Programs

- The program must be *benign*. A benign program is one that is designed not to hinder or degrade a group but, rather, to advance it—to create conditions of equal opportunity for it. The primary effect must not be to harm or discriminate against others, although that may be an unavoidable secondary effect.

- If the program uses *suspect classifications*—race, national origin, or sex—those suspect classifications are constitutional only if they can withstand *strict scrutiny*.
- Suspect classifications can only withstand strict scrutiny if they meet the following criteria:

  1. There must be a *compelling government interest,* for example, improving education or providing educational opportunity.
  2. The program must be *narrowly tailored* to achieve the government's interest. The program can go no further than is absolutely necessary to accomplish that compelling interest.

     - Admission policies that seek the proportional representation of minorities are not narrowly tailored; those that seek to prevent minorities from being isolated and becoming "spokespersons for their race" are narrowly tailored.
     - Admission policies that consider race or ethnicity alone are not narrowly tailored; those that consider a variety of elements of diversity in individual cases (for example, geography and economic hardship) are narrowly tailored.

1. Apply the criteria in Reading 10.4.3 to the affirmative action program described in Reading 10.4.1 (*Grutter* case) to determine whether that affirmative action program might have been found constitutional or unconstitutional.

    a. Is the program benign? Explain and support your answer.

_____

_____

_____

    b. Can the suspect classification withstand strict scrutiny (compelling government interest? narrowly tailored?)? Explain and support your answer.

_____

_____

_____

    c. How do you think the Supreme Court ruled in *Grutter v. Bollinger*—for Grutter or for Bollinger (University of Michigan Law School)? Explain your answer by showing what criteria you applied.

_____

_____

_____

_____

_____

_____

_____

2. *Web-Based Question.* You can find the *Grutter* case at http://caselaw.lp.findlaw.com/scripts/getcase.pl?court=us&vol=000&invol=02-241. (Read the "Held" section of the decision to find the answer.) Did you predict the ruling in the case correctly?
Website URLs sometimes change. Use a search engine to find *Grutter v. Bollinger*.

_____

3. Apply the criteria in Reading 10.4.3 to the affirmative action program described in Reading 10.4.2 (*Gratz* case) to determine whether that affirmative action program might have been found constitutional or unconstitutional.

    a. Is the program benign? Explain and support your answer.

_____

_____

_____

b. Can the suspect classification withstand strict scrutiny (compelling government interest? narrowly tailored?)? Explain and support your answer.

_____

_____

_____

c. How do you think the Supreme Court ruled in _Gratz v. Bollinger_—for Gratz or for Bollinger (University of Michigan's undergraduate admissions)? Explain your answer by showing what criteria you applied to particular features of the program.

_____

_____

_____

_____

_____

_____

_____

_____

4. Web-Based Question. You can find the _Gratz_ case at http://caselaw.lp.findlaw.com/scripts/ getcase.pl?court=us&vol=000&invol=02-516. (Read the "Held" section of the decision to find the answer.) Did you predict the ruling in the case correctly?
Web site URLs sometimes change. Use a search engine to find _Gratz v. Bollinger._

_____

5. Some critics of race-based affirmative action programs argue that they are racially divisive and they do little for the underclass. Those critics have called for affirmative action based on economic need, particularly in college and professional school admissions, as the most effective and fair way to promote equal opportunity.[5] Do you think it's appropriate for a state university system to use economic disadvantage as a criterion for admissions to diversify its undergraduate school and its professional programs—for example, engineering and law? Explain and support your answer.

_____

_____

_____

_____

_____

_____

_____

_____

---

[5]See, for example, Shelby Steele, _The Content of Our Character_ (New York: St. Martin's Press, 1990).

Reading 10.4.4 includes excerpts from Chief Justice Roberts's opinion and Justice Breyer's dissenting opinion in *Parents Involved in Community Schools v. Seattle School District No. 1* (2007). In that case—discussed in the introduction to this exercise—the Court ruled that race could not be used explicitly to determine which transfer requests to honor within school districts. School districts around the country had been using race as a factor in transfer requests in order to try to maintain integrated schools. Read Chief Justice Roberts's main rationale for striking down the use of race in making transfer decisions and Justice Breyer's main reason for dissenting from that decision, and then answer the questions that follow.

READING 10.4.4
Excerpts from Roberts's Opinion of the Court and Breyer's Dissent in *Parents Involved in Community Schools v. Seattle School District No. 1* (2007)

ROBERTS'S OPINION OF THE COURT:

. . . Before Brown, schoolchildren were told where they could and could not go to school based on the color of their skin. The school districts in these cases have not carried the heavy burden of demonstrating that we should allow this once again even for very different reasons. For schools that never segregated on the basis of race, such as Seattle, or that have removed the vestiges of past segregation, such as Jefferson County, the way to achieve a system of determining admission to the public schools on a nonracial basis is to stop assigning students on a racial basis. The way to stop discrimination on the basis of race is to stop discriminating on the basis of race.

BREYER'S DISSENT:

. . . Finally, what of the hope and promise of *Brown*? For much of this Nation's history, the races remained divided. It was not long ago that people of different races drank from separate fountains, rode on separate buses, and studied in separate schools. In this Court's finest hour, *Brown v. Board of Education* challenged this history and helped to change it. For *Brown* held out a promise. It was a promise embodied in three Amendments designed to make citizens of slaves. It was the promise of true racial equality—not as a matter of fine words on paper, but as a matter of everyday life in the Nation's cities and schools. It was about the nature of a democracy that must work for all Americans. It sought one law, one Nation, one people, not simply as a matter of legal principle but in terms of how we actually live.

Not everyone welcomed this Court's decision in *Brown*. Three years after that decision was handed down, the Governor of Arkansas ordered state militia to block the doors of a white schoolhouse so that black children could not enter. The President of the United States dispatched the 101st Airborne Division to Little Rock, Arkansas, and federal troops were needed to enforce a desegregation decree. . . . Today, almost 50 years later, attitudes toward race in this Nation have changed dramatically. Many parents, white and black alike, want their children to attend schools with children of different races. Indeed, the very school districts that once spurned integration now strive for it. The long history of their efforts reveals the complexities and difficulties they have faced. And in light of those challenges, they have asked us not to take from their hands the instruments they have used to rid their schools of racial segregation, instruments that they believe are needed to overcome the problems of cities divided by race and poverty. The plurality would decline their modest request.

The plurality [represented by Roberts's Opinion of the Court] is wrong to do so. The last half-century has witnessed great strides toward racial equality, but we have not yet realized the promise of *Brown*. To invalidate the plans under review is to threaten the promise of *Brown*. The plurality's position, I fear, would break that promise. This is a decision that the Court and the Nation will come to regret.

6. Roberts's opinion has been called the "color-blind" approach to the meaning of the equal protection clause of the Fourteenth Amendment, signifying that it requires equal treatment of all races, no matter what the context. Breyer's opinion has been called the "historical" or "contextual" approach, signifying that race neutrality cannot be a reality in the context of a society in which race is, in fact, not treated neutrally. What language from both opinions illustrates the difference in color-blind versus the contextual approaches?

_____

_____

_____

_____

_____

_____

_____

_____

7. Do you agree with Roberts or Breyer? Explain and support your answer. (You might want to consider the approach the unanimous Supreme Court took in the landmark _Brown v. Board of Education_ decision. See Exercise 10.1.)

_____

_____

_____

_____

_____

11

Civil Liberties

EXERCISE 11.1 The Tension Between Civil Liberties Advocates and Civil Rights Advocates: Campus Hate Speech Codes

---

INTRODUCTION

For most of twentieth-century U.S. history, advocates of civil liberties, like the American Civil Liberties Union (ACLU), and advocates of civil rights, like the National Association for the Advancement of Colored People (NAACP), have been allies in numerous causes. Those and other groups fought together to defend racial, ethnic, and ideological minorities against overbearing majorities and against government repression of dissent. Beginning in the 1970s, however, some hot-button issues, such as school busing, affirmative action, and hate speech codes, created tension between these old allies. A hate speech code imposes sanctions on any communication that disparages a person on the basis of a racial, ethnic, gender, or sexual orientation characteristic. Hate speech codes once promulgated by many colleges, universities, and cities brought into stark contrast—and occasionally into conflict—the sometimes contradictory values of freedom and equality espoused by civil liberties and civil rights advocates.

Civil liberties are anchored in the freedoms granted in the Bill of Rights. The first ten amendments to the Constitution involve the right to be left alone, to be free from government interference and arbitrary government action. Typically, civil liberties cases involve an individual asserting the right to live and express herself freely. According to civil libertarians, only a compelling government interest may restrict those liberties.

Civil rights are constitutionally based in the equal protection clause of the Fourteenth Amendment. Rather than asserting the right to be left alone by the government, advocates of civil rights have pressured the national government—particularly the Supreme Court—to dismantle political and social systems of discrimination and oppression. According to civil rights advocates, government enforcement of the equal protection clause is essential for minorities' attainment of the full rights of citizenship.

Most civil libertarians oppose hate speech codes. They believe that the right to freedom of speech overrides the objections of those offended by hate speech. Democratic public life, they argue, requires an open, vigorous debate, unimpeded by university authorities. Hate speech should be combated not by suppressing it, but rather by subjecting it to unyielding criticism and scrutiny in the marketplace of ideas. Civil libertarians do not, of course, defend the right of anyone to harass specific individuals with racist, sexist, homophobic, or religious epithets—so-called *fighting words*.

Civil rights advocates believe that hate speech, by its very nature, dehumanizes and undermines the equality of citizens. In the university setting, hateful attacks on minority students deny them the right to an equal education. At the very least, hate speech marginalizes those it targets, making them uncomfortable in the classroom and impairing their success. According to civil rights advocates, college and university campuses should provide a refuge for minorities from odious speech. (See Box 11.1.1.)

> ### BOX 11.1.1   Hate Speech Code Controversy
>
> **Hate Speech Codes as a Civil Liberties Issue (Opposes Hate Speech Codes)**
> - Based on the First Amendment (freedom of speech).
> - The emphasis is on the right to *individual* expression—to think and to believe as one wants.
> - Speech in a free and open debate has value—even if the speech is offensive.
>
> **Hate Speech Codes as a Civil Rights Issue (Favors Hate Speech Codes)**
> - Based on the equal protection clause of the Fourteenth Amendment.
> - Groups that have suffered a historical pattern of discrimination seek government protection under the Fourteenth Amendment.
> - The group objective is to achieve full participation in the educational community and to achieve educational objectives, not to be marginalized and made to feel uncomfortable in the classroom, on campus, and in college housing.

The constitutionality of hate speech codes has remained an issue, particularly at public institutions. Private colleges and universities have much greater leeway in defining prohibited behavior. However, under California's Leonard Law (1992), students at private colleges and universities were granted free speech rights. In 1995, Stanford University's Hate Speech Code was struck down by a California court.[1]

Federal district courts found unconstitutional hate speech codes at the University of Michigan and the University of Wisconsin.[2] The courts found the codes to be overly broad—meaning that the codes were so sweeping that they banned protected speech, such as speech that is merely offensive. In the courts' view, codes must be drawn narrowly to address "only the specific evil at hand." The courts also found the codes vague and imprecise, so that men or women with "common intelligence must necessarily guess at [their] meaning." Courts declare codes "void for vagueness" when reasonable people cannot determine from the language of the code whether their speech or actions are likely subject to the code's provisions. After these court cases, public universities narrowed the focus of their hate speech codes or dropped them altogether.

ASSIGNMENT

Study the hypothetical cases involving hate speech in Reading 11.1.1. Then answer question 1.

READING 11.1.1
Case Studies of Campus Hate Speech

CASE 1

The members of a prominent fraternity held an "ugly woman" contest in a university building. One of the contestants donned a black wig with curlers, painted his face black, and used pillows to simulate an exaggerated bust and buttocks. Several weeks later, the university dean, at the urging of several student leaders, disciplined the fraternity for engaging in behavior that perpetuated racial and sexual stereotypes. The fraternity appealed the discipline, contending that the expression—though perhaps offensive to some—was harmless and therefore protected by the First Amendment. University rules specifically prohibit speech and conduct that demean others on the basis of race, ethnicity, sexual orientation, and gender. A hearing has been scheduled for the appeal.

---

[1]*Robert J. Corry et al. v. The Leland Stanford Junior University et al.,* No. 740309 (Cal. Super. Ct. Feb. 27, 1995).
[2]721 F. Supp. 852 (E.D. Mich, 1989); 774 F. Supp. 1163 (E.D. Wis, 1991).

CASE 2

A female student at a community college in Texas charged that her English professor's continual references to sexual topics and use of profanity in class constituted sexual harassment. The college's recently enacted sexual harassment policy reads in part: "Conduct is prohibited that has the purpose or effect of unreasonably interfering with an individual's academic performance or creating an intimidating, hostile, or offensive learning environment." The professor acknowledged that his teaching style is sometimes provocative and confrontational, but he argued that he has taught this way effectively for years. The college administration put the professor on unpaid leave for one semester and required that he attend sensitivity-training workshops. After a lower court upheld the administration's actions, the professor appealed on the grounds that the college's sexual harassment policy violated his First Amendment rights.

CASE 3

A public university adopted a speech code that punished students "for racist or discriminatory comments, epithets or other expressive behavior directed at an individual or on separate occasions at different individuals, or for physical conduct, if such comments, epithets or other expressive behavior or physical conduct intentionally:

1. demean the race, sex, religion, color, creed, disability, sexual orientation, national origin, ancestry or age of the individual or individuals; or
2. create an intimidating, hostile or demeaning environment for education, university-related work, or other university-authorized action."

A student in a sociology class, during a discussion of homosexual marriage, stated, "If we allow gays and lesbians to marry, what's next? People will have the right to marry dogs and adults will have the right to marry children—even their own children." The professor and several students filed a complaint against the student for violating the university's speech code. He was subsequently expelled. The student challenged the expulsion in federal court on the grounds that the speech code was overly broad and vague, and therefore it unconstitutionally restricted his First Amendment right to free speech. He argued in court that his comments should not have come under the purview of the university's speech code because they were part of a classroom discussion of an academic issue. The university defended the code and its application of it on the grounds that it had a compelling interest in maintaining a campus climate free from discrimination and intimidation.

1. For each of the three cases, identify one possible civil liberties argument and one possible civil rights argument that would apply. Review the introduction to this chapter and Box 11.1 for more information.

Case 1

Civil liberties argument:

_____

_____

_____

Civil rights argument:

_____

_____

_____

Case 2

Civil liberties argument:

_____

_____

_____

Civil rights argument:

_____

_____

_____

Case 3

Civil liberties argument:

_____

_____

_____

Civil rights argument:

_____

_____

_____

Reading 11.1.2 presents some arguments for and against a proposed (and later discarded) hate speech code at the University of Michigan. Study the arguments and consider them as you answer question 2.

READING 11.1.2
The Pros and Cons of a Policy Covering Hate Speech at the University of Michigan[3]

PROS

1. Universities have a right and duty to provide an educational environment, a climate of civility, where all students can learn and live free from bigotry.
2. A university's objective is to educate and to instill within students fundamental values of human decency.
3. Numerous responses from students to the rights and responsibilities document last summer indicated that a significant proportion of the harassment experienced by U-M [University of Michigan] students comes from faculty. They described in-class harassment, racial harassment at a public event, harassment based on ethnic origin, and clear cultural bias in classroom settings.

---
[3]The [Michigan] *University Record*, February 8, 1993.

4. Speech codes publicly announce a university's support of civil rights and equal dignity of all persons; the failure to adopt a speech code implies that the University condones hate speech.
5. The University may be held liable for damages by persons who were subjected to harassment, if the University knowingly tolerates such conduct.
6. Faculty and staff, as well as students, should be prohibited from violating the rights of other members of the University community.
7. While harassment by faculty may be quite rare, it is important to have a mechanism for dealing with reported incidents and resolving misunderstandings that may be interpreted as harassment.

CONS

1. Any regulation of speech thwarts the truth-seeking process, inhibits the sharing of knowledge and encroaches on academic freedom.
2. The toleration of hate speech is the price to be paid for individual liberty.
3. Restrictions on hate speech represent a step down the slippery slope toward censorship and, ultimately, totalitarianism.
4. Universities are the last place where speech should be restricted, since the essence of a university is the free and unfettered exchange of ideas.
5. Those who are disciplined by codes become martyrs for the cause of free speech despite their hate-filled message.
6. Those victimized by hate speech are overly sensitive and self-conscious, the university's role not being to protect students.
7. Codes are not an effective means to stop hate, and only strong counter-speech prevents hate.

Source: Ejner J. Jensen, The University Record, February 8, 1993. Used by permission courtesy of the University of Michigan.

2. How would you decide each of the three cases in Reading 11.1.1? Consider Reading 11.1.2 as you explain and support your answer.

Case 1

Case 2

_____
_____
_____
_____

Case 3

_____
_____
_____
_____
_____
_____
_____

Web-Based Questions. Questions 3 and 4 are based on the American Civil Liberties Union's position on hate speech codes. You will find that position at http://www.aclu.org/free-speech/hate-speech-campus.

Web addresses sometimes change. If you can't locate a website, try an external search (e.g., Google) to find the website. Configurations within a website often change. If you can't find a particular link or article, for example, try an internal search of the website as well as an external search. Be resourceful! If you still can't find what you're searching for, move on to the next question.

3. a. Why does the ACLU oppose hate speech codes?

_____
_____

b. Do you agree with the ACLU's position? Explain.

_____
_____
_____
_____
_____

4. The ACLU affirms that racism, sexism, and homophobia are problems on college campuses.

a. How does the ACLU propose to address these problems while preserving free-speech rights?

_____
_____

_____

_____

_____

_____

_____

_____

_____

b. Do you agree with the ACLU's recommendations? Explain.

_____

_____

_____

_____

_____

EXERCISE 11.2   Sexual Intimacy and the Right to Privacy

INTRODUCTION

Americans take for granted that a constitutional right to privacy shields them from a wide array of government intrusions. Many citizens bemoan the erosion of the right to privacy, a perennial topic of national political discourse. A close reading of the U.S. Constitution, however, reveals no explicit grant of a right to privacy.[1] The Supreme Court inferred the right to privacy from certain language in the Bill of Rights (see Box 11.2.1). In *Griswold v. Connecticut* (1965), the High Court held that a Connecticut statute that prohibited a married couple from obtaining information about the use of contraceptives violated the couple's right to privacy. In *Stanley v. Georgia* (1969), the Court found that people have a privacy right to watch sexually explicit movies in their own homes. The Court also employed the concept of privacy to support a woman's right to an abortion (*Roe v. Wade*, 1973). However, the right to privacy does not protect the contents of trash bags left at the curb for pickup (*California v. Greenwood*, 1988). The Court used the right to privacy to allow the withdrawal of artificial life-sustaining measures as long as there is "informed consent," such as a living will, in *Cruzan v. Director, Missouri Department of Health* (1990). But the Court has not extended privacy rights to protect physician-assisted suicide, *Washington v. Glucksberg* (1997).

The Court ruled, in *Bowers v. Hardwick* (1986), by a slim 5–4 majority, that homosexual sex was not protected by the Constitution, thereby upholding the constitutionality of Georgia's antisodomy law, a law that applied to both hetero- and homosexual sodomy but that was enforced—albeit rarely—against gays only. In a landmark reversal of *Bowers*, the Court, in *Lawrence v. Texas* (2003), struck down a Texas antisodomy statute that had been aimed exclusively at homosexuals. Responding to a reported weapons disturbance in a private residence, Houston police entered Lawrence's apartment and saw him and another adult man engaging in a private, consensual sexual act. Under the Texas penal code, Lawrence and his partner were charged with "deviate sexual intercourse, namely anal sex, with a member of the same sex (man)."

BOX 11.2.1   The Right to Privacy

- The right to privacy was announced by the Supreme Court in a 1965 case involving access to birth control devices: privacy of the "marital bedroom."
- The Supreme Court based the right to privacy on inferences from the following amendments: 1 (freedom of assembly or association), 3 (prohibition against forced quartering of soldiers), 5 (prohibition against self-incrimination—freedom of conscience), and especially 4 (the right of the "people to be secure in their persons, houses, papers, and effects"). The Court also based the right on Amendment 9 ("the enumeration of certain rights [in the first eight amendments] does not disparage or deny others retained by the people").
- The right to privacy was later applied to abortion rights (*Roe v. Wade,* 1973)—that is, the privacy of a woman's body and the private relationship between a woman and her physician.
- The right to privacy, some argue, is also applicable to the right to die (physician-assisted suicide), random drug testing (see Exercise 11.3), and sexual relations between consenting adults (this exercise).

ASSIGNMENT

Reading 11.2.1 includes excerpts from the Supreme Court's opinion in *Lawrence v. Texas*. Justice Anthony Kennedy, usually a conservative voice on the Court, wrote the opinion of the Court. Reading 11.2.2 includes excerpts from Justice Antonin Scalia's stinging dissent from the Court's decision. Study both opinions, and then answer the questions that follow.

---

[1]Some state constitutions explicitly grant a right to privacy. Article 1, Section 1 of the California state constitution, for example, reads: "All people are by nature free and independent and have inalienable rights. Among these are enjoying and defending life and liberty, acquiring, possessing, and protecting property, and pursuing and obtaining safety, happiness, and privacy."

READING 11.2.1
Justice Kennedy's Opinion of the Court in *Lawrence V. Texas,* 539 U.S. 558(2003)

We deem it necessary to reconsider the Court's holding in *Bowers*. To say that the issue in *Bowers* was simply the right to engage in certain sexual conduct demeans the claim the individual put forward, just as it would demean a married couple were it to be said marriage is simply about the right to have sexual intercourse. The laws involved in *Bowers* and here are, to be sure, statutes that purport to do no more than prohibit a particular sexual act. Their penalties and purposes, though, have more far-reaching consequences, touching upon the most private human conduct, sexual behavior, and in the most private of places, the home. The statutes do seek to control a personal relationship that, whether or not entitled to formal recognition in the law, is within the liberty of persons to choose without being punished as criminals.

This, as a general rule, should counsel against attempts by the State, or a court, to define the meaning of the relationship or to set its boundaries absent injury to a person or abuse of an institution the law protects. It suffices for us to acknowledge that adults may choose to enter upon this relationship in the confines of their homes and their own private lives and still retain their dignity as free persons. When sexuality finds overt expression in intimate conduct with another person, the conduct can be but one element in a personal bond that is more enduring. The liberty protected by the Constitution allows homosexual persons the right to make this choice.

It must be acknowledged, of course, that the Court in *Bowers* was making the broader point that for centuries there have been powerful voices to condemn homosexual conduct as immoral. The condemnation has been shaped by religious beliefs, conceptions of right and acceptable behavior, and respect for the traditional family. For many persons these are not trivial concerns but profound and deep convictions accepted as ethical and moral principles to which they aspire and which thus determine the course of their lives. These considerations do not answer the question before us, however. The issue is whether the majority may use the power of the State to enforce these views on the whole society through operation of the criminal law. "Our obligation is to define the liberty of all, not to mandate our own moral code."

The present case does not involve minors. It does not involve persons who might be injured or coerced or who are situated in relationships where consent might not easily be refused. It does not involve public conduct or prostitution. It does not involve whether the government must give formal recognition to any relationship that homosexual persons seek to enter. The case does involve two adults who, with full and mutual consent from each other, engaged in sexual practices common to a homosexual lifestyle. The petitioners are entitled to respect for their private lives. The State cannot demean their existence or control their destiny by making their private sexual conduct a crime. Their right to liberty under the Due Process Clause gives them the full right to engage in their conduct without intervention of the government. "It is a promise of the Constitution that there is a realm of personal liberty which the government may not enter." The Texas statute furthers no legitimate state interest which can justify its intrusion into the personal and private life of the individual.

The judgment of the Court of Appeals for the Texas Fourteenth District is reversed, and the case is remanded for further proceedings not inconsistent with this opinion. It is so ordered.

READING 11.2.2
Justice Scalia's Dissenting Opinion of the Court in *Lawrence V. Texas,* 539 U.S. 558(2003)

I turn now to the ground on which the Court squarely rests its holding: the contention that there is no rational basis for the law here under attack. This proposition is so out of accord with our jurisprudence—indeed, with the jurisprudence of *any* society we know—that it requires little discussion.

The Texas statute undeniably seeks to further the belief of its citizens that certain forms of sexual behavior are "immoral and unacceptable"—the same interest furthered by criminal laws against fornication, bigamy, adultery, adult incest, bestiality, and obscenity. *Bowers* held that this *was* a legitimate state interest. The Court today reaches the opposite conclusion. The Texas statute, it says, "furthers *no legitimate state interest* which can justify its intrusion into the personal and private life of the individual." The Court embraces instead *Justice Stevens'* declaration in his *Bowers* dissent, that "the fact that the governing majority in a State has traditionally viewed a particular practice as immoral is not a sufficient reason for upholding a law prohibiting the practice." This effectively decrees the end of all morals legislation.

Today's opinion is the product of a Court, which is the product of a law-profession culture, that has largely signed on to the so-called homosexual agenda, by which I mean the agenda promoted by some homosexual activists directed at eliminating the moral opprobrium that has traditionally attached to homosexual conduct. I noted in an earlier opinion the fact that the American Association of Law Schools (to which any reputable law school *must* seek to belong) excludes from membership any school that refuses to ban from its job-interview facilities a law firm (no matter how small) that does not wish to hire as a prospective partner a person who openly engages in homosexual conduct.

One of the most revealing statements in today's opinion is the Court's grim warning that the criminalization of homosexual conduct is "an invitation to subject homosexual persons to discrimination both in the public and in the private spheres." It is clear from this that the Court has taken sides in the culture war, departing from its role of assuring, as neutral observer, that the democratic rules of engagement are observed. Many Americans do not want persons who openly engage in homosexual conduct as partners in their business, as scoutmasters for their children, as teachers in their children's schools, or as boarders in their home. They view this as protecting themselves and their families from a lifestyle that they believe to be immoral and destructive. The Court views it as "discrimination" which it is the function of our judgments to deter. So imbued is the Court with the law profession's anti-anti-homosexual culture, that it is seemingly unaware that the attitudes of that culture are not obviously "mainstream"; that in most States what the Court calls "discrimination" against those who engage in homosexual acts is perfectly legal.

Let me be clear that I have nothing against homosexuals, or any other group, promoting their agenda through normal democratic means. Social perceptions of sexual and other morality change over time, and every group has the right to persuade its fellow citizens that its view of such matters is the best. That homosexuals have achieved some success in that enterprise is attested to by the fact that Texas is one of the few remaining States that criminalize private, consensual homosexual acts. But persuading one's fellow citizens is one thing, and imposing one's views in absence of democratic majority will is something else. I would no more *require* a State to criminalize homosexual acts—or, for that matter, display *any* moral disapprobation of them—than I would *forbid* it to do so. What Texas has chosen to do is well within the range of traditional democratic action, and its hand should not be stayed through the invention of a brand-new "constitutional right" by a Court that is impatient of democratic change. It is indeed true that "later generations can see that laws once thought necessary and proper in fact serve only to oppress," *ante,* at 18; and when that happens, later generations can repeal those laws. But it is the premise of our system that those judgments are to be made by the people, and not imposed by a governing caste that knows best.

One of the benefits of leaving regulation of this matter to the people rather than to the courts is that the people, unlike judges, need not carry things to their logical conclusion. The people may feel that their disapprobation of homosexual conduct is strong enough to disallow homosexual marriage, but not strong enough to criminalize private homosexual acts—and may legislate accordingly. The Court today pretends that it possesses a similar freedom of action, so that we need not fear judicial imposition of homosexual marriage, as has recently occurred in Canada (in a decision that the Canadian Government has chosen not to appeal). At the end of its opinion—after having laid waste the foundations of our rational-basis jurisprudence—the Court says that the present case "does not involve whether the government must give formal recognition to any relationship that homosexual persons seek to enter." Do not believe it. More illuminating than this bald, unreasoned disclaimer is the progression of thought displayed by an earlier passage in the Court's opinion, which notes the constitutional protections afforded to "personal decisions relating to *marriage,* procreation, contraception, family relationships, child rearing, and education," and then declares that "[p]ersons in a homosexual relationship may seek autonomy for these purposes, just as heterosexual persons do." Today's opinion dismantles the structure of constitutional law that has permitted a distinction to be made between heterosexual and homosexual unions, insofar as formal recognition in marriage is concerned. If moral disapprobation of homosexual conduct is "no legitimate state interest" for purposes of proscribing that conduct; and if, as the Court coos (casting aside all pretense of neutrality), ""[w]hen sexuality finds overt expression in intimate conduct with another person, the conduct can be but one element in a personal bond that is more enduring"; what justification could there possibly be for denying the benefits of marriage to homosexual couples exercising "[t]he liberty protected by the Constitution." Surely not the encouragement of procreation, since the sterile and the elderly are allowed to marry. This case "does not involve" the issue of homosexual marriage only if one entertains the belief that principle and logic have nothing to do with the decisions of this Court. Many will hope that, as the Court comfortingly assures us, this is so.

The matters appropriate for this Court's resolution are only three: Texas's prohibition of sodomy neither infringes a "fundamental right" (which the Court does not dispute), nor is unsupported by a rational relation to what the Constitution considers a legitimate state interest, nor denies the equal protection of the laws. I dissent.

1. In *Bowers,* the Court ruled that the Constitution gives no protection to the practice of homosexual sodomy. In the *Lawrence* case, Justice Kennedy asserts that the real constitutional issue posed by Texas's antisodomy law has nothing to do with specific sexual practices or sexual orientation. What does he think the real constitutional issue is? Cite specific language from the decision to support your answer.

_____

_____

_____

_____

_____

2. a. Justice Kennedy concedes that many people have a deeply ingrained moral aversion to homosexuality. According to Kennedy, why is it improper to base the Court's decision on such moral objections? Cite specific language from the decision to support your answer.

_____

_____

_____

_____

_____

b. According to Kennedy, what is the fundamental constitutional issue on which the Court should base its decision? Cite specific language from the decision to support your answer.

_____

_____

_____

_____

_____

3. a. On what grounds does Justice Scalia criticize the Court's majority for maintaining that the state of Texas has no legitimate interest in prohibiting homosexual sodomy?

_____

_____

_____

_____

_____

b. What, according to Scalia, is the legitimate state interest that justifies prohibiting homosexual sodomy?

_____

_____

_____

_____

_____

4. Scalia accuses the Court's majority of pursuing a political agenda. What is his argument?

_____

_____

5. Do you agree with the Court's decision in *Lawrence* that private sexual relations between consenting adults—whether heterosexual or homosexual—should not be a concern of the government? Or do you agree with Justice Scalia that the government has a legitimate interest in the regulation of morals, as long as there is no specific constitutional prohibition against such regulation? Explain and support your answer. (Remember that Scalia is not explicitly defending the wisdom of the anti-sodomy law but, instead, arguing that the Constitution does not specifically prohibit such laws.)

_____

_____

_____

_____

_____

EXERCISE 11.3   Random Drug Testing in Public Schools

INTRODUCTION

According to civil libertarians, efforts to curb drug use often threaten individual privacy, especially when authorities search for and seize drugs in a person's home or automobile or on one's own body. (See Exercise 11.2 for more about the right to privacy.) One privacy issue involves drug testing and the language in the Fourth Amendment that protects people "against unreasonable searches and seizures" except when there is "probable cause." According to the Supreme Court, drug testing is reasonable for employees in "safety-sensitive" jobs, for example, railroad engineers, airline pilots, those who carry firearms, and those in sensitive national security positions. The Court also recognizes that some forms of drug testing are more intrusive than others. For example, breath and urine tests are less intrusive than blood tests, which require penetration of the skin. Many companies routinely test prospective employees for drugs as a condition for employment. Private businesses have more latitude in drug testing because the Bill of Rights protects citizens against government invasion of privacy to a greater extent than it protects against private entity invasion of privacy.

But the Court has not given a green light to drug testing under all circumstances. In 1997, in *Chandler v. Miller*, the Court struck down a Georgia law that required candidates for public office to pass a drug test to qualify for a spot on the ballot. According to the Court, the drug-testing requirement was not reasonable because the state of Georgia failed to demonstrate that drug use plagued a significant number of candidates for state office. In 2001, in *Ferguson v. City of Charleston*, the Court invalidated drug testing for indigent pregnant women who sought the medical services of city hospitals. A public hospital in Charleston, South Carolina, tested pregnant women for drugs—without their knowledge—to identify crack babies. The results of all positive tests were passed on to the police. In a 6–3 decision, the justices held that the hospital's failure to inform the women of the test, not to mention tipping off the police, violated the women's rights under the Fourth Amendment.

Although the courts have generally conceded that public school authorities have significant leeway in restricting minor students' rights (e.g., locker searches, censorship of school newspapers, and free speech and assembly rights), random drug testing in public school grades K–12 raises particularly controversial questions about the privacy rights of students. In the precedent-setting case, *Vernonia School District v. Acton* (1995), the Supreme Court ruled that schools did not exceed their constitutional authority by requiring random drug tests in a noncompulsory, after-school, competitive athletic program. Since that decision, the Supreme Court has expanded random drug testing in extracurricular activities. (See *Board of Education of Pottawatomie County v. Earls*, 2002, in Reading 11.3.2.) Courts have been willing to permit public schools much constitutional leeway because the judiciary is reluctant "to become a national school board" micromanaging the nation's schools. School authorities are typically found to have a *compelling interest* in maintaining the educational program and in exercising *custodial responsibilities* to protect students' welfare and safety. Critics of the courts' position contend that the judiciary has suspended the Constitution at the schoolhouse door. Nevertheless, a federal judge in Texas struck down what had been the nation's first school district policy requiring drug testing of all junior high school students in *Tannahill v. Lockney School District* (2001).

ASSIGNMENT

Study Reading 11.3.1, which is an excerpt from the Supreme Court's opinion in *Vernonia School District v. Acton* (1995). Then answer questions 1 to 4. The selection focuses on the Court's response to the claim that the student's privacy rights had been infringed on, that the privacy of the student's own body had been violated by the "search for and seizure of" his bodily fluids.

READING 11.3.1
Vernonia School District v. Acton, 515 U.S. 646 (1995)

The first factor to be considered is the nature of the privacy interest upon which the search here at issue intrudes. The Fourth Amendment does not protect all subjective expectations of privacy, but only those that society recognizes as "legitimate." What expectations are legitimate varies, of course, with context, depending, for example, upon whether the individual asserting the privacy interest is at home, at work, in a car, or in a public park. Central, in our view, to the present case is the fact that the subjects of the Policy are (1) children, who (2) have been committed to the temporary custody of the State as schoolmaster.

Traditionally at common law, and still today, unemancipated minors lack some of the most fundamental rights of self-determination—including even the right of liberty in its narrow sense, i.e., the right to come and go at will. They are subject, even as to their physical freedom, to the control of their parents or guardians. [A] parent "may . . . delegate part of his parental authority, during his life, to the tutor or schoolmaster of his child; who is then in loco parentis, and has such a portion of the power of the parent committed to his charge, viz. that of restraint and correction, as may be necessary to answer the purposes for which he is employed." Thus, while children assuredly do not "shed their constitutional rights . . . at the schoolhouse gate," the nature of those rights is what is appropriate for children in school.

Fourth Amendment rights, no less than First and Fourteenth Amendment rights, are different in public schools than elsewhere; the "reasonableness" inquiry cannot disregard the schools' custodial and tutelary responsibility for children. For their own good and that of their classmates, public school children are routinely required to submit to various physical examinations, and to be vaccinated against various diseases. Particularly with regard to medical examinations and procedures, therefore, "students within the school environment have a lesser expectation of privacy than members of the population generally."

Legitimate privacy expectations are even less with regard to student athletes. School sports are not for the bashful. They require "suiting up" before each practice or event, and showering and changing afterwards. Public school locker rooms, the usual sites for these activities, are not notable for the privacy they afford. The locker rooms in Vernonia are typical: no individual dressing rooms are provided; shower heads are lined up along a wall, unseparated by any sort of partition or curtain; not even all the toilet stalls have doors. There is an additional respect in which school athletes have a reduced expectation of privacy. By choosing to "go out for the team," they voluntarily subject themselves to a degree of regulation even higher than that imposed on students generally. In Vernonia's public schools, they must submit to a preseason physical exam (James testified that his included the giving of a urine sample), they must acquire adequate insurance coverage or sign an insurance waiver, maintain a minimum grade point average, and comply with any "rules of conduct, dress, training hours and related matters as may be established for each sport by the head coach and athletic director with the principal's approval."

Having considered the scope of the legitimate expectation of privacy at issue here, we turn next to the character of the intrusion that is complained of. We recognized in Skinner that collecting the samples for urinalysis intrudes upon "an excretory function traditionally shielded by great privacy." We noted, however, that the degree of intrusion depends upon the manner in which production of the urine sample is monitored. Under the District's Policy, male students produce samples at a urinal along a wall. They remain fully clothed and are only observed from behind, if at all. Female students produce samples in an enclosed stall, with a female monitor standing outside listening only for sounds of tampering. These conditions are nearly identical to those typically encountered in public restrooms, which men, women, and especially school children use daily. Under such conditions, the privacy interests compromised by the process of obtaining the urine sample are in our view negligible. The other privacy-invasive aspect of urinalysis is, of course, the information it discloses concerning the state of the subject's body, and the materials he has ingested. In this regard it is significant that the tests at issue here look only for drugs, and not for whether the student is, for example, epileptic, pregnant, or diabetic. And finally, the results of the tests are disclosed only to a limited class of school personnel who have a need to know; and they are not turned over to law enforcement authorities or used for any internal disciplinary function.

Taking into account all the factors we have considered above—the decreased expectation of privacy, the relative unobtrusiveness of the search, and the severity of the need met by the search—we conclude Vernonia's Policy is reasonable and hence constitutional. We caution against the assumption that suspicionless drug testing will readily pass constitutional muster in other contexts. The most significant element in this case is the first we discussed: that the Policy was undertaken in furtherance of the government's responsibilities, under a public school system, as guardian and tutor of children entrusted to its care. We find insufficient basis to contradict the judgment of Vernonia's parents, its school board, and the District Court, as to what was reasonably in the interest of these children under the circumstances.

1. On what basis does the Court claim that there is less right to privacy behind the schoolhouse door than beyond it?

_____

_____

_____

_____

2. What are the special circumstances in Vernonia School District's program that make the program constitutionally permissible?

_____

_____

_____

_____

3. How does the school district seek to protect the students' privacy?

_____

_____

_____

_____

4. Do you agree with the Court's decision in _Vernonia_, or would you have voted to decide the case differently? Explain and support your position.

_____

_____

_____

_____

_____

_____

_____

_____

_____

Study Reading 11.3.2, which is an excerpt from *Board of Education of Independent School District No. 92 of Pottawatomie County v. Earls* (2002). Then answer questions 5 and 6. In this case, the Supreme Court faced the question of whether random drug testing was permissible in *all* extracurricular activities, not just for athletics, as in *Vernonia*. (In practice, the drug testing in the Oklahoma school district had been limited to *competitive* extracurricular activities.)

READING 11.3.2
Board of Education of Independent School District No. 92 of Pottawatomie County v. Earls, 536 U.S. 822 (2002)

We first consider the nature of the privacy interest allegedly compromised by the drug testing. As in *Vernonia,* the context of the public school environment serves as the backdrop for the analysis of the privacy interest at stake and the reasonableness of the drug testing policy in general.

A student's privacy interest is limited in a public school environment where the State is responsible for maintaining discipline, health, and safety. Schoolchildren are routinely required to submit to physical examinations and vaccinations against disease. Securing order in the school environment sometimes requires that students be subjected to greater controls than those appropriate for adults. ("Without first establishing discipline and maintaining order, teachers cannot begin to educate their students. And apart from education, the school has the obligation to protect pupils from mistreatment by other children, and also to protect teachers themselves from violence by the few students whose conduct in recent years has prompted national concern.")

Respondents argue that because children participating in nonathletic extracurricular activities are not subject to regular physicals and communal undress, they have a stronger expectation of privacy than the athletes tested in *Vernonia*. This distinction, however, was not essential to our decision in *Vernonia,* which depended primarily upon the school's custodial responsibility and authority.

In any event, students who participate in competitive extracurricular activities voluntarily subject themselves to many of the same intrusions on their privacy as do athletes. Some of these clubs and activities require occasional off-campus travel and communal undress. All of them have their own rules and requirements for participating students that do not apply to the student body as a whole. For example, each of the competitive extracurricular activities governed by the Policy must abide by the rules of the Oklahoma Secondary Schools Activities Association, and a faculty sponsor monitors the students for compliance with the various rules dictated by the clubs and activities. This regulation of extracurricular activities further diminishes the expectation of privacy among schoolchildren. We therefore conclude that the students affected by this Policy have a limited expectation of privacy.

Respondents also argue that the testing of nonathletes does not implicate any safety concerns, and that safety is a "crucial factor" in applying the special needs framework. They contend that there must be "surpassing safety interests," or "extraordinary safety and national security hazards," in order to override the usual protections of the Fourth Amendment.

Respondents are correct that safety factors into the special needs analysis, but the safety interest furthered by drug testing is undoubtedly substantial for all children, athletes and nonathletes alike. We know all too well that drug use carries a variety of health risks for children, including death from overdose.

5. Explain the reasoning the Court used to determine that random drug testing in all extracurricular activities is not significantly different from drug testing in competitive athletics (*Vernonia*) and is therefore constitutional.

_____

_____

_____

_____

Question 6 is based on both the *Vernonia* and *Earls* decisions.

6. Do you think the Court's decisions in *Vernonia* and *Earls* have opened the door for random drug testing for *all* K–12 public school students? Explain and support your answer by citing specific language from the Court's decisions.

_____

_____

_____

_____

_____

Web-Based Question. Question 7 asks you to consider the pros and cons of random drug testing for public school students in grades K–12. The position in favor of random testing is stated in Reading 11.3.3. The position against random testing, "Just Say No to Random Drug Testing," can be found at the American Civil Liberties Union's website: http://www.aclu.org/drug-law-reform/aclu-op-ed-against-student-drug-testing.

READING 11.3.3
What Are the Benefits of Random Drug Testing?

Drug use can quickly turn to dependence and addiction, trapping users in a vicious cycle that destroys families and ruins lives. Students who use drugs or alcohol are statistically more likely to drop out of school than their peers who don't. Dropouts, in turn, are more likely to be unemployed, to depend on the welfare system, and to commit crimes. If drug testing deters drug use, everyone benefits—students, their families, their schools, and their communities. Drug and alcohol abuse not only interferes with a student's ability to learn, it also disrupts the orderly environment necessary for all students to succeed. Studies have shown that students who use drugs are more likely to bring guns and knives to school, and that the more marijuana a student smokes, the greater the chances he or she will be involved in physical attacks, property destruction, stealing, and cutting classes. Just as parents and students can expect schools to offer protection from violence, racism, and other forms of abuse, so do they have the right to expect a learning environment free from the influence of illegal drugs.

Source: Office of National Drug Control Policy, "What You Need to Know about Drug Testing in Schools," 2002.

7. Do you favor the extension of mandatory random drug testing to all students in grades K–12? Explain and support your position.

_____

_____

_____

_____

_____

EXERCISE 11.4   Offensive Speech: Jerry Falwell, *Hustler*, and Funeral Protestors

INTRODUCTION

Where does the right of the press to criticize—and even to mock—public figures end, and the right of the state to censor the press begin?

Censorship is an odious matter, conjuring ingrained fears of the state waging war against the right of free expression. But the First Amendment's freedom of speech protection demands that the nation's courts grapple with a thorny question: Which is the greater threat to the republic—the damage done by reckless, outlandish journalism, or the chilling effect of state censorship on public discourse?

The Supreme Court consistently has held that libel is not protected expression under the First Amendment. *Libel* is the defamation of character in print or by other visual means; *slander* is oral defamation. The Supreme Court has established the following categories of libel as it applies to individuals:

- **Public officials** are those who are elected or appointed to public office. In a landmark decision, *New York Times v. Sullivan* (1964), the Court held that a public official could not recover damages for libel unless that individual could prove actual malice or that an article was printed or a statement made "with knowledge that it was false or with reckless disregard of whether it was false or not." The Court's decision was based on the principle that public debate about a public official needs to be free, open, and uninhibited, even if that means a public official's reputation is tarnished. The necessity of a free press in a free society means that the public's right to know prevails over a public official's reputation. (*Public figures*, such as movie stars and other celebrities, are considered to have the same burden of proof as public officials.)

- **The Sullivan** standard does not apply to *private individuals*. In *Gertz v. Welch* (1974), a 5–4 majority of the Court held that private individuals do not have to prove malice or reckless disregard for the truth in a libel action. The effect of *Gertz* is to give private citizens more protection from defamatory statements than public officials or public figures have. In a libel or slander suit, private individuals need to prove that a statement was defamatory and false only.

The problem for the Court has been defining *defamation* in a way that does not undermine the First Amendment right to freedom of speech. The Court fears that defining defamation to encompass speech that is merely offensive will lead to a "slippery slope of censorship." If the Court allows the government to punish speech that is merely offensive, or a jury to award damages to those who find speech merely offensive, then all speech may eventually be regulated because someone, somewhere will find someone else's speech offensive. Concern about the slippery slope of censorship affected the Court's decision in the *Falwell* case in Reading 11.4.2.

ASSIGNMENT

Study Readings 11.4.1 and 11.4.2. Then answer the questions that follow.

READING 11.4.1
Reverend Jerry Falwell and *Hustler* Magazine

Hustler magazine is best known for its photographs of naked women in explicit sexual poses, not for satire. But in 1983, *Hustler* published a parody of an ad for Campari, an alcoholic beverage. The original series of Campari ads, which appeared in a number of magazines but never in *Hustler,* featured celebrities who, in interview format, talked about their "first time." At first glance, it looked as though the "first time" was referring to the interviewee's first sexual experience, but it was clear in reading the ads that the interviewees actually were talking about the first time they had experienced drinking Campari.

In the *Hustler* parody, Reverend Jerry Falwell was the celebrity and his answers to the interviewer's questions were of a decidedly sexual nature. In the parody, Falwell spoke of getting drunk on Campari and having sex with his mother in an outhouse. He also was quoted as saying that he often got drunk before delivering his Sunday sermons. At the bottom of the ad, in small but legible print, ran this statement in bold print: **AD PARODY—NOT TO BE TAKEN SERIOUSLY**.

Not surprisingly, Falwell, a televangelist and conservative commentator on politics and morality, took issue with the parody. He filed suit against *Hustler* and its publisher, Larry Flynt, seeking damages for invasion of privacy, libel, and intentional infliction of emotional distress. The jury found the parody was not libelous because no reader would have believed the words or the behavior attributed to Falwell in the ad. But the jury awarded Falwell $200,000 in damages for "the intentional infliction of emotional distress." After the award was upheld by a court of appeals, Flynt appealed to the U.S. Supreme Court. In *Hustler Magazine v. Falwell* (1988), the Supreme Court reversed the award for emotional distress in an 8–0 vote.

Source: Lee Epstein, Thomas G. Walker, based on material in *Constitutional Law for a Changing America: Rights, Liberties, and Justice*, CQ Press, 1992. Copyright © CQ Press, a division of SAGE Publications, Inc.

READING 11.4.2
Chief Justice Rehnquist's Opinion of the Court in *Hustler Magazine, Inc. et al. v. Jerry Falwell*, 485 U.S. 46 (1988)

This case *Hustler Magazine, Inc. et al. v. Jerry Falwell* presents us with a novel question involving First Amendment limitations upon a State's authority to protect its citizens from the intentional infliction of emotional distress. We must decide whether a public figure may recover damages for emotional harm caused by the publication of an ad parody offensive to him, and doubtless gross and repugnant in the eyes of most. Respondent would have us find that a State's interest in protecting public figures from emotional distress is sufficient to deny First Amendment protection to speech that is patently offensive and is intended to inflict emotional injury, even when that speech could not reasonably have been interpreted as stating actual facts about the public figure involved. This we decline to do.

At the heart of the First Amendment is the recognition of the fundamental importance of the free flow of ideas and opinions on matters of public interest and concern.

"[T]he fact that society may find speech offensive is not a sufficient reason for suppressing it. Indeed, if it is the speaker's opinion that gives offense, that consequence is a reason for according it constitutional protection. For it is a central tenet of the First Amendment that the government must remain neutral in the marketplace of ideas."

It is firmly settled that . . . the public expression of ideas may not be prohibited merely because the ideas are themselves offensive to some of their hearers.

[Falwell] is thus relegated to his claim for damages awarded by the jury for the intentional infliction of emotional distress by "outrageous" conduct [because he does not meet the constitutional standard for libel]. But for reasons heretofore stated this claim cannot, consistently with the First Amendment, form a basis for the award of damages when the conduct in question is the publication of a caricature such as the ad parody involved here. The judgment of the Court of Appeals is accordingly Reversed.

1. According to Supreme Court precedents explained in the introduction to Exercise 11.4, what characteristics of the *Hustler* Campari ad made it impossible to award Falwell libel damages against *Hustler*?

_____

_____

2. If *Hustler* had *not* written in bold print, **AD PARODY—NOT TO BE TAKEN SERIOUSLY,** would the jury have likely found *Hustler* guilty of libel? Explain and support your position. (Think about the satires you see on *Saturday Night Live* or *The Daily Show.*)

_____

_____

_____

_____

3. Because libel damages were not allowed against *Hustler*, the Supreme Court had to decide the case solely on the constitutionality of the jury's verdict that the parody inflicted *emotional distress* on Falwell. Why did the Court reject the argument that the infliction of emotional distress entitled Falwell to monetary damages from *Hustler*? Cite specific language from the Court's decision to support your answer.

_____

_____

_____

_____

_____

4. If you were on the federal court jury in Virginia that initially decided the case, would you have voted to award monetary damages to Falwell for suffering the infliction of emotional distress? Explain and support your position.

_____

_____

_____

_____

_____

5. In 2011, the Supreme Court announced its decision in the emotionally charged case of *Snyder v. Phelps* (No. 09–751). Members of the Westboro Baptist Church of Topeka, Kansas, had been protesting at military funerals, including that of Snyder's son, a Marine. Westboro Church members believed that U.S. fatalities in Iraq and Afghanistan were indicative of God's judgment on the alleged moral decadence of the United States, especially its tolerance of homosexuality. They held up signs with messages like, "America Is Doomed" and "God Hates Fags." A jury awarded damages to Snyder for Westboro's (Phelps) intentional infliction of *emotional distress*. In ruling that the First Amendment protected the Westboro picketers' speech and assembly, Chief Justice Roberts wrote, "Any distress occasioned by Westboro's picketing turned on the content and viewpoint of the message conveyed, rather than any interference with the funeral itself."[1] "Such speech," Roberts wrote, "cannot be restricted simply because it is upsetting or arouses contempt."

Justice Alito, the lone dissenter, wrote that "outrageous conduct caused [Snyder] great injury, and the Court now compounds that injury by depriving petitioner of a judgment that acknowledges the wrong he suffered. To have a society in which public issues can be openly and vigorously debated, it is not necessary to allow the brutalization of innocent victims like [Snyder]."

   a. Is the Supreme Court's decision in *Snyder v. Phelps* consistent with its decision in the *Falwell* case? Explain your answer.

_____

_____

_____

   b. Do the circumstances of the *Snyder* case cause you to change your mind about the decision in the *Falwell* case (question 4)? Why or why not? (Consider Justice Alito's dissent in formulating your response.)

_____

_____

_____

_____

_____

---

[1] Adam Liptak, "Justices Rule for Protesters at Military Funerals," *New York Times*, March 2, 2011.

APPENDIX 1

For Instructors: A Guide to Using This Textbook

Critical Thinking and American Government was designed to provide maximum flexibility for its adopters. In this appendix, the authors offer suggestions on using the text effectively.

SELECTING AND ASSIGNING EXERCISES

The exercises differ significantly in length, level of difficulty, type of skill development, and subject matter. Several exercises are divided into two or three parts to provide flexibility in making assignments.

GETTING STUDENTS STARTED

It is not uncommon for students to struggle with the first couple of exercises assigned. Depending on the skill level of your students, it may be advisable to discuss with them in advance the first couple of exercises assigned to increase their confidence level. It has been our experience that students become more comfortable with, and skilled at, the exercises as the semester progresses. You might elect to post answers to some of the exercises as you assign them.

INTEGRATING THE CRITICAL THINKING EXERCISES INTO CLASSROOM TEACHING

The exercises can be easily and productively employed to supplement and enhance subjects taught in class. Student completion of an exercise prior to class will provide the instructor with many openings to elaborate, clarify, and discuss the exercise in relation to the subject being studied in class. For example, Exercise 2.4, "Is the Federal Government or Are the States in Charge of the Minimum Drinking Age?" can be employed to clarify how the federal government uses categorical and block grant aid to secure state or local compliance with federal policy objectives. Another example, Exercise 7.2, "Evaluating Presidential Performance," can add a valuable dimension to the study of presidential power.

EMPLOYING THE EXERCISES AS GROUP WORK

The exercises are ideally suited to group work either in or outside class. The questions are focused to avoid the pitfalls of overly broad group discussion. At the same time, the questions invite collaboration and discussion. Exercise 1.1, "Reading the Constitution," is a good example. Some students will miss items when reading the Constitution that will be picked up by others. Exercise 4.2, "Gerrymandering," should spur student collaboration, too. Some students will be more adept at grasping the politics of gerrymandering than others, who may get tripped up by the concept of wielding political power by drawing district lines on a map.

The advantages of collaborative learning are well documented. So, too, is a major disadvantage: the lack of individual responsibility and accountability within the group. Too often the group's workload is not shared equally. This imbalance can build resentment and dampen enthusiasm for group work. Too often the brightest and most diligent students do the difficult thinking for the other group members.

We offer the following suggestions for overcoming the perils and pitfalls of group work:

1. Assign students to groups randomly, and reconstitute groups periodically.
2. Evaluate group work by having individual students answer written questions on quizzes and/or exams.
3. Evaluate group work by asking individual students to answer oral questions in class.
4. Ask students to evaluate their group. The evaluation instrument should identify the group, but student responses should be anonymous.

EVALUATING THE EXERCISES

Whether assigned for completion by groups or by individual students, the exercises may be evaluated in a number of ways.

1. Whether instructors collect completed exercises from groups or individual students, the evaluation process will be faster if instructors score only selected questions. We usually tell students in advance if this will be the grading mode, but we

don't tell them which questions will be scored. Some questions are more significant than others and more clearly reflect student understanding of the material. Some questions are more difficult than others, and minimizing or not scoring these may reassure students that the instructor's expectations are reasonable and achievable.

2. If instructors do not collect completed exercises for evaluation, students' comprehension can be checked with a brief written quiz in class. Take Exercise 1.1, "Reading the Constitution," for example. One could select a few of the more significant and easily grasped questions, put them on an overhead screen, and ask the students to provide short written answers. For this exercise, an obvious candidate would be: "Identify one enumerated power of the president." Another might be: "Identify one power the Constitution prohibits to the states." Informing students in advance of this mode of evaluation and assuring them that the quiz will focus on the most important questions in the exercise may encourage students to approach the text with fewer reservations.

3. Another option for instructors who don't collect the written exercises is to formulate variations on one or more questions in an exercise and distribute this as a written quiz to the class. This has worked well, for example, with Exercise 7.1, "The Electoral College." Questions 9 to 13 in this exercise ask students to apply their understanding of the mechanics of the Electoral College to electoral strategy. Instructors can vary the specifics of these questions to present students with different situations that probe their understanding of the material. Of course, instructors who don't collect the written exercises can formulate written or multiple-choice questions based on assigned exercises to integrate into their standard exams.

USING THE INSTRUCTOR'S MANUAL

The answers to the exercises are in the Instructor's Manual. These answers can be downloaded and posted for student use. As we have already noted, we have sometimes made the answers available to students at the time of assigning an exercise to facilitate their working through the questions. In this case, we explain how they will be tested on the exercise and caution them that—even though the answers are there for the taking—they must do the hard work of learning the material and how to apply it. When we post answers, we tell our students that if they are experiencing difficulty with a question, they can check the answer and try to determine how it was derived. Other times, we have withheld posting answers until the exercise has been turned in or until students have been tested in class on the material.

"We, the people." Three simple words are of profound importance and contentious origin. Every government in the world at the time of the Constitutional Convention was some type of monarchy, wherein sovereign power was bestowed from the top. The Founders of our new country rejected monarchy as a form of government and proposed instead a republic, which would draw its sovereignty from the people.

It is this very sense of empowerment that allows the "people" to influence our government and shape the world in which we live. We are among the freest people in the world largely because of this document. We are presented with multiple pathways to influence our government and better our lives.

ARTICLE I. The very first article in the Constitution established the legislative branch of the new national government. Why did the framers start with the legislative power instead of the executive branch? The framers truly believed it was the most important component of the new government.

It was also something that calmed the anxieties of average citizens. That is, they had experience with "legislative-centered governance" under the Articles and even during the colonial period. It was not perfect, but the legislative process seems to work.

SECTION 1. Section 1 established a bicameral (two-chamber) legislature, or an upper (Senate) and lower (House of Representatives) organization of the legislative branch.

A bicameral legislature offers more opportunities to influence the policy process, as you can appeal to both your Senators and your representatives through the lobbying decision makers pathway, or indirectly through the elections pathway, the grassroots mobilization pathway, or the cultural change pathway. If you do not like a law passed by Congress, you can appeal to the courts to invalidate it or to change its meaning.

SECTION 2 CLAUSE 1. This section sets the term of office for House members (2 years) and indicates that those voting for Congress will have the same qualifications as those voting for the state legislatures. Originally, states limited voters to white property owners. Some states even had religious disqualifications, for instance, if citizens were Catholic or Jewish.

There was a great deal of discussion about how long a legislator should sit in office before appealing to constituents for re-election. Short terms of office, such as the 2 years used in the House of Representatives, help force members to pay attention to the needs of their constituents.

CLAUSE 2. This section sets forth the basic qualifications of a representative: at least 25 years of age, a U.S. citizen for at least 7 years, and a resident of the state in which the district is located. Note that the Constitution does not require a person to be a resident of the district he or she represents.

Clause 2 does not specify how many terms a representative can serve in Congress, but some critics support limiting the number of terms members can serve in order to make Congress more in touch with the citizenry—and to overcome some of the advantages incumbents have created to help win elections. Currently the average length of service in the House is 9 years (4.6 terms).

APPENDIX 2

The Constitution of the United States
THE PREAMBLE

We, the People of the United States, in Order to form a more perfect Union, establish Justice, insure domestic Tranquility, provide for the common defence, promote the general Welfare, and secure the Blessings of Liberty to ourselves and our Posterity, do ordain and establish this Constitution for the United States of America.

Article I
THE LEGISLATIVE ARTICLE

Legislative Power

SECTION 1. All legislative Powers herein granted shall be vested in a Congress of the United States, which shall consist of a Senate and House of Representatives.

House of Representatives: Composition; Qualifications; Apportionment; Impeachment Power

SECTION 2 CLAUSE 1. The House of Representatives shall be composed of Members chosen every second Year by the People of the several States, and the Electors in each State shall have the Qualifications requisite for Electors of the most numerous Branch of the State Legislature.

CLAUSE 2. No Person shall be a Representative who shall not have attained to the Age of twenty five Years, and been seven Years a Citizen of the United States, and who shall not, when elected, be an Inhabitant of that State in which he shall be chosen.

CLAUSE 3. Representatives and direct Taxes[1] shall be apportioned among the several States which may be included within this Union, according to their respective Numbers, which shall be determined by adding to the whole Number of free Persons, including those bound to Service for a Term of Years, and excluding Indians not taxed, three fifths of all other Persons.[2] The actual Enumeration shall be made within three Years after the first Meeting of the Congress of the United States, and within every subsequent Term of ten Years, in such Manner as they shall by Law direct. The Number of Representatives shall not exceed one for every thirty Thousand, but each State shall have at Least one Representative; and until such enumeration shall be made, the State of New Hampshire shall be entitled to chuse three, Massachusetts eight, Rhode-Island and Providence Plantations one, Connecticut five, New-York six, New Jersey four, Pennsylvania eight, Delaware one, Maryland six, Virginia ten, North Carolina five, South Carolina five, and Georgia three.

CLAUSE 4. When vacancies happen in the Representation from any State, the Executive Authority thereof shall issue Writs of Election to fill such Vacancies.

CLAUSE 5. The House of Representatives shall chuse their Speaker and other Officers; and shall have the sole Power of Impeachment.

Senate Composition: Qualifications, Impeachment Trials

SECTION 3 CLAUSE 1. The Senate of the United States shall be composed of two Senators from each State, chosen by the Legislature thereof,[3] for six Years; and each Senator shall have one Vote.

CLAUSE 2. Immediately after they shall be assembled in Consequence of the first Election, they shall be divided as equally as may be into three Classes. The Seats of the Senators of the first Class shall be vacated at the Expiration of the second Year, of the second Class at the Expiration of the fourth Year, and of the third Class at the Expiration of the sixth Year, so that one third may be chosen every second Year; and if Vacancies happen by Resignation, or otherwise, during the Recess of the Legislature of any State, the Executive thereof may make temporary Appointments until the next Meeting of the Legislature, which shall then fill such Vacancies.[4]

CLAUSE 3. No Person shall be a Senator who shall not have attained to the Age of thirty Years, and been nine Years a Citizen of the United States, and who shall not, when elected, be an Inhabitant of that State for which he shall be chosen.

CLAUSE 3. This clause contains the Three-Fifths Compromise, in which American Indians and blacks were only counted as three-fifths of a person for congressional representation purposes. This clause also addresses the question of congressional reapportionment every 10 years, which requires a census. Since the 1911 Reapportionment Act, the size of the House of Representatives has been set at 435. This is the designated size that is reapportioned every 10 years. Based on changes of population, some states gain and some states lose representatives.

While the Constitution never directly addresses the issue of slavery, this clause and others clearly condone its existence. It ultimately took the Civil War (1861–1865) to resolve the issue of slavery.

CLAUSE 4. This clause provides a procedure for replacing a U.S. representative in the case of death, resignation, or expulsion from the House. Essentially, the governor of the representative's state will determine the selection of a successor. Generally, if less than half a term is left, the governor will appoint a successor. If more than half a term is remaining, most states require a special election to fill the vacancy.

CLAUSE 5. Only one officer of the House is specified, the Speaker. The House decides all other officers. This clause also gives the House authority for impeachments—the determination of formal charges—against officials of the executive and judicial branches.

Interestingly, this clause does not stipulate that the Speaker be a member of Congress. The House might choose an outsider to run their chamber, but this has never happened—and will likely not happen in the future.

SECTION 3 CLAUSE 1. This clause treats each state equally—all have two senators. Originally, state legislators chose senators, but since passage and ratification of the 17th Amendment, they are now elected by popular vote. This clause also establishes the term of a senator—6 years, three times that of a House member.

This clause is very important when thinking about pathways of change. For one, it creates a mechanism by which the minority, through their senators, can thwart the will of the majority. Each state has the same number of senators. A majority of senators, representing states with small populations, have the ability to control the process—or at least stall things. In our system "majority will" does not always prevail.

Also, 6-year terms give senators the chance to worry only periodically about an approaching reelection. Unlike members of the House, who come up for reelection so frequently that their actions may be constantly guided by a concern for pleasing the voters, this extended term in office offers senators some leeway to do what they think is best for their state and the nation, rather than what might be seen as popular.

CLAUSE 2. To prevent a wholesale replacement of senators every 6 years, this clause provides that one-third of the Senate will be elected every 2 years. In other words, in order to remove at least one-half of the Senators from office, two elections are needed.

Senate vacancies are filled in the same way as the House—either appointment by the governor or by special election. Currently the average length of service in the Senate is 11.3 years (slightly less than two terms).

CLAUSE 3. This clause sets forth the qualifications for U.S. senator: at least 30 years old, a U.S. citizen for at least nine years, and a citizen of a state. The equivalent age of 30 today would be 54 years old. The average age of a U.S. senator at present is 59.5 years.

CLAUSE 4. The only constitutional duty of the vice president is specified in this clause—president of the Senate. This official only has a vote if there is a tie vote in the Senate; then the vice president's vote breaks the tie.

The split between Democrats and Republicans in Congress has been tiny in recent years. Not surprisingly, the Vice President has been called upon to cast several deciding votes.

CLAUSE 5. One official office in the U.S. Senate is specified—temporary president, who fills in during the vice president's absence (which is normally the case). All other Senate officers are designated and selected by the Senate.

CLAUSE 6, 7. The Senate acts as a trial court for impeached federal officials. If the accused is the president, the Chief Justice of the U.S. Supreme Court presides. Otherwise, the vice president normally presides. Conviction of the charges requires a two-thirds majority vote of those senators present at the time of the vote. Conviction results in the federal official's removal from office and disqualification to hold any other federal appointed office.

SECTION 4 CLAUSE 1. Through the years this clause has proven to be a critical aspect of the elections pathway. By allowing states to regulate elections procedures (that is, until Congress acts), the types of citizens able to participate in the process have been limited. First, religious and property qualifications were common, and many southern states used this provision to discriminate against black voters until the 1960s. Many states barred women from voting in elections until the ratification of the 19th Amendment, and still others kept 18-year-olds out until the 25th Amendment.

Lingering issues include residency and registration requirements. In some states citizens can register to vote on Election Day, but in many others they have to take this step 30 days in advance. Indeed, many argue that residency and registration requirements unnecessarily inhibit voting, especially for young people who tend to be more mobile. Others argue that such laws help to reduce voter fraud.

CLAUSE 2. The states determine the place and manner of electing representatives and senators, but Congress has the right to make or change these laws or regulations, except for the election sites. Congress is required to meet annually, and now, by law, annual meetings begin in January.

SECTION 5 CLAUSE 1. This clause enables each legislative branch to essentially make its own rules. Normally, to take a vote, a quorum is necessary. But if no votes are scheduled, fewer than a quorum can convene a session.

CLAUSE 4. The Vice President of the United States shall be President of the Senate, but shall have no Vote, unless they be equally divided.

CLAUSE 5. The Senate shall chuse their other Officers, and also a President pro tempore, in the Absence of the Vice President, or when he shall exercise the Office of President of the United States.

CLAUSE 6. The Senate shall have the sole Power to try all Impeachments. When sitting for that Purpose, they shall be on Oath or Affirmation. When the President of the United States is tried, the Chief Justice shall preside: And no Person shall be convicted without the Concurrence of two thirds of the Members present.

CLAUSE 7. Judgment in Cases of Impeachment shall not extend further than to removal from Office, and disqualification to hold and enjoy any Office of honor, Trust or Profit under the United States: but the Party convicted shall nevertheless be liable and subject to Indictment, Trial, Judgment and Punishment, according to Law.

Congressional Elections: Times, Places, Manner

SECTION 4 CLAUSE 1. The Times, Places and Manner of holding Elections for Senators and Representatives, shall be prescribed in each State by the Legislature thereof; but the Congress may at any time by Law make or alter such Regulations, except as to the Places of chusing Senators.

CLAUSE 2. The Congress shall assemble at least once in every Year, and such Meeting shall be on the first Monday in December, unless they shall by Law appoint a different Day.[5]

Powers and Duties of the Houses

SECTION 5 CLAUSE 1. Each House shall be the Judge of the Elections, Returns and Qualifications of its own Members, and a Majority of each shall constitute a Quorum to do Business; but a smaller Number may adjourn from day to day, and may be authorized to compel the Attendance of absent Members, in such Manner, and under the Penalties as each House may provide.

CLAUSE 2. Each House may determine the Rules of its Proceedings, punish its Members for disorderly Behaviour, and, with the Concurrence of two thirds, expel a Member.

CLAUSE 2. Essentially, each branch promulgates its own rules and punishes its own members. Knowing exactly how each chamber of the legislature conducts its proceedings is essential for political activists. The lobbying decision makers pathway can be a potent means of shifting public policy, but only when internal rules are well understood. Perhaps this is one of the reasons why former members of Congress make such good lobbyists.

CLAUSE 3. Each House shall keep a Journal of its Proceedings, and from time to time publish the same, excepting such Parts as may in their Judgment require Secrecy; and the Yeas and Nays of the Members of either House on any question shall, at the Desire of one fifth of those Present, be entered on the Journal.

CLAUSE 3. An official record called the Congressional Record, House Journal, etc., is kept for all sessions. It is a daily account of House and Senate floor debates, votes, and members' remarks. However, a record is not printed if a proceeding is closed to the public for security reasons. Many votes are by voice vote, and if at least one-fifth of the members request, a recorded vote of Yeas and Nays will be conducted and documented. This procedure permits analysis of congressional role-call votes.

CLAUSE 4. Neither House, during the Session of Congress, shall, without the Consent of the other, adjourn for more than three days, nor to any other Place than that in which the two Houses shall be sitting.

CLAUSE 4. This clause prevents one house from adjourning for a long period of time or to some other location without the consent of the other house.

Rights of Members

SECTION 6 CLAUSE 1. The Senators and Representatives shall receive a Compensation for their Services, to be ascertained by Law, and paid out of the Treasury of the United States. They shall in all Cases, except Treason, Felony and Breach of the Peace, be privileged from Arrest during their Attendance at the Session of their respective Houses, and in going to and returning from the same; and for any Speech or Debate in either House, they shall not be questioned in any other Place.

SECTION 6 CLAUSE 1. This section refers to a salary paid to senators and members of the House from the U.S. Treasury. This clearly states that federal legislators work for the entire nation, and not for their respective states.

In 2010, the salary for members of Congress was $174,000; some leadership positions, like Speaker of the House, receive a higher salary. The Speaker receives a salary of $223,500. Members of Congress receive many other benefits: free health care, fully funded retirement system, free round trips to their home state or district, etc. This section also provides immunity from arrest or prosecution for congressional actions on the floor or in travel to and from the Congress. For example, few members of Congress have ever been charged with drunk driving.

CLAUSE 2. No Senator or Representative shall, during the Time for which he was elected, be appointed to any civil Office under the Authority of the United States, which shall have been created, or the Emoluments whereof shall have been encreased during such time; and no Person holding any Office under the United States, shall be a Member of either House during his Continuance in Office.

CLAUSE 2. This section prevents the U.S. from adopting a parliamentary democracy, since congressional members cannot hold executive offices and members of the executive branch cannot be members of Congress.

Legislative Powers: Bills and Resolutions

SECTION 7 CLAUSE 1. All Bills for raising Revenue shall originate in the House of Representatives; but the Senate may propose or concur with Amendments as on other Bills.

SECTION 7 CLAUSE 1. This clause specifies one of the few powers specific to the U.S. House—revenue bills. Since the House was intended to be more closely tied to the people (since members are elected more frequently and they represent fewer people than the Senate), the founders wanted to grant them the power of the purse.

Given that much of politics centers on the allocation of scarce resources (the distribution of money), this provision is a key piece of information for would-be political activists.

CLAUSE 2.   The heart of the checks and balances system is contained in this clause. Both the House and Senate must pass an identical bill and present it to the president. If the president fails to act on the bill within 10 days (not including Sundays), the bill will automatically become law if Congress is in session. If the president signs the bill, it becomes law. If the president vetoes the bill and sends it back to Congress, this body may override the veto by a two-thirds vote in each branch. This vote must be a recorded vote.

The systems of checks and balances, as well as a division of power at the federal level, allow many ways to pursue change by a variety of pathways.

CLAUSE 3.   This clause covers every other type of legislative action other than a bill. Essentially, the same procedures apply in most cases. There are a few exceptions. For example, a joint resolution proposing a new congressional amendment is not subject to presidential veto.

SECTION 8 CLAUSE 1, 2.   This power allows the federal government to deficit-spend (which most states are not allowed to do). Thus, when times of economic difficulty arise, individuals and groups can petition government for financial aid and relief with job shortages.

CLAUSE 3.   This is one of the most sweeping powers granted to Congress, because so much can be linked to interstate "commerce." Since the early twentieth century, the U.S. Supreme Court has defined interstate commerce broadly and thereby enabled Congress to use this power to pass antidiscrimination laws, criminal justice laws, and other statutes.

CLAUSE 4.   This provision helps us understand why Congress, rather than state legislatures, has been at the center of the recent immigration reform debate.

CLAUSE 2.   Every Bill which shall have passed the House of Representatives and the Senate, shall, before it becomes a Law, be presented to the President of the United States; If he approve he shall sign it, but if not he shall return it, with his Objections to that House in which it shall have originated, who shall enter the Objections at large on their Journal, and proceed to reconsider it. If after such Reconsideration two thirds of that House shall agree to pass the Bill, it shall be sent, together with the Objections, to the other House, by which it shall likewise be reconsidered, and if approved by two thirds of that House, it shall become a Law. But in all such Cases the Votes of both Houses shall be determined by yeas and Nays, and the Names of the Persons voting for and against the Bill shall be entered on the Journal of each House respectively. If any Bill shall not be returned by the President within ten Days (Sundays excepted) after it shall have been presented to him, the Same shall be a Law, in like Manner as if he had signed it, unless the Congress by their Adjournment prevent its Return, in which Case it shall not be a Law.

CLAUSE 3.   Every Order, Resolution, or Vote to which the Concurrence of the Senate and House of Representatives may be necessary (except on a question of Adjournment) shall be presented to the President of the United States; and before the Same shall take Effect, shall be approved by him, or being disapproved by him, shall be repassed by two thirds of the Senate and House of Representatives, according to the Rules and Limitations prescribed in the Case of a Bill.

Powers of Congress

SECTION 8 CLAUSE 1.   The Congress shall have Power To lay and collect Taxes, Duties, Imposts and Excises, to pay the Debts and provide for the common Defence and general Welfare of the United States; but all Duties, Imposts and Excises shall be uniform throughout the United States.

CLAUSE 2.   To borrow Money on the credit of the United States;

CLAUSE 3.   To regulate Commerce with foreign Nations, and among the several States, and with the Indian Tribes;

CLAUSE 4.   To establish an uniform Rule of Naturalization; and uniform Laws on the subject of Bankruptcies throughout the United States;

CLAUSE 5.   To coin Money, regulate the Value thereof, and of foreign Coin, and fix the Standard of Weights and Measures;

CLAUSE 6.   To provide for the Punishment of counterfeiting the Securities and current Coin of the United States;

CLAUSE 7.   To establish Post Offices and post Roads;

CLAUSE 8.   To promote the Progress of Science and useful Arts, by securing for limited Times to Authors and Inventors the exclusive Right to their respective Writings and Discoveries;

CLAUSE 9.   To constitute Tribunals inferior to the supreme Court;

CLAUSE 10.   To define and punish Piracies and Felonies committed on the high Seas, and Offences against the Law of Nations;

CLAUSE 11.   To declare War, grant Letters of Marque and Reprisal, and make Rules concerning Captures on Land and Water;

CLAUSE 12.   To raise and support Armies, but no Appropriation of Money to that Use shall be for a longer Term than two Years;

CLAUSE 13.   To provide and maintain a Navy;

CLAUSE 14.   To make Rules for the Government and Regulation of the land and naval Forces;

CLAUSE 15.   To provide for calling forth the Militia to execute the Laws of the Union, suppress Insurrections and repel Invasions;

CLAUSE 16.   To provide for organizing, arming, and disciplining, the Militia, and for governing such Part of them as may be employed in the Service of the United States, reserving to the States respectively, the Appointment of the Officers, and the Authority of training the Militia according to the discipline prescribed by Congress;

CLAUSE 17.   To exercise exclusive Legislation in all Cases whatsoever, over such District (not exceeding ten Miles square) as may, by Cession of particular States, and the Acceptance of Congress, become the Seat of the Government of the United States, and to exercise like Authority over all Places purchased by the Consent of the Legislature of the State in which the Same shall be, for the Erection of Forts, Magazines, Arsenals, dockYards, and other needful Buildings;

CLAUSE 5, 6, 7.   Congressional power over coining money, counterfeiting, and post offices provides the justification for the creation of many criminal laws that are handled by federal law enforcement agencies such as the Federal Bureau of Investigation (FBI) and Secret Service. Because these matters are specified as under federal authority in the Constitution, it is a federal crime—rather than a state crime—to counterfeit money and engage in mail fraud. Most other kinds of crimes, such as murders, robberies, and burglaries victimizing ordinary citizens, are governed by state law.

CLAUSE 9.   Congress is responsible for the design of and procedures used in the federal court system. The U.S. Supreme Court is the only court created by the Constitution (see Article III). The lower federal courts are created by—and can be changed by—laws enacted by Congress. When there are changes in the design of the federal court system, such as the creation of a new court, these matters are under the power of Congress rather than under the control of the Supreme Court.

CLAUSE 10, 11.   Although Congress possesses the exclusive authority to declare war, presidents use their powers as commander-in-chief (see Article II) to initiate military actions even when there is no formal congressional declaration of war. There have been periodic disputes about whether presidents have exceeded their authority and ignored the Constitution's explicit grant of war-declaring power to Congress.

CLAUSE 11, 12, 13.   These three clauses, clauses 11, 12, and 13, ensure that Congress is involved in foreign policy decisions; thus citizens and groups can appeal to Congress if they do not like the president's foreign policy decisions or actions. Giving Congress the power to make appropriations to fund the military is potentially a significant power they have in rivaling the president for influence.

CLAUSE 14, 15, 16.   These clauses establish what are known as the "expressed" or "specified" powers of Congress.

CLAUSE 17.   This clause establishes the seat of the federal government, which was first located in New York. It eventually was moved to Washington, D.C., when both Maryland and Virginia ceded land to the new national government, which then established the District of Columbia.

CLAUSE 18. This clause, known as the "Elastic Clause," provides the basis for the doctrine of "implied" congressional powers, which was first introduced in the U.S. Supreme Court case of *McCulloch* v. *Maryland* (1819). It greatly expanded the power of Congress to pass legislation and make regulations.

The "necessary and proper" clause increases the powers of Congress, granting the legislature a great deal more authority and influence in our system of government. It has proven essential in creating a strong national government and in placing Congress at the center of the policy process.

SECTION 9 CLAUSE 1. This clause was part of the Three-Fifths Compromise. Essentially, the new Congress was prohibited from stopping the importation of slaves until 1808, but it could impose a head tax not to exceed $10 for each slave.

Condoning slavery, from today's perspective, clearly clashed with the Declaration of Independence's assertion that all men are created equal. It is hard to understand the hypocrisy of a free society with slaves. Without this provision, however, southern delegates would have left the Constitutional Convention, and southern states would not have voted to ratify the new Constitution.

CLAUSE 2. Habeas Corpus is a judicial order forcing law enforcement authorities to produce a prisoner they are holding, and to justify the prisoner's continued confinement. Congress cannot suspend the writ of habeas corpus except in cases of rebellion or invasion. The writ of habeas corpus permits a judge to inquire about the legality of detention or deprivation of liberty of any citizen. This is one of the few legal protections for individuals enshrined in the Constitution before the Bill of Rights.

CLAUSE 3. This provision prohibits Congress from passing either bills of attainder (an act of legislature declaring a person or group of persons guilty of some crime, and punishing them, without benefit of a trial) or ex post facto laws (retroactive crimes after passage of legislation). Similar restrictions were put in many state constitutions. These protections were among the few specifically provided for individuals in the body of the Constitution before the creation of amendments.

CLAUSE 4. This clause was interpreted to prevent Congress from passing an income tax. When the Supreme Court struck down congressional efforts to impose an income tax, passage of the 16th Amendment in 1913 counteracted the Supreme Court decision and gave Congress this power.

CLAUSE 5. This section establishes free trade within the U.S. That is, one state cannot tax the importation of domestic goods, and the federal government cannot tax state exports.

CLAUSE 6. This clause also applies to free trade within the U.S. The national government cannot show any preference to any state or maritime movements among the states.

CLAUSE 7. This clause prevents any expenditure unless it has been provided for in an appropriations bill enacted by Congress. At the beginning of most fiscal years, Congress has not completed the budget. Technically, the government cannot then spend any money, and would have to shut down. So Congress usually passes a Continuing Resolution Authority providing temporary authority to continue to spend money until the final budget is approved and signed into law.

CLAUSE 18. To make all Laws which shall be necessary and proper for carrying into Execution the foregoing Powers, and all other Powers vested by this Constitution in the Government of the United States, or in any Department or Officer thereof.

Powers Denied to Congress

SECTION 9 CLAUSE 1. The Migration or Importation of such Persons as any of the States now existing shall think proper to admit, shall not be prohibited by the Congress prior to the Year one thousand eight hundred and eight, but a Tax or duty may be imposed on such Importation, not exceeding ten dollars for each Person.

CLAUSE 2. The Privilege of the Writ of Habeas Corpus shall not be suspended, unless when in Cases of Rebellion or Invasion the public Safety may require it.

CLAUSE 3. No Bill of Attainder or ex post facto Law shall be passed.

CLAUSE 4. No Capitation, or other direct, Tax shall be laid, unless in Proportion to the Census or Enumeration herein before directed to be taken.[6]

CLAUSE 5. No Tax or Duty shall be laid on Articles exported from any State.

CLAUSE 6. No Preference shall be given by any Regulation of Commerce or Revenue to the Ports of one State over those of another; nor shall Vessels bound to, or from, one State, be obliged to enter, clear, or pay Duties in another.

CLAUSE 7. No Money shall be drawn from the Treasury, but in Consequence of Appropriations made by Law; and a regular Statement and Account of the Receipts and Expenditures of all public Money shall be published from time to time.

CLAUSE 8. No Title of Nobility shall be granted by the United States: And no Person holding any Office of Profit or Trust under them, shall, without the Consent of Congress, accept of any present, Emolument, Office, or Title, of any kind whatever, from any King, Prince, or foreign State.

> **CLAUSE 8.** Feudalism would not be established in the new country. We would have no nobles. No federal official can accept a title of nobility (even honorary) without permission of Congress.

Powers Denied to the States

> This section sets out the prohibitions on state actions.

SECTION 10 CLAUSE 1. No State shall enter into any Treaty, Alliance, or Confederation; grant Letters of Marque and Reprisal; coin Money; emit Bills of Credit; make any Thing but gold and silver; Coin a Tender in Payment of Debts; pass any Bill of Attainder, ex post facto Law, or Law impairing the Obligation of Contracts, or grant any Title of Nobility.

> **SECTION 10 CLAUSE 1.** This clause is a laundry list of denied powers. These restrictions cannot be waived by Congress. States cannot engage in foreign relations or acts of war. Letters of marque and reprisal were used to provide legal cover for privateers. The federal government's currency monopoly is established. The sanctity of contracts is specified, and similar state prohibitions are specified for bills of attainder, ex post facto, etc.

CLAUSE 2. No State shall, without the Consent of the Congress, lay any Imposts or Duties on Imports or Exports, except what may be absolutely necessary for executing its inspection Laws: and the net Produce of all Duties and Imposts, laid by any State on Imports or Exports, shall be for the Use of the Treasury of the United States; and all such Laws shall be subject to the Revision and Controul of the Congress.

> **CLAUSE 2.** This section establishes the monopoly control of the national government in matters of both national and international trade. The only concession to states is health and safety inspections.

CLAUSE 3. No State shall, without the Consent of Congress, lay any Duty of Tonnage, keep Troops, or Ships of War in time of Peace, enter into any Agreement or Compact with another State, or with a foreign Power, or engage in War, unless actually invaded, or in such imminent Danger as will not admit of delay.

> **CLAUSE 3.** This final section of the Legislative article establishes the war monopoly power of the national government. The only exception to state action is actual invasion or threat of imminent danger.

Article II

THE EXECUTIVE ARTICLE

> **ARTICLE II.** This article establishes an entirely new concept in government—an elected executive power. This was a touchy topic in 1787. On one hand, there was great worry about executive power—it was seen as the root of tyranny. On the other hand, many believed that a powerful executive was necessary for long-term stability for the new nation. The right balance was a system with a strong executive, where the executive's power could be limited.

Nature and Scope of Presidential Power

SECTION 1 CLAUSE 1. The executive Power shall be vested in a President of the United States of America. He shall hold his Office during the Term of four Years, and, together with the Vice President, chosen for the same Term, be elected as follows:

> **SECTION 1 CLAUSE 1.** This clause establishes the executive power in the office of the president of the United States of America. It also establishes a second office—vice president. A 4-year term was established, but not a limit on the number of terms. A limit was later established by the 22nd Amendment.

CLAUSE 2. Each State shall appoint, in such Manner as the Legislature thereof may direct, a Number of Electors, equal to the whole Number of Senators and Representatives to which the State may be entitled in the Congress: but no Senator or Representative, or Person holding an Office of Trust or Profit under the United States, shall be appointed an Elector.

> **CLAUSE 2.** This paragraph establishes the Electoral College to choose the president and vice president. Each state can determine how electors will be allotted to different candidates. For instance, today 48 states give the candidate who receives the most votes from citizens all of its electoral votes. This "winner take all" system puts an important twist on presidential election strategy. The trick for the candidates is to amass 270 electoral votes from different combinations of states.
>
> Another implication of this system of choosing an executive is that it is possible for one candidate to receive more votes from citizens than other candidates, but still not become president. This has occurred four times in American history, most recently in 2000, when Al Gore received roughly 500,000 votes more than George W. Bush but fewer Electoral College votes.

CLAUSE 3. This paragraph has been superseded by the 12th Amendment. The original language provided for a House election in the case of no majority vote or a tie vote among the top five candidates. Now the number of candidates is three. The Senate is to select the vice president if a candidate does not have an electoral majority or in the case of a tie vote. The Senate considers only the top two candidates. The amendment also clarifies that the qualifications of the vice president are the same as those for president.

CLAUSE 4. Congress is given the power to establish a uniform day and time for the state selection of electors.

CLAUSE 5. The qualifications for the offices of president and vice president are specified here—at least 35 years old, 14 years' resident in the U.S., and a natural-born citizen. The 14th Amendment clarified who is a citizen of the U.S., a person born or naturalized in the U.S. and subject to its jurisdiction. But the term "natural-born citizen" is unclear and has never been further defined by the judicial branch. Does it mean born in the U.S. or born of U.S. citizens in the U.S. or somewhere else in the world? Unfortunately, there is no definitive answer.

CLAUSE 6. This clause concerns presidential succession and has been modified by the 25th Amendment. Upon the death, resignation, or impeachment conviction of the president, the vice president becomes president. The new president nominates a new vice president, who assumes the office if approved by a majority vote in both congressional branches. The president is also now able to notify the Congress of his or her inability to perform the duties of office.

CLAUSE 3. The Electors shall meet in their respective States, and vote by Ballot for two Persons, of whom one at least shall not be an Inhabitant of the same State with themselves. And they shall make a List of all the Persons voted for, and of the Number of Votes for each; which List they shall sign and certify, and transmit sealed to the Seat of the Government of the United States, directed to the President of the Senate. The President of the Senate shall, in the Presence of the Senate and House of Representatives, open all the Certificates, and the Votes shall then be counted. The Person having the greatest Number of Votes shall be the President, if such Number be a Majority of the whole Number of Electors appointed; and if there be more than one who have such Majority and have an equal Number of Votes, then the House of Representatives shall immediately chuse by Ballot one of them for President; and if no Person have a Majority, then from the five highest on the List the said House shall in like Manner chuse the President. But in chusing the President, the Votes shall be taken by States, the Representation from each State having one Vote; A quorum for this Purpose shall consist of a Member or Members from two thirds of the States, and a Majority of all the States shall be necessary to a Choice. In every Case, after the Choice of the President, the Person having the greatest Number of Votes of the Electors shall be the Vice President. But if there should remain two or more who have equal Votes, the Senate shall chuse from them by Ballot the Vice President.[7]

CLAUSE 4. The Congress may determine the Time of chusing the Electors, and the Day on which they shall give their Votes; which Day shall be the same throughout the United States.

CLAUSE 5. No Person except a natural born Citizen, or a Citizen of the United States, at the time of the Adoption of this Constitution, shall be eligible to the Office of President; neither shall any Person be eligible to that Office who shall not have attained to the Age of thirty five Years, and been fourteen Years a Resident within the United States.

CLAUSE 6. In Case of the Removal of the President from Office, or of his Death, Resignation, or Inability to discharge the Powers and Duties of the said Office, the Same shall devolve on the Vice President, and the Congress may by Law provide for the Case of Removal, Death, Resignation or Inability, both of the President and Vice President, declaring what Officer shall then act as President, and such Officer shall act accordingly, until the Disability be removed, or a President shall be elected.[8]

CLAUSE 7.   The President shall, at stated Times, receive for his Services, a Compensation, which shall neither be encreased nor diminished during the Period for which he shall have been elected, and he shall not receive within that Period any other Emolument from the United States, or any of them.

CLAUSE 8.   Before he enter on the Execution of his Office, he shall take the following Oath or Affirmation:—"I do solemnly swear (or affirm) that I will faithfully execute the Office of President of the United States, and will to the best of my Ability, preserve, protect and defend the Constitution of the United States."

Powers and Duties of the President

SECTION 2 CLAUSE 1.   The President shall be Commander in Chief of the Army and Navy of the United States, and of the Militia of the several States, when called into the actual Service of the United States; he may require the Opinion, in writing, of the principal Officer in each of the executive Departments, upon any Subject relating to the Duties of their respective Offices, and he shall have Power to grant Reprieves and Pardons for Offences against the United States, except in Cases of Impeachment.

CLAUSE 2.   He shall have Power, by and with the Advice and Consent of the Senate, to make Treaties, provided two thirds of the Senators present concur; and he shall nominate, and by and with the Advice and Consent of the Senate, shall appoint Ambassadors, other public Ministers and Consuls, Judges of the supreme Court, and all other Officers of the United States, whose Appointments are not herein otherwise provided for, and which shall be established by Law: but the Congress may by Law vest the Appointment of such inferior Officers, as they think proper, in the President alone, in the Courts of Law, or in the Heads of Departments.

CLAUSE 3.   The President shall have Power to fill up all Vacancies that may happen during the Recess of the Senate, by granting Commissions which shall expire at the End of their next Session.

CLAUSE 7.   This section covers the compensation of the president, which cannot be increased or decreased during his/her office. The current salary is $400,000/year. The prohibition against decreasing the president's salary was considered an important part of the separation of powers. If Congress were at odds with the president and also able to decrease his pay, then it could drive him from office or punish him by reducing his salary.

CLAUSE 8.   This final clause in Section 1 is the oath of office administered to the new president. Interestingly, the phrase "so help me God," is not part of this oath, but has become customary in recent years.

SECTION 2 CLAUSE 1.   This clause establishes the president as commander-in-chief of the U.S. armed forces. George Washington was the only U.S. president to actually lead U.S. armed forces, during the Whiskey Rebellion.

The second provision is the basis for cabinet meetings that are used to hear the opinions of executive department heads. The last provision grants an absolute pardon or reprieve power for the president.

Since the president is commander-in-chief, citizens and groups concerned with U.S. foreign policy (especially armed military conflicts) can hold the president accountable for policy decisions. Litigation, protests, marches, and electoral battles have all been used by citizens dissatisfied with presidential foreign policy decisions.

CLAUSE 2.   This clause covers two important presidential powers: treaty making and appointments. The president (through the State Department) can negotiate treaties with other nations, but these do not become official until ratified by a two-thirds vote of the U.S. Senate.

The president is empowered to appoint judges, ambassadors, and other U.S. officials (cabinet officers, military officers, agency heads, etc.) subject to Senate approval.

These powers are important to ensure the division of power between the three branches of our national government as well as the system of checks and balances. Sharing these powers allows for input by the people and organized groups. The Senate approves most treaties and most presidential appointments, especially if it is controlled by members of the same party as the president. But this is not always true; many treaties and appointments have been rejected, often because the Senate was responding to strong public opinion.

CLAUSE 3.   This allows recess appointments of the officials listed in Clause 2 above. These commissions automatically expire unless approved by the Senate by the end of the next session. Presidents have used this provision to fill jobs when the nomination process is stalled.

SECTION 3.   This section provides for the annual State of the Union address to a joint session of Congress. Presidents have learned that the ability to reach out to the public can be a source of tremendous power. The State of the Union Address is thus an important opportunity to speak directly to the American public, build support for initiatives, and shape the policy agenda. The president is also authorized to call special meetings of either the House or Senate. If there is disagreement between the House and Senate regarding adjournment, the president may adjourn them. This would be extremely rare. The next-to-last provision, to faithfully execute laws, provides the basis for the whole administrative apparatus of the executive branch.

SECTION 4.   This section provides the constitutional authority for the impeachment and trial of the president, vice president, and all civil officers of the U.S. for treason, bribery, or other high crimes and misdemeanors (the exact meaning of this phrase is unclear and is often more political than judicial). Impeachment proceedings have been undertaken against two presidents in American history: Andrew Johnson, in 1868, and Bill Clinton in 1998. In both cases the Senate failed to convict the president, and both were allowed to stay in office. Richard Nixon would have also confronted impeachment proceedings in 1974 for his involvement in the Watergate scandal, but he resigned from office and avoided the process.

ARTICLE III SECTION 1.   This section establishes the judicial branch in very general terms. It only provides for the Supreme Court; Congress must create the court system. It first did so in the Judiciary Act of 1789, when it established 13 district courts (one for each state) and 3 appellate courts. All federal judges hold their offices for life and can only be removed for breaches of good behavior—a very ambiguous term. Federal judges have been removed for drunkenness, accepting bribes, and other misdemeanors. To date, no justice of the U.S. Supreme Court has ever been removed.

The tenure of judges in office, which can be for life, is meant to give judges the ability to make decisions according to their best judgments without facing the prospect of removal from office for issuing an unpopular judgment. While this protected tenure is an undemocratic aspect of the Constitution in the sense that it removes federal judges from direct electoral accountability, it has been an important aspect of the judiciary's ability to enforce civil rights and liberties on behalf of minority groups and unpopular individuals.

This protected tenure is one aspect of government that makes the court pathway especially attractive to individuals, small groups, and others who lack political power. For example, federal judges acted against racial discrimination in the 1950s at a time when most white Americans accepted the existence of such discrimination when applied to African Americans. The salary of federal judges is set by congressional act but can never be reduced.

SECTION 2 CLAUSE 1, 2, 3.   This section establishes the original and appellate jurisdiction of the U.S. Supreme Court. Original jurisdiction cases are essentially limited to disputes between states. The 11th Amendment limited the ability of individuals to sue states. Even in these cases involving states, the Supreme Court now typically appoints a special judge to hear the evidence and make a recommendation to the justices rather than hold an actual trial at the Supreme Court. Since 1925, the Supreme Court no longer hears every case on appeal but can select which cases it will accept, which is now only about 75–85 cases per year. Although this provision mentions trial by jury in all cases, the Supreme Court's interpretations of the jury trial right, also contained in the 6th Amendment, limits the right to criminal cases involving serious crimes with punishments of 6 months or more of imprisonment.

SECTION 3.   He shall from time to time give to the Congress Information of the State of the Union, and recommend to their Consideration such Measures as he shall judge necessary and expedient; he may, on extraordinary Occasions, convene both Houses, or either of them, and in Case of Disagreement between them, with Respect to the Time of Adjournment, he may adjourn them to such Time as he shall think proper; he shall receive Ambassadors and other public Ministers; he shall take Care that the Laws be faithfully executed, and shall Commission all the Officers of the United States.

SECTION 4.   The President, Vice President and all civil Officers of the United States, shall be removed from Office on Impeachment for, and Conviction of, Treason, Bribery, or other high Crimes and Misdemeanors.

Article III
THE JUDICIAL ARTICLE
Judicial Power, Courts, Judges

SECTION 1.   The judicial Power of the United States, shall be vested in one supreme Court, and in such inferior Courts as the Congress may from time to time ordain and establish. The Judges, both of the supreme and inferior Courts, shall hold their Offices during good Behaviour, and shall, at stated Times, receive for their Services, a Compensation, which shall not be diminished during their Continuance in Office.

Jurisdiction

SECTION 2 CLAUSE 1.   The judicial Power shall extend to all Cases, in Law and Equity, arising under this Constitution, the Laws of the United States, and Treaties made, or which shall be made, under their Authority;—to all Cases affecting Ambassadors, other public Ministers and Consuls;—to all Cases of admiralty and maritime Jurisdiction;—to Controversies to which the United States shall be a Party;—to Controversies between two or more States—between a State and Citizens of another State;[9]—between Citizens of different States;—between Citizens of the same State claiming Lands under Grants of different States, and between a State, or the Citizens thereof, and foreign States, Citizens, or Subjects.

CLAUSE 2.   In all Cases affecting Ambassadors, other public Ministers and Consuls, and those in which a State shall be Party, the supreme Court shall have original Jurisdiction. In all the other Cases before mentioned, the supreme Court shall have appellate Jurisdiction, both as to Law and Fact, with such Exceptions, and under such Regulations as Congress shall make.

CLAUSE 3.   The Trial of all Crimes, except in Cases of Impeachment, shall be by Jury; and such Trial shall be held in the State where the said Crimes shall have been committed; but when not committed within any State, the Trial shall be at such Place or Places as the Congress may by Law have directed.

SECTION 2 CLAUSE 1, 2, 3.   This section establishes the original and appellate jurisdiction of the U.S. Supreme Court. Original jurisdiction cases are essentially limited to disputes between states. The 11th Amendment limited the ability of individuals to sue states. Even in these cases involving states, the Supreme Court now typically appoints a special judge to hear the evidence and make a recommendation to the justices rather than hold an actual trial at the Supreme Court. Since 1925, the Supreme Court no longer hears every case on appeal but can select which cases it will accept, which is now only about 75–85 cases per year. Although this provision mentions trial by jury in all cases, the Supreme Court's interpretations of the jury trial right, also contained in the 6th Amendment, limits the right to criminal cases involving serious crimes with punishments of 6 months or more of imprisonment.

Treason

SECTION 3 CLAUSE 1.   Treason against the United States, shall consist only in levying War against them, or in adhering to their Enemies, giving them Aid and Comfort. No Person shall be convicted of Treason unless on the Testimony of two Witnesses to the same overt Act, or on Confession in open Court.

CLAUSE 2.   The Congress shall have Power to declare the Punishment of Treason, but no Attainder of Treason shall work Corruption of Blood, or Forfeiture except during the Life of the Person attainted.

SECTION 3 CLAUSE 1, 2.   Treason is the only crime defined in the U.S. Constitution. Congress established the penalty of death for treason convictions. Note that two witnesses are required to convict anyone of treason.

Article IV
INTERSTATE RELATIONS

Full Faith and Credit Clause

SECTION 1.   Full Faith and Credit shall be given in each State to the public Acts, Records, and judicial Proceedings of every other State. And the Congress may by general Laws prescribe the Manner in which such Acts, Records and Proceedings shall be proved, and the Effect thereof.

ARTICLE IV SECTION 1.   This section provides that the official acts and records (for example, marriages and divorces) of one state will be recognized and given credence by other states. It is one of several clauses that were designed to create a strong national government. Concerns about this clause have taken on new importance in recent years, as the gay marriage issue has heated up in most state legislatures.

Privileges and Immunities; Interstate Extradition

SECTION 2 CLAUSE 1.   The Citizens of each State shall be entitled to all Privileges and Immunities of Citizens in the several States.

SECTION 2 CLAUSE 1.   This clause requires states to treat citizens of other states equally. For example, when driving in another state, a driver's license is recognized.

CLAUSE 2.   A person charged in any State with Treason, Felony or other Crime, who shall flee from Justice, and be found in another State, shall on Demand of the executive Authority of the State from which he fled, be delivered up, to be removed to the State having Jurisdiction of the Crime.

CLAUSE 2.   A criminal fleeing to another state, if captured, can be returned to the state where the crime was committed. But this is not an absolute (extradition). A state's governor can refuse, for good reason, to extradite someone to another state.

> **CLAUSE 3.** This clause was included to cover runaway slaves. It has been made inoperable by the 13th Amendment, which abolished slavery.

> **SECTION 3 CLAUSE 1, 2.** This section concerns the admission of new states to the Union. In theory, no state can be created from part of another state without permission of the state legislature. But West Virginia was formed from Virginia during the Civil War without the permission of Virginia, which was part of the Confederacy. With 50 states now part of the Union, this section has not been used for many decades. The only foreseeable future use may be in the case of Puerto Rico or perhaps Washington, D.C.

> **SECTION 4.** This section commits the federal government to guarantee a republican form of government to each state and to protect the states against foreign invasion or domestic insurrection.
> By mandating a republican form of government, the Constitution guarantees that power rests in the hands of the citizens and is exercised by their elected representatives. As such, citizens are able to appeal directly to their governing officials through several pathways, such as through the courts, via elections, or by lobbying.

> **ARTICLE V.** Amendments to the U.S. Constitution can be originated by a two-thirds vote in both the U.S. House and Senate or by two-thirds of the state legislatures asking for a convention to propose amendments. Proposed amendments, by either route, must be approved by three-fourths of state legislatures or by three-fourths of conventions convened in the states for purposes of ratification. Only one amendment has been ratified by the convention method—the 21st Amendment, to repeal the 18th Amendment establishing Prohibition.
> Thousands of amendments have been proposed; few have been passed by two-thirds vote in each branch of Congress. The Equal Rights Amendment was one such case, but it was not ratified by three-fourths of state legislatures. There have only been 27 successful amendments to the U.S. Constitution.
> Since both the federal and state levels of government are involved in amending the Constitution, interested parties have several strategies to pursue to increase the likelihood that a proposed amendment is successful or is defeated.

CLAUSE 3. No person held to Service or Labour in one State, under the Laws thereof, escaping into another, shall, in Consequence of any Law or Regulation therein, be discharged from such Service or Labour, but shall be delivered up on Claim of the Party to whom such Service or Labour may be due.[10]

Admission of States

SECTION 3 CLAUSE 1. New States may be admitted by the Congress into this Union; but no new State shall be formed or erected within the Jurisdiction of any other State; nor any State be formed by the Junction of two or more States, or Parts of States, without the Consent of the Legislatures of the States concerned as well as of the Congress.

CLAUSE 2. The Congress shall have Power to dispose of and make all needful Rules and Regulations respecting the Territory or other Property belonging to the United States; and nothing in this Constitution shall be so construed as to Prejudice any Claims of the United States, or of any particular State.

Republican Form of Government

SECTION 4. The United States shall guarantee to every State in this Union a Republican Form of Government, and shall protect each of them against Invasion; and on Application of the Legislature, or of the Executive (when the Legislature cannot be convened) against domestic Violence.

Article V

THE AMENDING POWER

The Congress, whenever two thirds of both Houses shall deem it necessary, shall propose Amendments to this Constitution, or, on the Application of the Legislatures of two thirds of the several States, shall calla Convention for proposing Amendments, which, in either Case, shall be valid to all Intents and Purposes, as Part of this Constitution, when ratified by the Legislatures of three fourths of the several States, or by Conventions in three fourths thereof, as the one or the other Mode of Ratification may be proposed by the Congress; Provided that no Amendment which may be made prior to the Year One thousand eight hundred and eight shall in any Manner affect the first and fourth Clauses in the Ninth Section of the first Article; and that no State, without its Consent, shall be deprived of its equal Suffrage in the Senate.

Article VI

THE SUPREMACY ACT

CLAUSE 1. All Debts contracted and Engagements entered into, before the Adoption of this Constitution, shall be as valid against the United States under this Constitution, as under the Confederation.

CLAUSE 2. This Constitution, and the Laws of the United States which shall be made in Pursuance thereof; and all Treaties made, or which shall be made, under the Authority of the United States, shall be the supreme Law of the Land; and the Judges in every State shall be bound thereby, any Thing in the Constitution or Laws of any State to the Contrary notwithstanding.

CLAUSE 3. The Senators and Representatives before mentioned, and the Members of the several State Legislatures, and all executive and judicial Officers, both of the United States and of the several States, shall be bound by Oath or Affirmation, to support this Constitution; but no religious Test shall ever be required as a Qualification to any Office or public Trust under the United States.

Article VII

RATIFICATION

The Ratification of the Conventions of nine States, shall be sufficient for the Establishment of this Constitution between the States so ratifying the Same.

    Done in Convention by the Unanimous Consent of the States present the Seventeenth Day of September in the Year of our Lord one thousand seven hundred and Eighty seven and of the Independence of the United States of America the Twelfth. In Witness whereof We have hereunto subscribed our Names.

Amendments

The Bill of Rights

AMENDMENT 1
RELIGION, SPEECH, ASSEMBLY, AND PETITION

Congress shall make no law respecting an establishment of religion, or prohibiting the free exercise thereof; or abridging the freedom of speech, or of the press; or the right of the people peaceably to assemble, and to petition the Government for a redress of grievances.

CLAUSE 1. This clause made the new national government responsible for all debts incurred during the Revolutionary War. This was very important to banking and commercial interests.

CLAUSE 2. This is the National Supremacy Clause, which provides the basis for the supremacy of the national government. This seems to be a rather straightforward issue these days, but until the conclusion of the Civil War, "national supremacy" was not a settled concept.

CLAUSE 3. This clause requires essentially all federal and state officials to swear or affirm their allegiance to and support of the U.S. Constitution. Note that a religious test was prohibited for federal office. However, some states used religious tests for voting and office qualification until the 1830s.

Realizing the unanimous ratification of the new Constitution by the 13 states might never have occurred, the framers wisely specified that only 9 states would be needed for ratification. Even this proved to be a test of wills between Federalists and Anti-Federalists, leading to publication of the great political work *The Federalist Papers*.

ARTICLE VII. In the end, all 13 states ratified the Constitution. But it was a close call in several states.

The first ten amendments were ratified on December 15, 1791, and form what is known as the "Bill of Rights."
    The Bill of Rights applied at first only to the federal government and not to state or local governments. Beginning in 1925 in the case of *Gitlow* v. *New York*, the U.S. Supreme Court began to selectively incorporate the Bill of Rights, making its provisions applicable to state and local governments, with some exceptions, which will be discussed at the appropriate amendment.
    Until the Supreme Court incorporated the Bill of Rights to include protections from state governments, citizens had to look to state constitutions for protections of civil liberties.

AMENDMENT 1. This amendment protects five fundamental freedoms: religion, speech, press, assembly, and petition. The press is the only business that is specifically protected by the U.S. Constitution. Freedom of religion and speech are two of the most contentious issues and generate a multitude of Supreme Court cases.
    These freedoms are crucial for nearly every pathway of change; without each fundamental right, individuals and groups could not pursue change without fear of reprisal. This amendment is perhaps the most crucial to guarantee a free society.

AMENDMENT 2.   Those who favor gun ownership, either for protection, hunting or sport, cite this amendment. This amendment has not been incorporated for state/local governments; that is, state and local governments are free to regulate arms, provided such regulation is not barred by their own state constitutions.

　　There is controversy as to the meaning of this amendment. Some believe that it specifically refers to citizen militias, which were common at the time of the Constitution but now have been replaced by permanent armed forces (state national guard units), thereby allowing the federal government to regulate gun ownership. Others believe that the amendment refers to individuals directly, therefore guaranteeing private citizens the right to own guns.

AMENDMENT 3.   It was the practice of the British government to insist that colonists provide room or board to British troops. This amendment was designed to prohibit this practice. Today, military and naval bases provide the necessary quarters and this issue does not arise. This amendment has not been incorporated and applies only against the federal government.

AMENDMENT 4.   This extremely important amendment is designed to prevent the abuse of police powers. Essentially, unreasonable searches or seizures of homes, persons, or property cannot be undertaken without probable cause or a warrant that specifically describes the place to be searched, the person involved, and the suspicious things to be seized.

　　People who believe that these rights have been violated have successfully used the court-centered pathway for protection, either by seeking to have improperly obtained evidence excluded from use in court or by seeking money damages from police officials to compensate for the invasion of a home or an improper search of an individual's body.

　　Many people feel that the rights of the accused are often given more precedence than the rights of victims. The Constitution does not contain rights for victims, but a constitutional amendment has been proposed to protect victims' rights. This does not mean that victims are unprotected by the law. States and the federal government have statutes that provide protections and services for crime victims.

AMENDMENT 5.   Only a grand jury can indict a person for a federal crime. (This provision does not apply to state/local governments because it has not been incorporated by the Supreme Court.) This amendment also covers double jeopardy, or being tried twice for the same crime in the same jurisdiction. This amendment also covers the prohibition of compelled self-incrimination. The deprivation of life, liberty, or property is prohibited unless due process of law is applied. This provision applies to the federal government, and there is a parallel provision that applies to state and local governments in the 14th Amendment. Finally, private property may not be taken under the doctrine of "eminent domain" unless the government provides just compensation.

AMENDMENT 2
MILITIA AND THE RIGHT TO BEAR ARMS

A well-regulated Militia, being necessary to the security of a free State, the right of the people to keep and bear Arms, shall not be infringed.

AMENDMENT 3
QUARTERING OF SOLDIERS

No Soldier shall, in time of peace be quartered in any house, without the consent of the Owner, nor in time of war, but in manner to be prescribed by law.

AMENDMENT 4
SEARCHES AND SEIZURES

The right of the people to be secure in their persons, houses, papers, and effects, against unreasonable searches and seizures, shall not be violated, and no Warrants shall issue, but upon probable cause, supported by Oath or affirmation, and particularly describing the place to be searched, and the persons or things to be seized.

AMENDMENT 5
GRAND JURIES, SELF-INCRIMINATION, DOUBLE JEOPARDY, DUE PROCESS, AND EMINENT DOMAIN

No person shall be held to answer for a capital, or otherwise infamous crime, unless on a presentment or indictment of a Grand jury, except in cases arising in the land or naval forces, or in the Militia, when in actual service in time of War or public danger; nor shall any person be subject for the same offence to be twice put in jeopardy of life or limb; nor shall be compelled in any criminal case to be a witness against himself, nor be deprived of life, liberty, or property, without due process of law; nor shall private property be taken for public use, without just compensation.

AMENDMENT 6
CRIMINAL COURT PROCEDURES

In all criminal prosecutions, the accused shall enjoy the right to a speedy and public trial, by an impartial jury of the State and district wherein the crime shall have been committed, which district shall have been previously ascertained by law, and to be informed of the nature and cause of the accusation; to be confronted with the witnesses against him; to have compulsory process for obtaining witnesses in his favor, and to have the Assistance of Counsel for his defence.

AMENDMENT 7
TRIAL BY JURY IN COMMON LAW CASES

In Suits at common law, where the value in controversy shall exceed twenty dollars, the right of trial by jury shall be preserved, and no fact tried by a jury shall be otherwise reexamined in any Court of the United States, than according to the rules of the common law.

AMENDMENT 8
BAIL, CRUEL AND UNUSUAL PUNISHMENT

Excessive bail shall not be required, nor excessive fines imposed, nor cruel and unusual punishments inflicted.

AMENDMENT 9
RIGHTS RETAINED BY THE PEOPLE

The enumeration in the Constitution, of certain rights, shall not be construed to deny or disparage others retained by the people.

AMENDMENT 10
RESERVED POWERS OF THE STATES

The powers not delegated to the United States by the Constitution, nor prohibited by it to the States, are reserved to the States respectively, or to the people.

AMENDMENT 6.   This amendment requires public trials by jury for criminal prosecutions. However, the Supreme Court only applies the right to trial by jury to serious offenses, not petty offenses. Anyone accused of a crime is guaranteed the rights to be informed of the charges; to confront witnesses; to subpoena witnesses for their defense; and to have a lawyer for their defense. The government must provide a lawyer for a defendant unable to afford one for any case in which the defendant faces the possibility of a jail or prison sentence.

There are serious questions about the adequacy of attorney performance and resources for criminal defense. In some jurisdictions, there are not enough defense attorneys for poor defendants, so that the attorneys spend little time on each case. In addition, the Supreme Court does not have strict standards for attorney performance, so some defendants have been represented by attorneys who know very little about criminal law.

AMENDMENT 7.   The right to trial by jury in civil cases will never be incorporated by the Supreme Court for application against state and local governments, because it would impose a huge financial burden (jury trials are very expensive).

AMENDMENT 8.   The Supreme Court has not clearly defined the limits imposed by prohibition of excessive bail or excessive fines. Thus these rights rarely arise in legal cases, and bail amounts in excess of $1 million will periodically be imposed for serious crimes or wealthy defendants. The prohibition on cruel and unusual punishments focuses on criminal punishments, not other contexts (such as the punishment of children in public schools or civil fines against businesses). Cruel and unusual punishments are defined according to current societal values and thus the definition of what is "cruel and unusual" can change over time. This provision bars punishments that are either excessive or torturous.

Capital punishment is covered by this amendment, as well as the treatment of prisoners inside prisons. Court cases challenging the constitutionality of capital punishment cite this amendment's language prohibiting cruel and unusual punishment. For a period of 4 years (1973–1976), the Supreme Court banned capital punishment as it was then being applied by the states. When states modified their statutes to provide a two-part judicial process of guilt determination and punishment, the Supreme Court allowed the reinstitution of capital punishment by the states.

AMENDMENT 9.   This amendment implies that there may be other rights of the people not specified by the previous amendments, but the wording gives no guidance about what those rights might be. Instead, when the Supreme Court has identified rights not specifically mentioned in the Bill of Rights, it has tended to claim that these rights, such as privacy and the right to travel between states, are connected to the right to "due process" found in the 5th and 14th Amendments.

AMENDMENT 10.   The 10th Amendment was seen as the reservoir of reserved powers for state governments. But the doctrine of implied national government powers, which was established by the U.S. Supreme Court in McCulloch v. Maryland (1819), undercut the words and apparent intent of this amendment. With the exception of a few decisions, the Supreme Court has generally deferred to assertions of federal power since the 1930s.

> **AMENDMENT 11.**   Article III of the U.S. Constitution originally allowed federal jurisdiction in cases of one state citizen against another state citizen or state. This amendment removes federal jurisdiction in this area. In essence, states may not be sued in federal court by citizens of another state or country.

> **AMENDMENT 12.**   This was a necessary amendment to correct a flaw in the Constitution covering operations of the Electoral College. In the election of 1800, Thomas Jefferson and Aaron Burr, both of the same Democratic Republican party, received the same number of electoral votes, 73, for president. Article II of the original Constitution specified that each elector would cast two ballots. It did not specify for whom. This amendment clarifies that the electoral vote must be specific for president and vice president. The original Constitution provided that if no candidate received a majority of electoral votes, the House would decide from the candidates with the top five vote totals. This amendment reduces the candidate field to the top three vote totals. If the House delays in this selection past the fourth day of March, the elected vice president will act as president until the House selects the president. The original Constitution provided that the candidate with the second highest number of electoral votes would become vice president.
>
> This amendment, which requires a separate vote tally for vice president, provides for selection by the U.S. Senate if no vice presidential candidate receives an electoral vote majority.

AMENDMENT 11

SUITS AGAINST THE STATES

[Ratified February 7, 1795]

The Judicial power of the United States shall not be construed to extend to any suit in law or equity, commenced or prosecuted against one of the United States by Citizens of another State, or by Citizens or Subjects of any Foreign State.

AMENDMENT 12

ELECTION OF THE PRESIDENT

[Ratified June 15, 1804]

The Electors shall meet in their respective states, and vote by ballot for President and Vice-President, one of whom, at least, shall not be an inhabitant of the same state with themselves; they shall name in their ballots the person voted for as President, and in distinct ballots the person voted for as Vice-President, and they shall make distinct lists of all persons voted for as President, and of all persons voted for as Vice-President, and of the number of votes for each, which lists they shall sign and certify, and transmit sealed to the seat of the government of the United States, directed to the President of the Senate;—The President of the Senate shall, in the presence of the Senate and House of Representatives, open all the certificates and the votes shall then be counted;—The person having the greatest number of votes for President, shall be the President, if such number be a majority of the whole number of Electors appointed; and if no person have such majority, then from the persons having the highest numbers not exceeding three on the list of those voted for as President, the House of Representatives shall choose immediately, by ballot, the President. But in choosing the President, the votes shall be taken by states, the representation from each state having one vote; a quorum for this purpose shall consist of a member or members from two-thirds of the states, and a majority of all the states shall be necessary to a choice. And if the House of Representatives shall not choose a President whenever the right of choice shall devolve upon them, before the fourth day of March next following, then the Vice-President shall act as President, as in the case of the death or other constitutional disability of the President.[11] The person having the greatest number of votes as Vice-President, shall be the Vice-President, if such a number be a majority of the whole numbers of Electors appointed, and if no person have a majority, then from the two highest numbers on the list, the Senate shall choose the Vice-President; a quorum for the purpose shall consist of two-thirds of the whole number of Senators, and a majority of the whole number shall be necessary to a choice. But no person constitutionally ineligible to the office of President shall be eligible to that of Vice-President of the United States.

AMENDMENT 13

PROHIBITION OF SLAVERY

[Ratified December 6, 1865]

SECTION 1   Neither slavery nor involuntary servitude, except as a punishment for crime whereof the party shall have been duly convicted, shall exist within the United States, or any place subject to their jurisdiction.

SECTION 2   Congress shall have power to enforce this article by appropriate legislation.

AMENDMENT 14

CITIZENSHIP, DUE PROCESS, AND EQUAL PROTECTION OF THE LAWS.

[Ratified July 9, 1868]

SECTION 1   All persons born or naturalized in the United States, and subject to the jurisdiction thereof, are citizens of the United States and of the State wherein they reside. No State shall make or enforce any law which shall abridge the privileges or immunities of citizens of the United States; nor shall any State deprive any person of life, liberty, or property, without due process of law; nor deny to any person within its jurisdiction the equal protection of the laws.

SECTION 2   Representatives shall be apportioned among the several States according to their respective numbers, counting the whole number of persons in each State, excluding Indians not taxed. But when the right to vote at any election for the choice of electors for President and Vice President of the United States, Representatives in Congress, the Executive and Judicial officers of a State, or the members of the Legislature thereof, is denied to any of the male inhabitants of such State, being twenty-one years of age, and citizens of the United States, or in any way abridged, except for participation in rebellion, or other crime, the basis of representation therein shall be reduced in the proportion which the number of such male citizens shall bear to the whole number of male citizens twenty-one years of age in such State.[12]

AMENDMENT 13.   This is the first of the three Civil War amendments. Slavery is prohibited under all circumstances. Involuntary servitude is also prohibited unless it is a punishment for a convicted crime.

AMENDMENT 14 SECTION 1.   This section defines the meaning of U.S. citizenship and protection of these citizenship rights. It also establishes the Equal Protection Clause, meaning that each state must guarantee fundamental rights and liberties to all of its citizens. It extended the provisions of the 5th Amendment of due process and protection of life, liberty, and property and made these applicable to the states. The due process clause has been especially important for the expansion of civil rights and liberties as the Supreme Court interpreted it in a flexible manner to recognize new rights (e.g., privacy, right of choice for abortion, etc.) and to apply the Bill of Rights against the states.

SECTION 2.   This section changed the Three-Fifths Clause of the original Constitution. At the time of ratification of this amendment, all male citizens, 21 or older, were used to calculate representation in the House of Representatives. If a state denied the right to vote to any male 21 or older, the number of denied citizens would be deducted from the overall state total to determine representation.

   This is the first time that gender was entered into the Constitution. It was not until 50 years later (in 1920 with the 19th Amendment) that women were granted the right to vote.

SECTION 3.   This section disqualifies from federal office or elector for president or vice president anyone who rebelled or participated in an insurrection (that is, the Confederate Army after the Civil War) against the Constitution. This was specifically directed against citizens of Southern states. Congress by a two-thirds vote could override this provision.

SECTION 4, 5.   Section 4 covers the Civil War debts; Section 5 grants to Congress the very specific authority to create legislation that will implement and enforce the provisions of the 14th Amendment.

Unlike the Bill of Rights, which is intended to protect individuals by limiting the power of the federal government, including Congress, Section 5 intends to empower Congress to create laws that will protect individuals from actions by states that violate their rights.

Although the 13th and 14th Amendments were designed to end slavery, and provide citizenship, due process, and equal protection rights for freed slaves and their offspring, they were interpreted very narrowly until the 1960s. Civil rights activists had to use the court-centered, cultural change, and grassroots mobilization pathways to force legal, political, and social change to allow all individuals, regardless of color or race, to enjoy full civil rights.

AMENDMENT 15 SECTION 1, 2.   This final Civil War amendment states that voting rights could not be denied by any states on account of race, color, or previous servitude. It did not mention gender. Accordingly, only male citizens 21 or over were guaranteed the right to vote by this amendment. Some states sought to defeat the intent of the amendment by adopting additional restrictions to voting rights (such as poll taxes, whites-only primaries and literacy tests) in order to block the participation of African-American voters. These restrictions were eliminated in the 1960s as civil rights activists effectively used several pathways for change: court, lobbying decision makers, and grassroots mobilization.

AMENDMENT 16.   Article I, Section 9 of the original Constitution prohibited Congress from enacting a direct tax unless in proportion to a census. Congress in 1894 passed an income tax law, levying a 2 percent tax on incomes over $4,000. In 1895, the U.S. Supreme Court in a split decision (5–4) found that the income tax was a direct tax not apportioned among the states and was thus unconstitutional. Thus, Congress proposed an amendment allowing it to enact an income tax. Once this amendment was ratified, the flow of tax money to Washington increased tremendously.

SECTION 3   No person shall be a Senator or Representative in Congress, or elector of President and Vice President, or hold any office, civil or military, under the United States, or under any State, who, having previously taken an oath, as a member of Congress, or as an officer of the United States, or as a member of any State legislature, or as an executive or judicial officer of any State, to support the Constitution of the United States, shall have engaged in insurrection or rebellion against the same, or given aid or comfort to the enemies thereof. But Congress may by a vote of two-thirds of each House, remove such disability.

SECTION 4   The validity of the public debt of the United States, authorized by law, including debts incurred for payment of pensions and bounties for services in suppressing insurrection or rebellion, shall not be questioned. But neither the United States nor any State shall assume or pay any debt or obligation incurred in aid of insurrection or rebellion against the United States, or any claim for the loss or emancipation of any slave; but all such debts, obligations and claims shall be held illegal and void.

SECTION 5   The Congress shall have power to enforce, by appropriate legislation, the provisions of this article.

AMENDMENT 15
THE RIGHT TO VOTE

[Ratified February 3, 1870]

SECTION 1   The right of citizens of the United States to vote shall not be denied or abridged by the United States or by any State on account of race, color, or previous condition of servitude.

SECTION 2   The Congress shall have power to enforce this article by appropriate legislation.

AMENDMENT 16
INCOME TAXES

[Ratified February 3, 1913]

The Congress shall have power to lay and collect taxes on incomes, from whatever source derived, without apportionment among the several States, and without regard to any census or enumeration.

AMENDMENT 17
DIRECT ELECTION OF SENATORS

[Ratified April 8, 1913]

The Senate of the United States shall be composed of two Senators from each State, elected by the people thereof, for six years; and each Senator shall have one vote. The electors in each State shall have the qualifications requisite for electors of the most numerous branch of the State legislatures.

When vacancies happen in the representation of any State in the Senate, the executive authority of such State shall issue writs of election to fill such vacancies: Provided, That the legislature of any State may empower the executive thereof to make temporary appointments until the people fill the vacancies by election as the legislature may direct.

This amendment shall not be so construed as to affect the election or term of any Senator chosen before it becomes valid as part of the Constitution.

AMENDMENT 17. Before this amendment, U.S. senators were selected by state legislatures. Now U.S. senators would be selected by popular vote in each state. Further, the governor of each state may fill vacancies, subject to state laws.

AMENDMENT 18
PROHIBITION

[Ratified January 16, 1919. Repealed December 5, 1933 by Amendment 21]

SECTION 1 After one year from the ratification of this article the manufacture, sale, or transportation of intoxicating liquors within, the importation thereof into, or the exportation thereof from the United States and all territory subject to the jurisdiction thereof for beverage purposes is hereby prohibited.

SECTION 2 The Congress and the several States shall have concurrent power to enforce this article by appropriate legislation.

SECTION 3 This article shall be inoperative unless it shall have been ratified as an amendment to the Constitution by the legislatures of the several States, as provided in the Constitution, within seven years from the date of the submission hereof to the States by the Congress.[13]

AMENDMENT 18. This amendment was largely the work of the Women's Christian Temperance Union and essentially banned the manufacture, sale, or transportation of alcoholic beverages. Unintended consequences of this attempt to legislate morality were the brewing of "bathtub gin" and moonshine liquor and the involvement of organized crime in importing liquor from Canada. The 21st Amendment repealed this provision. This is also the first amendment where Congress fixed a period for ratification—7 years.

AMENDMENT 19
FOR WOMEN'S SUFFRAGE

[Ratified August 18, 1920]

The right of the citizens of the United States to vote shall not be denied or abridged by the United States or by any State on account of sex.

Congress shall have power to enforce this article.

AMENDMENT 19. Women achieved voting parity with men. It took enormous efforts by a large number of women and men to win this right, spanning over 70 years (from the call for the right to vote at the first women's rights convention in Seneca Falls, New York, in 1848). Suffragists protested, sued, marched, lobbied, and were imprisoned in their battle to win equal voting rights for men and women.

AMENDMENT 20. Called the Lame Duck amendment, this amendment fixes the dates for the end of presidential and legislative terms. A new president is elected in November, but the current president remains in office until January 20th of the following year, thus the term "lame duck." Legislative terms begin earlier, on January 3rd.

AMENDMENT 20

THE LAME DUCK AMENDMENT

[Ratified January 23, 1933]

SECTION 1   The terms of the President and Vice President shall end at noon on the 20th day of January, and the terms of the Senators and Representatives at noon on the 3d day of January, of the years in which such terms would have ended if this article had not been ratified; and the terms of their successors shall then begin.

SECTION 2   The Congress shall assemble at least once in every year, and such meeting shall begin at noon on the 3d day of January, unless they shall by law appoint a different day.

SECTION 3   If, at the time fixed for the beginning of the term of the President, the President elect shall have died, the Vice President elect shall become President. If a President shall not have been chosen before the time fixed for the beginning of his term, or if the President elect shall have failed to qualify, then the Vice President elect shall act as President until a President shall have qualified; and the Congress may by law provide for the case wherein neither a President elect nor a Vice President elect shall have qualified, declaring who shall then act as President, or the manner in which one who is to act shall be selected, and such person shall act accordingly until a President or Vice President shall have qualified.

SECTION 4   The Congress may by law provide for the case of the death of any of the persons from whom the House of Representatives may choose a President whenever the right of choice shall have devolved upon them, and for the case of the death of any of the persons from whom the Senate may choose a Vice President whenever the right of choice shall have devolved upon them.

SECTION 5   Sections 1 and 2 shall take effect on the 15th day of October following the ratification of this article.

SECTION 6   This article shall be inoperative unless it shall have been ratified as an amendment to the Constitution by the legislatures of three-fourths of the several States within seven years from the date of its submission.

AMENDMENT 21
REPEAL OF PROHIBITION

[Ratified December 5, 1933]

SECTION 1 The eighteenth article of amendment to the Constitution of the United States is hereby repealed.

SECTION 2 The transportation or importation into any State, Territory, or possession of the United States for delivery or use therein of intoxicating liquors, in violation of the laws thereof, is hereby prohibited.

SECTION 3 This article shall be inoperative unless it shall have been ratified as an amendment to the Constitution by conventions in the several States, as provided in the Constitution, within seven years from the date of the submission hereof to the States by Congress.

AMENDMENT 22
NUMBER OF PRESIDENTIAL TERMS

[Ratified February 27, 1951]

SECTION 1 No person shall be elected to the office of the President more than twice, and no person who has held the office of President, or acted as President, for more than two years of a term to which some other person was elected President shall be elected to the office of the President more than once. But this article shall not apply to any person holding the office of President when this article was proposed by the Congress, and shall not prevent any person who may be holding the office of President, or acting as President, during the term within which this article becomes operative from holding the office of President or acting as President during the remainder of such term.

SECTION 2 This article shall be inoperative unless it shall have been ratified as an amendment to the Constitution by the legislatures of three-fourths of the several states within seven years from the date of its submission to the states by the Congress.

AMENDMENT 23
PRESIDENTIAL ELECTORS FOR THE DISTRICT OF COLUMBIA

[Ratified March 29, 1961]

SECTION 1 The District constituting the seat of government of the United States shall appoint in such manner as the Congress may direct:

A number of electors of President and Vice President equal to the whole number of Senators and Representatives in Congress to which the District would be entitled if it were a state, but in no event more than the least populous state; they shall be in addition to those appointed by the states, but they shall be considered, for the purposes of the election of President and Vice President, to be electors appointed

AMENDMENT 21. This unusual amendment nullified the 18th Amendment. The amendment called for the end of Prohibition unless prohibited by state laws.

This is the only instance of one amendment nullifying another. Here, governmental actions reflected the will of the majority. Initially, there was concern that the production and consumption of alcohol was detrimental to society, but as time passed, public opinion shifted. The public became less concerned about consumption and more worried about the illegal manufacture of alcohol and the subsequent growth of illegal markets and urban violence.

AMENDMENT 22. This amendment could be called the Franklin D. Roosevelt amendment. It was FDR who broke the previously unwritten rule, established by George Washington, of serving no more than two terms as president. Democrat Roosevelt won election to an unprecedented four terms as president (although he died before completing his fourth term). When the Republicans took control of the Congress in 1948, they pushed through the 22nd Amendment, limiting the U.S. president to a lifetime of two full 4-year terms of office.

AMENDMENT 23. This amendment gave electoral votes to the residents of Washington, D.C., which is not a state and thus not included in the original scheme of state electoral votes. Currently, Washington, D.C., has 3 electoral votes, bringing the total of presidential electoral votes to 538. Residents of Washington, D.C., do not, however, have voting representation in Congress. Puerto Ricans are citizens of the U.S. but have no electoral votes. Both Washington, D.C., and Puerto Rico are represented in Congress by non-voting delegates.

AMENDMENT 24.   The poll tax was a procedure used mostly in southern states to discourage poor white and black voters from registering to vote. Essentially, one would have to pay a tax to register to vote. The tax was around $34/year (sometimes retroactive), which amounted to a great deal of money to the poor, serving to disenfranchise a great proportion of the poor. As part of the fight for universal voting rights for all, the poll tax was abolished. Literacy tests, another device to disqualify voters, were abolished by the Voting Rights Act of 1965.

By banning this tax (coupled with other civil rights reforms), the United States delivered what the civil rights amendments promised—full voting rights for all citizens regardless of race.

AMENDMENT 25.   President Woodrow Wilson's final year in office was marked by serious illness. It is rumored that his wife acted as president. There was no constitutional provision to cover an incapacitating illness of a president. This amendment provides a procedure for this eventuality. The president can inform congressional leaders of his/her incapacitation, and the vice president then takes over. When the president recovers, he/she can inform congressional leaders and resume office.

The amendment also recognizes that the president may not be able or wish to indicate this lack of capacity. In this case, the vice president and a majority of cabinet members can inform congressional leaders, and the vice president takes over. When the president informs congressional leadership that he/she is back in form, he/she resumes the presidency unless the vice president and a majority of the cabinet members disagree. Then Congress must decide who is to be president. The likelihood that this procedure will ever be used is relatively small.

The most immediate importance of this amendment concerns the office of vice president. The original Constitution did not address the issue of a vacancy in this office. This amendment was ratified in 1967, only a few years before it was needed. In 1973, the sitting vice president, Spiro Agnew, resigned his office. Under the provisions of this amendment, President Nixon nominated Gerald Ford as vice president. As a former member of the House, Ford was quickly approved by the Congress. But a year later, President Nixon also resigned. Now Vice President Ford became President Ford, and he in turn appointed Nelson Rockefeller as the new vice president. For the first time in our history, neither the president nor the vice president were selected by the Electoral College after a national election.

by a state; and they shall meet in the District and perform such duties as provided by the twelfth article of amendment.

SECTION 2   The Congress shall have power to enforce this article by appropriate legislation.

AMENDMENT 24

THE ANTI-POLL TAX AMENDMENT

[Ratified January 23, 1964]

SECTION 1   The right of citizens of the United States to vote in any primary or other election for President or Vice President, for electors for President or Vice President, or for Senator or Representative in Congress, shall not be denied or abridged by the United States or any state by reason of failure to pay any poll tax or other tax.

SECTION 2   The Congress shall have power to enforce this article by appropriate legislation.

AMENDMENT 25

PRESIDENTIAL DISABILITY, VICE PRESIDENTIAL VACANCIES

[Ratified February 10, 1967]

SECTION 1   In case of the removal of the President from office or of his death or resignation, the Vice President shall become President.

SECTION 2   Whenever there is a vacancy in the office of the Vice President, the President shall nominate a Vice President who shall take the office upon confirmation by a majority vote of both Houses of Congress.

SECTION 3   Whenever the President transmits to the President pro tempore of the Senate and the Speaker of the House of Representatives his written-declaration that he is unable to discharge the power-sand duties of his office, and until he transmits to them a written declaration to the contrary, such powers and duties shall be discharged by the Vice President as Acting President.

SECTION 4   Whenever the Vice President and a majority of either the principal officers of the executive departments, or of such other body as Congress may by law provide, transmit to the President pro tempore of the Senate and the Speaker of the House of Representatives their written declaration that the President is unable to discharge the powers and duties of his office, the Vice President shall immediately assume the powers and duties of the office as Acting President.

Thereafter, when the President transmits to the President pro tempore of the Senate and the Speaker of the House of Representatives his written declaration that no inability exists, he shall resume the powers and duties of his office unless the Vice President and a majority of either the principal officers of the executive department, or of such other body as Congress may by law provide, transmit within four days to the President pro tempore of the Senate and the Speaker of the House of Representatives their written declaration that the President is unable to discharge the powers and duties of his office. Thereupon Congress shall decide the issue, assembling within forty-eight hours for that purpose if not in session. If the Congress, within twenty-one days after receipt of the latter written declaration, or, if Congress is not in session, within twenty-one days after Congress is required to assemble, determines by two-thirds vote of both Houses that the President is unable to discharge the powers and duties of his office, the Vice President shall continue to discharge the same as Acting President; otherwise, the President shall resume the powers and duties of his office.

AMENDMENT 26

EIGHTEEN-YEAR-OLD VOTE

[Ratified July 1, 1971]

SECTION 1 The right of citizens of the United States, who are 18 years of age or older, to vote, shall not be denied or abridged by the United States or by any state on account of age.

SECTION 2 The Congress shall have power to enforce this article by appropriate legislation.

AMENDMENT 27

CONGRESSIONAL SALARIES

[Ratified May 7, 1992]

No law varying the compensation for the services of the Senators and Representatives shall take effect until an election of Representatives shall have intervened.

AMENDMENT 26 SECTION 1, 2. During the Vietnam War, 18-year-olds were being drafted and sent out to possibly die in the service of their country. Yet they did not even have the right to vote. This incongruity led to the 26th Amendment, which lowered the legal voting age from 21 to 18.

Before the passage of this amendment, young people, being denied the ability to express themselves peacefully with the vote, often felt frustrated with their inability to express their concerns and influence public policy. With the passage of this amendment, those citizens over the age of 18 could pursue the election-centered pathway (and others) to instigate change.

AMENDMENT 27. This is a "sleeper" amendment that was part of 12 amendments originally submitted by the first Congress to the states for ratification. The states only ratified 10 of the 12, which collectively became known as the Bill of Rights. But since Congress did not set a time limit for ratification, the other two amendments remained on the table. Much to the shock of the body politic, in 1992, three-fourths of the states ratified original amendment 12 of 12. This reflected the disgust of seeing Congress continuing to increase its salary and benefits. The amendment delays any increase of compensation for at least one election cycle.

---

1 Modified by the 16th Amendment
2 Replaced by Section 2, 14th Amendment
3 Repealed by the 17th Amendment
4 Modified by the 17th Amendment
5 Changed by the 20th Amendment

6 Modified by the 16th Amendment
7 Changed by the 12th and 20th Amendments
8 Modified by the 25th Amendment
9 Modified by the 11th Amendment
10 Repealed by the 13th Amendment

11 Changed by the 20th Amendment
12 Changed by the 26th Amendment
13 Repealed by the 21st Amendment

3 Repealed by
4 Modie